POWER IN AMERICA:

THE POLITICS OF
THE NEW CLASS

Also by David T. Bazelon — The Paper Economy

DAVID T. BAZELON
POWER IN AMERICA:

THE POLITICS OF
THE NEW CLASS

*Why is light given
to a man whose
way is hid,
and whom God
hath hedged in?*
—Job 3:23

THE NEW AMERICAN LIBRARY

First Printing

Published by The New American Library, Inc.
1301 Avenue of the Americas, New York, New York 10019

Published simultaneously in Canada by
General Publishing Company, Ltd.
Library of Congress Catalog Card Number: 67–12119
Printed in the United States of America

This is a book from the Institute for Policy Studies.

For my son, Coleman David Bazelon

*"My brother, Huey, used to buy Congressmen,
but I have found it more economical to rent them."*
—Governor Earl Long of Louisiana

*"I knew they were crooks,
but I don't like to see it right on T.V."*
—from an opinion study of a mayoralty election

*"Everything begins in mysticism
and everything ends in politics."*
—Charles Péguy

CONTENTS

ONE The Starting Point 1

THE PROBLEM
American History

TWO Non-Rule and Some of Its History 29

THREE The House 58

FOUR Once More, the Parties Realign 91

THE ESSENCE
Our Emotions

FIVE The Myth of Individualism 133

SIX Where Religion Went 163

SEVEN Scientism—the Stultifying Style 185

EIGHT An Essay in Defense of Lying
by a Compulsive Truth-Teller 207

THE SOLUTION
Existential Coalition

NINE Apportionment and Majoritarianism 237

TEN Negroes in the Streets 270

ELEVEN The New Class 307

TWELVE The American Liberal 333

THIRTEEN The New Coalition 360

Author's Acknowledgments 394
Index 397

ONE

The
Starting
Point

1 I take as the starting point for a discussion of American politics that intellectuals favor ideals too much, and our more practical men lack both the ideals and the ideas that may lead to a new American realism. So the persistent effort underlying the pages of this book is to imagine—he must be imagined; he does not exist—a person with the virtues of each and the faults of neither.

This imagined person might do us a great service: he could perform on an elevated critical platform and instruct us all in the use of a fresh set of political gestures. The alternative to some such adequate instruction induces in me only despair compounded. If the money people, the practical ones, persist in inscribing upon our history the irrelevance of their primitive ideals, America will finally come to represent, despite the promise and the power of its short course, a botched opportunity amounting to one of the more devastating defeats of the human species. Such power as we have accumulated, being an unparalleled opportunity to transcend traditional historical evils, is not easily come by on this planet.

I will elaborate hereinafter that any such failure will be primarily a *cultural* one. Here, "culture" implies more than the accumulation of technique; it is *all* the heritage human beings may draw upon for their intended intervention in the course of events, including awareness of the why and what-for of technique. My effort to expand the meaning of this term will not emphasize abstract definitions. Mostly I will try to worm my way inside the American liberal mind, that warmest home of the working intellectual. He is a member of the New Class, so is and will be the bearer and custodian of culture—however defined or misdefined, used or misused—for the entire fateful passage from the old middle-class world of property and other supposed stabilities into the new overorganized and overpopulated planetary order which is, realistically, the single image of our future.

Of the two halves of our imagined new man, note that the trouble with the intellectual is that too often he has been finely honed to an edge of elevated irrelevance. This is the result of tradition; and this tradition was hardly established by accident or oversight. Up to a point, one is compelled to sympathize with the yearning of the man of affairs to continue to enforce the traditional prescription, that is, to deal with intellectuals as accomplished servants of technology and trained monkeys of spirituality. When as priests, in the past, they intervened in practical matters, the resulting confusion between the spiritual and temporal empires was not such as to encourage further experimentation. This (as well as—more obviously—the revolutionary potential of all ideas, both new and old) caused the tradition of caged irrelevance in the first place. But now all that is necessarily changed. In the new technological world, it is no longer merely a question of tolerating intellectuals: today they are needed, perhaps even essential. And if only the pure technologists are welcomed, without their humanist brethren, the practical men of affairs will suffer the evil consequence no less than the rest of mankind. Indeed, for my part, that is the core of the struggle with Communism.

Unfortunately, only the intellectuals can teach these and similar truths to the established men of power: I am not sanguine about the latter's picking up the information merely along the way, without careful tutorials and other seminars. Which, again unfortunately, means that the intellectuals, in preparation for their new utility, will first have to begin by clearing up a few ambiguities among themselves. But this effort strikes me as far and away the better opening and the sharper wedge. So to that effort this book is generally devoted: it is a preachment to the New Class, urging some neglected aspects of self-awareness, and indicating some iron choices to be made. And even a suggestion or two is advanced as to what we affluent Americans might do about getting beyond the stale pleasure of living out our lives as consumer-oriented pigs. (Many members of the younger generation, you may have noticed, are revolted by us.)

2 The simple "cultural" point being asserted here is that politics is so important as to be essential. There is, in the end, no other way than the political way to persist in being human. So any distaste for the various aspects of politics and power must be borne with human grace, even with an animal-like yielding to events. The "solution" of the deepest problems of human existence has one exterior end and object only, that is, action-in-history: *politics.* Even when it cannot in fact be accomplished, it must be placed up front, if only there to preserve what objective reference we may envision for our more poetic integrity.

But the ordinary mis-definition of "politics" in the United States is so pervasive as almost to be enlightening. Most commonly, it is understood as an old-fashioned circus-barker salesmanship, a rather low livelihood, in which some fellow's need for income and notoriety is sold with the loudest and most entertaining lies, in competition with similar efforts around the corner. In line with all good American salesmanship of a bad product, anything that isn't known for what it is comes off best of all. For example, politicians prefer off-year campaigning to that of the even-numbered years. One congressman has said: "The best speech is a non-political speech." Of these, a commencement speech is even better, because the listeners are "more prepared to like you and take you into the family than . . . at any other time."

This sneaky commencement speaker is not the only one to engage in our typically "non-political" form of politics. We all do it: because something like politics in fact occurs wherever there is an issue of power. Since this issue is seldom absent, the root-stuff of politics is everywhere. Much of our activity not thought to be political is intensely that, although no state official is elected in the process (at the very least that because a constituency, which will later oppose or support an elected official, is then being organized).

Most issues of power are perhaps resolved by an act of delegation —whether that consists of electing someone to represent me, acquiescing in the state's monopoly of armed force, or handing over a paycheck to my wife—and that is perhaps why the issues are not noticed or remembered for what they are. It may even be that delegation is the primary relation which initially separates-out "power" from other factors in living. But if so, this view of power would only serve to emphasize the broad inevitability of "politics," properly named and conceived.

Continuing with the more usual misconception, politics—that is, being, becoming, supporting, opposing a candidate for state office—is also noticed by the populace as being a frequent engagement of individuals, wealthy and otherwise successful, who choose "statesmanship" as an early hobby, or as something to occupy themselves with during the later period of retirement. But this is thought to be part of the inexplicable foolishness of the upper strata, exemplifying the kind of misdirected effort that only the wealthy can afford. "Real" politics remains a disreputable business in which an honest man can end up only by mistake or seduction.

On the next higher level of American sophistication, the people interested in politics are seen as special types called "power-hungry." The implication of this view is that politics is perhaps necessary (while remaining evil) in that it siphons off undesirable persons and thus sanitizes normal civil society, much as the regular army has been welcomed for gathering in bullies and potential murderers. In each case, the remaining problem for proper people is to steer clear of soldiers and of politicians—unless there is violence in the area, or you need to fix a parking ticket. But no matter where you start or where you end, "politics is a dirty business" in the common American understanding. Even some of the pros accept this definition: a male poll-watcher from Carmine De Sapio's Tamawa Club in Greenwich Village is reported to have said to a young female poll-watcher from the opposition Reform group: "What's a nice girl like you doing in a place like this?"

As we shall see, this notion was not all that wrong in the first instance, if that is taken to be the post-Civil War period. All in all, however, it has been one of the more destructive general lies embedded in our culture. And now it is an impossible lie to live with. Lacking leisure fulfillment in private, our lives are inevitably becoming more public—this needn't all take place in bars, etc. If politics has been dirty, it was mostly because the clean people spent their time elsewhere, mostly making money. Now that so many of us are transcending that passion, we can certainly brighten the political arena, too, as we go public in new ways. Also, many activities in America have for long been dirtier businesses by far, if only because they were more actively engaged in. And politics in America, while largely a low appendage of business, has entertained broad non-business motives more frequently and with greater effect than either business itself or the subsequent philanthropy of the big winners.

But a further problem with "politics" is that, at the mere mention of the word, everybody pirouettes into a prepared position and the ensuing exchange can have more in common with an adolescent snowball fight than with an adult effort to come to terms with an issue of power. Still, politics is unavoidable. My particular unavoidable point about politics is that we must reconceive the matter, noting first that it takes place almost everywhere, in all group-life, and not just in electing state officials; and secondly, that it is characteristically a struggle between old ideas and new needs. Power clings to the one, although it is required for the satisfaction of the other; the resulting conflict is called politics. It seems that it is most often an effort toward re-delegation of some kind.

And it is revealingly *not* what President Coolidge believed it to be. He opposed any kind of state intervention in the course of events. He said of public administrators (apparently including his own Office of the President): "They should remain silent until an issue is reduced to its *lowest* terms, until it boils down to something like a *moral* issue." (My emphasis.)

3 Morality is not really the lowest term. The lowest term in politics is self-delusion—leading at different times both to excessive giving-in and to flamboyant holding-out. For many Americans, morality has been the Higher Form of holding-out, while politics itself has been altogether understood as the Lower Form of giving-in. This is so silly—and I am so American —that I decided to object frequently thereto in this book.

The idea of morality's being what you do only when you are all boiled-down—what we might call the New England red-lobster conception of morality—amounts to a ferocious attempt to devote the moral and ideal and spiritual capacity of the human being solely to the preservation of an individual mental state: a state of grace by virtue of anointed omnipotence. A not inconsiderable by-product of this ultimate adoration of the self and its will is that the moral and ideal and spiritual capacity of the human being, in this way ferociously deployed, is not apt to interfere thereafter with anything important. It has been isolated and contained. With the existential decks thus neatly cleared, survival—and even prosperity—is almost easy. The remaining problem concerns only the off-chance that, for just a crucial moment or two, the champion of perfected moral isolation might relax his strenuously achieved and absolutely convinced adoration of self, and love something or other by mistake. If the object of this lapse were property or an obvious career-line, then no particular harm. But what if this Classic American lives in a city, or in the midst of some such form of organized life, and (not having slept well the night previously) he relaxes his will on one of the *persons* with whom his crowded environment is now filled? Why, then we have some more undermining of American Individualism, and another beginning of new forms of American moral and ideal and spiritual capacity.

Soon enough? That was the underlying issue Senator Goldwater presented in 1964. If too late, then too distorted. Perhaps not quite so perverse as the bizarre Senator suggested, but still sufficiently warped so that the sanguine view recedes, and we must then seriously entertain the image of America which all good Americans deny as they live—indeed, in order to live—as follows: this country could be absolutely the worst human desert on the planet; that has been clear from the beginning:

> We are too wealthy.
> We are too pure.
> We are too shallow.
> We are too young.
> We lack direction.

But mostly, we are simply too disjointed. I think that, reasonably well joined together, we could probably accomplish almost anything reasonable. Our big problem has been getting together—on acceptable human terms—enough of us to accomplish anything much at all.* But we are Individualists, despite our horrible hunger to get together. So still the great creative act in America is coalition-build-

---

* Perhaps this is why the military and the big corporation—industry organized on military principles—have created so much in America, and in the end have been accepted so profoundly by Americans.

ing. So still the great abiding question in America is whether the next necessary coalition will be created within the given limits of historical time, and on more rather than less democratic principles. I cannot even presume to suggest an answer to that ultimate question; but I am willing to, and I do, indicate the general outline of the next American coalition. This you will find in the last of the three sections of the book.

In the first section, the prevailing effort is to suggest what in the past happened to our chances for majoritarian democracy—what we ended up being like, to date, and why. This view of our history emphasizes the absence of a positive government for the continent; and the point is made apposite with a depiction of the House of Representatives, the democratic body intended by the Founders to assert the legitimacy of popular power. The House has not accomplished as much in this direction, in recent decades, as the Presidency, the Court, or even the Senate. Finally, the Big Doings of 1964 are evaluated; and the resulting Big Question confronted as to whether the long post-New Deal paralysis has in fact been overcome by something more than Johnson magic joined with Goldwater nonsense.

Apart from war, the New Deal was our greatest successful effort at positive government. And the main thing about the New Deal was not its ideological offering but the fact that out of the events of its day, it created a new political coalition. My thought is that the New Deal as a program is now finished—by Johnsonian fulfillment and other success; at least by the passage of time; and not least by the provision of jobs for working intellectuals in the administration of positive government. If this is so, then the time will soon be upon us to commence again the creation of another and the next New Coalition, because that is how our history gets accomplished and we continue to deny successfully that darker image of a narrow and repressive America.

But when we approach this project, which is both necessary and creative, we rediscover our fatal heritage—American moralism, and its nearly overwhelming emotional sources in the forms presented by our social order. The relation between the psychic furniture of idealism and the requirements of achieving historical effect is a continual subject of the exposition herein; but it is gone at all-out in the middle section of the book, where I probe the native myth of Individualism, and even the seemingly alien subjects of religion and "science" and lying are tied-in to America's political future.

4 Richard Hofstadter characterized our moral problem very nicely—"the United States was the only country in the world that began with perfection and aspired to progress." In our perfectly rational social contract at the beginning, our Original Conception substituting once-and-for-all for Original Sin, we were indeed nonpareil. While politics may have been too "dirty" here, everything else has been exceptionally "clean." We came here, the self-chosen people, and designed ourselves in abundant reasonableness to account for each and every defect of European history (not for all human history, but only because we didn't know enough about that). The Atlantic passage was the return to nature and true morality under the single prescription of Christ Returned, here in the welcoming wilderness. We are the revivalist nation, consecrated to the richly fulfilling proposition of around-the-clock renewal.

Notice this Beautiful American Statement by William Jennings Bryan:

A man can be born again; the springs of life can be cleansed instantly. . . . If this is true of one, it can be true of any number. Thus, a nation can be born in a day if the ideals of the people can be changed.

This, and not long hours in a library stocked with European books, is the root of the American intellectual.

My purpose, however, is to modify and not to eradicate this first principle of American sentiment, which has been variously referred to as Puritanism, moralism, grandiose individualism, Populism, Progressivism, Reformism, purism, and home-grown idiocy. The reason I decline the job of uprooting this primitive revivalism is that the country, in my opinion, could not survive the loss. These ideas and attitudes are not the expression of drop-outs: they are the staples of our better-educated and better-intentioned citizens. And this has been the fact for quite a while. We are not the revivalist nation because the latest issues of *The Observer* and *Les Temps Modernes* did not arrive: they are on the shelves, where they have always been— and, as always, they are well-worn from greedy reading. We are the revivalist nation because if we did not revive regularly we would drop dead—from the lack of a coherent national society and culture and government to begin with.

Also, I never grew up or out enough to book passage back, and I remain what I began as, an incurable American. So, for example, Bryan's statement expresses almost perfectly one of the two basic ideas of my own childhood. My first idea occurred as the startling, silent answer to the question, "But what is outside of 'outside'?" This childish reflection of endlessness, the first perception of infinity, is the core of an American's empty-continent Individualism: here, it provided not so much a metaphysical speculation as a practical program of action. The second idea of my childhood was the one specifically put forth by Bryan. The little boy expressed it to himself this way: If everybody stopped right now and agreed on what was the right thing to do, and then did it, unhappiness would end—especially mine but (*generously*) also everyone else's. We would all live happily ever after—together. I wouldn't be surprised if all schemes for living happily ever after together were attenuated elaborations of this first and grandest one that Bryan and I had.

One might almost define an American as a person with Bryan's and my predilection, and the specific problem that it occasioned, as follows: If I have moral ideals, do I need power, too? And what is power if it isn't money? (Both questions are utterly American, although the first is naïvely metaphysical and the second is abjectly historical.) The answers are: 1) And how! and 2) Un-American.

Power is intention and motivation in the real world of history, as contrasted with moral ideals in the psychic world provided solely by God and His intellectuals. If only this neat and brutal formulation resolved the matter! But it doesn't. Given the various disastrous circumstances of history, impossible ideals are integral with realistic motivation. If we need the latter, we are stuck with the former. (See Chapter Six as to why the former need not be traditionally religious.) I cannot claim to have resolved this great problem; but I have indeed strained mightily to argue that it is silly even to try to resolve it. It is not that kind of problem. As long as a social order requires impossible ideals as part of the substance of innovative motivation, intellectuals who do their duty have a messy problem that cannot be avoided or easily resolved. Certainly it is not enough, late in a life committed to awareness, to discover the iron character of the issues of power and effectiveness and then, simply, to invert your earlier ideal beliefs. Life could not possibly be that puerile.

I want to urge, in these chapters, that the locus of power lies espe-cially in the emotional organization of the individual, as well as in our institutional arrangements; that both, interactively, are the result of our extraordinary empty-continent history; and that, with consid-erable agony, the irresponsible power residing in our central insti-tutions *and* the powerlessness of our majority of well-intentioned individuals are each the evil flowering of the same cultural flaw. The trouble has been not only our inevitably hasty history, but our childish and greedy—and somewhat less than inevitable—miscon-ception of it. And of ourselves. And of anything else we found it convenient to misconceive. Convenient misconception has been Ev-erybody's Candyland in America. But we were too well-favored to have become and remained so indulgent: certainly for so long. With wealth and privilege goes responsibility; or else one travels to the edge of meaninglessness.

My major premise is this: There are *two* recurrent evils in the conduct of human history—power for its own sake, and morality for its own sake. These patterns of human failure have had strange and special careers in America. Most strange of all because both have been subordinated to new grotesqueries compounded of each: first, *business* for its own sake; and lately, *science,* likewise for its own sake.

5 The subject of politics is power: of this, there is no question. And there is also no doubt that jungle-animal power differs drastically from power in an organized society. The physical power of an individual survives in a society such as ours; but it is not significant—neither socially nor politically. The power that most concerns us in our effort to understand the mechanisms and possibilities of modern politics proceeds from or-ganizations. Indeed, we may readily begin by saying that power *is* organization. This cannot mislead us, and it may be of some help.

It would be a great deal of help if everybody knew right away what "organization" is: they don't. Instead of embarking on a long ex-cursus, we may merely note that organizations are "institutions"—which means a complicated set of habits existing in numerous indi-viduals—and these habits allow, facilitate, and finally require all of these individuals to carry on certain activities in common. The power resides in the habitude, and in the connection between a habit in one person and another habit in a second person. To which it may be added that ours is clearly a society made up of organizations, and of individuals living in and through organizations: the very size of the population depends upon the productivity of these patternings.

Why and how do these habits persist? *That* they do, creates the power; *why* and *how* they do, states the problem of power. Note that, when you are all done observing how big General Motors is, the habits comprising it still reside in individuals. So even though few people run away from the job at GM and the suburban bedroom it provides, still the monster lives in their habitude.

Modern power is, at the root, psychological. Habits are emotional; one's involvement in an institution, thus creating it, is emotional; and so the answer to the question, What is power? (and, How can I re-delegate some of it to friendlier agents or even back to myself?) must likewise be emotional. The term "emotional" here means the pattern of perception and ideas closer to motivation than abstract ideas and postures are, and therefore closer to action. In politics, we understand by doing. I suggest that this is true of power generally.

But look what actually happens to us: We begin with ideals, even very good or obvious ones, and proceed from this beginning to pieties and other rigidities which, as we all know, are a major prop of everything the ideals presumed to oppose. Why? Because the desire for change (ideals) is universal, while the effort toward it (power) is much more limited; and the two often lack effective connection. Can thinking, particularly thinking about the emotional context of motivation, have an effect on this schism? Can it make a difference? Yes, because politics is inevitable, because it exists, through action or inaction, wherever there is an issue of power—and there almost always is.

Politics is the purposeful effort for or against change; so the power that concerns us must somehow be different from a natural event like, say, a hurricane. Power is conscious and intended: it is the harness, if any, of the hurricane. And in America, it is the weakness of the harness—with a brass-studded strand here, and nothing but dimestore twine over there—that should concern us. We might even say that the problem in America is not power but powerlessness, especially the self-devised variety of the intellectuals. We have learned too well to live within our system, which does not provide adequately for the conscious, positive exercise of national, legitimate power.

Our emotional organization personally reflects this social flaw. The two go together. Therefore, American emotional patterns are, along with the institutional arrangements, an apposite point of attack. Certainly for an understanding of our society; and if we look for fresh political action, then the emotions of the potential actors are most important of all.

We tell so many lies about power in this country—and worse yet, to ourselves. Usually the lies are intended to sustain one ideal or another.* But lying is itself too great a power to be wasted on the manufacture of obscurantist ritual. And when lying is the usual thing in a particular area of life, a little truth goes a long way. Truth, too, is a rather considerable power: for your own self, when you tell it to yourself, it may be even better than lying, although the latter of course remains profoundly more effective as a social technique.

The nonsensical part of idealism derives from the need to have a perfect or a fulfilled or a secure future right next to you at all times *here in the present*, despite all evidence to the contrary, in order to act at all (or even to get through the rest of the day). From this very special nonsense comes the reluctance, and later the inability, to distinguish between what is In the Head and what is Out There. The present and the future can be separated somewhat more functionally, for many people, only as a strenuous act of faith. And here is where we come upon the special American difficulty: all our faith is used up believing in the value of money, before we ever find alternative uses for it. Money-faith has exhausted us, so that we cannot work for ideals but can only embrace them.

* J. K. Galbraith expresses this strained quality very shrewdly in *American Capitalism:* "The role of power in American life is a curious one. The privilege of controlling the actions or of affecting the income and property of other persons is something that no one of us can profess to seek or admit to possessing. No American ever runs for office because of an avowed desire to govern. He seeks to serve—and then only in response to the insistent pressure of friends or of that anonymous but oddly vocal fauna which inhabit the grass roots. We no longer have public officials, only public servants. The same scrupulous avoidance of the terminology of power characterizes American business. The head of the company is no longer the boss—the term survives only as an amiable form of address—but the leader of the team. It is years since the United States has had a captain of industry; the brass-bound officer who commands has now been entirely replaced by the helmsman who steers. No union leader ever presents himself as anything but a spokesman for the boys."

6 Money-making has been our history, no matter what the intellectuals were doing or failing to do. Until recently, that is, when the intellectuals, too, started to make money.

Most Americans, following our eighteenth century beginnings, have not only shared the national disease of elevating money to a measuring substitute for Everything, but have also insisted on its putative rationality—which is the craziest part of the whole story.

"A fierce debate raged throughout the country by 1874 over the question of whether the American currency system was to be 'hard' or 'soft,' gold or paper," Matthew Josephson tells us. "It was the historic, traditional form which political controversy between opposing classes and regions had taken in America ever since the eighteenth century." The American attitude toward money is rooted in the history of the debtor-creditor conflict which characterized our continental development. From the time of dealing with the Revolutionary War debt, through the Bank of the United States crisis, and the redemption issue regarding greenbacks and specie payment of war debts after the Civil War, to the great Populist revolt of the farmers against gold, culminating in the silver crusade of Bryan and well into the twentieth century, the issue was ultimately that of debtor against creditor. *The United States was an interior colonial development,* its character obscured only by the rapidity of its occurrence.

Our peculiarities concerning economics in general and money in particular derive from gold as an instrument of colonialism; from the fact that this country was the queen of colonies, the most magnificent in the whole history of such developments; and because the continental stampede occurred so quickly and achieved such immediate success. How is one to be reasonable about a great mutation? So the dollar in America is sound, stable, real, right, and so on. And that is how our national nuttiness on the subject became certified.

Until the Great Depression, that is—when the cow jumped over the moon, the kettle barked commands to the cook, and the American mind finally separated altogether from the American reality (also later referred to as "the end of the American Dream"). It is downright significant that the House of Morgan supported Roosevelt's gold policy—the abandonment of the Great Metal as a direct measure of the value of the dollar. Morgan could admit enough about the necessities of financial rule to acknowledge that gold, in the circumstances, was an absurd atavism: the colonial era had ended. Apparently he also knew enough to realize that the federal government was then and there required to take over a great deal of his role in ruling financially, with or without gold (never more than a means of ruling). The following Roosevelt dictum—November 1934—did not, it would seem, apply to Morgan: "One of my principal tasks . . . is to prevent bankers and businessmen from committing suicide!"

Arthur M. Schlesinger, Jr., also reports on the conflict of interest, in the New Deal group, regarding monetary policy as between the *rentier* class and the entrepreneur group. It was the *rentier*, represented by Lewis Douglas of Treasury, who tried to hold on to gold, apparently out of concern for international finance rather than for domestic recovery. Jesse Jones of the Reconstruction Finance Corporation, representing the entrepreneur-promoter class, opposed Douglas and his commitment to yellow metal. Of the un-golding RFC, Schlesinger states: "By January 1, 1934, it had disbursed two-thirds again as much money in its short twenty-three months of existence as the House of Morgan and its syndicates had disbursed in aggregate underwritings from 1919 to 1933." It was indeed utilizing a good measure of the power which dropped from Morgan's hands as the system became too big for him to handle. And note that the entrepreneur across the land willingly accepted the federal government as basic banker in lieu of Morgan.

Then Roosevelt most meaningfully said (writing to Colonel House, President Wilson's adviser):

The real truth of the matter . . . is, as you and I know, that a financial element in the larger centers has owned the government ever since the days of Andrew Jackson—and I am not wholly excepting the administration of W.W. The country is going through a repetition of Jackson's fight with the Bank of the United States—only on a far bigger and broader basis.

I think the foregoing suggests sufficiently the rich intimacy of our money-making history and the emotionality of the question of power. Money is so much less "real" than our history has made it, that one is continually re-amazed at the monstrous irony that has placed this buck-hungry nation first in line on the frontier of a post-money society. Money was never more than the measure of price and debt, even in the epoch of primitive accumulation (it was then, even as treasure, simply a store of power *over* price and debt, their vagaries and vicissitudes). Today, major price and debt are "artificial" issues of an institutional and political character, with little subservience to raw natural forces. Therefore, *a fortiorari*, money. Today, one might say that money is ministerial; price, and of course the legitimate price called "tax," are tactical; but debt is the strategic political question in our kind of paper society.

We have now come to a critical point on the matter of the federal deficit, which is the key to full and purposeful production. The issue posed is the need to devise original measures for financing "abundance" (also called "overproduction" when you can't sell it and are afraid to give it away). All the unoriginal measures have been exhausted, and so have we, waiting for our ship to come in. To continue indefinitely to view our surplus capacity (including our proven capacity to build more plants and produce more surplus) as a monstrous threat, would be a human abdication quite beyond description —like welcoming nuclear war. So, the line having been well held against the federal deficit for two decades, a change is due. But in its coming, it will amount to a convulsive spiritual revolution. (See Chapter Four for a discussion of the Johnson administration's efforts.)

Very simply, we must now begin, however slowly, to transfer our basic faith from money to values-beyond-money. This must be accomplished institutionally, in the end; but now it begins in the realm of the spirit. And the Working Intellectuals must lead the way—severely pushed from behind, one hopes, by the Negroes and the colorless poor. The money-makers and other natural leaders will find it spiritually difficult to follow, much less lead: they must be urgently *invited* into our abundant future, although a few of them can be expected to concur with the wealthy Edward A. Filene, who went along with New Deal taxation, saying: "Why shouldn't the American people take half my money from me? I took all of it from them."

7 Money is not so often or so easily reduced to an issue called "power." More often it is discussed at great length, not to say endlessly, under the heading of "economics."

Because of our money-making history, the received thought in America about economic matters so obscures the problem of power that one may not safely bypass it. This strenuous obfuscation is the unifying thread behind our beloved free enterprise ideology, that centerpiece of national idiocy. In his book, *American Capitalism*, J. K. Galbraith says:

> . . . the appeal of the competitive model was its solution of the problem of power. This is still the basis of its hold on the American conservative. Indeed, for most Americans free competition, so called, has for long been a political rather than an economic concept.

Apart from ideological models, the can-do and will-do built into the actual postwar economic system has been adequate to forestall the deepening of recessions, but was first not capable of achieving, and now (1966) not clearly able to maintain, full and purposeful production. We have not been able to get the best out of the system; what that might be, and how we might go about doing it, or whether we dare try, have been the essential issues dividing and diversifying our serious economists.

These issues are matters of political choice in a much more obvious way than some earlier issues put forward by economic thought. Less and less can the rational nay-sayers point to a natural purity of the system being corrupted by any particular policy proposal; more and more must they warn against that one additional step which will tumble us into the abyss. Moreover, it is now a political rather than an economic abyss that is regularly warned against. The central point everywhere and always is whether to resist or allow an expansion of the role of the central government, of a big "fisc," in designing and ensuring abundance.

As a consequence, the profession of economics in the old sense is deeply readjusting: it may even be breaking up into technicians and politicians and philosophers, because less and less can the traditional unifying presumptions be supported by practice or tolerated in reflection. For the time being, economics is finished as a coherent branch of theology.

What we need now is a method of social analysis going beyond scarcity: we require a candid catalogue of policy-making considerations: that is, a logic of power.

The problems of economics were always political at bottom. The historical reliance on private property and free competitive markets was a great effort to bypass the problem of power, on the theory that it would be properly distributed according to the ownership of property. With the widespread separation of ownership and control—that is, the separation of *property and power*—this is no longer a tenable presumption.

The revolutionary turnabout from capitalism to corporatism—which has shuffled social and psychological as well as economic categories like so many cards in a deck—is best revealed by noticing what has happened to property. It would have been a happy circumstance if "the managerial revolution" had been identified, instead, as "the property revolution." This might have helped us to understand somewhat sooner the meaning of the great change from the robber barons to the robber baronies. That is, if we had wanted help. I doubt that we did. What we have always wanted, I think, was to obscure the facts of power—as if to look upon them would be to stare directly at the godface of the sun, and risk annihilation.

Classic private property is full possessory property held and dispensed at the absolute discretion of an individual. It never existed—it was born and bred as an ideal. And although as anything like a fact it is dying and otherwise daily transforming its earthly state, the ideal persists: indeed, it seems to feed on the carrion of its own demise. (This may well be a characteristic of ideals, in their dangerous phase.) First of all, no discretion is or can be absolute because everybody lives in a society, even Hitler. (Especially Hitler?) Secondly, full possessory property requires the protection of a state devoted to its protection, which thus limits the other matters of that state's concern: but again, not absolutely, because states also exist in societies. Anyway, private possessory property was certainly a major historical means for the distribution of power to individuals. Property-owners had power instead of the state—and instead of non-property-owners. Both conditions are required for the ideal to wriggle into any real life down here in the historical mud: as property, has power, the propertyless and the state both suffer from a consequential powerlessness. (Also intellect and intellectuals, but who cares?)

This classic system (which never existed) has ceased—except in that warm wonderful area in which individuals store their irrelevant ideals. What happened in the other important areas was, as our theorist of these matters (A. A. Berle) has said: "Modern technical organization silently battered property into its component fragments." The fragments are paper and power. The delicate phrase "modern technical organization" is a euphemism for corporations, commissariats, and bureaus like the DOD and the Department of Agriculture, which presume to harness the thrust of productive technology, that is, science applied to the formerly existing society. Applied technology is the power above all other powers. So in our new world, possessory property, the image of owned things, is mostly laughable—until the warm wonderful areas assert themselves once more against our cooler conceptions.

As for "paper," Berle discusses it as being the passive part of fragmented property: power is the active part. Passive property he refers to as "liquidity," and in his recent work has been, on this point, at least as brilliant as usual:

> To accomplish this liquidity, it is necessary that the property
> . . . have no relation whatever to its owner *except* that relation
> arising from the owner's capacity to transfer it. Nothing can be
> liquid if any value assigned to it depends upon the capacity or
> effort or will of the owner.

So modern property is adequately alienated paper. The modern system, calling for the quick allocation of large blocs of capital, requires liquidity—and liquidity is passive property. (It is also, given an adequate market, about the same thing as money.) These blocs of paper are agglomerate acts of faith, as far as any definite real value is concerned; but that such acts of faith should exist in the first place, and that they should then be subject to allocation to the great works of a society, expresses a rather creative connection between faith and act: paper is a genuine god.

After bequeathing us paper or passive property or liquidity, the modern fragmentation of property leaves us at last with the unanswered problem of power. It leaves us, in a word, with the bureaus administering technology, and the effects thereof on all society. These are extensive beyond description. In America, the large corporation (thus engaged) has undermined not only property, but also material scarcity, and much else besides—most particularly the whole paraphernalia of powers and ideologies and forms of personality accompanying the property-idea.

On the bequeathed problem of fragmented property, we get first of all the following major proposition: *Active property, passive state; passive property, active state.* This formulation should fix in our minds the property-cause of concentrated power in big statelike organizations and in the state itself. The profitable enticements of technology induced property-owners to delegate power, initially to the masters of the corporations, and lately also to the federal government for the benefit of the corporations. The first adequately alienated property was debt, including bank deposits: the first concentrated power in this country was financial: the first major use of federal power (apart from military action and pure giveaways like land for the railroads and tariffs for everybody else) was the Federal Reserve System. Active possessory property and the full exploitation of technology were incompatible.

8 A hundred or more years ago, a pre-Marxist French socialist named Pierre Proudhon wrote an attack on the classic system entitled *What Is Property?* He said it was theft. But this particular crime has been dis-solved. Now public and police alike ask, What Is Power? This is the problem bequeathed to post-socialist thought—equally so, incidentally, as a result of the triumph of bureaucratic socialism in Russia and of the corporate order here in the United States. Organizational power has replaced the problem of property as the major query presented by Western history. How to live with and perhaps occasionally here and there get the better of organizations, and maybe improve them in some of the countless ways imaginable, is now the firm context of the problem of *personal* power. In the longer Western perspective, we have moved from God to property to power. As if a further and further distilled compound were bubbling from test tube to test tube, we deal with an ever-clearer essence. And it is now an emotional one, as God and property were; but with each refraction more self-consciously so.

(The essence was always, of course, the question of law: the enforcement of rules for the living together of strangers *en masse*—that is, joining and acquiescing in mutual expectations.)

Even though we had pragmatism instead of socialism here in America, as the basic modern tradition, post-socialist thought has perhaps more application in this over-advanced but under-developed country than elsewhere. This new tradition can here be more essentially itself, since it need not bother with a detailed critique of traditional socialist doctrine. Also, things being farther along here technologically, and more backward in all other ways, the purer case is presented on these shores of ours which face both East and West (as, in another day, there was a special relation between bourgeois developments on the Continent and in Britain).

But we have such a teeny socialist tradition or understanding in this country that the term "post-socialist thought" may produce a certain blankness in discussion. What I refer to, besides the point already made about property-and-power, is this: Very simply, Marx was wrong—but not altogether wrong. Indeed, few major thinkers have been quite so usefully right as he was; and he would be the first, in deep disgust, to leave a current Russian or Chinese room in which "Marxism" was being discussed. Where he was pertinently incorrect, I think, was in the identification of the historically active class. It turned out (he could hardly have guessed) that it was not the so-called working class that would make the revolution for itself: it was the New Class that would lead anyone who might follow to make a revolution for *itself*—as in an earlier day it was the bourgeoisie that led all who would follow in the magnificent effort to elevate the bourgeoisie. *The New Class is the cream of the proletariat: and the cream has been separated from the curd.* (This is an additional consequence of understanding how wrong he was in predicting the continued material impoverishment of the workers.) So post-socialist thought is properly concentrated on this class and its historical role. We owe Marx the idea that classes make revolutions, and that this "making" is the flywheel of history; but when computers replace flywheels, the complicated maneuvers of class-advance leave the barricades of 1848 street fights far behind.

So this book is a speculation in post-socialist thought for Americans, if to the foregoing assumptions about property-and-power is added the mutative emergence of the New Class, and the accompanying rearrangement of the non-unionized lower proletariat as a new

Under Class. The New Class—by educational certification, actual training, and organizational position—holds something better than union privileges, and more important than property ownership: it "owns," it is, it identifies with, the organizations themselves. It will, then, as a class, operate the power mechanisms of the new world. Thus, the essay in your hands—you are probably a member of the New Class if you buy or read books—is an early appeal to the New Class to do and to believe and to feel this-rather-than-that. There will be many more such books.

The decisive relation for the future will be that of the New Class and the Under Class (which latter now includes, and will later include more than, the Negroes). These two will "meet," politically, in the House of Representatives—there finally to pervert the country, or to form a New Coalition which will enact its potential. For the members of the New Class, this issue will occur, occurs today, as emotional, symbolic, spiritual: Shall we continue merely to worship the manufactured slogans of Moral Democracy? Or shall we take a leap, and make an early effort to choose to be either the new middle-elite of a rigidly rational hierarchy or of a human democracy? Which of these would you like to live in? And help to create? And take responsibility for?

9 The New Class is becoming the special carrier of ideals, if these are at all connected with education. But its members are also quite practical, in that their education affords them good organizational jobs; and the tenure and work connected with these are not merely ideal. The New Class will have its greatest effect on American society in the new mix of ideals and practicality which it will offer to or inflict upon us.

The day-by-day and most ready adjustment of ideals and practicality occurs in that expressive thing called "style"—which is why fashion, its *modus operandi,* is so irresistible, so disgusting, so evanescent. In the nature of the case, any adjustment between ideals and actual events can only be temporary (and often enough so temporary as not to be noticed at all).

When President Kennedy was killed, we experienced—behind the immediate shock of the event and the ensuing excitement of a new Administration—a rather decisive pause in our history. This was because he had constituted a genuine departure in American style: in this—in nothing else, certainly—he had been nearly radical, genuinely ahead of his times. As for the program distinct from the style, it was nothing more than watered-down New Deal in the first place, and the new President was, obviously to everyone, immediately impressive—much more so than the dead hero—in getting it enacted. A fascinating conjunction of larger-than-life events, especially if you are interested in enactments as well as style, or vice versa; and the truth is that most of us, members of the New Class in particular, are.

It was a great cultural and educational loss to the nation to have been deprived of a Kennedy-Goldwater style contest. Especially since, twelve years earlier, we had unfortunately not been deprived of the equally educational engagement between Eisenhower and Stevenson. In both cases, the result was foregone, which enhances the cultural quality of the event. Also, the issues were vaguely the same: stale New Deal vs. stale anti-New Deal; ethnic mix vs. WASP presumption; intellectual vs. merely muscular purity; etc. In the second go-round, the emerging style of the New Class would have recovered the image of power and efficiency and success which it lost to native Americanism in 1952. That would have been nice: but now the certification will have to wait until 1968 or 1972.

In the post-Kennedy pause, President Johnson is clearing the decks and consolidating his centrist coalition based on the inherited New Deal grouping. In effect, he is fulfilling—he almost embodies in his own person the fulfillment of—the previously existing political system. This view will or will not be accepted according to one's evaluation of what the New Deal was all about, and more particularly what it still means, thirty years later, as a present concern. (These matters are discussed in Chapter Four.) In this writer's view, the New Deal—"program" and coalition both—properly occupy the current center. Innovation in American politics will come from a new left faction within speaking and jabbing distance of this established center—perhaps the very one now being constructed so brilliantly by the Kennedy government-in-exile. Our weird rightists will remain, vocal and significant, but they can seriously contend for national power only on a fascist wave following upon a genuine social breakdown.

It was only the long, dreary period of domestic paralysis since 1938, highlighted by the sociological holocaust of McCarthyism, that seemed to present a contradiction of this picture. We had become overadjusted to our frustration. And we canonized the New Deal because of its interrupted enactment.

The New Deal was not a genuine "program" but rather a major innovative impulse growing out of the Depression—a confused but joyous effort to use federal fiscal and regulatory power in trying to see if something couldn't be done about the economic collapse. It never reached the level of coherent national planning which we traditionally practice in furthering our military efforts. Indeed, it was our productive effort in World War II which in fact "resolved" the Great Depression. And we have been somewhat more or less "at war," in this economic sense, since then.

The over-all military effect is perhaps the main reason why so many people did not notice the absence of domestic policy, that for a quarter-century there had been no significant domestic reform and no important increase in federal spending—which would itself be a reform and which most other reforms require—that was not occasioned or excused by a foreign policy or a military need. Not only the New Deal but also all positive domestic policy ended in 1938. The other big reason is that while we did not have any, we certainly had a lot of talk about it—about reforms and spending and programs and so on. At times, the noise was deafening.

It was often referred to as "the liberal program." I suppose it was; but I found the call letters embarrassing. It was merely a collection of periodically amended proposals designed to deal with some few of the needs, opportunities, and recurrent crises of a technological urban society. The common denominator of the proposals was no more than a willingness to employ federal fiscal power and regulatory initiative in facing up to these matters. But the proposals took on a distinctly stale character due to repetitious non-enactment. And finally they came to suffer as well from excessive shrewdness, heated insistence, and premature surrender: from, that is, the effects of frustration.

As the common denominator was deficit, so the primary locus of the opposition had been the House of Representatives—constitutionally, the purse-string side of Congress. Whether one was observing Truman's impetuous and impassioned style, the lackadaisical fumbling of the Eisenhower years, or the elaborate managerial calculations of the Kennedy administration, the blockading paralysis remained highly consistent. This was, of course, the work of the conservative coalition in Congress that took over from the New Deal in 1938 and so nobly kept us bottled up in the Thirties. (One of the members of this coalition, explaining why he ever bothered to go onto the floor of the House, where nothing important ever happens, said: "Many bills which are essentially the same come up year after year; House attendance helps you acquire the background of basic legislation.")

Then, with President Johnson rather than the coalition dominating the 89th Congress, the so-called "liberal" program was finally more or less enacted. And, with the Negro voting bill, a further giant step was taken in the legal revolution supporting the Second Reconstruction (not a part of the New Deal, incidentally). From the perspective of post-New Deal frustration with which we had lived so long, it was all marvelous and wonderful and so on. But, we have to admit, strangely unsatisfying—indeed, almost uninteresting. Why? Because it was not like a burst of fresh income—a big raise with a promise of more to come, one's value to the firm finally recognized— but rather like a final award of back-pay after a long, irritating litigation.

President Johnson will give the country an inadequate program covering each and every identifiable need, from youth unemployment to water pollution. Mostly he will ensure prosperity—any kind and at any price. And the center will thus be established.

Once established, it will, I trust, be pushed and shoved from all directions.

The aspects of American politics presented in this book, and the kinds of power discussed most closely, are selective. I was looking for the factors usually neglected by the liberal book-reading public, and for other such openings to understanding. So this is not a comprehensive treatise on the subject of power. Foreign and military matters, the corporation and the union, and so on—these mechanisms of Big Power are hardly talked about at all.

We are in such an unresolved condition domestically that in truth (or at least in my opinion) we have nothing to offer the rest of the world, except for our military power devoted to the containment of Communism. We are not able to offer any real alternative after or even while Communism, that unwelcome face of the future, is being held back by these merely military means. Our agricultural and industrial surplus is a greater international weapon by far than missiles or Special Forces, but domestically we have not been able to find the political trigger. So while nothing is more important than to avoid a nuclear engagement and at the same time present livable alternatives to technological totalitarianism, we are just not up to it (because of our domestic political default) on the larger arena of this planet. The surplus that *can* be utilized, and perhaps with decisive effect, is the surplus capacity to think and act generously which is afforded to many Americans by their affluence. This is personal and immediate, so it seems reasonable to approach it directly by analysis and exhortation, thus encouraging a more self-conscious and effective use of this surplus. We Americans are experiencing a new condition: its qualities are untested: someone ought to try. The following chapters are my effort to present an ideal-but-realistic view of the American situation for the consideration of our New Class—of which I count myself a nervous, tenuous member.

We are not yet formed: let us now participate in our own formation.

THE
PROBLEM

American
History

TWO

Non-Rule
and Some of
Its History

1 The first great issue in American history was whether we were to have a continental government at all; its final resolution took about a hundred years. The second great issue of American history—which remains unresolved after another hundred years—is whether the continental government, now that we have it, is ever going to be allowed to govern.

There are two major and two minor exceptions to this formula for our history. War and some other foreign relations have always been the province of the national power. Without the pressure proceeding from these imperatives, the national government, once it had completed its second major function—namely, to assist in collecting and distributing the lands of the continent—would probably have become purely ceremonial. As for the "minor" exceptions, the first has been to contribute slightly to the managing of the liberties, the welfare, and the general utility of the population, while the second—and potentially more important—has been the role of the national government, inherited from the bankers during the Great Depression, in averting the domestic disaster which lies just beyond a conventional slowdown of production.

All other purposes and non-purposes of the continental government have been converging on this no longer minor exception, and around it the fresh dynamisms of our history are currently expressed, repressed, distorted, and contained. We now have a society and an economy neither of which can work adequately without somewhat more positive central authority than we have been accustomed to. I take it as fully self-evident that the technological society called the United States is too big and too complex, too dynamic existentially and metaphysically too desperate, to continue its existence under the jurisdiction of the inherited principles and techniques of non-government. From this self-evident premise, one may deduce a summary crisis of American history, involving most pointedly the eternal issue in that history—our refusal or inability to become a coherent nation.*

The institutional and ideological ground of the crisis has always been there: what brings it forward now is the present overriding need of genuine, positive, effective, national, legal, democratic, American government. The ideological ground is, in essence, our exasperatingly profound and equally absurd idea that money is a thing in itself, that there is never enough of it, that it is a private matter, and that the federal government, being public, should therefore have as little to do with it as possible. All this centers now on the qualities of the budget (and on devices, such as the price guidelines, for protecting its effect), and especially on the deficit in the budget. Other ideological matters—mostly the rags and tatters of free-enterprise theology—cluster around this one and are subordinate to it.

The general subject of this chapter is our historical non-rule in America; my particular thesis is that American individuals and institutions give profound evidence of peculiar attitudes toward power. These peculiarities are especially gathered under and around negative notions of power—initially, a deep reluctance to think in terms of the concept at all, and thereafter, when an element or issue of power has finally been identified, a strong impulse simply to consider it an evil and to "oppose" it. A great deal of politics in America, both thought and action, consists of little more than an opposition to power: especially public official power, and especially national legal power. In other words, we are not yet a nation in the full responsible sense, and it is still a question when we shall become one. From this

---

* I can see only one objection, logical or otherwise, to this deduction: the whole course of American history, from the beginning, gives the uneasy appearance of crisis.

point of view, we can discern a consistent framework to American history despite the frontier hurly-burly involved in settling and industrializing a great continent: the ever-present issue of just what that government in Washington was supposed to be doing there.

Our current problem is not so much that the "wrong" political decisions have recently been taken, and certainly not lack of awareness as to the generally indicated direction of fresh and adequate policy: the paralyzing problem is the abysmal capacity of the country for rear-guarding negativism, which has been unearthed and expressed, organized and overorganized, in the past thirty years. This is power derived from the anti-national and anti-majoritarian features in the very *structure* of our system, and it is asserted on behalf of a non-program; in many respects, the protagonists of this negative power do not even pretend satisfaction with what they are preserving by its exercise. (Perhaps this is why our conservatives have recently become "radical.") I cannot believe that this non-program represents a national consensus. It is only a minority of the nation who have confronted the newness of our day and have then and there decided that they cannot bear it, that they will not deal with it, that they will instead live within a spiritually "livable" image of the world whatever the historical and obvious facts of the matter may turn out to be.

2 So the issue of our history has been whether we were to have a federal government that would rule. The state of irresolution of this issue just prior to the Depression is suggested by the following pronouncement by President Coolidge:

> If the Federal Government should go out of existence, the common run of people would not detect the difference in the affairs of their daily life for a considerable length of time.

(One may well ask, President of *what*?)

So that was the "issue." But the chief "event" in American history was that so many people made so much money so quickly—and with so little sense of responsibility to anything other than their own active intent to do so. This was well expressed by C. Vann Woodward in *The Origins of the New South* when he characterized one of Morgan's agents in the building of that great instrument of colonial power, the Southern Railway, as follows:

Smith operated the Louisville and Nashville [a component of the Southern Railway] for thirty-eight years on the theory that, in his words, "society, as created, was for the purpose of one man's getting what the other fellow has, if he can, and keep out of the penitentiary." His chief complaint lay against government interference with the game.

The purpose at the beginning was very possibly otherwise. Certainly the personnel of government was different. But all the elite capacity of the Virginia Dynasty and the principled New Englanders was not adequate to create the country on another model. Whether one assigns the primary deficiency to the quality of these two regional cultures, to some flaw in the original constitutional deal, or to the basic unmanageability of the problem presented by this tempting continent, the Civil War did happen and then did usher in the true and new and real businessman's America, which is the one we still have to deal with today.

The problem of moving people West, and commercial money into the colonial South, was indeed one of the great problems of human history—that is, to accomplish it in a civilized manner; but somewhat more in the way of civilization might well have been achieved under a different conception of rulership. And this might have been in fact forthcoming from cultures somewhat richer and deeper than those offered by the colonial North and South. The gravest faults in the beginning, and which persisted, were the excessive rationalism of the Founders—subsequently to be applied ferociously to the subjects of money and property—and the dark, deeply irrational and intractable issue of slavery. Between them, these fissures weakened the original constitutional system to the point where it never had a fair chance to constitute a governing authority for the westward move and the Southern renovation. I share the heretical view that, so far from the Constitution's being our greatest blessing, the really astounding consideration is that the country has survived it this nicely.

It has been a fine system for preventing national tyranny. But it accomplished this at the expense of preventing national government as well; and finally of promoting other forms of tyranny, to account for the lack of such government. To the extent that any national government of any kind is necessary and consequently does occur (even if only in limited areas and for limited periods), the system ensures that such government shall be more authoritarian than it would be if it were constitutionally provided for or realistically understood. Legal and effective national government in the United States has been an *occasional* thing, a result of crisis, usually of a military nature. What happens—apart from straight grab and give-away—is that a specific area of activity will require the use of legal national power, and just exactly enough of it will be borrowed and established as the cementing item in an *ad hoc* institutional arrangement with the relevant non-governmental powers. There are numerous examples: it is a very basic American pattern. (As a general illustration, the so-called regulatory agencies represent such a use of legal federal power.)

Perhaps the primary irony of American history is that a purposely perplexing system established for an eighteenth century colonial gentry was inherited and used by a very un-genteel group of post-Civil War winners. A system having been set up to favor the rule of a superior class, it was subsequently discovered that this so-so class was easily overwhelmed; not by the propertyless, as had been feared, but by the new-propertied. The established restraints were then exaggeratedly worked thin by the grossest group of plutocrats and spoilsmen imaginable, most of whom had nominated themselves from off the streets. The original system, based on an intricate web of impossibility, required the highest order of class responsibility to function as a government at all—at least as high an order of responsibility as that of the Framers. It was never achieved again. The achievable national purpose since the Civil War has been on occasion to slow down the pace of stealing. Not much more was possible.

Concerning this early period, Richard Hofstadter says:

A properly designed state, the Fathers believed, would check interest with interest, class with class, faction with faction, and one branch of government with another in a harmonious system of mutual frustration.

And the Important People were expected, one supposes, to resolve each and every impasse with a neat application here-and-there of the lace trimmings of eighteenth century wisdom. But the very simple point is that there are only two "reasonable" political systems: an aristocratic one and a majoritarian one. The Constitution was established to forestall majority rule in the new country, without reliance on monarchy. The difficulty with our history has been that during most of it there has been no aristocracy able or willing to rule in place of the majority. Moreover, the successful effort to talk the masses out of trying to rule themselves (and on occasion to suppress their efforts) has been deeply corrupting in the absence of this viable aristocratic alternative. The alternative-in-fact has been the narrow rule of business, of money-making by any means and for any purpose.

"The liberties that the Constitutionalists hoped to gain were chiefly negative," Hofstadter adds. What was established was mainly a web of protection for property interests against numerous real and imagined assaults thereon. Hofstadter sees the Federalist/Republican conflict as a conflict between two kinds of property-owners, the Northern investing class and the Southern landed class. He says of the agrarians that "their primary goal [was] essentially negative"—to keep governmental power out of the hands of the non-agrarian property-owners.

A great inhibition currently observable in the creation of positive national government in the United States proceeds still from the Southern obstructionist bloc; and this was true in the very beginning. The checks and balances of the system were written into the original charter by the Southern states in order to ensure that they would forever be able to protect the institution of agrarian slavery. When national power was required to complete the industrial conquest of the continent, the Civil War was fought against the Southern proposition. But a major effort of the Civil War, as we know, was never completed. Full federal law was never brought to the South. Moreover, the political system had been established in such a way that, in the post-Civil War period, the resulting national power was not that of the legal central government but rather that of a greatly expanded private government of finance and industry. The democratic elements in our society have from the very beginning—and I mean, beginning with Jefferson—been ruinously compromised by the racial issue. This was as true of the New Deal, for instance, as ever it was in the past.

The Civil War was "completed" in the Hayes-Tilden election of 1876—the major "bought" election in our history. This seems to have been the fateful moment when the Northern business interests realized that the "Southern remnant" need be fought no longer, was indeed defeated, and now could be preserved as a buffer against popular action: a doomsday decision. For the history of the Negro in this country, it was the most important election since 1860 and would remain the most important until 1932, and perhaps more important than both; because it was at this time that the Northern Republicans finally returned the South—necessarily including the Negroes—to the Southerners. It was also certainly the end of Radical Republicanism, and of all the ideals of the Abolitionist movement (and therefore of New England as well).

> The hour had come at last when the Republicans and their northern capitalist allies no longer needed to "use" the freed Negro as a pretext or as an ally, for the forceable control of the political government,

says Matthew Josephson in *The Politicos*. So the political basis for Southern independence, along with a new Southern opportunity for continuing the enslavement of the Negro, was established. This system of *de facto* slavery was finally canonized in *Plessy v. Ferguson* twenty years later. The major benefit of the Civil War thus ended up in the hands of the Eastern business interests, although numerous other classes had joined in the great effort, including homesteading farmers, workers, other immigrants, and cultured New Englanders.

The remnant of Eastern class responsibility began to reappear with Henry Adams and the Mugwumps; and was most forcefully expressed later by the Progressives. (The cultured Southerner appeared again mostly in fiction.) Hofstadter's shrewd picture of the Progressive movement is drawn from the circumstance that the great accumulation of wealth in the post-Civil War period upset the balance of society by reducing the stature of the previously secure class of inherited wealth, culture, professional intellect, etc. These people were galvanized into an attack on the new wealth, and what it was doing to the country socially and politically (especially including them). And finally, more than a generation later (as Schlesinger beautifully states it):

> Before a crowd gone mad, T.R., strong as a bull moose, challenged his followers to stand at Armageddon and battle for the Lord. Across the nation young men rose to his call. . . .

But one young man of that generation (Frederick R. Coudert), writing to a friend during the New Deal days, could say:

> When you and I first began to practice law . . . one hardly needed to know that there was a Federal Government until one went abroad.

(Referring, of course, to the utility of consular services: *noblesse oblige,* indeed.)

The problem of the radical social critic in the United States is a simple and disastrous one—there has been no established national power to criticize. I suggest that it is time to recognize this fact, however embarrassing the resulting orientation may turn out to be. The consequence of continuing not to face up to it is a crushing burden of confusion, which is intolerable culturally even if one imagines it to be insignificant—or even "helpful"—politically. One cannot even attack the stupidity of "our ruling class" in good faith, because we do not have one entitled either to the name or to the assault. They haven't got sense enough to rule. ("Rule," I said, not "steal": I make this distinction because many Americans do not readily recognize the difference.)

It's early, but let's summarize: The sum of our history is that we have had a very makeshift ruling "class" and a constitutional system that could be run only by a very good one. The result has been a mess. This is what it means to say, and I say it, that we are not a nation. Note that law—to say nothing of justice—issues from power: what law we have is given us—yes, in response to our demand as well as our entreaty—but still given or allowed to us by our powerful groups. (Whom we in turn also "allow," of course.)

What a job they have done—on us. It is a wonder that there is any law left in this country: on race in the South, and on corporate power across the country, there is in fact little to speak of. Oh, the grand irresponsibility of money-making, when taken as the ultimate devotion! Galbraith says of Andrew Mellon, in the days preceding the Great Crash, that he was "a passionate advocate of inaction"—as the Secretary of the Treasury, that is, and facing a runaway credit inflation. The bankers and all the others, they either didn't know or just couldn't admit what they were doing. Schlesinger reports:

Hoover summoned leading bankers to secret meetings in the fall of 1931, and invited them to pool their funds in order to provide a credit reserve for their weaker brethren. To his chagrin, most of the group insisted that *this was the government's responsibility.* (Emphasis added.)

This put the final sign of the Great Kibosh on the default of the bankers for the system from which they had benefited most and from which they then ran. How truly American they were to decide finally that the *government*—that they had kept from coming into existence—had the responsibility to exercise the power that they alone held!

And our situation is similar today. Note that, because power is in process of being transferred from the *rentier* to the corporate segment of the New Class to the governmental segment (add military) —because it is *in transit*—no one alone has enough actual, usable power to work with. In Congress, the essential democratic institution, we have enthroned—as a historical result of the efforts of this ruling class of ours—a "rationally" derived system that amounts to the most desperate form of legalistic obstructionism yet made available to so important a segment of mankind.

First, there was vicious competition for the wealth of the continent, and then something like a money-making order formed out of all that money-making activity. Now we require a real and responsible national elite that goes beyond the established money-making cabal: actually to do away with that fun-group is past our capacity. But we must somehow get beyond it, by adding some kind of managerial overlay: we must.

3   With the sad demise or default of the original ruling class, after they had blessed us with our rationalistic constitutional system, we ended up with Jacksonian farmers and post-Civil War money-makers. The latter won all the big battles. So the money-men were mostly in charge of creating the private government that substituted for the legal public authority our "classless" money-making history had denied us. (We had money-making instead of class—that's one of the reasons money remains so spectacularly peculiar in the affections of the American people.)

The history of the United States, certainly since the Civil War, is the history of dual government—public official government on the one hand, and private financial-industrial government on the other. Except for war and other crises, our private government has been far and away the dominant one. But since the 1929 collapse, additional governing has been called for by the geometrically progressing complexity of the technological system, as well as by the needs and presumptions of the military economy. (I think we all understand that if there had not been a Cold War, we would have had to invent one —or suffer a political revolution.) A substantial amount of such governing authority has finally been relocated in Washington, D.C., as originally intended by the pre-Civil War rationalists.

Both governments are necessary in running a technological democracy. It is not a matter of either/or. And neither is an effective government without the other: in fact, the destructive aspect of the conflict between the two has resulted in each being less effective in its own sphere than it might otherwise have been. Even halfway properly articulated, the two powers with their inherent independence could provide the necessary counterbalance which is our desired bulwark against common nightmares of tyranny. But it is not possible realistically to provide against tyranny if we will not admit to ourselves where the power is. To provide against federal tyranny only, while ignoring or denying the obvious facts of concentrated private power, is a deep disservice to each and to the ideals of American pluralism. We all want a limited government, if the alternative is an unlimited one. Of course we want a limited government, in *both* the public and the private spheres.

It may very well be that banking, as represented by the achieved power of J. P. Morgan, was the first form of national power created in this country—after the westward move began, and apart from the national role of the army in fighting the Southern rebellion and the Indians and other prior occupants. In any event, national continental power was first created in this country by finance and industry (under credit-type capitalism, banking is a primary form of political organization). The federal government assisted the money-making interests in building *their* national power; it did not build one in contradistinction to theirs. This trend is pre-Civil War: Hofstadter says of the Bank of the United States during Jackson's term, "As a fiscal agency it was comparable in magnitude to the government itself." In 1837 Nicholas Biddle wrote: "As to mere power, I have been for years in the daily exercise of more personal authority than any President habitually enjoys."

If that was the situation in 1837, then for extension we may note that in 1902 it was Mark Hanna and Morgan who brought about a settlement of the great anthracite strike which Teddy Roosevelt was powerless to resolve on his own. This also reveals the division of power between the private government and the public government.

One cannot avoid the impression that the political leaders of the Republican Party, after the Civil War, acted as if they were agents of another, more "real" government than the one they were officially charged with tending. The official government was for them a way of making a living. It was used mostly, as with the tariff and railroad-building, to distribute advantages to business interests—that "other" government. This also served the defensive function of ensuring that potential governmental power was not allowed to "lapse" (so to speak) into the hands of the populace. When one has said all this, it seems to me one has said the main thing. That's mostly what the government was. That's mostly what the politicians did.

Let us refer, as an example, to the long history of tariff regulations. Tariff was a federal grab-bag from which business interests, acting on a passive government, took what they needed and what they could get (which was a great deal) to establish their own national power. In the tariff agitation of 1866, the ironmongers of Pennsylvania wanted an increase in their protection (according to Josephson), although "iron was at $80 a ton here as against $32 in England." This was the "borrowed" basis of Andrew Carnegie's empire. The advantage of the tariff accrued to private business interests, not to the government. The same general story would be true of the giveaway of natural resources. Indeed, one of these "resources" was the governmental power available to be expropriated—as with the tariff—by entrepreneurs. (And then they took the duty receipts and redeemed Civil War greenbacks in specie, also for their benefit.)

The Spoilsmen of the Republican Party were known as "the tariff gang." They administered the organized grab, and certainly made money out of it. First of all, the customs duties provided the federal patronage—the "spoils" in the spoils system. (Customs duties were the main source of income to the federal government through most of our history.) And they also took money directly from the business interests being benefited. The tariff was *joint* taxation by business and the party controlling the government: it became the chief form of theft. (Today, tax preferences have played a similar role.) If one credits Hofstadter, this system, too, had early beginnings: "It was tariffs, not slavery, that first made the South militant," he says (but notes as well that the balance of population—which was about equal in 1790—had shifted substantially in the North's favor before the Civil War). Once established, both parties lived off the tariff system: in the election of 1892, Henry Havemeyer, head of the Sugar Trust, contributed as usual to both parties. Testifying before a Senate Committee in 1894, he said: "We receive a good deal of protection for our money." (So did Al Capone's customers, incidentally.) What he wanted was to be sure that if the Republicans were elected, he would get a positive benefit out of the tariff, and that if the Democrats were elected, they at least would not remove the existing Republican tariff. He bought both positive and negative insurance. The situation had been "organized."

One of the more superb crises in our system of dual government, until recently, was the extraordinary one represented by NRA at the beginning of the New Deal. NRA was the unsuccessful attempt of American business to govern itself—but to *govern*. Business accepted wage levels above the "natural" ones, and in return it was permitted to fix prices legally: the underlying *raison* of NRA was the almost unanimous business demand for price-fixing in order to halt the headlong deflation. Also, and most significantly, the first effort of business to govern, naturally enough, followed a military pattern. Schlesinger pinpoints this neatly as follows: "The child of the War Industries Board, NRA was the father of the War Production Board." And also naturally enough, NRA was a revivalist debauch. Led by the Billy Sunday of economic engineering, General Hugh Johnson, the enthusiasm generated by the magnificent advances of the unbelievable—"over two million employers signed up"—was like nothing so much as a national camp meeting. (If it had been televised, it might have stuck—at least as entertainment, if not as policy.) But Schlesinger adds:

> . . . NRA paid a price too, for Johnson, in transforming a government agency into a religious experience, had put over all too well a millennial vision of rising wages, spreading work, and six million new jobs by Labor Day.

Nothing was more American than the Blue Eagle—for the initial enthusiasm accompanying it, its apocalyptic character, and its nasty, abrupt demise.

But when the noise quieted down, and the New Deal (that is, the necessary adjustment between the two governments) began in earnest, I think that what happened was more or less similar to the pattern of railroad-building, etc.: business quickly learned how to use government to its own advantage, no more and no less than was useful; and finally to create its own style of minimal, and still largely private, governing—and mostly for its own limited advantage (that is, still within the concept of scarcity). A. A. Berle, who was there, says of the New Deal: "Never as far as I could see was great change less revolutionary." If one *assumes* the existence of national power, then indeed almost nothing at all happened except that some of it was used—in a typically wild and experimental American fashion, to begin with. But even so, what the New Deal represented was the first major non-military meeting of the American people with the inherent negativism of their government—*which engagement they somehow won.*

I have characterized our dual government at such length because it, and our ignorance of it, provide the most enduring institutional source of our absurd attitude toward power. After all, our full and easy acceptance of extensive corporate authoritarianism must be given at least equal weight with our loud and righteous rejection of central governmental authority. As Galbraith has put it: "In the American liberal tradition, a finding that private economic power exists has been tantamount to a demand that it be suppressed." Which it never is. In another strand of the American tradition, any discovery of non-military public power is also accompanied by a demand for early suppression. Which we have also not yet gotten around to. (Please note that the private corporate government of which I speak is, as much as the other one, very much a *federal* system—that is, national, but loosely so.)

Our constitutional system inhibited the creation of a legal national government, *and made inevitable the establishment of private national governments.* These latter were and still are illegally derived: by "illegal," I mean exercising power "not officially constituted"—that is, unconstitutional.

4 America is different—*how* different we hardly dare admit to ourselves. Mostly we are different, I think, because in the Atlantic passage we were traveling not only far but also light as for cultural baggage; and in the westward continental move, we traveled just as far and even lighter. The heritage was spread exceedingly thin, with the consequence that the resulting society was rudimentary: it was mostly created, in a rough-and-tumble, by the travelers themselves, without much assistance from pro-consuls who might have instituted a fuller range of the older cultures from which we derived. We early rid ourselves of our colonial governors. And never was a segment of humanity so tempted by the Eden-like fruit of conjoined natural bounty and ripe technology. It was like letting a bunch of kids loose in a candy store—hardly anybody behaved well.

Pointed against the imagined fullness of human capacity and purpose, such a society is shallow; being shallow, it is necessarily fantasy-ridden (to make-up by making-believe); the fantasies in a society of shallow cultural forms could be expected to be deeper, greater in quantity, and more "private" in nature. Our depth tends to be individual rather than social, and nearly incommunicable. Paradoxically, the shallow society forces ideal Individualism on its members while providing them with reduced and insufficient means for its practical attainment—each effect is the result of the same social shallowness. It is like demanding greatness from a son set adrift without much material or spiritual inheritance: he may in fact be forced to spend himself merely surviving.

A Big Principle for understanding the American power structure is that it is a grouping of gangs. Or, if the term is too unpleasant, let us say that it is a collection of disparate constituencies. There is no clear movement in this country from the emotional pattern of the family to expanding communities which organize essentially the same emotions in something like the same patterns, albeit for different uses. Despite all our efforts, neither the bar nor the office is a home. Instead, what we have is a basic interruption in the family emotional pattern shortly after puberty. There is no room for both sexuality and growth, for a genuinely maturing animal individuality, within our family pattern; that form, under pressure of animal growth, does not so much expand with freedom as collapse in the street. The result is that non-family public life is ganglike, beginning with the well-known street gangs of adolescence. (Note also the severe significance of college—even high-school—classmates.) This discontinuity between private family emotional patterns and the expansive emotionality which is organized for extra-familial and more public life, persists throughout one's career. This dooms us, first, to an extremely overheated family pattern in later life, with an astounding concentration on children as children: the horrible hunger to relive one's own interrupted childhood. And then there is that grab-bag of "left-over" emotions available largely to a demeaning of public life, which is especially characterized by a lack of tenderness, a lack of concern for the next generation-in-large, a similar and even more characteristic lack of concern for the previous generation-in-particular, and a concentration on grab. Thus we convert public life into a foraging arena in which movables can be commandeered and transported back into the private emotional cave which is the natural habitat of spiritually sundered animals in this spiritually divided jungle of ours.

One point may be added to "balance" this picture: upon the failure of this overheated private family life, and the projection of the emotion derived therefrom and formerly devoted thereto upon the larger public scene, the result *can* be something quite beyond pathos —it can be genuinely dangerous. (We ought to be thankful for television, that saving invasion of the private *even* with spurious public fantasies.)

For politics, a big consequence of the gang or constituency form— based on the schism which sets aside primary emotions and relieves public life of their benefit until they have reached a distorted pitch at which they are a public burden—is that the higher form of politics in America is brokerage (including even the accommodation of various hysterias). Brokerage is the relation between constituencies. Brokerage politics is inevitable in a shallow society, one in which there are no formal classes, and therefore no formal relations between groups: as for power, there are money and institutional position to be considered, and the subjectivity of people who will broker their money status for other status, and vice versa. One reason money is so important in America is that we have very little else of a general nature to hold us together: and that is also why we are so rigid about it.

This leads, for instance, to a heavy concentration on the importance of the job, which is not merely a source of income but also our major foray into the public arena; and beyond that, upon the familiarity with techniques which qualify us for our jobs. We are in effect an anarcho-syndicalist society: no social form other than or superior to "work"; and, with immense irony, the first society in which actual work is becoming genuinely redundant and the term itself confusing.

To recapitulate a bit: The subject of politics is power; power is an aspect of emotional organization; emotional organization is a result of culture, or at least results in culture, and in any event is tied to it by reason of the personality of the generations. Having, for our speculative purposes, thus connected politics and culture, we then notice the peculiar deficiencies in the American culture-power complex. The general proposition is that we are an *ad hoc* society. It is a major effort just to hold the situation together. Our first necessity is always accommodation according to the given circumstance. This puts brokerage up front.

Our regionalism is no less shallow for being small and narrow-minded. National power, national jurisdiction, national law, national culture—namely, America as a nation—that is what we need to press for. Meanwhile, there is very little true local community or government in the United States. We are a collection of shallow and spurious and artificial communities, and it is one and the same thing to say about us that we need more national government and that we have hardly any real local government at all. Gunnar Myrdal has noted that we have a heightened and unfortunate need for federal intervention precisely because our traditions of local organization are inadequate, much inferior to those in many European countries. And what we do have—mostly the corporations and similar "private" organizations—is barely recognized for what it is.

The basic gang structure of American life resulted from the fact that we came over here in gangs, we got off the ships in gangs, we moved West in gangs, we exploited the continent and made money in gangs. The criminal gangs we read about simply imitated the basic American pattern while operating in forbidden areas.*

* The story of the Whisky Ring in the Grant administration suggests that

5 Immediately important, for our purposes, has been the ganglike quality of our political parties. They are especially American—and not less specially so because unaccounted and unprovided for constitutionally. In *The Politicos*, Josephson says of the American political party:

> It had its own rules (many of them secret); tactics, and ends; its own store of knowledge and experience. It was something "organic." It was virtually a tribal institution—as distinct as the church or the nobility in older lands—risen among the American people, rooted in the climate of the new democratic nation from the very beginning.

Politics got its dirty name in America from local operations like that of Boss Tweed in New York City and, nationally, from the extensive indecorum of the Republican Party in the Grant administrations. Whatever local and national differences one elaborates, the two misbegotten operations battened off and serviced the same client —business. "The parties of the period after the Civil War were based on patronage, not principle; they divided over spoils, not issues," says Hofstadter. And Josephson goes on to add:

> In short, the new capitalism gave an immense impetus to official and political venality—blindly, by its own disorderliness and fiercely competitive character rather than out of regard for its own deeper interest.

Later, what political commodities business required it would buy at wholesale (under Mark Hanna's tutelage)—or even go into the manufacturing end. But right after the Civil War, there was a very brisk retail trade.

Of course, we all know that Jackson created the "spoils system" in dethroning the Virginia Dynasty (whose management of the govern-

---

some aspects of organized politics in America are an outgrowth of organized crime, rather than the other way around; that at first they were the same, and then later the particularly illegal part of the operation was spun-off with the provision that a continuous ground rent, so to speak, be paid in tribute to the party for later protection, or non-recognition.

ment and other patronage was not called "spoils" because such well-born people were involved). But it flowered in administration after money-making won the War Against the States. Then, there was one-party rule *for* business, no matter which party happened to be tending the store.* It would appear that after the Civil War the parties finally reached a level and a character of organization whereby it could be said that we had parties instead of a government. Or, at least, they gave us the *kind* of government identified by Horatio Seymour, writing to Samuel Tilden after the overthrow of Tweed in New York: "All people want men in office who will not steal, but will not interfere with those who do." (You can see the strain that might put on the office-holder.)

I would not attempt to review even the highlights of theft in those glorious days, not even the *Crédit Mobilier* scandal. But I want to make a point about Morgan's famous "preferred list"—the collection of distinguished men, including leading politicians, who were invited to participate in lucrative underwritings. What is often overlooked in all the hullabaloo about the preferred list (a root-source of the currently discussed "conflict of interest") is that everybody has one—that is part of the gang structure of the country. I doubt if it would have been much remarked on had it not included politicians, who approach the "take" from left field, although its character would have been nearly the same. Everybody operates in and through a circle of acquaintances; and money or other items of value are naturally exchanged wherever good and useful friends get together in America.

Reformers and other outsiders have operated in gangs, too. The great John P. Altgeld of Illinois built up a personal machine in his efforts to win the governorship. In Wisconsin, Robert La Follette builded so well that his machine ended up as a dynasty. The gang structure of politics in America can cut both ways—and I suggest it *should* cut the "other" way more often than it does. Indeed, this sort of personal machine ought to afford more mileage today than it did in the past (more resources are available). But reformers don't like

---

* It seems fairly obvious that Cleveland put the Democratic Party back in business after the Civil War by imitating the Republicans, just as Thomas E. Dewey did for the Republican Party after Roosevelt. Me-tooing is endemic in our party system. Hofstadter characterizes Cleveland deliciously as follows: "Out of heartfelt conviction he gave to the interests what many a lesser politician might have sold them for a price. He was the flower of American political culture in the gilded age."

machines, or the disciplined use of energy and resources implied thereby. Indeed, when they belong to a gang they don't like to admit it even to themselves.

Why? Why this stand-offishness on the part of those valuable persons who are interested in something more than money? Why can't they gang up American-style with less distaste and more effect?

Well, I have thought about this and I have an answer: they are Americans, too. This is not, in fact, a nation of money-grubbers: it is a nation of money-grubbers *and* moralists. Money and morality are of equally exaggerated importance in the shallow society, so Americans look to their moral status just as they study net-worth statements, all the time accumulating values in either line. Preferably in both: you never know how the "market" is going to turn.

Intellectuals and other beyond-money people in America have never come to terms with the dominant fact of our history, namely, that there is not a cultured ruling class to which their own culture could be realistically referred. So money and morality are intermixedly confused; so the essential and unpleasant question of power—particularly where it hurts, in relation to culture and ideal values—does not come wrapped in cellophane, like everything in America should. It is personal and immediate and ambiguous: it is existential. (That is, if it is valid—otherwise the issue goes by default. Which has been much more typically American.)

On this central subject, Hofstadter is wonderfully good: for his very useful scholarship, his excellent analysis—*and* for exemplifying the problem in his own attitudes. These latter come through clearly because he is such a good writer. He is very perceptive in tracing the moralism and the Puritanism in our history—this seems to be his main concern—especially as it is revealed in our two great reform movements, Progressivism and Populism. He is duly attracted to and embarrassed by Progressivism. But Populism holds an ugly fascination for him, and he never manages to overcome his revulsion at the screaming primitive moralism that was situated at its center. (Even so, he sets up the discussion of these matters quite expertly.)

But Populism was our great revolt against the private financial government that had been so successfully established in the United States: it is revealingly unreasonable to expect the protest to have been refined. The revolt was carried forward with the cultural materials available, *not* with the best imaginable. This was a raw country, and the oppression being protested against was equally raw; so I think that Hofstadter's cultural disdain and fear of Populism are overemphasized.

Harry Truman, for instance, was something of a latter-day Populist—with the rousing campaign cry uttered by the audience itself, *"Give 'em hell, Harry!"* which echoed the famous line of Mrs. Mary Ellen Lease, one of the leading Populists of the revolt of the 1890's—*"What you farmers need to do is to raise less corn and more Hell!"* For political emotion, you can't beat it. Without this kind of political emotion, we would have had very little "politics" at all in America, at least as practiced by ordinary people. The terrible problem is that so many intellectuals look back with yearning upon the days of the Virginia Dynasty, the only approach in America to responsible class government. But culture out of context can be just as bad as morality out of context. This revulsion at the Populists can be easily overdone. After all, this is America.

And after all, what the farmers wanted was *more money*—and, with parity, they finally got it. This was their complaint and their demand from the time of the Jacksonian attack on the Bank of the United States—indeed, from the time of Jefferson's conflict with Hamilton, or even beginning with the role of the Treasury and the payment of the debt of the Revolutionary War. It was always the same. The farmers wanted money.

Of the two strands of reformism which culminated in the New Deal, it was Populism that was the first to demand a federal government with the power to act positively on behalf of the mass of the people. (Most significantly, the farmers' protest was occasioned in large measure by the fact that they were experiencing our first "overproduction" problem.) The fact that the furor ended with the Scopes Trial and parity is certainly a large piece of history, and difficult to digest without Alka-Seltzer. But I deeply appreciate our primitives for their positive approach to power. Meanwhile, Hofstadter says of the Jeffersonians and Jacksonians and Progressives and other pre-New Deal reformers: "Their conceptions of the role of the national government were first largely negative and then largely preventive."

Now doesn't it turn on a bulb in your head that the New Deal not only greatly carried forward the positive role of the federal government in achieving reform but was also a sharp departure, as Hofstadter notes, in reversing "the ideological roles of conservatives and reformers"—that is, the excessively moral position was abandoned by the reformers, who became practical, and the morality was picked up by the conservatives, who then espoused a principled program of inaction? The conservatives inherited both the morality and the conjoined negativism. My point is, let 'em have it, and good riddance: with this exchange accomplished, the liberals will at last—and clearly—be more truly American than the old-fashioned Native Americans.

In the sense that so many elements of it were then at last revealed, our history crested in the New Deal—seen as a non-moralistic coalition of reform elements. But we have not gotten much beyond this Period of Revelation. Meanwhile, the brokers, who have always dominated our business civilization, have been busy just holding things together. Their model—appropriately enough a congressional figure —was Sam Rayburn. The Age of Rayburn is ended, however. He and it were probably more of a factor in our recent history than either Truman's Populist-minded attempt to revive the New Deal or Eisenhower's silly effort to adapt house-broken McKinleyism to twentieth century uses. The compelling *sense of departure* conveyed by the late President Kennedy was, no matter how much or how little substance it involved, his very startling contribution. It *is* time for a departure.

And it is this Congress of ours that blocks the road. No nation without it: no nation, apparently, with it. This country cannot be run properly without a positive-acting legislature. Congress is the problem. But the Congress is tolerated—if not actually created—by the Democratic Party. The reason the Democrats are the majority party is that they most often do not act like a party and therefore cannot properly use a majority position. In any event, the post-1938 Democratic Party is a holding action—and now it is pretty clearly holding us back (as we will see in the afterglow even of Johnsonian magic).

Our peculiar American political parties have served as bridges between the two governments of our dual system: that is the key to their character. But to the extent that these two governments and their relations change, so must the parties. Otherwise, their function in relation to serious movements is, taking Populism and Progressivism as examples, to betray the primitivism of the one and misdirect the refined moralism of the other. Thus the shallow society is held together, and deepening change is denied or obscured.

6 The party—gang or not—is a greatly creative form of power in post-monarchical society. The discovery was made, throughout the Western world, that the principle of legitimacy conferred by virtue of a rational constitution (rather than by the family principle of monarchic succession) resulted in the creation of parties, and their elevation to the role of a primary mechanism in politics. It is a kind of power that has not yet been developed to its highest form—it has not kept up with the corporation, for example (except in Russia, where it was used to create the corporation).

Whether a grabbing-gang or an ideological grouping, the party provides an emotional structure for action in history. In this it complements the exclusive rational legality of the constitutional state in which it operates, and which requires its existence in order itself to operate. But it is thereby so much more effective than the state that it continuously threatens to overwhelm it, and become "total." (This could be corrected if that state were genuinely majoritarian rather than merely rational.) At its fullest expression, a big-city machine more or less displaces the municipal government it has captured; and of course the Leninist, or later and more refined Maoist, party is designed to overwhelm the state, and has most obviously succeeded in doing so. But whether or not the party accomplishes this, and for how long, depends on its relation to the class or class-coalition it represents. Here the main thing is whether the class is established and merely defensive, or is aggressively demanding more state power to fulfill itself—the difference, say, between Mark Hanna's Republican Party and the crusade led by Bryan.

The key analytical terms are state, class, and party: class is the basic factor, party the organized active force, and state power—its use or the prevention of its use—is the prize. In America, the "party," in the distinct sense of a disciplined, aggressive group acting as a conscious historical unit, has been limited to factions within our flabby official parties (when they bothered with the parties at all: many business factions, during the "retail period," did not bother). Seldom does a faction take over a whole party for long; and hardly ever does a faction in one party represent inclusively a major social element, much less a class. Classes in America have never been well organized. The highest level of organization achieved is probably still what Mark Hanna inveigled out of big money in fashioning the Republican Party into a chosen defensive instrument for them. And even that beautiful concert consisted mostly of the bag-operation. For us, it is much more likely that money rather than people will succeed in getting organized adequately.

For our American purposes, the elements of party are money and people. The more people, the more capacity they have, the more active and disaffected they are, and the better their disaffection is organized, the less need there is to rely on money—that is, the promise of something immediate and practical to the participants. But note the fate of the Leninist party: Stalin overwhelmed it by organizing the self-interest represented by the new state bureaucracy created after the October Revolution. Djilas says that this is the standard fate of the party—that it creates the class and is consumed by the class. But he is conceiving party almost exclusively as an ideological historical vehicle (designed for the total capture of the state). We should know, however, that ideology does not exist apart from material class conditions—certainly we know it if we remember any Marx at all. (Djilas, being a Leninist, remembers not enough Marx as he needs to.) It must be that the class precedes the party, so Djilas must be wrong. Probably elements of the unformed class—unknown to Djilas and other enthusiasts—created the party in the first place.

The essence of party is money and people—and it's hard to manage with the one and without the other. If you rely entirely on people, then eventually these people you rely on will require some money, and this will change the party. Better to face facts to begin with and rely not on people alone, and not on money alone.

The special American problem has been to bring together this congruent reliance on people and money, avoiding the concurrent sins both of moralism and corruption. We have been cursed with the opposition of idealists, on the one hand, and what have come to be called the practical professional politicians, on the other. But the virtue of a matured and useful culture is that it provides a rationale for the mixture of spirituality and practicality in the same person, in the same act, for the same purpose (and in something of an atmosphere of candor). A living culture is valuable to the extent that it accounts for both sides of the body-mind dualism, and resolves it sufficiently to allow action to go forward. My point here is that culture is *validated* by its livability, and especially its livability accompanied by cumulative political action. It is politics that validates culture; and it is thus culture that makes politics into something more than an extension of business by other means.

7 A settled component of the American attitude toward power, I have discovered, is that a true native can accuse you of conniving to appoint yourself dictator of Everything, and, in the same sentence—without pause or apology or benefit of comma—accuse you of not having done enough for him lately.

Further in line with this abysmal confusion: Have you noticed that most political questions here are argued on metaphysical grounds? The issue is seldom *how* power is to be used, but whether it is to exist in the first place or have its existence acknowledged in the second. In this sense, all of our political arguments are "wrong" as such—but "right," of course, from the national metaphysical point of view.

Since politics is concerned entirely and exclusively with the uses of power, it is possible to say that we have not yet arrived at politics in this country; that we are still carrying on the work of the Founding Fathers—that is, creating an American system in which the uses of power may eventually be discussed and the thing itself, politics, occur.

This negative, know-nothing view of power is perhaps the distinctive aspect of the American character. This personal metaphysics of ours usually occurs as a conflict between need and propriety—the former requiring a positive, and the latter preferring a negative, approach to power. It subsumes our notorious Puritanism, but is not limited to it. It relates to the Puritanism in that all *private* power—whether exercised by you in relation to your child or by the management of General Motors with respect to the structure of urban life—is so completely overjustified from a spiritual point of view that in practice it is no longer recognized as power at all. (The proof is simple: try to use the word "power" in discussing any of these private relations, and many Americans will act as if they had been insulted.) But this power-denial, this moralism, this Puritanism, has become so hard-pressed by the challenges of modern complexity that it now requires a kind of paranoid screen on which to project a negative image of the power, or need of power, it fears to acknowledge. That negative image has become the federal government—*public legal power*. (Only war, which opens up the perspective of external hostility, is exempt from this prescription.) The radical right-wingers are nearly as paranoid about our own government as they are about the Soviet government; and they are simply worse than the rest of us, not all that different at bottom. And the Viet Nam Anti-War Enthusiasts on the left are prepared to find their way through the rice paddies of Asia with the help of little more than a fantasy-map of Washington, D.C.

The subject of power is nearly infinite. Indeed, the main trouble with the concept is the difficulty of determining just what in the whole range of human experience it really does not include. The reason I pursue the concept anyway is that it is hardly possible to discuss modern experience without it. (If you don't believe this, try it some time: we even speak of the power to love.) But if power is so close to life itself, then I think we can say that there are really *two* kinds of power: 1) the power for you *to* do; and 2) the power to keep me *from* doing. The main thing is the positive or negative use of power. Talleyrand's view of the dichotomy is useful: "To have said and done nothing is a tremendous power; but it should not be abused."

At this early stage, perhaps we can move forward by stating a few propositions:

1. Little people may become "powerful" by using the little power they have to give them the feeling of even more power: this feat can be accomplished only by an exercise of the power to refuse—to say no, and leave things as they are, against the other's powerful innovation.

2. My strength may be based on your weakness. Therefore, in seeking power, I must devise and encourage your weakness.

3. Your power to allow me to exercise my power is a real power. You must control yourself to accomplish this. Your negative power is exercised where it *should* be exercised when you keep yourself from doing something to me that you know you ought not.

4. Puzzling about the distinction between power and event, it occurs to one that power may be exclusively the *threat* of an act. Even

if my power brings about an event, still that event represents power only by its threat of repetition. In any case, power is mostly threat: if I have the power to kill you, and do, I lose my power over you. If I kill everyone, I lose all my power.

5. The powers in America have managed to achieve control of the very sense of belonging to life itself: with this, why bother to kill anyone?

6. Or take the distinction between power as capacity, and power as the desire to use the capacity. This may afford a clue as to the difference between ancient and modern power, because at one time there was not enough technique for men to accomplish what they wanted to do—and now there is too much.

7. Where power comes from outside, where it is afforded you by your situation or office, the imperatives may be simple: either you try to control it, or it will succeed in controlling you. That is, your actions will be merely "determined" unless you exploit the situation and "corrupt" it to your own subjective use.

8. As you make the effort to see matters from the other person's point of view, you are observing in power terms—whatever you may end up doing with the knowledge thus derived. If you cannot, or refuse to, see matters in this way, you are stuck with the innate inefficiency of ideals, ideology, and lies—your own lies to yourself—whatever prior knowledge you may use to enrich the same.

9. I suggest that the essence of the problem of power, this unequaled social problem, is whether you obey the life force or the death force. I say this while understanding that no one lives by either alone, and that it can even be difficult to know which is which. Notice also that with this life-death definition of power, we reach a certain level of subtlety whereby two *very* powerful but *equally* powerful parties may be absolutely helpless, weak beyond recognition, if power is defined to exclude cooperation, and both can die. In that circumstance, all power is reduced to the power of self-destruction. This is probably the most common type—and the main reason why power is such a problem.

10. The kind of power individuals may have in highly realized communities (as in Europe) is different from what it may be where the larger situation is not settled (as in America). In the latter condition, individual power must be more creative—it has less of the given to rely on. There are no easy adults in a society of gangs.

11. Finally, power is a concept of concern mostly as an apposi-

tional idea in relation to our traditional Christian moralism—without the one, the other is not so necessary. The need and the utility of distinguishing-out "power" from "life" occurs most readily in an excessively moralistic environment that stifles life. And in such an environment, people fear not only the power of others but their own as well.

8 The national power denied by our history is desperately needed today, both at home and abroad. As to the first: an advancing technological society cannot exist ungoverned; without more coherent government than we have now, we will end up crushing each other—perhaps even physically, as now psychologically. With more and more people living together in increasingly complicated and interdependent patternings made possible and imperative by the astounding pace of technology, fewer areas of social life can safely remain free of governing. Each time we wait for problems to solve themselves we deny the palpable world around us, thus seeking a disaster we must ultimately find. Health, education, employment, the organization of our living and working areas, along with the development of the scientific technology which is the source of all our blessings and troubles—all these require some decisive support or control by the national government, some positive use of central power. But wherever a need is noted, the deeper American propriety regarding power intervenes, and it is frustrated. The justifying arguments are legion, but always boil down, first, to denying the existence of the need and, finally, the existence of the power to satisfy the need, or the propriety of so using it.

In the second, worldwide arena, this matter of our national power is a daily one of life and death; and with the current primary reliance on military posture, it must remain so. In the absence of further and deeper agreements with the Soviets, the only road forward is that of non-military initiatives; also, the more agreement we achieve, the more such initiatives—based on the benchmark of our domestic power—will dominate the world scene. Here lies the true unilateral path. This is the only way to force the Soviets to agree; or, with their agreement, to rule the nuclear world; or to deal with the abiding conflict after they agree. If we were to adapt the army, say, to the purposes of massive developmental aid, or build a new technical organization to dispense and utilize $10 billion or $20 billion annually in this kind of "war," the Soviets would have to respond in kind. This would certainly make them more amenable to arms reduction and joint nuclear control, since they are not nearly equal to us in over-all capacity and would be hard put to find the necessary resources. We would in effect be "spending them into submission"— or, at least, reasonableness. The idea of spending them into submission is regularly advanced in support of all new or redundant armament. To spend them into submission by means of developmental aid would be infinitely more effective and desirable from all points of view. But this alternative is not available to us, we are told, because the need is not recognized, or because the power does not exist, or because it would be improper to use the power for that purpose. Or, when the argument gets hot, all three at the same time.

To this juncture has our history brought us. The issue: to be not merely a geographical federation of constituencies, but a nation— and that for more than military reasons and by more than military means. Reading American history with hindsight, we see that our deepest difficulty has been the sustained, positive use of national power, to an extent that nations with more duration and less real estate can hardly imagine.

It seems that just before the civil rights bill was passed, the whole conscious segment of the country was shocked into awareness of the role of Congress as the torchbearer of American power-negativism. All of a sudden—perhaps because the initial verve and the top-flight press releases of the Kennedy administration cruelly revived memories of the New Deal—many people realized that domestic amelioration and reform had been almost entirely blocked, tabled, and dribbled out for a full quarter-century. The military umbrella had previously obscured this fact. Yet I would suggest that what had been obscured was a cultural, even spiritual, factor—and not a matter of how the seniority system works. Nor will Lyndon Johnson's magic and muscle by itself result in transforming the congressional institution: his achievement has been to understand and utilize Congress-as-it-was. But the brokerage mechanisms he mastered as a member of the Class of '36 in the House and kingpin of the Senate establishment of the Fifties, and then exquisitely exploited as President, are tied to the character of a generation and are evanescent in the longer perspective.

Congress expresses the profounder contradictions in our history: it represents the true effort of this nation toward a majoritarian rule of law. It dominates the Judiciary just as statute is superior to decision; and the Executive can initiate for the most part only ideologically when it does not carry Congress. It is easy for the Executive or the Judiciary to make believe that we are a completed nation, but it is impossible for Congress to do so. Where Congress acts, there a nation acted. There is no distortion and no backwardness in, around, and under our incomplete nationhood which is not represented and over-represented in Congress. So Congress cannot possibly be viewed as an unfortunate collection of technical details. That institution is, indeed, the major structural problem in our history, and never more so than today (despite the Marvelous 89th). *But structural means spiritual, not technical*—although this is one of the hardest propositions for an American to understand, with his traditional confounding of the two categories. What is wrong with Congress is wrong with us: Congress is in fact a discouragingly true simulacrum of our democracy. The crisis of this institution is the crisis of American character and per-sonality. Congressional non-rule perfectly expresses our personal unwillingness to abandon our adored image of infinite Individual-ism, and enter gracefully, or at least energetically, into a generous age of technological abundance. No President and no court can ever finally save us from this fact: we will have to save ourselves, if at all. And we will have to do it in the committee rooms and cor-ridors of Congress.

THREE

The
House

1 The House of Representatives
represents us so perfectly that something really ought to be done
about it. Because the House—not the Senate, the Presidency, the
Court, nor the corporate order—is our major democratic opportunity: this was the one big chance provided by the Fathers. So the
weird patterning of this congressional institution reveals the startling state of our national effort toward democracy. The facts of the
House tell us about ourselves, as to people, what the tariff and then
the dollar-prism of the Internal Revenue Code have told us, as to
wealth: almost as if the arrangement of a gypsy's tea leaves com-
prised rigorous and revealing data.

De Tocqueville noticed, in 1831, that some of our Representatives
were not able to read or write. Today, they are studious in their research, one of them asserting: "I read forty-eight weekly newspapers and clip every one of them myself." Besides research, there is
forceful communication with the public: "The shopping bag is the
best gimmick in the world. . . . Just remember to have your name
printed on both sides so it will be sure to show." In the quaint old
days, according to Neil MacNeil in *Forge of Democracy*, there was a
certain Jeremiah "Sockless Jerry" Simpson of Kansas, "who wooed
votes by refusing to wear socks; and James Watson of Indiana, who
clattered about his Congressional district in wooden shoes to impress

his Dutch constituents." And other contributions to American culture: the word "bunk" comes from a remark by Felix Walker in 1820, a Representative from North Carolina whose district included Buncombe County. When he made a speech merely for the benefit of his constituents, he indicated to his colleagues that they needn't hang around—"This is for Buncombe," he would say. But a liberal intellectual congressman has remarked, more than a hundred years later: "I have two degrees in government and I learned more in my first year in Congress than I did in six years of college "

From 435 miscellaneous areas of the continental and other United States a like number of citizens come to Washington, D.C., every two years, there to mingle with their fellows as ambassadors each for some several hundred thousand neighbors. They deal with each other as to their clienteles' desires and assorted images of the future, all the while personally striving to stay in business and get ahead in the world. From an additional 50 non-functional areas come 100 more ambassadors plenipotentiary for a more dignified stay in the social hothouse on the Potomac. And each time this is, in truth, the American continent and people in Congress assembled, yet once again.

One supposes that, after all, Washington, with its area ambassadors, is the real melting pot of America. Particularly with the Potomac heat. This may be the reason why the national government was placed physically in the middle of a swamp, where it would not so much grow firmly in stature as simply mush in heated turmoil toward a single national blob.

What follows is not a Big Treatise on Congress, its structure and function. What follows, by means of an institutional illustration, is an impressionistic unburdening as to the state of democracy in America. I think that when you look at our political history you either say, No, I'd rather not belong—or you burst out laughing. (I compromise with a furious chuckle.)

The real story of Congress is that of the parties and the people. Our two parties provide a deep and more or less meaningless—i.e., perfectly businesslike—difference. For whom? Against whom? To what purpose? Occasionally, a party threatens to achieve form. Then, following a frantic burst of activity, the imminence is averted. Through all this, our history happens.

While writing this essay I have had two symbols always before me. The Capitol building against a kaleidoscope sky—really very beautiful—and a clipping from the front page of the New York *Times* for August 18, 1961, being a photograph of Nelson A. Rockefeller and Louis J. Lefkowitz, each embracing the other (and the camera) with the lead "Lefkowitz Backs Special Session" and the legend "Governor Rockefeller demonstrating support of Louis J. Lefkowitz yesterday at Republican meeting at Commodore." I will always remember those two diverse blintz-eaters in smiling public embrace: the camera caught them *in medias res,* still trying to achieve mutual political joy.*

And I like the Capitol building: it's immense and round; and it borrows frantically from Europe. Moreover, there is an image of a Free Lady on top of it. What more could one ask for, here in America?

2 I started out by saying that the House represents us "perfectly." I was kidding. We couldn't possibly be that bad. The House does not even manage to represent the worst of us fairly. (Can you imagine our having fostered anything so contrary to native boosterism?) It has been so wildly malapportioned, and artistically gerrymandered, and then fancily financed, that we have actually ended up looking a great deal worse than one was entitled to expect, given an honest crap game. After all, who would bother getting all wrought up about a rotten borough here or there; a few comforting rituals designed to ease the late years of aging public servants; or even some imaginative techniques for balancing family budgets? But that is not the situation. Instead, the situation is that three hundred years or more of geographical passion, gorgeously hard work, and impressive yearning, has resulted in this very particularly distorted democratic institution. And then, congressmen are in business—in the business of being congressmen. This is much more strenuous than it sounds. You have to get elected every two years, which means that you are running, running, running all the time. (The traditional line is, "A congressman is the shortest distance be-

---

* A reporter is supposed to have overheard Governor Rockefeller mumbling to his new wife's inquiring face, as they boarded their honeymoon plane to Venezuela, "No, dear, you have to smile *all* the time."

tween two years.") Now lots of Americans act like this, but when the congressman does it, his panic is structurally serious.

Let's go back to the unrepresentative character of the Congress.* In a practical way, the indictment reads as follows: Not every citizen has an equal chance to achieve representation; even if he did, Congress is not adequately organized to carry out the majority will of such properly selected representatives. The first is an ancient scandal; we soften the point of it by imagining ourselves to be more homogeneous than we are—but the Negroes have lately been making our heterogeneity harder to ignore.

The unrepresentative quality of our system of representation derives from various disfranchisements. Briefly, the *de facto* system favors whites over Negroes, rural over urban, permanent residents over mobile types, and, of course, the wealthy over the poor. Clearly, it favors the more conservative groups. So much so that, with their vested attachment to the present imbalance, the belief and willingness of conservatives to participate in the formal democratic system are being—or have already been—undermined. This is most obviously the tragedy of the South, but it is not limited to that area. Southerners are not the only Americans to have become so accustomed to unfair advantages that they can no longer bear to contemplate the possibility of fair disadvantages—which is a capacity very important to maintain in a democratic order.

The worst of the whole matter is the coerced denial of the right of Negroes to vote in the South.† This aspect of the *de facto* system does not exist even under an excuse of law. White voting registrars have simply refused to register Negroes: when the point needs to be driven home, the lawlessness of the white community—working through the police as well as volunteers—accomplishes whatever may be needed. Jobs are lost, loans are called, arrests are made, shots are fired. Whatever may be needed. The result is an *ad hoc* apartheid shaped in a deadly social battle directed by the Southern racial vigilantes against both the conscience of the nation and the

---

* We will go into the matter of apportionment more generously in a later chapter; but here we simply mention the characterizing circumstance as part of our over-all impression of the House.

† It is not likely that the 1965 act, providing for federal registrars in the worst counties, will alone re-do the Southern system. In the first year of enforcement, there were persistent reports of the continuing inhibition effected by private economic pressure. But increased voting should help toward economic advance; and that in turn may further support the voting power; and that's the way it goes in the Second Reconstruction.

legal police power of the federal government. In a way, it is worse than South Africa—worse for the whites, I mean. Because the black-and-white spiritual triumph of the white, which is the whole point of the absurd effort, is ever-beckoning and ever-denied. The entire purpose of racialism is to simplify life, but the white Southerners have in fact complicated everything almost beyond bearing. After awhile, all that is left to them in this impossible situation is to wallow in the process of losing—and, by their own unspeakable definition, losing everything, not merely the imagined pleasures of racialism. (Meanwhile, some Negroes may go to pieces in the process of winning, because they also consequentially defined their victory as "everything.")

But the disfranchisement creating a distorted Congress proceeds beyond the guerrilla apartheid of the South. It concerns malapportionment of congressional districts selectively across the land, which makes one man's vote worth a good deal more than the vote of another. The man with the more worthwhile vote, as noted, always lives in a rural area: the apportionment patterns give over-full representation to our vanished farm population and the culture once sustained by it. They give power to place rather than to persons. The facts have been quite amazing. In fifteen states, the difference between the smallest and largest district was in a recent Congress (prior to the Supreme Court's reapportionment decision in *Wesberry v. Sanders*) approximately equal to the apportionment factor itself—410,000 persons for each Representative. The difference between the smallest and largest in the whole country in the 87th Congress—1,015,460 for an urban district in California and 177,431 for a rural one in Michigan—was more than twice the factor.

There is much additional distortion at the threshold of congressional power. According to James MacGregor Burns, "Aside from the Negro, the most unfairly treated group of voters in America is the big mobile population." Since one out of every five Americans moves annually, a wide range of local residence requirements results in a good deal of disfranchising. Indeed, there are all those clever registration difficulties which Richard M. Scammon (the Census Bureau expert on voting) credits with being "the most important single factor" depriving us of the characteristically much higher voter turnout in other countries, most of which have automatic registration: a recent election in Italy, for example, achieved a 90 per cent vote as against less than 65 per cent for us in 1960, which was a "good" year; it was a fraction less in 1964. Canada, closer to home, gets 80 per cent. And then, our infamous literacy tests in nineteen states, which the majority of the Presidential Commission on Registration and Voting Participation characterized as "a remnant of class discrimination"—noting that it is the "poor and depressed" who ordinarily suffer from illiteracy. The Commission concluded: "Literacy tests have no more place in a modern democracy than property tests, which we have long since abandoned." (If you seriously want a "rational" electorate only, then you are certainly going to have to exclude a large number of people who read adequately.)

Voting for Representatives typically falls off sharply in non-presidential years, and is a few percentage points below the presidential vote even in the fun years. The reader may be surprised—I was—that the vote for the House has been as low as 30.1 per cent of the eligible vote in 1926, and was no better than 46.4 per cent in 1962. Representative Howard W. Smith, one-time mighty deacon of the Rules Committee, was elected in 1962 by the positive preference of 10 per cent of the eligible voters in his district. In the hot presidential year of 1960, he got better than 20 per cent.*

And gerrymandering, which assists greatly in predetermining the winner if all else fails. This maneuver (we pursue it further in Chapter Nine) can determine what the winner shall be as well as who he may be. A liberal Democrat who had his district reshaped without being made safe for his liberalism remarked:

> I could have been a statesman . . . if they had cut off a few of those conservatives. Now I'll have to continue going this way and that way, back and forth. I'm a cracker-ass Congressman— and I could have been a statesman.

3 It cannot be said that in the United States we have as yet achieved full and fair adult franchise. Notice what, all in all, we are up against: Beyond numerical malapportionment lies much institutional sludge, including gerrymandering; beyond gerrymandering we come upon the character of cam-

---

* This was his second district, incidentally—the first was shot out from under him by a suburban bazooka. And finally, in the Democratic primary held on July 12, 1966, the time-bomb of redistricting and new Negro voting destroyed "Judge" Smith's magnificent career of thirty-six years of congressional obstruction.

paign financing; beyond that and election there is the encounter with some further details of the sludge—the seniority system, the Rules Committee in the House, the filibuster in the Senate, and much more of that sort of negative power. And beyond all this is the capstone of structural issues: the ideological coherence and business discipline of the party system, since the sloppy characterlessness of our national parties derives from the underlying structural mess. Then the final issue, the relation between elected governmental power and the power of business, finance, and other private institutions. In confronting these issues and controlling the military, we can become a coherent democratic nation. And not until then.

Imagine for a moment that the positions of chairman of the Senate Finance Committee, the House Rules Committee, and the Senate Judiciary Committee had recently been national elective offices. Would you have voted for Byrd, Smith, and Eastland? Do you think the American people would? In fact, do you think they *did*? Well, I do. They may not have known they were doing so, but they did it. As one despairing M.C. said: "The people back home don't know what's going on." Congressional disarray derives from genuinely American attitudes toward power, whereby a citizen's God-given right to say *No*—even if he is the given-god of the Rules Committee—shall not be infringed. To the adolescents who comprise our major gangs, nothing is so precious as established anarchy.

The "conservative coalition" in Congress, which so well expressed this kind of power, was created in the course of marshaling the great reaction against the achievements, especially the achieved electoral successes, of the New Deal. It was first put together, or it was first noticed that events had put it together, in 1937 when the Democrats controlled the House by 333 to 89 (a horrible fact to conjure with). The meat on which this fledgling Caesar fed was the Court fight and the attempted congressional purge of 1938—and more important than anything else, following these Rooseveltian errors, was the fact that the approaching war diverted the President's attention from what he knew to be his major domestic political concern, kept him from correcting his errors or deepening his attack on the new coalition, and with military expenditure provided a whole new way of political life which seemed to solve all these difficult domestic matters by transcending them. At the end of the War, the coalition naturally gathered unto itself the usual postwar reaction.

But notice that the anti-New Deal response included Republican

Me-tooism as well as the congressional coalition. If, with the Goldwater phenomenon, we are about to see the end of this Me-tooism on the previous grand scale, I suggest that it is because the coalition has had its back to the wall and thus failed to equivocate sufficiently in favor of the Me-too posture. The negative power position in Congress is far more important, for the social forces concerned, than the opportunities of Me-tooism. The coalition was cracked by the liberal sweep in 1958 and then by the Rules Committee fight at the beginning of the Kennedy administration; its fundamentally desperate state was revealed by the civil rights enactment in 1964.

Even so congenial and consistent a glorifier of the House as Neil MacNeil has said: "In terms of power, the House's latent hostility to the President's program, reflecting the House's gathering commitment to conservative policies, was purely negative." This negativism is now inadequate in power terms: it relied more than it knew on the pallid positive posture of Me-tooism and on the substantial positivism of adequately expanding military expenditure. Hard-pressed, it now requires a purer and more aggressive negativism—that is, Goldwater-type and the hard-core South.

The coalition was forced in 1964—for the first time—"to go to the people." It did not do very well. That was revolutionary—it put too much up for grabs—and it contradicted the source of the coalition's power, namely, the special structure of Congress expressing a paralyzed party system. They should have been the last to fool around with party realignment, and now it appears that they have been the first (apart from the abortive Wallace campaign) in the post-New Deal era. This self-destructive daring could only have proceeded from desperation.

"GOOD NEWS FOR BUSINESSMEN, WHOEVER WINS CONGRESS"—this was the headline of an article on the coalition, March 14, 1960, in that funnel of Real Truth called *U.S. News & World Report.* The article meowed over a defeatist liberal analysis of the coalition which credited the conservative grouping with 130 Republican, 80 Southern Democratic, 9 Border State, and 6 Northern and Western Democratic votes, for a 225 majority in a 437-member House. But when President Kennedy counted the House after his election, he found 180 for him and 180 against, on his general domestic program, with seventy-odd "negotiable." The "negotiables" were mostly urban Republicans and some Populist-minded rural types, both South and West. In the Rules Committee fight, the final vote under Rayburn's leadership was 217-212, the official or formal bloc membership being 174 Republicans, 162 Northern and Western Democrats, and 99 Democrats from the Southern and Border States.

The conservative coalition was based on fiscal negativism more than on race, so it is not yet dead. It was no coincidence that the blockading role of Congress had fallen primarily upon the House of Representatives, which was designed constitutionally to exercise the original jurisdiction in fiscal matters.* The Senate, which was supposed to decelerate expression of the popular will, has become the more "liberal" chamber, notwithstanding the power of filibuster and Southern chairmanships (or the higher ante). The Senate is more "liberal" because the characteristic county-type malapportionment in the House is avoided, but less "liberal" basically because New York and Nevada both have two representatives in the chamber. The design has thus been inverted. (According to MacNeil, since 1939 and until recently the Senate had increased House appropriations by close to $3 billion annually. MacNeil tells a number of revealing stories to the effect that House members count on the Senate to increase appropriations in conference; they even plead with Senators to do so.)

But the entire constitutional design—not merely the relation of the House to the upper chamber—is now badly out of whack because of the social backwardness and democratic reluctance of the House of Representatives. The Supreme Court has been dangerously burdened with political initiatives by the necessity of taking up the congressional slack (the alternative, however, would have been disastrous—to revise the Constitution in favor of congressional ineptitude). And as for the Executive, it could have been described in the past as alternately benumbed and hysterical; now, with President Johnson, it is of course "magical." The President's method of dealing with Congress is perfection itself, given the *previous* facts of the matter. Is that enough? To answer this Big Question, we will have to look (we do so later) at the character of any new facts and needed daring.

---

* A Republican member of the coalition stated the ideology obnoxiously as follows: "The battle we are fighting is similar to the role of the stern parent as opposed to the parent who gives the child everything he wants. In the long run, I am sure it is not good for the child to have everything he wants. But you get awfully tired of being the stern parent, subject to abuse and accused of not being interested in your fellow human beings." And we get tired, Mr. Congressman, of being treated like children.

The problem of this country has always been the South and the unspeakable hypocrisy of the white view of Negro existence there.* But the deepest aspect of the problem, for the fate of the national culture, has never been simply the white or the Negro but rather the hypocrisy bequeathed to the national polka-dot children, deriving from much more than mere racial variety. Without viable polka-dot kids, we are in terrible trouble: because of the potentially irretrievable corruption of the entire polka-dot culture, race in America is like race nowhere else in the world; we are the melting-pot nation—we must melt *or else*. A serious congressman has said: "The only way we can pass legislation that is liberal in economics, whether it be education, housing, or airports, is by a substantial attrition of Southern votes." Do away with the need for this "substantial attrition," and you have changed the direction of the history of this country. Also true, nothing else will—not even Johnson "magic." We now at last must finally face the Problem of the South—which has, in modern times, become primarily the Problem of the Democratic Party. I am not suggesting a punitive attitude toward the white Southerner, although, guilty as he especially is, he can imagine nothing else. (Guilt is not that good a technique; and in the instance of the white Southerner it goes so deep that he no longer recognizes it for what it is.) The Southerner does have a way of life; but at the base of it is something quite unacceptable to the national majority. It has become "acceptable" to the South itself only by error, misrule, and Northern compliance. But for the lasting benefit of everybody concerned, it must end. Some substantial show of force will be required, as it is for any acceptance of law—North, South, or on the moon. But not vindictive. And certainly not in repetition of the errors of the first Reconstruction, as if the whole thing were another frontier effort to make a fast buck while somebody sat on the Indian. No, *this* time for non-business reasons.

---

* If the popular movement of the Nineties, for example, had not been so distorted by racism, it might well have achieved more—perhaps have established a decisive tradition—in controlling the growth and the character of American corporatism, even that historical monster.

4 The decisive fact about our legislature is that it has built up its own unique system of organization in default of party organization. Most particularly because of the numbers involved, and also because so many of the better men go on to better things, this *ad hoc* system has its worst effects in the House of Representatives. The decline in power of the party caucus and the Speakership—each at one time a dominant organizing factor —has deepened the non-party mess. This tells more harshly on the Democrats because they are the looser confederation (embodying within themselves the contradiction of the racial issue); thus they are the grouping to manage less well, as a national party, under the resulting system which elevates obstructionism and conceives positive policy enactments as a kind of Congressional Medal of Honor for heroes only.* In a rough way, the Republicans have (had?) more of a party in any event, since they represented the more committed money-makers and so had more money available for their party purposes. And since money-making *is* the American system, the Republicans needed only to defend it; they did not have the innovating problem of the Democrats. (Obstructionism accords well with defense.) Meanwhile, as long as the program of innovation remained a symbolic exercise anyway, the Republicans were free to play that inconsequential game as well.

So the special structure of the House derives from the absence of coherent party control, especially on the part of the Democrats. The Big Point to take home with you and think about is that this absence begins in the districts. My suspicion is that existing congressional party power that can be made effective back in the district—patronage, pork-barreling, big men on the platform, important long-distance dialing, etc.—is the monopoly of the seniority survivors, the professional "leadership" cabal.

Very simply, most congressmen, being in business for themselves,

* Writing of the lame-duck session in 1933, Schlesinger says: "James E. Watson, Hoover's leader in the Senate, hoped by blocking legislation in January to force Roosevelt into a special session in March, presumably on the theory that the new President would be caught without a program." Even at the depth of the Depression, this obstructionism was the order of the day in Congress.

put together personally-based coalitions in the district, where the party often enough does not exist at all except in a technical sense. They therefore do not answer to party discipline when they arrive in Washington: they do not owe their election to a national party. The irresponsible trading mess which has resulted can become clear as branch water on this one assumption of the nonexistence of the Democratic Party at the root-level. The cure is equally obvious: reinstitution of the party caucus in the House, based on effective power in the district, not as an absolute substitute for seniority and the other peculiarities of the system, but as an effective overlay—Otto Passman and Judge Smith and similar persons are told what and when, or out. Very likely, this effort cannot be accomplished quietly on the inside. It may well be necessary, in the first instance, to go back to the districts and begin at the beginning. This used to be understood as "democracy"; the understanding should be revived.

Also, the House is too large—there are simply too many members. "The original House of Representatives contained only 65 members," MacNeil informs us, "but, inexorably, the membership increased— to 106 in 1790, to 186 in 1810, to 242 in 1830, to 357 in 1890, and finally to 435 in 1910." The end result of this increased size has been to elevate the committees, reduce floor debate to insignificance, exaggerate seniority as an organizing principle, and generally to make the indigenously difficult problem of coherence *cum* responsibility nearly insurmountable. The members must narrow their view drastically: in effect, they stand in line to specialize. They hardly understand most matters they vote on; there is nothing like a fully or even adequately aware majority vote on most issues before the House. So the committees rule.

Professor Walter F. Willcox of Cornell University, testifying before a Judiciary subcommittee in 1959, suggested a technical plan for reducing the size of the House gradually. (Vice President Barkley had been in favor of bringing the number down to 300 members.) A congressman on the subcommittee objected on the ground that members have such a great workload just minding the needs of their voters that to increase the size of the constituency would aggravate an already severe burden. He did not take into account the fact that the population has doubled since 1910, when the last permanent increase in House membership was made. Also, the workload difficulty could and should be resolved by augmenting staff, so that more of the routine constituency work might be delegated. This would be

desirable in any event, since it takes the congressman-in-person out
of the "service business" (valued for its reelection utility) and puts
him more into something like legislative politics.

Because of the large number of Representatives, the House requires a large order of organization to function at all. Without the
strength of a coherent majority party, its "organization" tends inevitably toward a ganglike form which favors obstructionism. Then,
even positive moves in one line are bargained for with the currency
of negative threats in another. But no matter how organized, and
whether or to what extent the natural emphasis on obstruction is
utilized, power must be centralized somewhere in the House, since
the alternative is chaos. The usual defense of seniority, for example,
is that it is the most readily available means for avoiding the chaos
of continual argument as to who belongs *Where* and is valued at
What.

A brief taste of history may enliven this House *bouillabaisse,* and
make it somewhat more palatable. The highwater mark of positive
congressional rule, after Jackson dethroned King Caucus, was that
of the Radical Republicans, especially as represented in the conflict
with President Andrew Johnson over Reconstruction policy. This
was party power, based on war fervor and the reduction of the Democratic opposition. Finally, corruption reduced the Republican Party,
its dominance and discipline; the Democrats returned also to play
for the new spoils and to continue in the modern phase their long
career of successful obstructionism. They exploited the rules and
procedures of the House, as a defensive minority will, by negative
threat, which was played off against the need of the House for some
organization-against-chaos. Thomas B. Reed, one of the great Republican Speakers, remarked that the "only way to do business inside
the rules is to suspend the rules. . . . The object of the rules appears to be to prevent the transaction of business."

So he changed the rules. One of the more important items in the
repertory of Democratic obstruction had been the ability to defeat a
quorum by sufficient members' refusing to answer "present" although in fact present in the chamber. On January 29, 1890, Reed
executed his famous coup, consisting of the simple expedient of
counting members physically present but refusing to answer a
quorum call. Matthew Josephson says: "Amid the rioting and shout-

ing that lasted for three days Reed reiterated tirelessly his thesis that the object of a parliamentary body was 'action and not stoppage of action.' " Subsequently it became necessary to bolt the doors on a quorum call to inhibit the wild Democratic dash for the lobbies. (One big fellow kicked down a door on behalf of States' Rights, but this never became a settled custom in the House.)

Having thus increased the power of the Speakership, Reed completed the structure of its ascendancy by enlarging the function of the Rules Committee. (At this time, the Speaker was automatically chairman of Rules as well, since this committee was first conceived as a tool of the leadership to expedite the party program.) Reed developed the concept of the "special rule," which to this day is the core of the Committee's power: a special rule governing a piece of legislation can limit the number and kind of amendments which may be proposed, as well as the time in which to propose them or to debate the issues at all. (This obvious *Ja-Nein* tyranny is excusable only because of the patent impossibility of extended debate, and freedom to engage in the variety of amendment-maneuvering, for 435 ambitious statesmen.) But, at the beginning, Reed was quite charming about all this: after devising a rule with his Republican colleagues, he would inform the Democratic members of the Committee, "Gentlemen . . . we have decided to perpetrate the following outrage."

The height of the combined power of the Speaker and the chairman of the Rules Committee was achieved by Reed's Republican successor, Joe Cannon. By this time, the Republican Party itself had become defensive of an established system—against both Populist and Progressive onslaught. Cannon was a tyrant, and his tyranny was finally overturned in 1910-12 by a revolt of Republican Progressives in alliance with liberal Democrats. Note that this was not an intraparty revolt, which perhaps excuses the fact that the method of reform chosen was not to strengthen and democratize the party caucus but to separate the power of the Speaker from that of the Rules Committee—the Speaker was forbidden to be a member. Which set the stage for the worst aspect of the present organization of the House.

In the 1920's, Phillip Campbell of Kansas perfected the full force of the independent power of the chairman of the Rules Committee. "You can go to Hell," he informed the House. "It makes no difference what a majority of you decide. If it meets with my disapproval, it shall not be done. I am the committee. In me reposes absolute obstructive powers."

5 Perhaps the quickest way to lay a stethoscope on the heart of the House is to imagine a true parliamentary system, and then compare. The noises one hears can be frightening.

This approach goes all the way back to Woodrow Wilson's *Congressional Government*, published in 1885: his deep penetration of the theoretical problem undoubtedly contributed to his performance in actually putting together an *ad hoc* parliamentary system during the first two years of his administration. He did not have the kind of crisis working for him that FDR did; he had only the opportunity presented by a shaken-up situation on which he imposed a temporary order by virtue of intellectual power and main force of will. It occurs to one that there had to be the fact that Wilson *wanted* to use the power available—that he had been thinking of our peculiar power structure, its defects and opportunities, for a lifetime.

This benchmark parliamentary view based on the classic (English) system is a favorite of political scientists. They are entitled, and it is indeed helpful: without a benchmark of some kind our system is quite difficult to understand. But a reactive consequence seems to be that another large group of political scientists, understanding deeply that we are not English—that opportunity was thrown away in 1776—and are not apt to become such soon, has developed a vested interest in the descriptive characterization of the resulting difficult mess. My favored approach is that the system is indeed zany, but not at all incomprehensible if you dare to understand America; and care enough, even after that, to keep your eye on the bouncing ball of party factions. And remember and admit that the original system as conceived was a rationalist monstrosity. With this approach, you need join neither the benchmark nor the messy-emphasis schools but, acknowledging the character of our eccentric experience on this continent, take what you need from each.

The Founding Fathers set up a constitutional system that—no matter how good a deal at the time for the needs of the time—could not grow, *legally*. There has been a great deal of development, and very little by simple amendment. Instead, we had the Marshall enlargement of the Supreme Court from the very beginning: the largest part of our constitutional order is "unwritten," or written by the Court. This is particularly true of the boundaries between the different departments of government: these are altogether the result of historical struggles. The whole thing works only by virtue of party activity, and the party was not an original conception of the original order (the original conception was class). Indeed, the Federalists denied that they were a party. But Jefferson ruled by means of party —and the congressional caucus for several of the early decades even chose the president.

Professor Wilfred E. Binkley, as he appears in *President and Congress*, is a benchmark thinker. He says: "The Executive as an organ of American government got off to a bad start in the colonial period where it originated in the office of the colonial governor." The prerevolutionary tradition of asserting colonial legislative power against the Royal governors was the historical basis, he suggests, of the separation between the Executive and the Legislative, and the attempted primacy of the latter, in America. Thus the intense feeling in the colonies against the English monarchy and all its works was transformed into a standing animus against executive power itself. Binkley adds: "A consequence of colonial experience was the conviction that political power, particularly executive power, is so dangerous that it must be checked with power."

But of course this original impulse toward government by the popular assembly was itself frustrated, otherwise we would have developed a form of cabinet government.* It is the awful balance between neither that has caused so much trouble, and has produced our characteristic neither/nor negativism.

Once the Constitution was adopted and the government set up, a live issue involving cabinet-type government did in fact develop around the Treasury Department. The House, acting on its constitutional prerogative with respect to fiscal matters, attempted to make the Treasury its own organ rather than a department of the Executive branch. And Hamilton first established relations with Congress on the reasoned order of English ministerial procedures.

It was only later, under Jefferson, that the counteraction occurred

---

* Granted the disjunction between the Legislative and Executive branches, the committee system in Congress can indeed be viewed as "a form of cabinet government"—a horrible form.

and the committee system in Congress began to function regarding the Treasury: "The Republicans in the Third Congress proceeded in the demolition of the Federalist system of executive leadership, through a system of sabotage." Congress was rediscovering the capacity to obstruct the Royal governors as the basis of its true power. Thereafter, according to Binkley, our history records a deadly struggle between the presidents and the Congress whereby each weak president was the occasion for the establishment of further congressional power. This process was interrupted or reversed only by the "strong" presidents. Thus, the status of Congress may be seen as an accumulation of various presidential incompetencies. (Binkley's general view is that, at the beginning, the commercial interests in the country were for a strong central government; after Jackson, however, they became legislative supremacists, in alliance with various sectional interests.)

How the country survived the Civil War, with its heritage of division of powers, remains a marvel to contemplate. Binkley says: "Unquestionably the high-water mark of the exercise of executive power in the United States is found in the administration of Abraham Lincoln." (Followed, we note, by *legislative* high-water.) But much of this administration was in effect illegal. Lincoln himself stated: "I felt that measures, otherwise unconstitutional, might become lawful by becoming indispensable to the preservation of the Constitution through the preservation of the nation." Again and again, in creating and operating the government of the United States (conceived broadly), illegal and non-legal actions must be taken. This is the heritage of the rationalism with which the Constitution was adopted, and the moralism of the people who thereafter attempted to create a government under it.

James MacGregor Burns, in his very effective book, *The Deadlock of Democracy*, has carried the thesis of president/Congress conflict to the point where it dominates and displaces the history of the parties. He asserts that there are now and always have been four parties rather than two—that the difference between the presidential and the congressional grouping in each party is as significantly party-like as the difference between the parties themselves. Of this four-party pattern, Burns wrote: "This system is rooted in our constitutional arrangement, electoral behavior, party institutions, and machinery of government." The four-party view is a dramatic way of stating the problem; but once the curtain comes down on the presentation, the utility of the drama fades somewhat. Why only *four* parties? Why not a closer analysis of a larger number of gangs? When the president dominates, Burns calls the resulting system "Jeffersonian"; and when the president fails to dominate, he calls it "Madisonian"—going back to the original rationalistic image. But he characterizes the latter this way: ". . . under the Madisonian system personal factions would grow up around each office-holder and office-seeker, from President to fence viewer, and would buttress the constitutional and legal checks and balances with political and human forces."

This is the thesis of gang structure—and if a president manages to put together a dominant coalition of gangs which manages for a while to rule, this does not change the underlying structure one little bit: it is simply *one* possibility inherent in it. We still have gang rule rather than class rule. Indeed, a president's ability to put together a ruling coalition may be an even finer expression of the underlying structure than the weaker colleagues' inability to do so. Lincoln was elected in 1860 with 40 per cent of the total popular vote. Wilson also was elected as a minority president. It is a strange fact of our system that these two minority presidents were two of our most effective leaders, in that they managed to get considerable positive legislation through Congress. That must have something to do with the tension of the coalition, the adhesive factor. The threat from the outside holds the gangs together and makes them for a time responsible. It is coalition that rules in America; but whether Congress is the true forum where coalitions are created and recreated, or whether the real power lies in the hands of a strong president, it is Congress which holds the national legitimating power—for use or for non-use. Without this legitimating power, boys will be boys, and gangs remain gangs.

In line with our persisting inquisitiveness about power, we may note that the coalition with the weakest foundation and yet with the greatest reach was the deeply heterodox one managed by Lincoln under duress of our greatest crisis. And he will always be, I suppose, our paramount public figure—for the crisis he got us through, for his political cunning conjoined with achieved spiritual expression, for his prose. So we note with special care Richard Hofstadter's insight: "Here, perhaps, is the best measure of Lincoln's personal eminence in the human calendar—that he was chastened and not intoxicated by power." That is why Lincoln is so great in our history: he is the spiritual apex of the American response to the positive style in the use of power. And that is perhaps why he has been such a lonely figure in our history.

6 Next most revealing after Lincoln was the second Roosevelt. I'll be frank with the reader: I didn't care much for him, while he lived. I was, during much of his time, something of a doctrinaire socialist, or in the process of becoming one—and it was very clear to most people of my persuasion that he was a master conniver holding off a needed social revolution. Now, I think my understanding of socialist doctrine was superior to my early comprehension of American political life in its broader range. Since then I have stepped firmly off the transatlantic ship, and with each farther step into the interior I am more impressed with FDR's growth in stature. He more or less invented politics for us of the currently middle-aged generation: in any event, there has been precious little invention since his time, so he remains the classic genius of modern American coalition politics.

The amazing thing about Roosevelt was the extent to which his personality mirrored the country—and, one is tempted to say, vice versa. I succumb to the temptation: his personality did indeed provide a cultural form of use to others, in a wide range of areas of public performance. . . .The godlike grandeur of his voice issuing from the new Nowhere of radio; the absurd daring of his ebullience and confidence; the truly magic popular touch (so unlike the merely forceful representativeness of Harry Truman) which in a believing democracy like ours is granted only to a charismatic aristocrat; the wide hiring of intellectuals followed by playful juggling of their product; and not least, the Protestant-hypocritical awareness of the *nation itself* that, behind this gorgeous public image, there was working for all of us a tigerish ruthlessness in pursuit of a cornucopia of practicalities at any moment to be snatched from the selfish hands of The Powers. How that man understood the mixed bag of necessities and opportunities which are the real reservoir of American power! And unlike his cousin, he actually accomplished something; and unlike Wilson, he was no slave to righteousness. (Let's say that as to Wilson's Shelley and TR's Tennyson, his range was Byronic: later, John F. Kennedy died a Keats.)*

Schlesinger reports that "Roosevelt averaged about ten times as much daily mail as Hoover." This indicates the mutative departure in the significance of the presidency under Roosevelt's stewardship. We do not yet fully appreciate this massive change in our system— that big government in a big society necessarily means a big president; this factor matured with Roosevelt. Reflect even on the immobile Eisenhower: in Coolidge's day, he would have entered the history books as a smiling Coolidge. In Eisenhower's day, we would have had to make believe that even Coolidge was big; and he would probably have had to smile every once in a while.

It is important, as another example, that presidential initiative regarding legislation has been an occasional matter through much of our history, occurring mostly during military crises, and has been a regular thing only since Roosevelt. (The great exception, of course, was the first two years of Wilson's administration.) FDR added still another piece to our patched-up parliamentary forms: "By according the press the privilege of regular interrogation," says Schlesinger, "Roosevelt established the presidential press conference in a quasi-constitutional status as the American equivalent of the parliamentary question period—a status which future Presidents could downgrade to their peril."

And Roosevelt understood the importance of Congress; he perhaps had learned why and how to be a parliamentary leader from the example of Woodrow Wilson. He claimed to have spent three or four hours a day in conference with congressional figures during the whole period when Congress was in session. All of his personal talents and political wiles were brought to bear on the problem of organizing Congress for action; and an army of "special" liaison agents besides. But with all he had working for him, his success—like Wilson's—owed a good deal to internal changes in Congress itself: the Democratic Congress that President Roosevelt dealt with when he took office in 1933 contained 150 new and inexperienced congressmen—looking for leadership, so to speak. Luckily, they were "de-

---

* It occurs to one that Kennedy and Johnson are each half-a-Roosevelt— the one for style, the other for effect. But Kennedy reborn would beat Johnson again—once the fact of his incumbency had been dissolved into the campaign—in 1968. America yearns for style.

prived" of the previous Speaker, John Nance Garner, who had been promoted to the Vice Presidency at the 1932 convention. Garner later said: "The office is almost entirely unimportant." He regretted that he had not continued as Speaker of the House during Roosevelt's terms. He thought he could have been a "check" on FDR. "I would not have tried to tell him what he could do. But there would have been times when I would have told him what he could not do." (In the usual non-rule mode.)

So FDR, by parliamentary accretions and by political, even spiritual leaps, magnified the Presidency once and for all. And always the gay and uninhibited manipulator. For instance, his shrewd reason for financing social security through payroll taxes levied on the worker was to ensure that the benefits would be vested, so that, as he said, "no damn politician can ever scrap my social security program." This very nicely illustrates the relation between technique and policy, whereby the requirements of the latter can askew the former—even properly so, at the time. But today, with a long history of election-year expansions of social-security benefits, this form of payroll tax is becoming seriously regressive—more and more of a burdensome sales tax, and increasingly so as medicare initiates a trend of financing broader medical benefits in this unfortunate manner. (In 1964, before the tax cut and the social-security increase, payroll taxes were equal to one-third of individual income taxes.)

The Presidency has been magnified most profoundly in our hopes and dreams and other such areas of belief. For action, we still need a legislature, whether led by or leading a president in the parliamentary manner. Who led whom, for instance, in reducing the proposals for federal financing of medicine from the comprehensive Murray-Wagner-Dingell bill (defeated under Truman) to Kennedy's sales-tax medicare for burdensome parents? A non-acting Congress, I think—the cumulative non-acts of which had tended to transform the presidency (in domestic affairs) back beyond Wilson's good years to the noisy inventions of Teddy Roosevelt.

Kennedy, very much like TR, was an ideological leader—projecting an ideology of youthful and more or less humane managerialism —whereas Franklin Roosevelt was not an ideological leader at all, really, but rather a great political leader with major insights into the nature of American politics and personality. Roosevelt left ideology to his subordinates, who happened to have been loaded with it. To this purpose, he included in his government people with very contradictory positions, and allowed them rather full expression of their prejudices. What actually issued from his own mouth or hand was determined by his instinctual sense of the political moment. *He effected a beautiful orchestration of American gang structure.* That was his greatness.

We will not have another Roosevelt or Lincoln: they were too original. But we will have more great presidents. And more of the other kind, too—more McKinleys, whom William Allen White described so beautifully: "He walked among men like a bronze statue . . . determinedly looking for his pedestal."

And all will find one, now that Roosevelt has re-created the office.

7 What kind they are, both pedestal and statue, will depend on Congress as well as on their own inner qualities and the outer qualities of the crisis, if any, commanding them to greatness.

And all commands—both to greatness and to business-as-usual—must pass through the committees of Congress. Not especially to the appeals committees of the Senate, but more particularly to the committees of first instance in the House.

The committees are bastions of baronial power, as everyone knows. But let's be very clear about the matter: the committees are not instruments of the House; they are a full and complete substitute for it. It would even be stretching the truth to describe the House as an important appendage of the committees: that would require caucus-power, and there isn't very much. (One study asserted that 90 per cent of the legislative work in Congress occurs in these snug little gangs.) The late Representative Clem Miller from California, who wrote a book about his experience, characterized the situation this way: "Congress is a collection of committees that come together in a Chamber periodically to approve one another's actions." (Wilson said the same thing.) Other Representatives have added the following:

1. "All committee chairmen are despots."

2. "Committees are virtually autonomous bodies."

3. "The important work of committees takes place in closed rather than open sessions."

4. ". . . the committee selection system is pure and simple government by crony."

Whatever majoritarian democracy exists in the United States is up for grabs as soon as it arrives at the threshold and then enters into the deeper confines of the committee system of the House.

The House *sans* party, we have noted, is a brokerage agency. It is populated by people who are in the business of getting elected every two years, which means all of the time, which activity has as its object getting elected often enough to inherit a significant committee or subcommittee chairmanship. In a recent Congress, there were 167. The remaining 268 congressmen were reduced to concentrating on getting elected some more, and hanging around some while longer (or waiting for their party to return to power). Given the established committee system, it is the "hanging around" that sets the tone for the special exercise of power there. Murray Kempton, who sees the House as a kind of national small town, has this to say:

> The House . . . functions as a trade association for little enterprisers, and it depends for its life on those small hypocrisies and careful manners which people need to live together in small towns.

A fair look at the House leaves one with a perception of extreme coziness, considering the business at hand, and provides at least one firm principle of citizen belief: *anything at all* to shake up the situation—the web of relation is too rich.

Everybody also knows that the heart of committee rule is the seniority system. In this, apparently, everybody is wrong. For one thing, committees are an old feature of Congress, while seniority as a "system" has been called (by MacNeil) "a political development, actually a political phenomenon, of the twentieth century"—when, it may be noted, the Republicans joined the South in obstruction. In the nineteenth century, the average term of members was much shorter—indeed, only one Congressman, "Pig-Iron" Kelley, served the twenty years between 1861 and 1881. "In 1961 the average service for members of the House was almost ten years." And it was not Southerners but the Maine delegation that, toward the end of the last century, discovered the deep wisdom of returning the same Representatives to the House rather than rotating members, which had been the previous practice of local politicians.

Charles L. Clapp in his wonderful book, *The Congressman: His Work as He Sees It,** indicates that seniority is not the main thing in making committee assignments—it is important *after* the member is placed on the committee. Before that, the main things are his views, and whether these are acceptable to the "leadership," so called. Thus one congressman is quoted as saying: "Sometimes you begin to think that seniority is little more than a device to fall back on when it is convenient to do so." And another seconded this view: "Seniority is more of an excuse than a governing factor." Overall, Clapp's discussion of committee assignment indicates that (whether ideologically or more directly) specific interest groups more or less "own" particular committees. This seems to be the center of the power structure— and this center is the first thing to be preserved, with seniority coming second. But there are no young chairmen: the majority have been around for twenty-five to forty years.

The baronial power of the chairmen, the non-party irresponsibility it expresses and ensures, is based on both outside-of-Congress and

---

* Mr. Clapp's book is a perfect triumph of suggestive fact gathering and arranging, to which I am seriously indebted. What the author did was carefully to select and set up two panels of congressmen, Republicans over here, Democrats over there, and to record the ensuing talk, which ranged over all aspects of congressional life and business. The casting (something under twenty each for both parties) did not include the bosses, which again shrewdly carried forward the opportunities for candor. Several years in preparation, the basic work was done in 1959 with members of the 86th Congress. The wonderfully suggestive quotations with which the volume is filled are not ascribed to named participants; but a number of these are identified at the beginning of the book. It is nearly *all* quotes. And it is strangely similar to the *Statistical Abstract* (for purposes of American social analysis, my favorite volume after *Notes from Underground* and *Studies in Classic American Literature*), with the difference that suggestive personal quotations are substituted for suggestive public numbers. Mr. Clapp's substantial contribution of connective and summary tissue is valuable, and the slyly matter-of-fact tone is a real help in working one's way through the volume. But this book is not to be read as a narrative argument: it is to be daydreamed and speculated over.

Doing so, it occurs to me that academic work in political science may be on a substantially more acceptable level than that in standard college-teacher economics. Why? Because poli. sci. never got close enough to the cash register, where all piety begins. And also because, compared to money and business, the subject itself—*that is, the government of the United States of America*—was never important enough to attract the meddlesome interest of the trustees. Until recently, of course; and now, hopefully, it may be too late to put the poli. sci. departments through the same spiritual meatgrinder. (Even economics, in the new academic growth market, is getting a hold of itself.)

inside-of-Congress factors. Outside, there are interests backed by money or numbers or both, achieving more or less effect also according to their know-how and quality of organization. Inside, the factors are myriad, but consist mainly perhaps of the mutual fear and ambition and division of the members, their various states of personal development and commitment, and most deeply their isolation from sustaining sources of power: they are often alienated from their constituents on all but the lowest levels, thus representing all too nicely the mass alienation of their constituents from each other. And by and large, the party provides no community.

8   I would not attempt anything like a list of the shenanigans which are the coin of committee trading in the House. Reading from the analogue of maneuvers in law and business, none but a front-running practitioner's list is ever worth much, in any event. A good guiding principle in a society like ours is that very little is really tied down; and when strong men insist, even grandmothers will be exchanged. Remembering the point of the game—to become acceptable enough and get reelected enough to inherit a chairmanship—I choose two examples which appeal to me as especially absurd, and therefore more interesting than some others: the practice of release of votes and the role of expertise.

Under the Rayburn system, the demand of the hierarchy was the famous prescription: "To get along, go along." The reward (also, for some reason, stated as a command) was the equally famous Rayburn-Martin Rule: "Vote your district first." On occasion, these two monuments of practical wisdom could produce spiritual conflict, calling for the utmost in judicious dealing. Thus one of the bigger problems in the House is to use the inherent pressures of the hierarchy to persuade a man—sometimes to demand that a man—vote along with a measure at the risk of being hurt back in his own district. Carl Albert, the Democratic Whip, has said: "If a fellow keeps begging off . . . we tell him that it's his turn to take the heat the next time." A brokerage House has to operate under effective insurance.

One frankly discouraged Representative has said, "I don't think votes mean a thing"—referring not to ours, of course, but to his. I take it he meant that all the trading-off for purposes of appearance

—whereby a man can work like a tiger to defeat a bill and then, failing to accomplish anything more than the best professional emasculation, vote for it on the final roll call—has reduced the significance of the vote. I have to disagree: I think all these junk maneuvers testify to its importance. What our discouraged statesman should have said is that votes don't mean what they appear to mean—they frequently signify more, if only we could capture the significance. We certainly cannot capture it with "liberal" or "conservative" ratings: depending on the character of his district, a fellow who goes along can, apparently, order any kind of rating that fits him well, at the teller's window where all sizes are dispensed. But it is reported that great drama pervades the House when, on a close roll call, the storekeepers on each side are called upon to exert themselves to move inventory, and some of the fellows end up with vests that are hard to button, shoes of the wrong size, and even once in a while with tight pants.

The manipulation of votes for the sake of appearance bridges the two chambers. Often enough the Senate and the House will divide the work of the nation so that everybody who wants to, in one chamber, can get a piece of the action on a bill that, by prior general understanding, will subsequently be killed in the other chamber. In a really tight situation, everybody who has to on either side of the Hill can vote his "district" in the knowledge that a particular provision will be lopped off behind the closed doors of the conference committee. But these are emergency weapons, and in the ordinary course of business the ordinary arsenal of the House is adequate to guard the ramparts. Douglass Cater has pointed out:

> Chairman Howard W. Smith, of the House Rules Committee, claims that his real strength lies in the need for someone to take the rap for killing bills which weaker members would be afraid to vote against.

Note the last phrase, "to vote *against*": Smith voted against it for them, by institutional proxy.

Chairman Smith was the greatest expert on the Hill because he was the expert on how to vote against—a procedural expert.* The late

* The Eisenhower administration, surprisingly, also evidenced procedural expertise of a kind. During those days there happened to be a good deal of griping among congressmen simply because they did not know what the administration's position was on a particular bill. This might properly be termed "non-rule by virtue of concerted indifference."

Clarence Cannon, chairman of the Appropriations Committee for a quarter of a century, was primarily a great expert on voting against appropriations. But Chairman Smith was an expert on voting against *anything*. He served, of course, as the leader of the Southern bloc, the members of which must be prepared to vote against everything that might facilitate voting for anything: to be in a position to do this has been their Southern idealistic reason for bothering to get elected to Congress in the first place.

Nearly every congressman is an expert on something; he has to become one in order to get along (after going along, with the help of vote-maneuvers). This is one of the great sources of power for the aging congressmen who have become chairmen. Becoming experts, congressmen have preempted the role of staff in order further to secure their special individualistic power. (One of the consequences is that Congress is badly understaffed.) The "expert" on foreign aid is Otto Passman; and the "expert" on taxation is Wilbur Mills; these men are single experts for the nation, with no one in a real position to argue their expertise. Who could imagine an intellectual system less adequate for dealing with the complexities of our society? Even universities are not organized that badly.

I suppose it is understandable that many people are impressed on hearing that some Joe who never went to Harvard at all is Our Leading Expert on sugar quotas, the actuarial details of social security, or even a master of the horrors of the Internal Revenue Code. Still, I cannot accept any such consensus. For men who exercise power properly, experts are hired hands. If they are sufficiently expert, they will not only be able to do a much better job on the technical stuff than the boss, but also will know how to explain to him just what he requires to know—in order to be a boss, that is. He should be able to hear good, and so be an expert boss: that's plenty for one man. (Indeed, it is easier to be an expert—if you get into and through Harvard, of course; otherwise, it's tough.)

Most congressmen, and especially the insecure ones from two-party districts, are very busy getting reelected, as we have noted. They all complain about the extent of their case work for constituents (but wouldn't think of abandoning any of it), and are quite busy as well with more generalized personal contact: 90 per cent send out a newsletter of some kind; one admitted he had 13,000 visitors in his first two years; and in 1962 the House "handled nearly 23,000,000 pieces of incoming mail." (The principle underlying the permanent and perpetual campaign was nicely put by one of them as follows: "You can slip up on the blind side of people during an off-year and get in much more effective campaigning than you can when you are in the actual campaign.") All this necessary activity leaves little time for dealing with legislation, so that many of them will acknowledge even in public that they most often don't know what they are voting about. One of them was candid enough to say: "Time after time we go on the floor not knowing anything about the subjects to be discussed." And if this is true of the ordinary Joe, it must be even truer of the energetic prospective expert—he's attending the Harvard-on-the-Hill and certainly has no time for extracurricular reading outside his chosen field, such as moon probes. What the hell could he know about the dull details of medical finance that Wilbur Mills didn't tell him?

Nobody on the Hill knows more about the details (and less about the purpose) of foreign aid than Otto Passman. He's the expert, and that's that. That is especially that because these home-grown experts make certain that all "foreign" expertise is kept well under thumb. In 1963 there were approximately 4,500 employees on the House side, most of them secretaries, phone-answerers, and assorted constituent-handlers; of the professional staff, half are lawyers—although four-fifths of all bills are drafted in executive departments, and there is besides a Library of Congress service available for that sort of thing. (They are lawyers because lawyers like politics—you would, too, if you were a lawyer.)

The lack of staff on a number of major committees is quite scandalous, considering the work at hand. And the "staff" provided for—when provided for—is perhaps too often consecrated to the uses revealed to the newspaper public in the course of the 1964 primary campaign in New York which resulted in unseating Representative Charles A. Buckley, the Bronx power guy who headed the Public Works Subcommittee. Some of his men had hardly seen the Washington Monument, they were so engrossed in the details of running The Bronx.

I can just imagine former Congressman Buckley responding to an enlightened inquiry on this matter of experts: *Experts?* he might say. *I need a kid with a Phid. from Fordham maybe to tell me who got a contract coming? Sure I do. Also I need a hole in the head—for being in this business in the foist place.*

9 The idea of reforming Congress regularly occurs to people who take a long look at the institution. I sympathize thoroughly with the impulse, and I would guess that most congressmen do, too, when they are daydreaming. In one sense, reform is nearly impossible; in another, it happens all the time. Depends on how you look at the matter.

The word "reform" should be understood as a slogan—much as we have witnessed the word "poverty" becoming a slogan since 1963. Both are appropriate slogans for the educated middle class. Reform was very big in early '63; poverty is showing a nice turnover since then. But reform will come back, I believe, because it is a hallowed term, and because its underlying thought is in fact more serious. Indeed, with a little reform accomplished here and there we might be able to discuss and legislate regarding the use of our wealth and the condition of our population without cramming these comprehensive subjects into the sentimental nineteenth century handkerchief box called "poverty."

Reform is the preferred word for a formal shift in power relations to reflect already (or mostly) accomplished historical shifts. It is preferred because it seems always to imply something rather more noble than that. For me, there is hardly anything more noble we human beings ever manage to attain than to bring our formal relations somewhat into line with the changed facts. But the general run of educated humanity disagrees with me: for them, the biggest thing is to stop doing wrong, start doing right, and thereby make things better by making them over—all *right now*.

But not Senator Joseph S. Clark, currently the chief congressional reformer. He is a politician with a large, educated, middle-class constituency, and so would hardly be moved to avoid any nobility lying easily to hand. But he knows what he's doing, and in the bills he has proposed, the floor action he has taken, and the books he has published on the subject, he quite definitely has not limited himself to skimming the noble cream. The patrician Senator from Pennsylvania began his second term by taking on the bosses in public. This was not mere noble posturing but a calculated opening salvo in what he knew would be a long and dangerous campaign which he could begin effectively only by putting his own career in jeopardy, which he did.

The Senate Establishment, published in 1963, is a transcript of Senator Clark's speeches on four days in February 1963. What he undertook to do was to complain in detail about the decisions of the Democratic Steering Committee as to the granting or denying of the assignment preferences of the greatly augmented liberal bloc of Democratic Senators. They made out badly. While Clark was supported on the floor by Douglas, Proxmire, and some others, it would be stretching things to call it a debate (as usual, only a handful were present). The Majority Leader, Senator Mansfield, participated ("I really dislike to wash our dirty Democratic linen in public, but I suppose it has to be done every once in a while"), mostly to defend, however, his own past effort to be fair. Senators Russell and Byrd, the hearts of the matter, did not participate.

As the reader probably knows, senatorial discourse is burdened with incredible politeness. But what emerges, by reason of the Senator's effort, even through this veil, is that: 1) the big committees—Finance, Appropriations, Armed Services, Foreign Affairs—have been defended by every means against encroachment in any way on the control of the conservative bipartisan establishment; 2) these means include invoking or ignoring seniority as the purpose may be served; 3) members from whatever area who vote against amendment of the cloture rule have done conspicuously better than those voting for it; and 4) the conservative and mostly Southern Democratic members of the Club, or Inner Sanctum, or Establishment do about as little as their Republican allies to help provide liberal Senators with the kind of assignments, etc., which could be expected to assist in their reelection.

Congress: The Sapless Branch extends the analysis to the House, and contains a long schedule of desirable internal and external reforms. It is a good, clear, popular exposition of the problem of Congress—along with a very suggestive capsule history of previous congressional reform. The latter is particularly useful for demonstrating that Congress always changes, purposefully as well as haphazardly, and that "reform" is therefore most decidedly not the exclusive pastime of political science professors. (Their exclusive pastime is Proposed Rational Reform, which is another matter.) There are also some bright insights; for example, Clark suggests that the archaic atmosphere on the Hill provides a functional mystique for befuddling the new member, whose befuddlement is essential for the continued prosperity of the whole system: the biggest danger to the established powers, perhaps now and always the only real danger, is the threat of a Young Turks' revolt.

And most perceptively, in both the speeches and the *Congress* book, the Senator returns in his ruminations about reform to the great examples of such revolts which paved the way for the unique first two years of Wilson's administration—the dethroning of Speaker Cannon in the House by a Progressive-Democratic coalition, and the capture by the President's men of the Democratic caucus in the Senate. But we should speculate also on the relation between these bases of Wilson's two unique years of peacetime parliamentary rule and the following summary statement of the Senator's thesis:

> In the absence of crisis, Congress cannot and will not act affirmatively except under a strong President who has a clear mandate from the people, not only because of the separation of powers and the way Congressmen and Senators come to office, but also because of the congeries of rules and customs which favor inactivity.

Wilson had no clear mandate from the people, being a minority president; and he was able for a while to be a strong president only because of the Young Turks' revolt in the House led by Norris (a Republican) *two years before Wilson's election.* My simple point is that there must be a great deal more to the occasional functioning and the ordinary malfunctioning of our strange system than merely the determination of a Chief Executive to be "strong."

As the Senator certainly knows, the real problem is the Democratic Party. Representative Richard Bolling knows this, and states it forcefully in his shrewd and candid account, *House Out of Order:* "The failure of the House is the failure of the Democratic party of which I am a member." Characterizing the current House as "a lobby for arrogant brokers of special privilege," Bolling's prescription for reform is not to avoid the issue of power but to encompass it by use of the caucus. He sums up this way: "Basic flaws in party organization are reflected in the power structure of the House. They are entirely the responsibility of House Democrats, and the Democrats alone have the means at hand to correct them."

When we are all done analyzing Congress, including "the rules, parliamentary procedures, practices or precedents of either house

of Congress, or the consideration of any matter on the floor"—
which language Senator Russell excised from the Clark-Case resolution which he then kept from floor consideration by denying
unanimous consent (thus utilizing one of the sweeter precedents to
forestall reform)—it is clear as crystal that Congress was created,
both originally and developmentally, by the South; and that today
the last stronghold of the South is not merely in Congress but more
particularly in the Democratic Party—and in Congress mostly
through *that* position. Legislative obstruction was developed to the
level of a high art, utilizing any passing procedural debris—like the
Parisian art forms of *objet trouvé* and *collage*—by the South and
only by the South. Others are mere imitators, e.g., the later Republicans who adapted Southern premises and techniques to enforce non-
rule for the benefit of the plutocrats, when it came to suit their purposes to do so.

But their purposes change: at one time, a Republican will perfect
his control by destroying an element of Southern obstructionism—as
with "Reed's Rules" in 1890. Later, he will, failing of full control and
becoming himself a minority obstructionist, join with the Southern
artists in a new collaborative work of art.

So the primary problem remains party; the details of reform are
secondary. And behind party is money, which must be understood as
including the patronage Senator Clark disdains—certainly including
this junk until the patricians (like the good Senator) put more new
money behind more effort for newer and stronger party factions.*

The revolt against Speaker Cannon, making possible Wilson's special years, reformed the House by separating the considerable
powers of the Speaker from the even greater powers of the Rules
Committee. (In England, incidentally, the Speaker is a mere neutral
technician.) The most piercingly screamed-for reform in recent
times is to subject the powers of the chairman of the Rules Committee to the party leadership—first among whom is certainly the
Speaker.

What then, in perspective, is "reform"?

Reform as the "right" thing to do is a waste of time in politics
unless it is shrewdly hypocritical. Naturally, we all desire to live in a
perfectly ordered and honest world. But those of us who are in a big

* The history, for instance, of the Reformers in New York City makes it
quite clear that only decent *rentier* money can, initially, save us from the
unpleasantness of "patronage."

moral hurry about it do not serve their own stated purpose. *There is no perfect "system" to deal with imperfect circumstances inhabited by imperfect persons.* What, feasibly, requires reform, are the terms and counters of a power struggle; but a struggle for power is called for to accomplish such reforms. There is no way out of this tunnel except Forward.* The desire for a perfect system is something real that should be appealed to: when it is, and according to how it is, this desire itself can be an element of power—and thus, and only thus, honors the desire. That is its proper use; that is the proper use of all ideals. Improperly used, ideals substitute a Second World for the nasty one down here, which is so obviously dominated by issues of power. The Second World exists to inform the first, not to substitute for it (except as desperate personal occasions demand; but never as a regular, practical thing).

I think I will assert that genuinely balanced hypocrisy is not hypocrisy at all, but is the Holy Ghost of relation between the Second World and This (which relation, incidentally, requires a new name). Anyway, not all hypocrisy is equal—equal, for instance, to that of the Goldwater race strategy, which refurbished and nationalized traditional Southern duplicity on the subject. The critical point here—and the point to criticize—is not the simple one of duplicity, but the view of the second and first worlds implied in any *particular* duplicity. I was not against the Goldwater people because they were liars; I was against the lies they told, and the manner of the telling.

---

* *To the lawyers:* Proposed congressional reform is reform of procedure. We have, in the law, a rich history of attempted and achieved procedural reform and innovation. Our professionalism has, on occasion, allowed us to rearrange the terms and counters of the power struggle which *is* our profession. And we know that reformed procedures do not substitute for our power struggles, but are quickly adapted thereto. The net gain? More interesting—more professional—terms and counters, as law continues to mirror an imperfect society.

FOUR

Once More, the Parties Realign

1 Hardly ever before has so much political history been crowded into a single year as was jammed into 1964—especially if we imagine a "fiscal" political year extending from November 22, 1963, to November 3, 1964. The urgent need, in coming to terms with an overflowing period of this kind, is historical perspective.

I suggest the following basic one: *The political events of 1964 make possible, and all but ensure, the early completion of the New Deal.* To fill out this hypothesis, we must be clear about what the New Deal was, and wherein its lack of completion lay.

In most respects, the New Deal, given the facts of our history, was a very great triumph—equal in stature to the Colonial revolution and the Northern victory in the Civil War. But it did not solve the problem of the Great Depression: its only broad attempt to do so was the NRA, mere pieces of which survived; and the problem was actually "solved," of course, only by war production. What the New Deal, all on its own, did, was to interrupt a cataclysmic deflation. And, expressing a profound political decision by the overwhelming majority of the American people, it bequeathed to the federal government the continuing responsibility to forestall any such uncontrolled deflation in the future.

The completion of the New Deal revolution, which has been delayed for a quarter of a century, required both political and policy moves—and none of the Democratic leaders who expressed the willingness, showed as well the capacity, to carry these through successfully. The major policy move was to institutionalize budget deficits in pursuit of full production and employment. The political moves required to round out the New Deal coalition were the subordination of the Southern minority, in order to "contain" the explosive racial issue, and the inclusion of a significant element of corporate power in the coalition as a means of engineering the acquiescence of business and finance in efforts toward full production—meanwhile ensuring the distribution of the benefits of economic advance to the various constituent elements of the coalition. The New Deal grouping, great creation that it was, did not have the power to issue orders to the "second government" of big business. Certainly not, without an imminent economic collapse; certainly not, without a disciplined congressional majority, which would have had to include the Southerners. Caught between big business and the South, the New Deal was stopped short of fulfillment. And with the rise of the military economy, "fulfillment" often enough seemed like a wayward impulse to gild the lily: both taxes and deficits for military purposes were nicely accepted; nor was there any lack of "cooperation" on the part of big business (or the South) in achieving full production by the military route. So the New Deal was not only caught in the crossfire between business and the South; it was outflanked by the military-industrial complex.

Now all this has been changed, or the firm basis for the change provided, by the Big Year of 1964. The congressional sweep, the Civil Rights Act, the actual and the potential increase in Negro voting, and the defection of the convinced racists to Goldwater (and beyond), all invite a renegotiation of the basic arrangements of the Southern bloc within the Democratic coalition. The pro-deficit tax cut in 1964, followed by a $5 billion welfare deficit in the post-election budget—and assurances of further revenue cuts and deficits as needed—have pretty clearly established, however minimally or merely in principle, the long awaited full-production fiscal policy. Moreover, the painfully slow and careful assessment of the post-Cuban *détente*—the effort to carry forward what will necessarily be-a long-term effort to secure the right flank—remains a background factor of substance despite the Viet Nam overinvolvement.

But the greatest political event of 1964 has been the inclusion of a glittering section of the national corporate community within the Democratic Party. And this political event is solid because it was occasioned or encouraged by the basic policy now adopted, even including the new minimal welfare-ism represented by the anti-poverty program.

The main question in everybody's mind after November 3, 1964, was whether the "Goldwater results" would turn out to be transitory, because based on a monumental goof by the Republicans. I suggest that these events were lucky but are not in the least transitory. The Goldwater movement was the apotheosis of anti-New Deal sentiment which was due and coming, and which, with immense irony, provided the last link in the chain of historical events leading to the triumph of the New Deal revolution. But to believe this, one must understand that the New Deal was a *social* revolution only in creating status and jobs for administrative intellectuals, and was otherwise overwhelmingly a *political* revolution devoted to the preservation of the corporate order—by applying governmental power to make it workable. To see this, we must look as far back as 1912, when the cohesion of the previously governing coalition gave way and the pieces thereof began to arrange themselves in the pattern which became the New Deal.

Both Roosevelts intended an Establishment government, based on the facts of modern life and the model of the early Republic. But, with ordinary American irony, it was left to the barefoot genius from Texas to wind up their efforts successfully.

2 When the Republican Party was founded, Major Alvan E. Bovay chose the word "Republican" because, as he said, "It is the only one that will serve all purposes present and future. . . ." The word probably will, but the party has not. With this end in view, the party indeed had a magnificent beginning: the minority coalition which elected Lincoln was probably the wildest mixture in our history, ranging all the way from elements of the Know-Nothing Party to radical intellectual New Englanders. And whether or not it served all purposes, the party served

sufficient interests to hold power until 1912, with the slight interruptions of two Cleveland administrations.

The Republicans should have maintained their dominance long enough to mature into an adequate Establishment party. But American history is not subject to sustained fits of rationality. So in 1912 (with some lingering help from 1896) the turn was made, and the majestic process of dissolving the great Northern coalition was begun, along with the complementary process of putting together a new national coalition, this time based—absurdly—on the surviving party of the South. That this was necessary enough to happen, exposes the raw and often laughable mechanisms of American history in a fashion similar to the blinding sociological light of McCarthyism, and the recent low intellectual comedy of the Cowboy Pretender.

In retrospect, the Republicans perhaps failed because they represented imperialism rather than nationalism: the imperialism of Eastern industrial-financial forces. These, having occupied the South—first militarily and later, after the Hayes-Tilden deal, as a self-governing colony—then went on to subdue the West (meaning the farmers), which was accomplished with the defeat of Bryan in the great battle of 1896. But the party of Mark Hanna dissipated the powerful national coalition on which it was based; and the historical mutation of Teddy Roosevelt brought about the premature showdown of the Republican Party with American history. By 1912 it was all over—they were just too tightly tied to big, irresponsible money— and the Democrats once again had the opportunity forced on them to take up the burden of American history, as their predecessors had done before in the other worlds of Jefferson and Jackson.

Following the defeat of Bryan (James MacGregor Burns has noted), there was a steady decline in the exercise of the franchise to a low point in 1924. Perhaps this decline should be seen as the dissolution of Republican power, providing the opportunity for the growth of national Democratic power. This culminated, of course, in 1932, but it was in motion before that. Samuel Lubell has pointed out that the Republican hold on the cities was dissolved by Al Smith, not by FDR. The Republican plurality in the twelve largest cities shrank from 1,638,000 in 1920 to 1,252,000 in 1924, and in 1928 the Democrats achieved a plurality of 38,000. Having been the party of the South and the party of the West, the Democrats were now becoming the party of the North. Hoover's insane devotion to the myth of Individualism and the principles of federal non-rule speeded the process and helped achieve the final debacle: the Republicans lost forever the majority of the Negroes and the workers and, along with them, the sincere and well-to-do Progressives. (FDR set out, with self-conscious determination, to catch his cousin's former supporters, the enlightened minority of the middle and upper classes, the idealistic Bull Moosers: Ickes is an obvious example, but not the only one.) Highlighting this switch, once accomplished, Seymour Martin Lipset says: "In 1948 almost 80 percent of the workers voted Democratic, a percentage which is higher than has ever been reported for left-wing parties in such countries as Britain, France, Italy, and Germany." ("Left-wing" is the wrong word here; but no matter.)

This should never have happened. The default of the Republicans has cost us a half-century of development, or has forced upon us a half-century of unnecessary floundering. It should not have happened because there can, at this early stage of our history, be no adequate national government in the United States *without* a large portion of national corporate power or *with* too much of the South: not in the absence of a genuinely revolutionary reordering of social power.

But it did happen. And the members of the Progressive middle class were locked into the Democratic Party, there to squirm in the embrace of the sick South. They have been stuck with the Democrats —"the organized incapacity of the country." Those remaining with the Republicans achieved even less, with their embarrassing ties to the troglodytes and with their pallid Me-tooism. Explaining the source of the latter, Walter Lippmann (in his column of January 28, 1964) went back to the 1912 fight and the loss, never to be regained, of party control by the "progressive nationalists." (As to this continent, TR made nationalist rather than imperialist noises.) He put it this way:

> For when the party split in 1912, it surrendered to the Democrats the initiative in the selection and formulation of issues in domestic and international affairs. By surrendering the initiative, the party organization surrendered the vital center of American politics to the Democrats.

By "vital center" I presume he meant the ready possibility of putting together a national majority coalition. Without initiative, the center can be taken only with Me-tooism.

Lyndon Johnson, with his genius-like "sense of the center," has stitched together a Big Wigwam with the hides of any number of past and present political leaders. New Deal heritage; the Truman common-man touch; the Kennedy "program"; and, indeed, any salable Me-too merchandise ready to be remaindered. Even including Eisenhower: look at the electoral maps of the 1952, 1956, and 1964 results—and notice their near-identity. Goldwater lost very much as Stevenson did; Johnson won an Eisenhower victory.

One's deepest feeling when Eisenhower won in 1952 was that not a political but a *cultural* disaster had occurred. That was certainly confirmed by events. With the interregnum of the Kennedy regime, the achievements of which were largely cultural (referred to regularly as matters of "style"), the 1952 event has now been extended—almost, one might say, institutionalized. Although I would guess that the American people generally disliked Goldwater more than Stevenson, and certainly had more positive feeling for Eisenhower than for Johnson, the fact remains that the American majority now wants an imprecise if not actually innocuous symbol of national unity, a true centrist, at the helm. Out of their desire they have created an unhallowed Eisenhower out of Johnson, with his expert Me-tooing assistance. (And for ideological fervor, only the liberal adoration of Stevenson has matched the right-wing passion for Goldwater.)

It was Eisenhower who finally killed the Republican Party. He was their last chance to make up for the 1912 mistake, and subsequent defaults, in pursuit of the necessary effort to retake the center. He blew it; and I don't suppose that needs to be demonstrated. How anyone can imagine that anyone else is apt to have anything like as good an opportunity in the foreseeable future is quite beyond me. He was the one non-politician that broke the party's back: they needed a winner, but they needed a master politician rather more. And even if Goldwaterism is decisively squelched (an unlikely outcome), that it could ever have happened remains an enduring curse for a party aspiring to the center.

A genuine and comprehensive center party implies a right and a left as well. So I suggest that we are moving now toward a three-party system in the United States—right, left, and center. For nominalists, American parties have not realigned significantly since 1856. But one should be casual—realistically to follow the course of our realignments—not only about names but also about the major parties themselves. Our realignments are of *factions*, the parties serving as little more than battlegrounds—and, later, stockades. (Tipping his hat to the President after the 1964 election, Richard Nixon called him "the Robert E. Lee of modern political warfare.") There can be no majority politics in America that is not coalition politics: more than that, the coalitions, as we have noted, are often enough downright hilarious. Seen from this perspective, party realignment is a continual matter, but occurring mostly undercover— obscurely, as well as humorously. Every once in a while a big battle is fought in the open, a whole division defects to the opposing army, some prisoners escape (or are liquidated), and everybody notices a Big Rearrangement. One such occurred in 1964. It was brought about primarily by the slow shift of history, and the catalytic activism of the Negroes. But whether or not it holds, involves the prospects for the continued inclusion of corporate power in the coalition. No center without them. So to this equally difficult and crucial matter we now turn.

3 On July 23, 1964, President Johnson hosted a luncheon attended by 242 business leaders, the ostensible purpose of which had something to do with civil rights— these Influentials were supposed to use their what-with "to persuade others [sic] that the law of the land must be obeyed." (The Civil Rights Act had been passed, and Senator Goldwater had been nominated.) It was the first such well-attended presidential luncheon, and the physical planning was unavoidably off-form. The National Airport across the river in Virginia was not able to handle the crush of "more than ninety company planes"; two Jet Stars and "a dozen humbler" aircraft were diverted to Dulles Airport. The Washington Post also reported: "An operations worker . . . remarked that 'every big corporation you can think of' was represented." (No one has ever thought to ask, but where indeed did they park all the horses at Runnymede, three-quarters of a millennium earlier?)

Anyway, the barons met—and the President was Democratic. So be it, for the eccentric and de facto character of the new Magna Carta.

Whatever fresh and compelling attractions a revived Republican Party may be able to offer big business in 1968 or later, the underlying point is that a startlingly significant vanguard of the corporate barons has begun the serious institutional and political approach to Washington—and to the Democrats, at least for the time being. This does not consist merely of personal moves into administrative positions, which has been going on for quite a while. (These early ones were outriders scouting the terrain, warily looking for Indians.) And finally they have come not to obstruct but to participate in the political development of the nation. A part of the basic thinking behind the new move was indicated by Lammot du Pont Copeland, president of the big chemical company, in a speech to the New York Chamber of Commerce on February 10, 1964:

> Whether we like it or not, the Federal Government is a partner in every business in the country. . . . We are confronted . . . with a condition and not a theory. . . . As businessmen we need the understanding and cooperation of government in our effort to throw the economic machine into high gear.

Slogans primed—"it is possible to disagree without being disagreeable"—the barons have moved forward. On July 2, 1964, the president and second leading officer of the Bank of America returned from a trip to Europe and told reporters how impressed they were with the extent of cooperation there between business and government. "They are doing what we are talking about," the president said. The very important news in this report was that "we" are now talking about it.

There are a slew of excellent reasons for this big shift in business attitudes—so many, indeed, that it is easier to explain its happening than it would be to account for its not having happened. What keeps us from readily recognizing this, is the ordinary image of "business" as a monolith, and moreover one with an eternal and unreasoning allegiance to the Republican Party. But business is not a monolith, and the degree of national irresponsibility involved in traditional attitudes of "business" is no longer appropriate to the large national corporations. The suggestion here is that a "natural" division in the business community has now matured—with profound political consequences.

After the Goldwater nomination, the *Wall Street Journal* (July 22, 1964) reported: "A big majority of executives clearly favor the Arizona conservative." But the *Journal* also cited a Research Institute of America survey of 8,000 businessmen to the effect that one out of three would vote for Johnson, whereas four years previously Kennedy received only one out of five. Which one out of which three, the *Journal* didn't say. Eileen Shanahan, assigned for several months by the New York *Times* to cover the story of business defection during the campaign, wrote directly to this point in her report on the Northeast and Midwest (September 16, 1964): "The business executives who expect to cast the first Democratic Presidential vote of their lives are nearly all affiliated with large companies." She noted "the general rule that small businessmen are remaining Republican." Additional differences, borne out by later reports from other regions, were that Johnson was getting more support in the East, in big cities, among middle-aged rather than younger or older men, and from "businessmen who have previously been involved . . . in public affairs. . . ." In her report from the South, she quoted a large-firm executive from Winston-Salem: "Businessmen in the South felt a sense of relief when Johnson came in. We knew him . . . we knew from the start that he was not anti-business." She noted a "less pronounced" shift in the Far West; and added the further distinction that the defection was greater in port cities like San Francisco, New Orleans, and Boston, and among businessmen with international interests.

Also, defense contractors favor government spending and tend to roll with the paymaster-party in power. The effort of the Goldwater forces to identify *all* of Johnson's business support as being of this character was, however, patent nonsense. Another difference: among intellectuals, engineers have traditionally been distinguished by their overwhelming Republicanism. But in 1964 the scientific elite organized an effective action group—Scientists and Engineers for Johnson and Humphrey. The Organizing Group of forty-seven scientists was exceptionally distinguished—George Kistiakowsky, Jerome Wiesner, Detlev W. Bronk, James M. Gavin, Benjamin M. Spock, Gerard Piel, Harold C. Urey, Paul Dudley White, Warren Weaver, and other leading professors and administrators. *Also*, scientific corporate officers of IBM, CBS, Hallicrafters, Gillette, Northrop, Hughes Aircraft, Lockheed, Aerojet-General, Litton Industries, North American Aviation, The Martin Company, RCA, and the president of MIT. How many run-of-the-mill engineers went along is not clear. But a scientist or an engineer nowadays is never far from a big organization, including big business corporations (and the major universities are coming to be something strangely like corporations).

The first name and the biggest name was that of Henry Ford II. He was one of the early and really important business leaders to announce publicly for Johnson, and he later became one of the forty-five sponsors of the National Independent Committee for President Johnson and Senator Humphrey—the elite and willing-to-be-mentioned big business group behind the President. But having started things rolling, he rather retired from view.*

Mr. Ford is important not alone for being Mr. Ford, but also for having headed up the Business and Finance Committee for the Reduction in 1963, which lobbied among the barons for support of the big tax cut. This group was organized in April 1963, and a month later reported a membership in excess of four hundred. *Note the date:* seven months before the assassination, fifteen months before the Goldwater nomination. In this early organizing effort Mr. Ford was joined by the president of Westinghouse, for instance; and by Stuart T. Saunders, then president of the Norfolk and Western Railway, who has since become chairman of the board of the Pennsylvania Railroad. Addressing the elite Business Council (probably the single most august organization of barons in the nation) on October 17, 1964, Mr. Saunders proclaimed the tax cut to have been an unqualified success—he noted an increase in after-tax corporate profits of 18 per cent over the previous year. The *Times* reported that Mr. Saunders "emphasized, in a news conference following his speech, that he did not want his remarks taken politically." Two weeks before the election, that is. (Further on the Business Council: M. J. Rossant, writing in the New York *Times* for August 17, 1964, cited a member as saying that 60 per cent of the group intended to support President Johnson—a fabulous fact, if true, indicating an avalanche rather than a drift.)

Henry H. Fowler, a Washington lawyer appointed by President Kennedy to the politically active Under Secretary post in the Treasury Department, was the administration liaison in setting up the Committee for the Reduction. Having meanwhile left the government, he was also one of the organizers of the campaign committee. He is reputed to have been the central "executive" figure in the

---

* A man by the name of Ford who is the head of the Ford Motor Company is a prisoner of that corporation's advertising program: one continues to sell cars to hard-core Republicans, and I mention this consideration as a warning to future researchers. Also: I have no special information, but Mr. Ford could have been corralled, on the highest level, by Robert McNamara, a former employee. This detail is mentioned only to illustrate that while I rely on the drift of history for my analysis, I understand that history drifts in special ways, and that a little "contact" can accomplish wonders in helping the *Zeitgeist* along.

corporate-Democratic *rapprochement*. Mr. Fowler is a Democrat (since appointed Secretary of the Treasury). The leading Republican figure seems to have been Robert B. Anderson of Texas, Eisenhower's Secretary of the Treasury and a close friend or fellow-Texan President Johnson. Among other things, Mr. Anderson is a partner in the Wall Street firm of Carl M. Loeb, Rhoades, as is John L. Loeb, another organizer of the National Independent Committee. The three additional named organizers were Sidney J. Weinberg of Goldman, Sachs; Carter L. Burgess, chairman of the board of American Machine & Foundry; and John T. Connor of Merck & Co. (since appointed by the President as Secretary of Commerce).

A list of the forty-five "sponsors" of the political committee was published in the New York *Times* for September 4, 1964, following an organizational meeting at the White House. Perhaps the most impressive grouping in the list was that of investment bankers (concentrated in New York and Boston), including, besides those already mentioned, Thomas S. Lamont; Lehman Bros.; Lazard Freres & Co.; Eugene R. Black; Lewis W. Douglas and Mariner S. Eccles (both from New Deal days); and some Boston Cabots. Other well-known names (of individuals or companies represented by a leading executive) were—Kaiser; Curtiss-Wright; Inland Steel; American Electric Power; Burroughs; Ralph Lazarus of Federated Department Stores (current owner of Goldwater's department store); Hunt Foods; American Can; Tennessee Gas Transmission; Western Pacific Railroad; and Texaco.

Not exactly the *Fortune* list, to be sure. But it is presented as a list of *public* sponsors, not a survey of supporters and non-supporters. Businessmen are new at this public game; traditionally, they discuss and contribute privately. (Eileen Shanahan reported that "almost none" of the new Democratic supporters "will permit use of his name.") Moreover, whatever a true survey might reveal, there is the fact—noted proudly in the White House release—that three-quarters of the Johnson supporters were traditional Republicans.

Within a month, Citizens for Goldwater-Miller responded defensively with a full-page ad in the *Wall Street Journal* for October 1, 1964, listing 519 businessmen who were backing Goldwater. This was also not the *Fortune* list, although it included some national corporations: Armstrong Cork, J. I. Case, Cluett Peabody, Eli Lilly, Quaker Oats, and others. Upon closer analysis, the hidden surprise in this list was that the Goldwater supporters were heavily concentrated in Illinois, California, and Ohio. Along with Texas, with its well-known excess of right-wing wealth, *these were the four big states the Goldwater strategists said they had to win in order to put their man over.* (There was also an intriguing concentration among steel and steel-related business.*) The persuasive implication here is that the Goldwater maneuver from the beginning involved a schism in the business community—more specifically, a power play by regional (plus steel) interests to shift the *business* balance of power, using the Republican Party as the vehicle. Or was it a response to a power shift begun in the East?

Let's say both. In the East—and for the more national corporate interests nominally headquartered there—the basic policy toward the government was undergoing a change; elsewhere, the considerable growth of regional business wealth was producing a natural assertion of new independence and power. For representative persons, think of Douglas Dillon and George Humphrey—each a leading spokesman on the basic divisive issue of a purposeful federal deficit. (Miss Shanahan said: "It is on the issue of Government deficits that the division of opinion between small and large businessmen emerges most dramatically.") On this issue, under George Humphrey's tutelage (along with the pull of his own primitivism), Eisenhower failed—*failed as a centrist.* And the tragi-comedy of Richard Nixon, of course, is that he made himself into a centrist of the Republican Party, not the American nation—a serious oversight for a wily politician. It remained for Kennedy to plow the ground, and Johnson to harvest the seed-grain, of the new American center. Each in his own way (which turned out to be marvelously complementary) understood the New Deal heritage and its imperatives, and the consequent vulnerability of the Republican posture.

So business is not a monolith. The classic view, which produced the image of the business monolith, is simply the distinction between property-owners and the propertyless; the distinction to replace this classic one concerns personal proprietorship and sparsely populated areas as against highly organized property tenure and use in densely populated centers. With the natural *caveat* that young people are not very realistic, and old men hate to change their views, this formulation can be quite useful in evaluating diverse business opinion.

* I am indebted for these notions to a former student of mine, Elinor Graham.

4 It will soon be recognized that 1958 is a pregnant date, like 1929 and 1896 and 1912 and 1964, and so on. What happened in 1958 was that the postwar inflationary boom came to an end—by something like "administrative decision." In 1958, the powers that could have in 1928, made the decision they should have made then. And they made it in the light of the political decision the American people had meanwhile made in 1933: that is, the *repeal* of natural deflation. Big business and big money finally accepted the facts of life, including the fact of the New Deal: they "signed on" historically. For American society, it was like being born again.

What led them to this departure was the built-in (by the New Deal) and unintended (by Eisenhower) deficit of $18 billion in the first six months of fiscal 1959 which, after much effort, washed out as a $12 billion deficit for the full year. This was a unique financial event in American history. What it demonstrated was the submerged power of the potential deflation—the "bust" in boom-and-bust America—which had been turned over to the federal government in 1933 for general safekeeping, periodic exorcising, and ultimate liquidation. Because there was so much more to be destroyed in 1958, and perhaps also because big money and big business had been through it once before, the decision was taken *not* to go for broke again. The inflationary boom, presided over by the congressional Republicans and then the Eisenhower administration, had been played out; a slowdown was instituted. Indicating the administered quality of this decision is the fact that the corporate powers initiated in 1958 an expensive advertising campaign around the slogan, *"Inflation is the cruelest tax of all."* Perhaps they were not a "they" until they read the book C. Wright Mills wrote about them; but if one looks at the sponsors of the anti-inflation ads, one may be led to doubt this shrewd hypothesis. In any event, price inflation more or less ended in 1958, while the stock market paused decisively. Raising prices became a "bad thing."

When U. S. Steel, reportedly squeezed by its own inefficiency, attempted to get a little spiral going again after a few years, President Kennedy reacted on the part of the government as if the non-boom policy had not been an act of unilateral discretion on the part of the barons, but was in fact a kind of *joint* program of business and government. The emotional reaction to this presumption, you will remember, was extreme. But it was mostly emotional: U. S. Steel swiped a piece of cake a year later, but the policy was not abandoned. It still is in effect, as are the administration's wage/price "guidelines." These are a highly amateur effort at price control, or reasonableness, which can be "enforced" only by the profoundest quantum of voluntary cooperation on the part of business. The point is that *this has been given.*

Let's talk about inflation for a moment. There are two kinds: the ordinary one is price inflation; the overlooked one is paper inflation. Veblen emphasized the ways in which the first is a condition of the second; perhaps it is now time, following the repeal of natural deflation, to notice the quasi-independence of the latter. While the aggregate value of capital paper, so far as we know, is ultimately limited by the price level, the outer limits of this debt and capitalization are not very clear under the system of government responsibility for the potential bust. In the postwar period, paper inflation has far outdistanced price inflation, although the latter has been by far the more notorious.

Until the resumption of price inflation toward the end of 1965, prices had roughly trebled since the bottom of the Depression and doubled since the War. Total public and private debt, however, had gone from $200 billion in 1935 to something under $1,200 billion in 1964—at least twice as great an advance as the increase in prices. Meanwhile, the market value of stocks listed on the New York Stock Exchange went from about $46 billion in 1940 to $76 billion in 1950, $170 billion in 1955, $219 billion in 1957, $196 billion in 1958 (notice the decline), up again to $277 billion in 1959, and on January 1, 1965, stood at $474 billion. While prices were doubling since the War, values on the New York Stock Exchange went up ten times over in twenty-five years; total private debt had gone up five times over; state and local debt better than quadrupled; and apart from the Second World War itself, federal public debt had gone up no more than 20 per cent—including deficits attributable to *all* Cold War expenditures.

The basic postwar inflation has been a capital paper inflation, not a price inflation; and it has not included the federal government as a benefiting participant.

But capital values have continued to increase since 1958, while prices have been held fairly steady. The paper has grown, not in a primitive response to price increases, but as other opportunities permitted. This is a new situation, which can bear much hard thought. Without too much hard thought, note the following considerations: 1) prices rise by standing still, if costs go down and sales increase; 2) when there are no recessions to discount, because of growing assurance as to anti-recession policy, financial decisions concerning inventory and expansion become more sophisticated and less expensive; and 3) the actual anti-recession policy has been heavily slanted in favor of direct advantages for business.

In the middle of May 1964, Mr. Donner of General Motors pointed out that the company had not raised its "basic" auto prices since 1958. Then he pledged that "we're going to do our part" to hold the line on prices, etc. The following January, General Motors announced the greatest annual profits of any single corporation in the history of the human race. Now what could possibly induce the still-sane gentlemen from GM to yearn for Goldwater purism in such circumstances? I suggest that it is only the liberal intellectual's traditional and excessive downgrading of business intelligence that even raises the issue.

Following the decision to forgo a runaway boom, big business seemed willing to settle for high-level stagnation—about 80 per cent of capacity—and preserve the achieved level of paper values and reasonably expected growth thereof. But Sputnik had occurred in 1957; and there was in 1958 also the warning of the liberal congressional sweep. (Later warnings have concerned the pace of automation, the expected increase in the labor force, the new Negro activism, the general intractability of unemployment—and after Cuba, the threat of arms reduction.) When the 1958 recession began again too quickly in 1960, some enlightened elements began to see the light.

The choice then seemed to lie between an uncertain course of continued high-level stagnation and embarking on a series of planned deficits. The Democrats, under Kennedy and Dillon, demonstrated that there was no good reason to settle for that particular stagnation. With sneaky and then overt deficits, they gave business and most of the rest of the country six years of good growth and no recession (through 1966). This "New Economic Policy" was sold as a tardy imitation of proven centrist procedure in Europe, which I suppose it was. (Edwin L. Dale, Jr., of the New York *Times* had written the same piece on this point at least three hundred times in the course of two or three years in the early Sixties; I was in awe of his endurance.) It has worked extremely well, bringing about the longest postwar period without recessions. This policy is the proper and fairly secure basis of an Establishment government.

It is becoming clear that the real beginning for Kennedy was not the initial task-force noise or the Bay of Pigs, but Vienna. Khrushchev did not take the young man seriously—not until the Cuba confrontation in 1962. Before that apocalyptic event, the ambiguous missile gap of the campaign and the Berlin crisis were the occasions for increases in military expenditure. This economic policy, continued from previous administrations, postponed any fresh moves in fiscal policy. The first serious intimation of any occurred in the wake of the steel-price maneuvering, the subsequent stock-market shudder, and the talk about a tax cut—all in the spring and summer of 1962. The revised depreciation guidelines offered by the Treasury, and later depreciation benefits to business by virtue of congressional enactment, were definite pro-deficit moves—worth $2 to $3 billion annually.

But in the period of the post-Cuba *détente*, what the Democrats did was genuinely entitled to be called the New Economic Policy: it was a major departure. Under the thinnest veneer of a reform bill, a $10 billion-plus tax cut was advertised and finally enacted (later opinions put it at $14 billion). Thus were taken the first baby-steps toward a purposeful deficit. This was then buttressed by another advertising program which encompassed the embarrassing $1 billion "war on poverty." Meanwhile, a great deal of conversation and other newspaper action about defense cutbacks occurred. And rumors about further tax cuts. All this was designed to induce spending wherever possible in the private sector, and to prepare the necessary groundwork for non-military public spending, should the political occasion arise. (Thus the *détente* might be deepened without economic disaster.) To help the people understand their government's policy moves, President Johnson personally turned out the lights in the White House.

But the substance of all this indirection should not be lost sight of: consistent deficits were incurred (and surpluses avoided)—$3.9 billion in 1961, $6.4 in 1962, $6.3 in 1963, $8.2 in 1964, and $3.4 and $2.3 achieved for 1965 and 1966. If by one means or another—

indeed, if by any means—a ten to twenty billion dollar annual deficit attempt is institutionalized,* we shall have finally passed a major post-New Deal point of departure, and later historians will treasure the indirection as consummate shrewdness. (We have for two decades needed nothing quite so much as an attempted annual non-military deficit of adequate size.)

It is a *policy*—a wonderful, workable one—that has corralled enlightened, national business for the Democrats. The prospects for the firmer inclusion of this business element in the Democratic coalition rest primarily on the future success of the policy, and secondarily on the ability of the Republicans to Me-too it persuasively. The odds on the first are much better than those on the second.

Before we pursue this intriguing point, we may pause to note a special irony—the irrational difference in the attitude of big business toward Kennedy and Johnson. The President cannot be accused any more than his predecessor of wooing business: he simply did much better at it. Indeed, the NEP was Kennedy's creation—Johnson was the *executive* President. Business opposed Kennedy no matter how hard he tried to please them, and he tried very hard (the story is well detailed by Hobart Rowen in *The Free Enterprisers: Kennedy, Johnson and the Business Establishment*). They accepted Johnson —*and* the policy, when offered by him—almost immediately. This is where Kennedy's "style," especially including that of the intellectuals around him, was quite important: businessmen detest intellectuals.

In long-term perspective, Harry Truman understood (and tried to fulfill) the New Deal as the near-victory of Populism. John Kennedy saw it as the near-victory of enlightened managerialism. But President Johnson sees it more clearly as the great national political coalition that, in its essence, it truly is. Style must wait on the future—which future, I sense, is being carefully constructed by the Kennedy government-in-exile, headed by the dead President's brother, Robert.

* The deficits have been regularly less than projected in the administrative budget, e.g., $2.3 instead of $6.4 in fiscal 1966.

5 The major point is that if the NEP works so well and we are in fact going to have it, then business must participate in the governing political decisions by one institutional means or another. Which implies a further abrupt turn, on the order of that instituted by the New Deal and by the military economy.

In the course of President Johnson's famous (or at least notorious) *ad lib* performance before the annual mass meeting of the Chamber of Commerce in Washington on April 27, 1964, he detailed the government's beneficence toward business, and then said:

> But I must apologize to you this morning—we haven't done anything for business this week. But please remember, this is only Monday morning.

The government may "do" things for Chamber-type business—but if there is going to be any "doing" done on the upper level, the barons will do for themselves, thank you.

If they must be in politics in a new way and more seriously than before, then two things: 1) they cannot ignore the governing and majority party; and 2) the bigger bargain lies with the Democrats—they have the more usable coalition, and it is already there. (When a big corporation enters a new field, it almost always begins by buying into a good going concern.)

So Lyndon Johnson, Me-tooing Eisenhower politically and accepting the direction of Kennedy's shrewdly constructed economic policy, has now put together the elements of a competent Establishment —*using the Democratic Party as the instrument.* A significant element (still a minority) of national corporate power has joined in responsible national government, accepting the Democratic Party as the vehicle rather than the directly legitimating processes of the State. So be it. For liberals who have never faced up to the overriding facts of corporate power, and whose politics is derived from a glowingly fuzzy remembrance of New Deal things past, the event—when and as they own up to it—will be spiritually disquieting in the extreme. For their more realistic companions, who recognize the New Deal to have been a major innovative effort to save the corporations from themselves,* the event will be taken with a deep sigh of relief —and as an occasion for some fresh political thinking. The simplest and most important facts of our political life are and have been for some time: 1) That there can be no adequate government of the United States without the participation and cooperation of the major corporations—they are in fact all by themselves the major part of "*the* government of the United States"—and 2) that there has not yet been created in this country a power equal to the task of issuing *orders* to the corporations. Therefore, it has been, and remains, necessary to negotiate their compliance with federal policy.

What died in 1964 was 1940 Me-tooism. On the matter of deepening the new party realignment, the issue after 1964 is whether there will be a new 1968 or 1972 one. The Republican Party cannot avoid survival of some kind; the important question is whether the Me-too group can devise and execute a *new* Me-tooism. The old one is properly dead. Since it was a calculatedly pale reflection of Democratic initiative, the new form of the latter must emerge clearly before Republican Me-tooism can be newly recalculated with properly functional paleness. Barring the intervention of genius, this is a serious number of years off.

Meanwhile, the Republican Party is, from the most generous point of view, riven. The so-called moderates certainly gained no advantage from any lil' ole Goldwater diversion: they didn't even "clear the air." If that was their fantasy, it was as silly as the Goldwater-do itself. Indeed, sillier. Because the moderates are defined by little more than being in the business of "winning"; most significantly, this is *not* true of the Goldwater people. They couldn't care less; the one thing certain to destroy the conservative group would be for them to win their way to a position of responsible power. (Whether the country would survive the lesson is another matter.†)

Unless the Goldwater people dry up and blow away, the Republican Party—a distinct minority even when united—will suffer continued

---

* It would seem to be about time now to go back and study the NRA with a microscope: that scribbled blueprint seems increasingly relevant and clairvoyant as subsequent history accrues.

† Incidentally, the useful meaning of the word "fascism" for the present is this: a large group of politically activated people, making a mass appeal, who begin with a deep hysterical commitment to a particularly effective aspect of precedent unreality. That is also an objective, even historical, definition of social insanity—which is exactly what I intended.

reduction. The Goldwater group, broadly conceived, severely limits the flexibility required to create the new and necessary Me-tooism. Meanwhile, the grouping does not appear to be impressed with its loss, apart from a disappointment with Goldwater himself, who will be returned to Kiwanis fund-raising, where he belongs. They can hardly be thrown out, and it is difficult to believe that they will quietly return to their previous captive status in the party. Moreover, the "success" of John Grenier's Southern strategy is a new, intractable factor that will plague the moderates. It took an economic earthquake and a lot of history to bring the majority of the Negroes into the Democratic Party while it included the Southern racists. Now the racists are oozing away from the Democrats, at just the moment when the national racist policy of the Goldwater campaign has produced the massive defection of Negroes from the Republican Party. How can the moderates get them back, especially if the administration pursues its anti-poverty program and puts real force behind Negro registration in the South? And how can they win in the cities without the Negroes? Paradoxically, urban Republicans may have to become, like Javits and Lindsay, *more* liberal than the ordinary run of Democrat in order to win in the North.

The shocking helplessness of the Republicans, not merely the fact of the Goldwater takeover, was the big revelation of the black Republican year. It is not credible that the leaders were unaware of what the Goldwater group was about to accomplish. (Four years previously, the Democratic leaders were well aware of what the somewhat similar Kennedy machine was about to do.) Still, they acted like men waiting for a miracle. And what could that have been? It seems to me they could only have been waiting for Eisenhower to lead, Rockefeller to get out of the way, or the big money to arrive (and give orders all around). Leaving the special phenomenon of Rockefeller aside for the moment, they would have had to be sizably desperate in the first place to count on that General to lead their army. I think they were waiting for the money, and that it never arrived.

The eye-opener for me, chronologically, was the speech delivered by the reluctant Governor William W. Scranton on March 4, 1964, to the big guns of the Economic Club of New York (where he would have to do business if he was ever going to do any business at all). The speech was so clever that I thought at first it had been written by an apostate Kennedy intellectual. But the facts pointed to staff, beefed up by Malcolm Moos.

Scranton-Moos adapted Professor Burns's thesis concerning "the deadlock of democracy": it was cleverly and almost accurately laid off on the Democratic Party instead of on Democracy Itself. The title of the speech was, "The Republican Challenge: A Call to Leadership —a proposal for the Republican Party to become the majority." But it consisted as well of an effort to detail the history of the Republican Party as if many things had not happened, including 1912, 1932, and Eisenhower. Read with historical sensitivity, the stated party achievements—"The Republican party gave us the Morrill Act which set up the land grant colleges"—were as tombstones to all the lost possibilities. And the essential Goldwater-congressional themes were woven into the text, with adroitly meaningless hemstitching. In New York they didn't hear him, and in San Francisco they clubbed him to death. Then he essayed the role of caretaker, hanging around for '68. We will see what happens to *this* squelched Me-tooism in its stale Armageddon with the formerly deadlocked Democratic Party.

Governor Rockefeller, with his nearly limitless staff, has been the best Me-tooer since Thomas E. Dewey retired from the scene.* It may be suggestive as to the future of national Republican Me-tooism, therefore, that he has not been able to sell much pizza outside of the state. Some people, and I am one of them, do not believe that his divorce and remarriage were what did him in. I think he just doesn't have it: his boyish smile and heavy sincerity wear poorly. And I can imagine that what he does have—too much money—could be a real disadvantage in that it reduces the size of all regular party supporters: other than to pay off one's mortgage, it strikes me as almost presumptuous to write a thousand-dollar check payable to somebody named "Rockefeller." His 1964 presidential primary campaign is supposed to have cost $5,000,000. When a New York *Times* reporter asked about the cost, however, the quote goes this way: " 'I even hate to think about it,' he said, smiling." Notice that the answer was that of a man who thought he had been asked what it cost *him*.

The apparent utter collapse of the moderate or Me-too wing of the Republican Party became widely known after the California primary in the spring of 1964 and the subsequent cancellation of Rockefeller's self-financed one-man show. At that point, even amateurs and

* Rockefeller was still at it in 1965 with a welfare spending-spree in New York; but more recently he has seemed to be overwhelmed by the downstate dust being raised in the wake of the youthful Mayor Lindsay's push to a newer and more vital Me-tooism.

outsiders could see that the money had not arrived. On the great newspaper issue—Will the Good Guys Get the Party Back Again?— Milton Viorst had the right idea in a pre-election piece in *The Nation:* if you measure the all-around effort later required by the moderates, you must notice that it does not even approach what would have stopped Goldwater before California. Why was the effort not made? I suggest that it was because the money that made the difference in the past was lacking; and it has today even less reason than it had then to come back home. Eastern and national corporate money abandoned the Republican Party because the Goldwater group raised the ante: there is today too much primitive money, West and local, for the Big Men to try to match. And why bother? It costs less to buy into the going Democratic coalition; also, you win. They would rather buy I-too than Me-too, until Me-too comes down in price—or turns out better merchandise.

The Republican Party, as distinct from a reconstituted and smarter Goldwater grouping, could possibly take power again on a conservative (not-yet-fascist) wave—based, say, on foreign reverses. But more reasonably, they can win again only on the basis of a new and clever Me-tooism; or perhaps with the Fundamental Me-tooism of the Tories in England—we can do the same thing better because we are better people. They don't have it in sight as yet; and judging from the important National Committee meeting in January 1965, contradicted by nothing that has happened since, they are concentrating on more familiar targets. The Bliss-for-Burch exchange (and a one-year moratorium on insults) amounted to a retreat to the party professionals, with a minimum of ideological noise, to see what the regulars can salvage, find out, rearrange, etc.

And if the current managed prosperity continues through November 1968 and even more Novembers?

6   If the Democrats have truly become the party of an Establishment, wide recognition of the fact will certainly constitute the final kiss of death to the Republicans, who can survive anything except second place in the propriety scramble. In any event, the President has several years to consolidate and further prove out his creation. My guess is that he will succeed. He will clear the decks of hangover New Deal legislation, so

that there will be a "program" to deal with Everything; he will—unless he is much less of a "pure" politician than one imagines (or he insists)—register more and more Negroes in the South and further isolate the racists, forcing them deeper into the Republican Party, thus also ensuring the Democratic Northern majorities; and he will use federal money to back up the working congressional majority he is so eminently able—by training, talent, and unprecedented opportunity—to create. He could even reach out imaginatively to a Northern and urban Democratic-Republican coalition in Congress to replace the deeply damaged Southern Democratic-Republican coalition, which, along with Thomas E. Dewey's shattered Me-tooism, had ruled the nation domestically since 1938. This would certainly be a proper accompaniment to the new Establishment government. And it would follow naturally enough as a reasonable deal on behalf of the President's new business allies and as generally realistic politics, if the Northeastern Republican Party (with urban allies elsewhere) remains in business but does not re-achieve its dominance of the national party. This seems to me a likely event: the barons of the National Independent Committee agreed as an organizing principle to support *only* Johnson and Humphrey, leaving themselves free to continue their usual localistic interests. In some instances, this might not even be so bad from the President's point of view, since it would give him a fairly good handle in local party affairs (and even more of a handle in Congress). After all, if "we" are going to become as serious as the conservative coalition in Congress has been for several decades, we might recognize organizationally the fact that Democratic/Republican contests in some states are of less concern than primary fights in other states.

Also note that if enough big businessmen (a majority is not necessary) enter into the politics of the Democratic Party at the presidential level, and also abandon their camouflage backing of the screaming free-enterprisers in and out of Congress, they could easily build a congressional majority behind "their" President. One million dollars a year—chewing-gum money—puts $20,000 apiece into fifty congressional campaigns. Five million dollars a year—pipe-tobacco money—puts $25,000 into each of enough campaigns to elect a majority of the House. Ten million a year . . . well, you get the idea.*
Thus, the Establishment could easily create—in the absence of *new*

* It needn't be cash, but can be the simpler "assignment of staff," use of postage-meter machines, loan of air-travel cards, etc.

opposition—an *ad hoc* parliamentary system as backing for whatever it happened to be establishing that year.

One of the most enduring political/cultural questions in the United States has been the perplexing relation between the backwardness enthroned in Congress and the basic industrial-financial power in the country. The relation of congressmen to local business interests seems painfully clear. But what about the managers of big business? Is congressional backwardness a necessary social/political camouflage for big business? Or is this corporate power culturally incapable of confronting the social base of Congress? Or is it both—in that business may utilize the camouflage because it cannot overcome the backwardness? (In the latter case, big business might go to school and learn how to overcome it.) Take General Electric, and you have one answer; with IBM and Ford, perhaps another. The model may be the relation of big business to smaller firms in the National Association of Manufacturers (NAM), where the shouts of the free-enterprisers are clearly a screen of noise to obscure the bigger, surer managerial power in the background.*

It was the ingrained irresponsibility of big national business that complicated the understanding of this matter for so long. They may have done nothing about what Congress had been doing to the country for the simple, silly reason that it had not occurred to enough of them that it was anything but the other fellow's problem. Irresponsibility of this high order, however, creates irrelevance, so that their dominant power ended up immobilized (on that particular issue).

The deepest "malapportionment" in our whole system, then, may well be this profound structural irresponsibility of corporate power. Power is quantitatively limited: if they have it, whether or not they use it, it means that we don't have it, even if we would use it. The big corporations have been exaggeratedly frightened of federal power in the abstract, but deal with it easily and well enough for their own limited purposes (*vide*, military procurement). Perhaps they were so preoccupied with their cat-and-mouse maneuvering vis-à-vis the Executive that they did not get around to noticing Congress as a separate problem (also, things went so "smoothly" there in the past). More likely, they were so unreasonably fearful of the potential power of the Executive in relation to their own that they did not feel able to

---

* What do you do with this fact? "A poll taken in 1935 showed that Chamber of Commerce members were almost 3 to 1 for continuing NRA, while NAM members opposed 3 to 1." (Hofstadter.)

dispense with the native troops supplied by congressional suzerains, just as they still have not been bold enough to dispense altogether with traditional NAM balderdash.

The political possibilities are numerous and interesting; the eventualities will depend, however, on the success of the new centrist *policy:* the New Deal-Establishment coalition—with whatever additions, subtractions, and rearrangements—is coalescing behind a *policy*. And doing so only because it works so well; therefore, not necessarily any longer than that. The NEP can break down because of runaway technological unemployment, renewed and uncontrolled price inflation, or inadequate deficits.* In this wealthy country, only superhuman and super-shortsighted greed could engender the kind of anti-historical stupidity that might make these matters unmanageable. Clearly the next step is indicative planning American-style, i.e., gross voluntary planning executed by the government with the cooperation of the big corporations. Then very likely, later, some police-muscle will be required to keep wayward individual producers within the scope of wage/price reasonableness (across-the-board price control is out of the question short of a big war). Realistically, the more immediate issue is the growing acceptance of a growing deficit. I don't see why most people should care—especially the corporate sector *engagé* which I believe to be critical.

Meanwhile, everyone becomes more and more committed to the continuance of the incredibly continuing prosperity. These commitments are substantial, and thankfully need have nothing at all to do with ideology or sentiment: it will be the *present*, not the *future*, that is being "proven." Business, even in the South, cannot countenance racial actions which interfere with good business (including sales to Negroes). Therefore, one may expect non-militant and unexciting compliance with the Civil Rights Act and what we may call "calculated utilization" of the anti-poverty program. Since an educated work force becomes increasingly important to industry, one must be a psychoanalyst to imagine determinative reasons for business' re-

---

* Throughout, I am forgoing discussion of the possible effects of foreign/ military matters. Yes, including Viet Nam. Economically, the military action there could even have the beneficent effect of excusing some price-and-wage controls for the year or two of "bulge"—excessive demand not including the possibility of a major multi-front war with China—while the recently established anti-poverty programs, etc. continued in effect. This could assist the historical transfer of these useful controls from the one kind of war to the other. I am also forgoing discussion of a nuclear exchange and other acts of God.

fusing to allow the government to bear more and more of the cost of educating our substantially undereducated population (up to a *point*, that is). And now that big business has experienced with the unions enough fringe-benefit action to understand the game, it may even allow the government to help it cover the health and retirement costs of the working population. And by all means, the government must underwrite purchasing power to protect the achieved level of capital values, especially including that involved with consumer debt. As a final tasty, the government might try a little harder to open up the possibilities of trade with the Communist bloc before Western Europe and Japan take it all for themselves.

If the President can divide Eastern and bigger business from smaller and Western, older from newer money, managerial from fee-simple types, and include those he gathers in the Democratic Party while holding most—a majority but not all—of the current Democratic coalition, he will have at last re-created a national Establishment party. Which could and probably would govern this mass technological society—but naturally *not* to anyone's ideal satisfaction; that is not the business of a center.

Where does all this leave the "captured liberals" in the Democratic Party? It leaves them with an organizational problem. Which, we may note, they had all along but were not sufficiently compelled to deal with during that long post-New Deal hiatus when they thought they *were* the Democratic Party. They were not, and now it will become clear to everyone, even including them. Moreover, the enactment of the hangover New Deal program will leave them bereft—specifically, of a program. There are five *domestic* considerations,* or issues, or sources of issues, to replace it: 1) the main one is to count on the collapse of Johnson's "big tent"—because his policy will prove to be too little and too late, or not flexible enough to arrest urban decay and contain technology—and so prepare for a later polarization and Armageddon with the right wing; 2) next in order of importance is the size of the deficit as needed in the absence of

---

* Under tutelage of the *savants* of the New Left, of course, domestic considerations are for the time *passé*. The effort to save the Vietnamese peasants from the effects of American armament is now immediate, crucial, transcendent, etc. Thus our non-political politics leaps forward, and we are thus and once again spiritually renewed. As for the same peasants being "saved" from the effects of Communist armament, that is clearly the spiritual opportunity subsequently to be made available to all 148 Soviet poets, and their unnumbered allies in Eastern Europe.

military spending; 3) how the Establishment pie, granted a successful baking in its own oven, is divvied up, i.e., the social direction of
the deficit spray; 4) the fate of the newly devised *ad hoc* muscle being
marshaled behind the front of wage/price reasonableness; and 5)
issues of style and taste—what we might begin calling crypto-political
matters of culture—e.g., not whether there is a program in education
and housing, or its dollar value, but what *kind* of education and
housing it is apt to or did produce. Enough to keep anybody busy.

As between the Bland Corporatism being described here as an Establishment government, and the New Fascism adumbrated by the
Goldwater movement, I have no difficulty choosing. If you choose
along with me, we "liberals" establish a respectable enemy on whom
we can rely. Thus back to the original constitutional conception—of
a responsible Establishment—on which the country was founded. I
know it is a terrible thing to say, but, in my opinion, Senator Goldwater was as wrong as George the Third.

Toward the end of the 1964 campaign, that impressive political
stylist, former vice-presidential candidate William E. Miller, enunciated a warning—in a university town, Champaign, Illinois—that a
"fatal alliance" was being formed by the Other Fellows, which he
termed "the political wedding of big business, big labor, and big government." Being inexperienced with educated audiences, he went on
to point out unnecessarily that such alliances had once backed Hitler
and Mussolini (although he did not bother mentioning that big labor
"joined" these alliances afterward). When Mr. Miller and his colleagues rediscover Perón as well, their inventory will be complete,
and they can then give us an opportunity to choose a shrewder echo.
Meanwhile, we are getting an Establishment corporatism which
should be able to make the trains run on time—and without closing
too many grade crossings.

One of the insights Mr. Miller and his friends will have to come
upon is that it is not one *big* man who makes a dictatorship, but
rather a great number of small people who demand it. Speaking of
Perón and lower-class fascism, Seymour Martin Lipset very pointedly
says: "In a conservative dictatorship, one is not expected to give total
loyalty to the regime, to join a party or other institutions, *but simply
to keep out of politics.*" (Emphasis added.) So authoritarianism requires quietism; and, inversely, the one produces the other. Thus,
there is some very good basis for saying that America has for some

while been a conservative dictatorship in this exact sense. I almost add, whether or not we choose Bland Corporatism—except that the New Fascism will obviously require a great deal of strenuous morale-building, even more than we had during World War II.

(Incidentally, the *new* generation has not yet had *its* politics; it has begun to make its moves, and should crest by 1980. It is only the Depression-and-War generation that will now close out the remaining New Deal business.)

7 With a center established and the New Deal completed, the focus of American politics necessarily shifts to the character and capacity of the left faction of the Democratic Party. All clear on the right, all clear at the center: and what, helmsman, of the left? What will the post-New Deal liberalism be?

We will be discussing elements of the new liberal and his program (or at least the proper sources of it) for most of the remainder of the book. Here, I would like to wind up our brief inspection of the institutional/historical problem on the assumption that, in the beginning, no great political departure will be effected by the new generation, and no great new crisis will occur.

My guiding principle is that the House of Representatives is still, as it was for the Fathers, our one true chance for institutional "democracy." If this seems overly wishful to the reader, I urge him to reflect that our entire sense of the House is a result of the stymied New Deal we lived with so long; a deep dependence on the Presidency, bequeathed by FDR; a mistaken conviction as to the immovability of the conservative rear-guarding coalition centered in the House; a style-preference for the culture and dignity of certain leading senators and presidential candidates; a hallelujah enthusiasm for Supreme Court thunderbolts; and a generally negative attitude toward politics. The more genuine the politics we have, the more important the House will become. An established center implies a left as well as a right: we should not be confused because the American left has been slower to get organized: it literally couldn't begin until there was an adequate center. Now there is one, and the obvious staging area for the left—which no longer will have to carry the burden of a make-believe center—is the Democratic Party in the House of Representatives. This implies, however, a sophistication and a level of organization not previously attained by that messy grouping identified, after the New Deal, as "The Liberals."

But for openers, note that we still tend to have gangs instead of parties, or even solid factions, in this country. Parties are not based on mere physical contiguity and immediate practical imperatives, but on a somewhat more extensive community of interest responsive to a deeper need for getting together in larger aggregates. Street gatherings are gangs; trade associations are often parties, one imagines. Corporations can be either, depending on how the relevant members conceive of themselves. The Democratic Party need not forever remain a confederation of going gangs; it could become a select group of coherent factions, doing nice and necessary business with each other, within a party. When achieved, this will constitute a very great event in American history. One of the profundities of our political history to date has been the failure to achieve anything like this except on special occasions. Will Rogers was painfully accurate when he spoofed, "I belong to no organized political party—I am a Democrat."

But now we are stuck with them. When we note all that militates against party rule, and remember that only parties can make the system work, our hearts must sink at finding ourselves so solidly and finally in the Democratic Party. Sometimes I think that the greatest negativism of all is this marvelous "two-party system" of ours, where nothing is ever really serious, where the primary activity expressed through our desperately makeshift party structure only rarely rises above "business" to engage in the history-making of an incomplete nation.

"Many new members of the House express surprise that so little pressure is exerted by the party leadership regarding voting," says Charles L. Clapp. That refers to new members. After they have been around awhile, the deeper meaning takes hold: "Congressmen are shocked by the 'utter and complete lack of party discipline.'" This lack of direction occurs in the House maze where "the member is part of a system he does not fully comprehend and may never master. Its mysteries are often difficult to unravel. . . ." Mr. Clapp discusses "House leadership" * (another name for the lack of caucus and party direction) by pointing out that it is almost impossible to

---

* He quotes a legislator to the following effect: "The very ingredients which make you a powerful House leader are the ones which keep you from being a public leader." Now that's worth thinking about.

locate it. Junior members can hardly identify "the real wielders of power." The leaders are "catalysts for party groups and are generally remarkably responsive to situations existing within their party." That is, they are brokers. The leaders amalgamate with other power, and use whatever power they themselves have, in order to broker. That is all they can do without *more power* proceeding from outside Congress—whether from the Executive or from the people.

The liberal Democrats are aware of the absence of party responsibility, but do not see their way out of the tunnel. One remarked:

> All this talk about caucus is just a dream anyhow. The Democrats are so deeply split in philosophy that they cannot encourage anything which might divide them even more. Unlike the Democrats, the Republicans are a disciplined group and therefore they can use the caucus.

It is then suggested that the reason the Republicans have the necessary discipline is because there is a centralized capacity to finance campaign expenditures, which the Democrats lack. That's a pretty good reason—or rather, it *was* a pretty good one.

Those who fear the rigors of a party caucus, and the authoritarian potential in the parliamentary organization, should note that the same thing is achieved in any event by the peculiar structure of the House—but that the "caucus" thus created is responsible to the interests of irresponsible individuals and serves no coherent party or programmatic purpose. (In *Power in Washington,* Douglass Cater cited a scholarly study by Richard Fenno, Jr., to the effect that the fifty-man Appropriations Committee has an amazing record of reporting bills unanimously. Now *there's* a real caucus!) The lack of ideological coherence in the non-party structure of the House means that the individual interests of the seniority survivors take up the slack and thereby provide the substance of the power structure.

It is likely that the reason Rayburn operated the way he did, by the interior action of a network of friendships rather than by overt party leadership, was that he understood the basic divisions in the Democratic Party and did not want to exacerbate them. The important point is that he based his career of rule on this assumption.* But if

---

*Richard Bolling, who was his protégé on the liberal side, has said: "As Speaker, Rayburn used his strength sparingly. He subscribed to the belief that oftentimes withheld power is preferable to committed power that may not carry the day." I imagine the "withheld power" was often worth

they are not merely playing king-of-the-hill, just what have the Democrats gained by incorporating the Southern enemy in their camp? If the South cannot be controlled more, it should be let out altogether. At the very least, it is necessary to bargain with the Southerners as a bloc—to bargain with them about committee assignments, chairmanships, the whole works. They are *not* regular Democrats from the point of view of the Northerners, and there is no good reason for the Northerners to continue to contrive to treat them as such.

So an effective Democratic caucus, being directed necessarily toward the disciplining of the South, chances the loss of the South. What would happen? Why, the conservative coalition which ran Congress in the past might then have the opportunity to organize Congress—and take responsibility for what happens. Is that so terrible? Indeed, is that so *different*? Moreover (and Goldwater aside), the easygoing days of the coalition ended not with the death of Rayburn or with the Johnson sweep, but earlier, with the overthrow of Martin: it was the Rayburn-*Martin* system of brokerage that we had gotten used to. When Halleck replaced Martin, the meaning of the event was that the Republican caucus was being tightened—less freedom to "vote your district first." I suggest this was because the position of the coalition was endangered: note the date, 1958, the year of the 86th Congress and the Northern liberal sweep. Murray Kempton—who, you will remember, sees the House as a national small town—characterized the event this way:

> The Republicans had delivered themselves to a street fighter; in Charles Halleck the institution of the House confronted those dark passions which are the underside of every small town and which are meant to be kept from public sight.

Like the Republican deliverance to the Goldwater people. I say that all this was the beginning of the end of the effective resistance to a national urban caucus, led without the South by the former party of the South, thus fulfilling a half-century of "party realignment."

---

as much and no more than an ace nestling, not among the down cards, but in the undealt deck.

8 The lack of party—and thus of caucus—begins in the districts. The congressional districts seem to be currently a central area of gang-type power. The reasons: the districts are the right size; a gang-type dollar goes farther; and big national power, money or otherwise, less easily achieves its effect in the districts. For the most part, the districts have been ignored from the national viewpoint.

"If we depended on the party organization to get elected, none of us would be here," said one Republican Representative. A Democrat added: "I don't think there is any element of the party that is particularly interested in or concerned with the election of members of Congress." Discussing "the first election," Mr. Clapp remarks that party organizations in the district are not essential and frequently are not even important in the initial victory. Pointing out that in American politics it is everyone for himself, Professor Burns concurs. "Candidates," he says, "depend more on their own personal followings than on the collective efforts of the party organization."

The flimsiness of structure in the district, and its consequent vulnerability, has become known to the lobbyists. One of the more important developments in lobbying in the recent past has been a process of decentralization—what is called "grass roots" lobbying. (If you want a bargain, watch where the shoppers go.) MacNeil, in *Forge of Democracy*, quotes a railroad lobbyist as follows:

> I have the impression . . . that most of the Congressmen, particularly those living in the smaller states and in rural districts, depend for their support upon a comparatively few men in each county in their respective districts. If we could reach the men upon whom a Congressman depends for advice and assistance in his political campaign, we could go far toward having the problem solved.

Along this line, MacNeil reports that the AMA often operates by tracking down the family doctor of a congressman, and having *him* make the pitch. (It is said that one of Wilbur Mills's problems with the medicare bill was the standing challenge by the AMA to pour contrary money into his district if he ever listened seriously to the wrong people. I would imagine the President had to give him some kind of protection in 1965.)

The House has represented the most localistic and wayward elements in the national power structure. The solid basis for this lies in the districts, where penny-ante personal coalitions can be effective. These in turn are based on general apathy and specific money. But one congressman, admitting the lack of party-effect in the districts, added: "On the other hand, you will find small businessmen or lawyers or dentists taking a pretty substantial financial interest, generally on the grounds that they know the man and are interested in seeing him go to Congress." The price is cheap: while a contested first campaign in a big city may cost $100,000 or more, this is rare and the more usual price is about $25,000; in rural areas and in uncontested campaigns the price can drop well below this figure. To put the issue in context, note Professor Burns's pre-1964 characterization of the districts: "Almost half of the House seats never change party hands. Another quarter, roughly, switch only on rare occasions." There were supposed to be about 150 Republican and Democratic seats that "never" switch. "Reasonably competitive districts number about 125 out of a total of 435." And: "Most one-party districts are made up of villages, small towns, and small cities. They have a heavily rural bias." *

Because of the nature of campaign financing, the House has over-represented local ownership capital. If you accept, as I do, the hypothesis that most lawyers do not cease to represent clients when they go to Congress, the following figures are an aid to understanding: in the 88th Congress, 315 of 535 members of both chambers were lawyers—including 74 out of 106 Southerners. This is way out of line with the situation in other countries; and most of these men are not from the big-firm managerial elites, but are small-town lawyers—that is, true proprietors (or at least wholly-owned subsidiaries).

An accurately suggestive depiction of political finance in the United States would be unpublishable; it would also be a lifetime job to compile and defend. The governing laws are a moralistic shambles, which the critic may join the practitioner in ignoring. Al-

* Lipset says: "Since its centers of electoral strength . . . are in the 'provinces' rather than the large metropolitan cities, the Republican party can be more properly accused of being the agent of the small-town bourgeoisie than of big business." Which suggests that big business has hidden behind this action rather than being truly identified with it.

most all political money is devious, and much of it is seriously illegal. Jack Anderson in *Parade* (October 27, 1963) quotes an experienced political fund-raiser:

> There isn't a major campaign that doesn't receive illegal contributions. The candidate may not know, or pretend he doesn't. But the Corrupt Practices Act is broken, bent, twisted, ignored and circumvented all the time.

Ask yourselves how many people make their "livings" from politics in the United States? (You will have to ask yourselves, because I certainly don't know.) Then ask, How many proper ways of doing this are there? You have to say "proper" not "legal," because otherwise, in this gray area with its long history of proven corruption and shrill moralism, you forestall understanding: for instance, certain utterly political and wasteful patronage is legal, and other utterly unexceptionable contributions are not. The arithmetic is simple and the answers are obvious: political activity costs time and money, and disinterested mass contributions of both are the only "proper" sources. To stimulate and facilitate this more or less nonexistent factor is the underlying point of most proposals for reform.

An excellent summary statement of the reform problem is Philip M. Stern's "A Cure for Political Fund-Raising," in *Harper's*, May 1962. The core issue, he affirms, is the narrow base of political giving—"the overwhelming majority of Americans make no political contributions and few are even asked for any." As for the 1960 election, Gallup said 15 per cent were asked and 9 per cent gave. Big Givers are even rarer, of course. So the "remedy for this situation is to find a new source of campaign funds." The key proposal, endorsed by likely reformers from TR to JFK, is government financing (which has been in operation in Puerto Rico since 1957). There are many clever details already worked out to ensure fairness, etc., in the system: an attractive one is to provide U.S. Treasury drawing accounts for specified expenses, with the amounts to be determined on the basis of previous vote received (and a minimum guaranty to minor parties); funds for primary campaigns could be reimbursed to serious contenders; and to bring about genuine disclosure, federal funds could be available on a matching basis to other sums deposited with the Treasury for proper disbursement; and so on—out into the suburbs of ingenuity.

But a problem remains (as Mr. Stern recognizes) which is known to indoor-sports lovers as "raising the ante." This could end up leaving us nearly where we are today—with no feasible, enforceable means of enticing full disclosure or preventing quiet contributions. Nevertheless, house chips would let the pikers in and start a lot of action. All to the good. I would even go further, and help the project along by having the government pay $10 a head to everybody who votes—at the very most, a billion-dollar tax refund.

We do ourselves a favor to recognize ahead of time, however, that the better, shrewder reforms in campaign financing involve just about the same underlying questions as the frequently proposed reforms of Congress: they are power issues, to be resolved only by a determined caucus strong enough to manipulate the situation in favor of majoritarianism and other democratic participation—which the caucus will do only as the member believes that he and his will prosper additionally under the revised situation. There is no panacea for anything as current and important as campaign financing—every "good" idea will create a not-so-good one in reaction—and all that one can reasonably hope for is a Forward amendment of the rules.

The dream of sanitized power is boring. Also, it is an absolute contradiction. I will settle for the more reasonable dream of power-in-community: remember, power is organization, and our need is to create communities out of our lives-in-organization. That is what our power must come from if it is not to rest as anti-power, or power-for-its-own-sake, or power against life—*our* life.

9   My purpose in writing this book is to set forth choices. That is why I keep talking about power: without power, and without seeing things in terms of power, there are no choices to be made or worth making—except in the head alone (and I disapprove of that). The basic choice, I suppose, is always Hamlet's, whether to act at all: to live in the head, or not to live in the head, that is the question. Living in the head, in politics, is properly called "apathy," no matter how hysterical it may in fact be.

The notion that the public governmental system is democratically constituted, that it is egalitarian and therefore just, and anything that is wrong with it is our fault, is nonsense—one of the great myths sustaining the present actual maldistribution of power in our society. This is so, even though the system is not, all in all, such a bad one (which is true as well of the corporate order). That it is not so bad, however, does not make it any more democratic, or just, or anything of the kind. The human being is a spiritual animal, and a prosaic reliance on the fact that the situation isn't-so-bad-after-all would be untenable over the full course. The potential of this mistake could not be more evident than it is today in America, where most problems, for many people, are even now becoming predominantly spiritual. We are quite well fed, no question. And while some of us will die from overeating, many more of us are dead and dying already from spiritual starvation.

Insofar as thinking makes any difference, political apathy is the result of not thinking in power terms. The other terms are moral or religious or something like that, and are initially constructed to remain snugly in the head: they predominantly represent a preference for views-of-life over the thing itself (and I disapprove of that, too). Initially, ideals are part of a desire to live; only later do they displace the impulse. *Everybody who has chosen a view-of-life to compensate for experienced lacks in the real thing, knows in his heart when it happened to him.* So admit it; it is a basic datum, for many purposes. The point is that if power does not mean "life" and "community," many people are just not interested: they prefer to wait in weakness. While waiting, they naturally rearrange the furniture of their minds to make themselves more comfortable. Then the posture becomes complicated and is called "apathy."

In *White Collar*, the late C. Wright Mills said that "the problem of political apathy, viewed sociologically, is part of the larger problem of self-alienation and social meaninglessness." Which acknowledges our presence in the existential vineyard, still nurturing the grapes of meaning with our bare hands. In a general sociological way, I suppose there is no longer any question that the main thing wrong with democracy is the lack of interest in it by the democratic majority. We will have to pay attention to this: before it became a sociological fact, it was a disaster. Since I don't really know what a "sociological fact" is, it remains a still undigested disaster for me, and for many others.

Our American system of non-rule, or power-negativism, goes so deep that even people who detest it are afraid to abandon it. Professor Binkley (in *President and Congress*) finally says:

Such is the complexity of American society, with its conflicts of interests and of sections, that a resort to prompt settlement of its major issues by the simple majorities implicit in a parliamentary system might prove positively explosive.

What is wrong with this view is that it assumes a continuing lack of explosion as long as there is inactivity. That is wrong on the face of it; also, "promptness" is hardly any longer an explosive threat. We have achieved just about all that we can achieve by political inactivity on this continent. Our society is changing greatly, and the changed society can be disrupted as much by a lack of adjustment as by anything else. Since our government functions only in a crisis, for instance, it then becomes necessary for the society to create a crisis in order to have a government. When this created crisis consists of the Cold War and related involvements, the danger of awaiting crisis in order to have a government is abundantly clear. This situation is so thoroughly overripe that we must literally take our chances with despotism. (We already have a great deal of it as a result of our ill-advised efforts to avoid it.)

We may now step back from the arena of sound and fury and take note of the awful truth: the incredible structure of our democratic blessing, the House of Representatives, is based on the apathy and ignorance of the people. It is a silly, flimsy structure that seems as strong as iron only because genuine politics has not yet come to this nation, except spasmodically. Even so, what political consciousness and intensity and willing money there is in the country could be expressed much more effectively even in the intricate network of personal back-scratching which constitutes the current structure of the House. For one thing, little winds make little weathervanes tremble. There is enough urban-aware force in this country, properly organized, to achieve a major effect on the character of the House—even in the face of the one-five-ten million dollars of the barons.

We ought to do it: the structural deficiencies in our history are pressing in upon us today in some kind of final fashion. It is time to sum up American history in action; if we do not, it may end. I mean it will not be a recognizable America any longer. "America" was the conquest of a continent, and a particular contradiction underlying the style of accomplishing this. We have now come to the point where this contradiction must be somewhat resolved; we could survive it in the conquest of the continent, but not in the utilization of

the fruits of the conquest. Two very different matters; we are compelled now to constitute ourselves the vanguard of humanity in preparing a new attitude toward wealth. There *will* be a new America. It
can be democratic, in the sense that everybody will be "included-in"
on some kind of minimal-share terms; or it can be authoritarian, in
constituting a continuously harsher preservation of historically be-
gotten privilege. This is the American contradiction which must now
be somewhat resolved. To counter the authoritarian potential, the
Negroes must be raised, and the Negroes cannot be raised without
bringing up along with them the poorer whites.

This is one imperative; it is joined by another—the quality and
style of life of the educated masses and other privileged groups
snugly within the affluent sector of our society. The cultural needs
and desires of this group require a responsible national power as the
basis of a responsible national culture as much as the Negroes and
other poor require that same national power to effect their inclusion
in the growing abundance of our technologized continent. The alternative America must very clearly be an ever firmer injunction
against the fulfillment of these *two* motives: it can only be a negative injunction against the aspirations of the New Class, and the
needs of the Under Class.

And in my view, the quality of the culture is everything. More
important than the non-cultural fruits of power; much more important than religion and morality, which are occasional derivations
from it; more important even than rationality, which is only one of
its occasional tools. It is culture that leads one to politics, because
culture is based on politics, not on God. It's a rough proposition, but
there you are. T. S. Eliot was right to nag us with the fact that culture had to have a historical basis, could not exist for long in its
nineteenth century disembodied state; but that transplanted Tory
was about as wrong as George the Third in his notion of what that
basis had to be.

Why am I so strong for culture? Because this savage here no
longer feels so noble: out of nature, culture is all there is, for us and
for our children. If it wasn't for culture, you could say that some of
us were dead already—indeed, some time ago. Unfortunately, animals don't last, not even for a "lifetime" as we measure and construct it nowadays. So we are stuck with the reality of culture—the
heritage of humanity—living off it and leaving it. And, being histori-

cal, it rests on nothing firmer than politics (or, without that, chance).

Let me conclude by quoting *my* kind of congressman: "It is the second- and third-termers who really have to lead the rebellion."

It is all us second- and third-termers everywhere who will have to lead the next rebellion—and the one after that—and the one after that . . .

THE ESSENCE

Our
Emotions

FIVE

The Myth
of Individualism

1   "Myth" is an important word
again. What it means in its fresh career is what ideology or belief used to mean—with the addition that, having a myth, you are wrong to begin with. But after the end of the ages of belief and ideology, it was necessary to find a term that could describe the same sort of human thing under altered circumstances. A "myth" is an extended view of existence which presumes to explain it in a deep way, while at the same time unabashedly revealing the dearest personal wishes of the expositor. So myth is something other people suffer from. And since we don't notice non-political and unimportant ones, myth is the new word for *functioning political lies*.

The fundament of American myth is Individualism—still. American Individualism is the profoundly preferred mode, in this shallow society, of escaping experienced complexities in favor of a moral and otherwise uncomplicated view of existence.

I grant that *all* human beings escape the complexities of experience, in *all* historical periods, and in *all* national areas. In one sense, this is properly called "culture." Until science invents a pill for death, I expect the activity to continue. So all human beings tend toward the moral view; and we are not here approaching the either/or of being human, but rather the *form* of characteristic retreat. The form changes historically. One can become aware of the meaning of these changes, however, only by forestalling the escape at least long enough to look closely at the how and what-from. That is the purpose of this chapter.

So American Individualism is a cultural form to be understood and criticized, not in order to root out once and for all the disease beneath, but to use it more relevantly, if we are desperately stuck with it; or to search out a more relevant form, if happily it turns out that we have the capacity to do so.

My premise is really very simple—it is that our notorious belief in Individualism belongs to the uncrowded cowboys, the intense farmers, the lusting immigrants, and all the rest of the hurried American past; we need not in the American present be that shallow: in our Now, we may uncover personal and social alternatives which do not, out of initial spiritual perfection, so embarrassingly ensure our later powerlessness. If we are serious Americans, this spiritual opportunity to be effective is worth looking into. We can, if need be, learn to live without these traditional wide-open inner spaces.

For instance, I very much believe in being an individual; but when I take inventory on the matter, I measure my personal options rather than my state of mental grace. That is because I do not expect to satisfy my desire to be individual according to the fate of a mere image. On the contrary, I know that individuals require power in order to be or remain such, and I am convinced that power in our society, certainly in my educated urban part of it, is seldom separate from some aspect of organization bigger than any single person. Therefore, I never view my individualism as prospering in an inverse relation to the extent of organization. I am not a damn fool; but many of my countrymen are.

When you demand to be an individual in the desperate way required by the myth of Individualism, you necessarily end up applying power, whether derived from property or organization, in a negative and defensive way. That is because you could not possibly have enough power to satisfy the demands of the myth—and then some left over to do something else with. There just isn't enough power in the world for that. As an American Individualist you cannot be responsible, candid, perceptive, or fruitful on this matter of power: you worship a god with an infinite appetite, and your business in life must be limited to feeding him. (If it is an intellectual god, why then you feed him raw intellectual meat.)

Images of infinity and omnipotence are the special underpinnings of American Individualism. As a social theory—and it presumes to be just that—it is so grotesque as to reveal resoundingly the Major American Fact, that is, the lack of a society about which to construct a social theory. Infinity and omnipotence belong to God; but in this country we had to retrieve the gift in order to settle the continent. Then we formed our personalities around these fundaments, due to the shortage of other cultural materials. America is not a society with a religion, because it is a religion instead of a society.

Thus, the American boom-or-bust personality. In *The Great Crash*, Galbraith says, "at some point in the growth of a boom all aspects of property ownership become irrelevant except the prospect for an early rise in price." What a fit image for our basic emotional organization! Any aspect of anything may be abandoned, as one pursues the pilfered cash of infinity. Also, nothing is what it seems to be, since it may be transformed momentarily. Note this remark by a political leader of an earlier day, James G. Blaine: "The poverty of the frontiers is indeed no poverty. It is but the beginning of wealth, and has the boundless possibilities of the future always opening before it." Could Senator Goldwater, our disgruntled cowboy, have improved on this?

Individualism is the primitive ideology of the primitive personality. So no one is quite so individualistic as that quintessential American, the Southerner. W. J. Cash, in his eccentrically brilliant book, *The Mind of the South,* says of the "basic Southerner" (Cash himself was a rarer Southerner): "In some respects, perhaps as simple a type as Western civilization has produced in modern times." Remarking on the Southerner's "intense individualism," he adds: "The simple man in general invariably tends to be an individualist." He also tends to be violent. Cash points out that "the South had become peculiarly the home of lynching" *before* the great Negro-hatred which followed the Civil War: "of more than three hundred persons said to have been hanged or burned by mobs between 1840 and 1860, less than ten per cent were Negroes. . . ."

The more we emphasize the ideology of traditional Individualism, the more we undermine the immediate possibility of the actual strength and effectiveness of mere individuals. We tie ourselves, instead, to defense and negation. The rigidly hysterical devotion to Individualism that Goldwater was selling requires a harrowing degree of personal blankness. In the modern environment, this approach has become deadly. A person who takes a subsidy from the federal government, for example, whether through a tax privilege, a tariff preference, a loan, or any other of the many available offerings, who accepts this dependence in his life *in order to* sustain an absurd notion of traditional property-based Individualism, is a terrible danger to himself and to the whole world. This amounts to a use of federal power further to maintain the fantastical dissociation of the factual elements of social and cultural reality. The federal government in this instance is literally subsidizing insanity.*

2 It is the myth of Individualism, of course, that lies behind our ordained belief in Free Enterprise. This latter is not an economic concept at all: it is a psychological/religious category. What it means is that individuals shall compete for the goods of the world, and the winners shall be entitled to hold on to their winnings. And further, that all winnings are irrefutably the result of such individual competition. The ideology serves but one purpose: the anointment of winners. It describes and analyzes nothing other than this specific aspect of our secular theology. To the extent that it is related to competitive theory in economics, it merely borrows that special logic of scarcity in order to consecrate the traditions of scarcity in our institutions, and more especially in the form of our personalities. Anti-scarcity (abundance) is currently a great threat to our main status-distinction—the one separating anointed winners and pagan losers.

We can get a sense of where this emotional mess comes from by recalling de Tocqueville's designation of the leading American trait —egalitarianism. Whether trait or condition or commitment, equality in fact is unbearable if unrelieved—it comes out as "sameness," and requires for its maintenance the squelching of occasional excellence as well as the designed ignoring of more frequent inferiority. Enter Competition, which against all these odds assures hierarchy by providing losers. Losers are much more essential than competition

---

* If we require a poverty pledge for ordinary welfare payments, might we not also ask for a similar admission of status from standees on the business and property dole—a sort of affluence or capital-growth pledge?

ever was—as the naïve reaction of the Goldwater group to the penny-ante anti-poverty program revealed. But in traditional American terms, the troglodytes are right: it isn't the money, it's the *principle* that counts.

All the talk about freedom of opportunity and the chance to get ahead, which Jackson and Lincoln enunciated and which persisted down through Wilson and Hoover, was an ideological stance that appealed to the whole nation, perhaps, but was obviously designed for the benefit of less than the whole nation. Not everybody could succeed. Viewed somewhat more cynically, this was the ideology of grab and get ahead—and quickly get it certified. Once the ideology was established, only a quantitative historical issue remained as to how many people were going to be allowed, in fact, to grab, etc.

But now we have only frontiers of organization; everything else has been grabbed. We remain consistently American, however, in attacking these remaining frontiers fully wrapped in the Mother Hubbard of American Individualism and traveling forward in the covered wagon of its treasured memory. Thus we roll on to glory, carrying a spiritual Winchester across our knees. Hallelujah or bust. (Or both.)

Richard Hofstadter says of our pure Individualists, the Progressives: "At bottom, the central fear was fear of power, and the greater the strength of an organized interest, the greater the anxiety it aroused." Note: *any* interest.

According to our traditions, power should be only individual, God-given and self-managed, without social basis. It should be so thoroughly individual that it ceases to be recognized as power at all— power being, as we ordinarily discuss it, social.

Indeed, under anarchy, who has power? Under anarchy, the issue of power is ignored—and results in inevitable authoritarianism. This is the classic pattern. A seeming exception was the Spanish anarchist movement before Franco destroyed it: but noble Spanish anarchism was mostly the political expression of a pre-existing and genuinely organic subculture designed to assert itself *against* a thoroughly alien state. Look closely at anarchist thought and you will notice that it always *assumes* a pre-existing organic society while also assuming a lack of real involvement with the existing state. Which should reveal—even to my friend, Paul Goodman—the exquisite inappropriateness of this style of thought in the United States. Except on occasion regionally, we have been the farthest

thing from an organic society yet attempted by distraught humanity.
And we are a national society at all only as an occasional derivation
from the State and statelike institutions.

If it is helpful to categorize in European terms, American Individualism is a kind of bourgeois anarchism. As it attempts to remain
serious and consistent, it tends inexorably to the New Fascism; indeed, when joined with WASP-hysteria, it is clearly the main source
of that native phenomenon. Only with continuously refurbished hypocrisy does it manage to leave its victim sane. But we are a serious
people, and hunger after sincerity. Ordinarily, we need only be told
that we are kidding ourselves—not even lying, exactly—in order to
be moved then and there to make a big effort to straighten up. Still,
only energetically creative people can presume to this high level of
seriousness. In this respect, our eyes have always been bigger than
our stomachs.

Professor Hofstadter buried a brilliant insight concerning the Progressives in a footnote at the bottom of page 228 of the Vintage
edition of *The Age of Reform.* Quoting Woodrow Wilson—"If America is not to have free enterprise, then she can have freedom of no
sort whatever"—he suddenly realizes how the pre-World War I Progressives, the same people, could become post-New Deal conservatives; and more and more of them have, those that Roosevelt didn't
catch or that the ADA didn't hang onto. He says (my emphasis),
*"they had held to the same ideas with great constancy; it was history
itself that was inconsistent, and the world at large that had
changed."* *

This view is especially convincing if the Progressives are taken,
like the Populists, to be moral pastoralists to begin with. Of Progressivism, Hofstadter says:

> Its general theme was the effort to restore a type of economic
> individualism and political democracy that was widely believed
> to have existed earlier in America and to have been destroyed by
> the great corporation and the corrupt political machine; and
> with that restoration to bring back a kind of morality and civic
> purity that was also believed to have been lost.

Rugged Individualism, it is written, ended with Herbert Hoover
and the Great Depression. Well, I don't think so. There was every

---

* Note, as evidence: McCarthy came from La Follette land, and Susan
La Follette has been a right-wing activist.

reason for it to end then, but I don't think it did. Rugged or warped, it penetrates too deeply. It will end when it is replaced. It cannot be replaced until it is understood. It must be understood as a more or less necessary result of our primitivism—especially the primitivism of the Success motif, which is basic to our social order. Hofstadter remarks:

> Hoover was one of those bright and energetic businessmen who, precisely because of the ease with which success has been attained in their immediate experience, refused to learn deeply from anything outside of it.

In the responses of Hoover and Roosevelt to the problem presented by the Great Depression one sees what must really be called *two* Americas. Hoover's reaction was the epitome of negativism, based on sound American principle; Roosevelt's regime emerged as a triumph of innovative American personality. To the absence of coherence in American life the one response was rigid ideology centered around overwrought Individualism; the other (equally individualistic, but not ideologically so) ended up groupish and gayly manipulative. There is a great lesson in and around this experience: Roosevelt's engagement, which is not yet understood in adequate perspective, was the Shakespearean burst heralding a new American emphasis on emotion—away from compensatory Individualism, beyond Al Smith's ethnic urbanism, all the way into the modern world of a spiritual adjustment to the technological environment created by manipulation, and requiring continued manipulation to live in. And that means manipulating each other, not just the machines. (There is poetry and manipulation in life; there is not, seriously, much else of equal significance.)

And now American society is closing up. If you have education or some other kind of seniority, you can get a job; otherwise, you can get relief under one designation or another. But the whole thing is closing up in the press of *numbers*—masses who have accepted organization out of necessity rather than out of desire or rationality or purpose. And don't kid yourself that the past was so awfully gorgeous: when America was more "open," it was mostly open to self-interest and self-assertion. Big continent or not, there is never enough room for *that*.

Perhaps the main trouble with people in America has been that they all wanted to live, and so many of them persisted in living, as if their milieu were a novel—and further, as if the outcome of this novel depended on each of them as the author. The ultimate in Individualism. (I would like to see somewhat less of this—and a little more straight poetry and manipulation.)

3 Individualism is to be blamed mostly on the farmers, but one cannot avoid disgust with the urbaners for allowing themselves to be so deeply influenced by the farmview of life. The farmers were perhaps entitled; but the myth of Individualism in the city is frighteningly silly. A city is *nothing but* organization.

The Individualism of farmers at one time had some basis in fact. Physical isolation could always be confused with physical independence, and there were many genuine aspects to the latter. When the farmer got up in the morning he confronted nature, his own handiwork, and his own family—no masses and no bosses. He might even own his land outright. But this Robinson Crusoe idyll could be shattered abruptly by the need to sell his product and even to buy a few things for the family and the farm. Also, America being great quantities of land for the taking, the vision of a noble fee-simple empire projected by Jefferson was soon corrupted by land speculation. In his searching portrayal of American farming in *Absentee Ownership and Business Enterprise in Recent Times* (1923), Veblen pointed out the extent to which farmers had been more interested in buying and selling land than in using it to grow crops. Much of their notorious financial difficulty resulted from overextending themselves in this commercial activity. Confirming Veblen, Hofstadter says: "What developed in America was an agricultural society whose real attachment was not to the land but to land values."

So, early enough in our history, rural Individualism began to lose some of its natural nobility in favor of a rather narrow, trader's shrewdness. And the farmer's "rampant, suspicious, and almost suicidal individualism" caused him endless suffering and nearly destroyed him before he honed its edges sufficiently to learn the lessons of organization. It was his canniness, moreover, not his pastoral perfection, that finally achieved the high order of rural socialism that goes by the name of parity; and that was accomplished mostly through the determined exploitation of unearned but strategic political positions, over many decades. The revivalist burst of Populism, that great defeat, mainly achieved an end of innocence. Finally, the farmer was shrewd enough to give up and go to the city (taking his Individualism with him, unfortunately). The decade beginning in 1880 was the first in which our cities began to grow faster in population than rural places. By 1920, more people lived in urban than in rural areas. The rural population (a Census definition) has been more or less static since 1910, while the national population has doubled.

When the farmers got up and went, they left behind—perhaps as their forebears in Europe had done—both the established and the impoverished. The latter is entitled to whatever myth he can scrape together; he has little else. The former, however, is the great perpetrator of the myth of Individualism. The local banker and manufacturer, the feed-and-grain merchant, the large mechanized farmer, the hardware man, the soft-goods man, the supermarket owner, and the offspring of previous residents who simply inherited real estate —in short, the rural or small-town winner—is the current culprit. What holds this crew together, under the canopy of the myth, is not so much the activity of farming as the community of small-property interests—local and possessory property, as distinct from national corporate property (along with the malapportioned political power they had taken over from the vanished farming population, and are now losing under reapportionment). But the proprietor's ready reference-back is always to the Idea of the Farmer as the one pure and fundamental property-owner—the H_2O, so to speak, of business enterprise.

I suggest that we have historically passed beyond the profundity of the farmer-city dweller apposition. In the business of food and textile production, we are certainly over the hump, technologically: here in America, it still utilizes but is no longer based on the mass exploitation of individual producers. The distinction replacing this classic one concerns personal proprietorship in sparsely populated areas as against highly organized property tenure and use in densely populated centers. The former has appropriated rural ideology to its own uses. The more important point, however, is that the latter has not yet developed an ideology of its own. When, in default of one, the recently or hardly displaced farmers now living in cities try to believe the same things they did before they moved there, a uniquely

dangerous condition comes into being.* There is, if the belief is genuinely embraced, an accompanying commitment to irrelevance and
unreality which literally implores political exploitation. Fascism is
the strategical deployment of such unrealities. The portending New
Fascism is exactly this, applied to specifically American materials—
but, with pertinent ambiguity, in an age of affluence.

That most of us, despite our rural past, have ended up in a city is
felt—by the patsies of the New Fascism—to be a kind of monumental error in traffic direction. So there they sit, in the sylvan realm of
the psyche, waiting for the light to flash green. They will arrive for
real only when the city becomes psychically livable: that means the
creation of an urban, non-property-owning ideology not too far distant from the facts of the city.

If the cities remain confused, the regional proprietors could do us
in (but, after reapportionment, only if they carry enough of the suburbs with them). Analyzing the vote that put Hitler in power, Professor Lipset states (his emphasis) *"the larger the city, the smaller the
Nazi vote."* Also, he notes a high correlation of the Nazi vote with
both proprietorship and regionalism in Germany. It was the people
who were against Bigness who embraced that *particular* bigness. (In
this rapidly changing world, the conservative must become radical
even in attempting to remain conservative.) Lipset sums up:

> The ideal-typical Nazi voter in 1932 was a middle-class self-
> employed Protestant who lived either on a farm or in a small
> community, and who previously voted for a centrist or region-
> alist political party strongly opposed to the power and influence
> of big business and big labor.

The regional or small-property view concentrates on the fantasy of
self-centered Individualism, supported by some real or imagined organic culture—always local. The urban view, almost by definition,
must be that of a people who live under the god of organization:
good, bad, or indifferent—but organized. The urbaner will ignore no
aspect of organization, any more than the farmer would fail to size
up the sky or neglect peculiarities of terrain. He is a born psycholo-
gist, and quickly becomes a sociologist as well, certainly as a status-
analyst. He is always looking out for himself, parry and thrust, but

---

* If socialism was the first and basic ideology of the farmer displaced to
the city, we can now note *another* unfortunate aspect of its absence in
this country.

never overrates his capacity. Quixote dies in a city: if he wants to fight an organization, the urbaner joins with others to create an organization. Since his whole world is a man-made fantasy, he relaxes by thinking realistic thoughts. He knows that he must ration out his moments of dreaming, or else he may fall into the black pit of Ever-dream. He prefers humor to tragedy, wit to description, and only when he is exhausted from laughing does he burst into tears. He lives in a city.

The urbaner spends all of his time knowing that he is surrounded by people, even when the doors are closed or his eyes are shut. And most of his time he is actively engaged with others, which includes thinking their thoughts—often in order to determine his own, rhetorician that he is. He continuously alternates between devising a role for himself and taking the role of the other. He needs always to know what they are doing, what they can do; and he has the same need with regard to himself, who is Object Number One. He thinks in power terms. To admit this, and to share it with another doing the same, is for him a refreshing act of love.

He is all actor and politician. Nothing comes too naturally: everything must be expressed, rather than released. And personal silence is no true refuge, being as common as death. Since he does not begin by knowing the next person he may encounter, meaning itself is ambiguous, self-created, a continuing problem. So much of his life has become art that he genuinely needs to be a practicing artist of some kind in order to experiment with the emotional materials of his life. Like all artists—bad, mediocre, and superb—he loves to get good-and-lost every once in a while. Like all artists, he has his moments—and the rest of the time struggles to turn out hackwork.

Let's pretend that there are just two ways of looking at the world: one of these moves toward a perception of what the world actually is, the other asserts what one would like the world to be like. Let's then say that we will refer to the first as a "power analysis," and to the second as a delineation of religious feeling or a "myth-and-moral analysis." The power analysis occurs when you know why you do something or want something—you make your interest explicit, at least to yourself. You are concerned with motivation more than with morality, real action rather than desired action. The religious or moral "action" distinctively occurs when you cannot or will not make your interest explicit. The distinction is mostly between a description of present patternings as perceived and a statement of what the world might be if your successful human insistence were included in the patterning.

Generally, it is the weak or the uneducated who have the greatest need to dissemble; but their inexplicit myth-making acts may often be, as well, an effort to overcome their deficiencies. Thus the lower classes are the true source of religious feeling. They are both victims and creators of the important myths. These express their effort to achieve strength and awareness, while not disrupting their social subjection too rapidly.

The proper approach to a dreamer is not merely to tell him that he is dreaming but to help him to dream better, which involves an intrinsic criticism of the dream as well as an extrinsic criticism of its relation to whatever may be imagined to be reality. Power analysis does not substitute altogether for the myth-and-moral approach; rather, it informs and perfects it: so, finally, every man his own Jesuit-confessor.

Meanwhile, the reality itself has changed fundamentally. And we had better, too. The two big changes still to come are, first, to abandon the dichotomy of morals vs. power. That is a city-farm difference, and therefore irrelevant. It is based on the omnipotence of farmers in uncrowded areas: note that omnipotent people, by definition, do not have to distinguish-out "power" in their thinking. And, secondly (as good urbaners), not to overrate ourselves, recognizing that the awareness of myth, not myth itself, must be the issue for us. Only the quality of organization, not willful individuals, can refurbish myth-bound lives.

Those are the two big changes required. Few of us are ready for Jordan. The big problem? That the human race in its advanced state has simply not had enough opportunity to learn the human principles of advanced organization through *experience*. (Deducing them "scientifically," as I will elaborate in Chapter Seven, has been an unrelieved mess.)

4 The myth of Individualism, then, is still our unfortunate substitute for a genuine culture of the city. Since numerous city problems have been delineated at length, and much city experience expressed in many forms, isn't it an act of

untoward disaster-mongering to suggest that we do not have an adequate "culture of the city"? I say, No. Because facts alone, even enlivened with some savvy, will not create and cannot constitute an adequate culture. There must be an ideology, a myth at the center. People require to dream out loud. It is useful for some of them to recognize the distinctions between a dream and the rest of experience: this helps to keep us from trying to fly too far without the assistance of Boeing and Douglas. But motivation (as well as morality) is lost to the outside world if all dreams are left at home. After a while, nobody bothers getting up in the morning: they may act as if they do, but they don't really. They just drift downtown and put in a few hours with the *corps de ballet.*

The whole man requires room and reception in the real world. Otherwise, *pari passu,* he only makes believe he leaves home, and—wonder of wonders!—the real world out there becomes just exactly as make-believe as the fantasy he thought he left at home.

I realize that the foregoing only states the problem without solving it. But, on the other hand, so what? These are obviously very complicated matters we are now presuming to discuss. To illustrate: An interesting statement of this issue of dream and motivation appeared in *Commentary* for April 1964—"The Revolt Against Ideology," by Henry David Aiken. I think I share ground with the author of this essay, but there are many better reasons for you to read it. Professor Aiken provides a substantial setting for a critique of our leading "end of ideology" thinker, Daniel Bell. I read his point as being, roughly, that Bell manages to dispense with ideology—or makes an ideology out of anti-ideology—because he has concurrently dispensed with the perspective of change. But Bell has actually dispensed only with Marxist ideology (and socialist enthusiasm), which he once found indispensable—the clincher for him was the end of *that* ideology—and he has instead become a hardworking sociologist, which is considered by many to be very broad-gauge, if not exactly ideological.*

---

* In a reply (*Commentary,* October 1964), Professor Bell showed how hurt he had been by the attack—he traced the historical evolution of the term "ideology" and insisted that he had always been a democratic socialist. This did not sway Professor Aiken, who replied to the reply by noting that time is running out on certain kinds of misuse of intellect certified with socialist credentials (he was probably thinking more of the senior mentor, Sidney Hook, than of Daniel Bell). Whether or not Bell had been placed in the proper rogues' gallery, Aiken's persistent

Marxism did, in fact, answer too many questions—but this could be a consideration such as to wipe out the category, by reason of the specific failure, only for the type of people who are mostly interested in ideology or myth or dream for the number of "questions" it answers. The point, for me, is the purposes it serves, which point is based on my conviction that we humans never stop dreaming, and dreaming of wholeness.

Seymour Martin Lipset, one of Bell's fellow anti-ideologists, concludes his study, *Political Man*, by remarking that the Big Idea of socialism has now become (his example is Sweden) a question of "whether the metal workers should get a nickel more an hour," etc. Then he hits us with a Big Thought characteristic of the "end of ideology" school:

> This change in Western political life reflects the fact that the fundamental political problems of the industrial revolution have been solved: the workers have achieved industrial and political citizenship; the conservatives have accepted the welfare state; and the democratic left has recognized that an increase in over-all state power carries with it more dangers to freedom than solutions for economic problems. This very triumph of the democratic social revolution in the West ends domestic politics of those intellectuals who must have ideologies or utopias to motivate them to political action.

In this misdirected post-socialist thought—still too-Marxist, in an inverted way—a few nuances are missed: 1) the political problems of the industrial revolution—unless the future is reduced to the nineteenth century—hardly exhaust our repertory; 2) the *extension* of workers' "citizenship" (ugh), in the community of the industrial corporation, could well be more engaging than the immediate effects of the Wagner Act charter; 3) *radical* conservatives are dis-accepting the welfare state; 4) I am on the democratic left and I recognize no such thing; and 5) some triumph.

Do you hear the quiet music of this blue guitar insinuating not merely the end of ideology but nearly the end of history as a special complication? And if not quite that, then at least the end of the unmanageable part of the unconscious mind in history? This has the

point was that no one—least of all the anti-ideologists—escapes ideology, in the extended meaning he had given the term (taking meanings from usage, he insisted). With this I agree. On the other hand, Bell is not "really" against change as such, he simply lacks imagination regarding it.

neo-classical *odeur*. The Fifties and thereabouts were indeed a period of restraint and ratiocination. But the dream is always there, even if tightly chained. And I am guessing that the "end of ideology" group has published its findings and asserted its mood just about in the nick of time (as these scholarly things go). I look for considerable energetic adjustment in the near future to "the fundamental political problems of the industrial revolution," etc. (What an old-hat phrase that is!)

I am not a fancy romantic; and like all high school graduates, I have my neo-classical moments. I will, and I think we all should, discuss the importance of the differences between harmless and harmful dreams. But the human race is not going to give up dreaming, or acting out its dreams, or complicating the intellectual endeavor thereby. Period. Let's hope, in agreement with the *pffft!*-ideology fellows, that more real thought is applied to social and political problems. And that's that.

An underlying point, involved with dreams and dreamers, is something rather more serious called "community." In America, the shallow society, the desperate need for community, derived from the agonizing lack of it, is the source not only of ideological passion, both left and right, but also of flamboyant privatism, of poignant ethnic emphasis, and of numerous intellectual absurdities. Being concerned with these effects, we are dealing with *secular theologies* (discussed in the next several chapters); not merely with "alienation" as an academic concept, but with the more interesting extenuations of its actual existence. The perception of these requires analytical distinctions between the mass society responsive to organized technology and the ideas of other imagined societies which everyone carries around in his head. Our political sensibility often results from the tragic working out of this essentially emotional conflict.

Power is the mode of thought appropriate for building the community that does not pre-exist. To the extent that power is lacking, myth acting to accomplish its effects will be created. And this myth will itself be an element of power. The progressive liberal view that man's rational consciousness necessarily catches up with the development of his actual circumstance, without the intervention of myth, is a terrible illusion. Indeed, it would seem that there is not only an unconscious mind affecting the destinies of individuals, but also unconscious experience affecting whole groups—and perhaps even classes and nations. These would consist of the particular dreams underlying what is called "tradition." And just as with individual consciousness, so also our social consciousness never adequately reflects our actual experience.

Our particular American mythical fate involves something we have decided to call "freedom." By this, as used, incredible term, Americans mean the God-given and even constitutional right to make-believe, to live in the head, thus to assert the moral realm, and generally to go about their business so convinced of their perfect anointment as to ignore, with a near-passion of ignoring, most existential un-freedom more reasonably perceived. In this high-octane atmosphere of willed freedom, life-in-history hardly emerges as a problem at all. *Our national notion of freedom is willed mental freedom-from.* This freedom-from may be valuable to preserve youthful perspective; but all of us get older even if we don't grow up. After a while, the complicated side of freedom must assert itself— freedom-to, involving positive choice, engagement, power: e.g., the more limited or apposite freedom Marx was thinking of when he defined it as "the recognition of necessity." We Americans begin by defining freedom as the escape from necessity, and end by celebrating it as the hysterical submission, not then to anything as dignified as necessity, but rather to some kind of unknown social compulsion. Finally, if you conform to the worst in America, you are fully free. American "freedom" means freedom through negation.

We are always escaping from something. I say it is always the same thing: the lack of community in the shallow society. The better escape, in this impossible situation, is from the society; the more common escape is from oneself. Neither is anything to write home about; and, in the end, they don't differ all that much.

A nearly "normal" escape for us is back to the ethnic cocoon: inverted nationalism in the inverted empire constituting this nation. There are immigrant groups from Sicilian villages whose second generation is now living in the same tenement. This sort of thing is considered so decidedly normal that many people think it is harmless. The reason sectional and ethnic groupings have meant so much in our history—and still do—is that there was nothing else to compete in meaningfulness. William M. Dobriner in *Class in Suburbia* says that "ethnic and religious variables figured importantly" in the choice of a place to settle in the suburbs. If this "retreat to the ethnic" continues to be a favored solution even in the newest and most extensively extroverted part of our society, then we are in for some dark days. No failure in America is equal to this one. *If America does not melt, it will explode.*

But it continues to happen—and not just in the suburbs or the slums. It happens also as a direct result of any kind of quick move into the new world without a new idea of American humanity included in one's baggage. A leading doctor in a large metropolitan area described to me what happened as his profession underwent speedy specialization. Previously, there had been one medical society for the whole area. Then, quite naturally, the ob-gyn people "caucused" at the regular meetings—also the heart men, the internists, the psychiatrists, etc. The caucuses were formalized as businesslike specialty sections. Then it was noted that the good-fellowship character of the old medical society had been lost in this process. So good-fellowship was reconstituted as a specialty, too: Jews in one group, Protestants in another, Catholics in a third . . . .

A halfway nation populated by halfway people—and getting more so, apparently, as the pace of organization quickens. Organization, that is, from which so much of each of us remains alienated.

5 How do these "American effects" work themselves out politically? Well, now we get to that: the main thing is to identify the emotional constituencies of the shallow society: this would be the crucial political *background.*

For political Americans, I believe that the segment of the modern experience that clings to our days is McCarthyism. If we were talking about the life of an individual, we could say that McCarthyism was that indigestible event which one can never understand but to which one forever returns. The *McCarthy-effect* has dominated both the liberals and the right wing. It revealed to the latter that its most far-out ideas might one day seize the headlines; and it uncovered for the liberals the emotional depths involved—for proponent, objector, and audience alike—in the simplest ideas of the inherited national repertory. McCarthyism turned idiocy into food for thought, and thus irremediably widened the area of discussion: after Tail-Gunner Joe, nothing is so clearly insane as to be dismissed forthwith—and no mistake of an intellectual character is easily forgivable. It was the most disastrous collapse of community (even of our thin one) that this nation has ever experienced, and it has nearly ruined us. How can we ever trust each other again? Or, without such trust, deal with any Real Problem?

We will be a long time winding up the work of Joe McCarthy. His phenomenal rise to a quite new form of power in this country revealed, with deafening echoes, a profound structural hollowness in our system of being: he thus occasioned the trauma of an entire society. We have not yet digested the McCarthy phenomenon, but have simply managed to forget its worst aspects for a time; this only indicates our reluctance to face the facts of emptiness that his power revealed.

To begin with, what the McCarthy experience asserted about the background of liberal opinion in the United States was "known" to a large group of people before he occurred. The influence of Soviet Communist notions upon the liberal community in this country was a dreary and discouraging fact, appreciated and reacted to more than twenty years before McCarthy elaborated it into a new form of insanity. For understanding of any kind, he was an excrescence. But this background certainly gave him a footing; and he parlayed this unearned toehold into a weirdly effective attack on the American system itself. The durably terrifying result of McCarthy, moreover, was *on* the conservative mood, and *in* what he revealed about the nature of conservative power in this nation. It says an immense amount about our society that well-placed conservatives here did not understand until quite late that McCarthy was attacking *them* as well as the liberals. The body of responsibly conservative opinion in this country was as susceptible to the devastation of McCarthyism as the liberals were. Neither group has fully recovered from the attack: but the liberals, having suffered more, have learned more. The conservatives are just beginning their education; they have a lot to learn.

They also have a distance to go to find some decent teachers on their own side of the fence. The current crop of right-wing intellectuals (many of them recruited after substantial left-wing training) are not serious Burkeans, or indeed serious anything of philosophical stature. Their appeal lies in their PR deftness in accomplishing the impossible, that is, continuing the hard-sell of cheap, stale ideological merchandise. The position they take is almost entirely a reactive one: it is their simple inversion of the dominant liberal ideology that provides their line of argument and distinguishes them from more obvious hacks. Notice that, by newspaper consensus, they are called

radical right-wingers. Their views are a very poor excuse for a genuinely conservative position. They are not in fact in favor of "con-
serving" anything; and they are not so much profound reactionaries
as shallow reactivists. Also, relying so much on used-up popular materials, they are, intellectually, merely argumentative rather than
creative—and embarrassingly vulgar. They are the ridiculous, hard-
sell end of old-fashioned American propriety.

But the full right wing constitutes an important social guerrilla
action. This is the significant aspect: we needn't bother defrosting
the cultural icing provided by a handful of *National Review* intellectuals. They are dangerous, if at all, only for the disease they carry
and that they take for culture—the revolt against history. They
hardly represent any genuine social interests whatsoever, their class-
cultural negativism runs that deep (in this sense of client service,
they are lousy ad men). And the right-wingers have ended up making liberals more significant than they truly are, as any honest liberal
knows; they have done this by identifying all the indigestible history
since the Great Depression as a liberal conspiracy. The painfully
achieved *ad hoc* action undertaken by Roosevelt to deal with the prerevolutionary situation at the depth of the Depression, and carried
on by his followers both domestically and in our new world relations,
are seen by the right-wingers as a coherently rational conspiracy.
Some hotsy-totsy conspirators! It is downright sidesplitting to picture
Roosevelt, Hopkins, *et al.* as big-plan Leninists.

But American governmental history since 1933 does in fact give
much evidence of *ad hoc* heresy regarding the Given Truth of the
myth of Individualism. The right-wingers are true believers of that
myth—that is their main significance—and therefore passionate
heretic-hunters. So the proper answer to them should have been a
defense of heresy. But large sections of the genuinely conservative
community, as well as a good portion of the liberal group, have not
been able to present such a defense effectively because they have not
rooted out the residual emotions of the myth in themselves.

*This reluctance of others is the great strength—indeed, it is the
sole strength—of the radical right-wingers.*

There is no true intellectual conservatism in the United States. Of
course, there is no lack of concern—even vaguely reflective concern
—with conformism; and, contrariwise, with the emotional consequences of rebellion—or even simple freedom, for that matter. But
the drive for conformity here is so overwhelming (because the emp-

tiness it promises to conceal is so terrifying) that those who would tend thereto in any event are denied the sense of having thought their way into a daringly perverse position. Their impossible problem is how to conform by means of ratiocination. The conformism in America that presents itself with an air of original discovery fraught with effort is phony. (T. S. Eliot, with more sense, went to England.) This phony conformism tends readily toward despair and cynicism. And given such, along with a certain amount of public disaster, all this could turn into something revolutionary and distorted, similar historically to European fascism. Modern industrial man is not securely permitted such lapses from simple consciousness and perception as have been tolerated in the United States.

The radical right is indeed more radical than conservative: its adherents make a desperate effort to embrace the future. The image that compels them would not be radical if they were merely enthralled with the past; but it is truly radical because by means of it they lust after the future. Conservatives have a need to become "radical" in order to preserve the purity of the emotional underpinning of their desire to conform. But this radicalism signifies that they have already lost the historical battle, and the going issue is what they will now destroy in commemoration of their personal loss. Having suffered this time-fate, they become hysterical, symbolic, and otherwise insanely pure. It is this impulse toward madness which made fascism, which made McCarthy, which started to make Goldwater, which will plague us until the distorted tradition of that generation is denied.

A personal anecdote: Perhaps a year before the Goldwater nomination, I was cursed with the opportunity to observe a Real One at an indecently intimate range—I spent all night with him on a radio show. *Yaddita, yaddita, yaddita.* The key to this man (also a lawyer) whom I was forced to study so thoroughly was the kind of terms he never used, I realized at four-fifteen in the morning: at no time did he refer to historical trends or social forces or any pseudonyms therefor. His hatred of liberals had displaced history (or, to be subtle, vice versa). Everything that had happened since the beginning of the New Deal had been—his view—under the absolute control of the liberals. So he naturally and reasonably hated them. As I began a sentence containing the prize words—*"New Deal"*—he started to turn red; I stopped in the middle of the sentence and called his attention to the neurological symptom. He smiled sheepishly (a psycho-cultural phenomenon) and admitted the problem he had. Now the magic: if he hated the omnipotent liberals enough, what they did was undone: *and thereby the history as well would disappear.* So his hatred of the liberals-in-history was ferocious. His attitude toward me personally was quite friendly in a schizophrenic way (which incidentally meshes, with certain adjustments—this fellow was no poolroom *bon vivant*—with Richard Rovere's brilliant psycho-portrait of McCarthy). I do not hesitate for a moment to say that this man was in training for some future fascist action—certainly for nothing else. By some mysterious mental process, his large intellectual ineptitude—joined with his small rhetorical talent—had been consecrated by an unknown collegium as dynamic wisdom: he didn't win or lose arguments, learn or not learn, meet or fail to meet a thrust, but under the press of necessity merely went on to a likelier jousting area. (When five-thirty A.M. and freedom arrived, I knew I had had it: *all* of it.)

Look at the zany, long-term situation in America: the causes of the Civil War and the war itself destroyed for a hundred years or more the possibility of serious class leadership in the United States. Genuine conservatism in the absence of class-rule and class-responsibility is absurd—a sociological parody. The robber barons and other big winners in the post-Civil War period may very well have believed literally in a radical Individualism—they were certainly entitled to such belief: also, on a reduced scale, the multitude of local winners around the country, the quarter-million-dollar-net-worth types in real estate and retailing, etc. But their heirs were not entitled to believe in it, could do so only under considerable personal strain, and on the more sophisticated levels did not bother to believe in it but merely hid behind it. With or without belief, however, they decided they needed it; and so they used it.

For many, winners or not, it is too cold to live in this frontier culture without puristic ideological clothing. That has been the deep, sad, non-class, irresponsible, and devastating truth about this experimental continent of ours.

6 To continue our story: The so-called liberals, too, were desperately needful of ideology throughout the disturbing Thirties. Anyone who was around at the time and kept his wits about him knows that they were sickeningly influenced by Communist Party ideologues and fellow-traveling intellectuals. There were probably never as many as 100,000 members of the Communist Party in this country; the party no more here than elsewhere in the world ever attempted to achieve mass membership; and here, moreover, they achieved nothing much with the working class. But the intellectual and organizational influence was great. Communists, operating in the new world disorder, offered a coherent ideology which explained everything. Relying on the overwhelming fact of the Russian Revolution, and continuously justifying the Stalinist order in Russia and in the Third International, this coherent ideology was a hopeful one: it not only explained but also promised everything. It was thus very American emotionally—especially for recent apostates from the similar nonsense of the American dream and the myth of Individualism. It was particularly effective in this regard because, under the strategic concept of the Popular Front, it made room for a large spectrum of partial belief. (Participation required disaffection more than belief, and very little insight into the sources of the apparent disaffection or the nature of one's real beliefs.) A liberal did not have to sign on the dotted line on the last page of a completed bible of Communist ideology; rather, he was allowed to skip-read and initial isolated paragraphs. Doing so, he was treated with more or less friendly contempt and was allowed to proceed unmolested with a large placard on his back reading "Confused Liberal." Too confused to be a Communist, but not quite so confused as he would have been without the help of Communist "thought."

There was no liberal ideology in the United States prior to the Great Depression capable of surviving that event. Neither Populism nor Progressivism was equal to the challenge; and FDR's ebullient amalgam was, being polite, ideologically thin. That is precisely why the liberal community was subject to such ferocious and successful rape by a "foreign" ideology which was ostensibly appropriate to the

times, and was in fact only a decade or so into the process of dis-
proving itself once and for all.

Hofstadter says of Populism that it

> was the first modern political movement of practical importance
> in the United States to insist that the federal government had
> some responsibility for the common weal; indeed, it was the first
> such movement to attack seriously the problems created by in-
> dustrialism.

Progressivism, except as it incorporated the Populist impulse, did not
share this relevance. It expressed the mood of the middle classes in
the city, that cultivated minority of reasonable status-holders and
status-seekers. It was against Bigness and against Corruption: it was
a revolt, as much cultural as political, against the spiritual consequences of organization. If Populism is to be understood as the
sharp, primitive urge of the farmer and the small-town fellow
against the complexity of the new American existence, Progressivism was equally simplistic even if more "cultured." And, contrary to
its own presumptions, I think it was inferior to the other because it
lacked the coherence of definite self-interest which the farmers had.
(Both had more pervasive effect as nominees for a national style of
life than as lasting political perspectives.) But both movements were
involved with an extreme exertion of native American Individualism, as if no other cultural resources were available: and none were.

Yes, I am suggesting that it was the intellectuals out of the old
Progressive tradition who became fellow-travelers.* Devastating
American moralism was the basis. All of our reform efforts have
been motivated by a simple and extreme form of Protestant morality; and along the way of American history this has turned sour—
and more so each day. The American fantasy (why call it a dream?
"dream" is a better word) is over. There is too much human diversity
on this strange continent to be dealt with adequately by means of
simple Christianity, no matter how fervently indulged. The problem
of life in America is indeed religious: our society has no sufficiently
deep structure other than a religious one, and therefore cannot dis-

---

* Ethnic groups with a socialist tradition did not, except for some recent
Russian Jews, whose feelings involved a large measure of "national"
loyalty based on Czar-hatred.

pense with it. But nothing that simple will do much longer: it **is** leading us into terrible trouble.*

The desperate emotionality underlying the acceptance of Communist ideology by the liberal community during the Thirties is all too painfully evident in the reaction to the Moscow Trials, the labor camps, and the Nazi-Soviet Pact. Faith in the distant Russian dream was childlike. It was taken (it was even enforced) as a religious issue of belief, complete with the guilt of apostasy, intellectual hell-fire, and so on. Indeed, the emotionality was exaggerated, as ordinarily with converts: every convert is always an apostate as well, so he begins his second career of belief with extra guilt derived from the failure of his first. Those who gave a Russian inflection to the American dream, or altogether "abandoned" the one for the other (cashed it in, really), were terribly guilt-ridden people. They became, too many of them, "totalitarian liberals," and were subject to considerable manipulation by virtue thereof. Thus another phase to the disaster of American Individualism.

It was not until after the War—including the ridiculous Golden Period of Soviet-American friendship during the conflict—that, as the cold war mushroomed and Russia's intentions were revealed, adherence to Communist ideology began to appear in the guise of treason. When what had previously been proper and quite comfortable came to be viewed as treason—instead of what it obviously had been all along, namely, emotional childishness supported by ample stupidity—the liberal community split in two, the ADA, canonizing the New Deal, was formed on one side, and the previously dominant fellow-traveling group erupted in its final swan song, the Wallace progressive movement. And then, naturally enough after that sort of thing, McCarthy.

* In the long run, only the institutional accretions of history can dispense with religion in this secular sense. England, for instance, can get along without simple religion because the English have preserved so much of their history in their institutions. Finally, a country's history itself becomes a secular religion and the remaining problem is to make certain that the whole process comprises the future as well as the past (currently, a real problem for England). The key to England is that, in the face of industrialism, it remained a traditional society. (The key to pre-War Germany is that it did not, but tried to.)

7 McCarthyism represented the general cultural embarrassment of the country. Everybody participated. Look at the roster of default—that the right could reduce itself to accept it, that the left was so hopelessly guilty before its onslaught, that the established centrist powers so deviously tolerated and abetted it.

Pound for pound, Joe McCarthy must have been about the luckiest politician who ever lived. A warm match dropped into a gasoline tank—and the image is doubly apt, since he himself was destroyed in the resulting explosion. A decade and more later, it can be quite difficult to recall the days of McCarthyism: they are the kind of painful memory it is so tempting to hide from view. But let's make the painful effort: it's important.

In April 1954, when the decisive TV episode of the Army-McCarthy encounter began, Senator Joe McCarthy was a law unto himself. Part of the nation believed him to be the best law Congress had ever allowed; the rest of us favored outright repeal. Both factions were transfixed by the undeniable power of the man, his style, and his issue: these, along with the inner horror he revealed to and about us, were in a bundle called "McCarthyism." This phenomenon began—a month after Alger Hiss had been convicted in 1950—when the first-term Senator from Wisconsin delivered a speech in Wheeling, West Virginia. He waved some papers in the air and suggested that the State Department was in the hands of the Communists. Thus began the most meteoric political career in our history. Within a matter of weeks, Joe McCarthy had become a supplemental form of government in the United States.

The papers that really counted in his career were not the ones he waved in launching it, but the millions of tons of newsprint that each day arrange our image of the world. Joe McCarthy dominated that image. McCarthyism derived from the culminating event of the Hiss case; but it was created and maintained by the press—and finally destroyed by the newest, and then most uncontrollable, form of the press, television.

"It's good to get out of Washington and back to the United States," McCarthy would say in beginning his typical local speech. He was attacking the federal government of the United States, that and only that: anti-Communism was the means, not the end. The not-so-wrong assumption of his attack was that the federal government had been created by the New Deal (add, the Civil War—much of which government was later "retrieved"); and then he went on to say that this event was alien to America, and that all true believers would therefore oppose it. It was this very deep sentiment that McCarthy mobilized in the period of the first hysterical response to a nuclear world. And this anti-government feeling is mostly what has survived McCarthy's downfall—it is at the center of the current right-wing movement, and of embattled traditional American spirituality everywhere.*

In brief, McCarthyism grew out of the political rubble of the post-war world. It constituted the American spasm of dismay, which was then shaped by a deft hand into boundless suspicion. What had happened was that the failure of an entire generation had been ridiculously summed up in the lifeline of one man, Alger Hiss. Hiss was an ex-golden boy who had been convicted of perjury in a court of law and of treason in the high-powered tribunals of the press. Joe McCarthy parlayed these two convictions into a thousand accusations. At the height of his power, he operated a star chamber in newsprint by which he convicted contemporaries of Hiss, and any vulnerable liberal with a taint of radicalism in his past, of a new custom-made crime, "implied treason." In this manner did our history bear bitter fruit: the liberal errors of the Popular Front, the soft feelings of wartime partnership, the shattered hopes of the grand alliance against Hitler so soon replaced by nuclear terror, the frightening efficiency of Soviet espionage, the queer nightmare of Korea—all these were tied into a simple political package. McCarthyism was our last great effort to escape a historical reckoning: with a drunken bullyboy leading the way, we celebrated a Black Mass: like half-Christianized Indians, we held a hateful wingding—here in America, with its revivalist culture appropriate to the shallow society.

But notice particularly that McCarthyism was not just caused—it was also permitted. The daring young Senator from Wisconsin had received a certified license to accuse—freely, endlessly, mercilessly.

* In part, this anti-government feeling first galvanized by McCarthy was a delayed reaction to the death of Roosevelt. The big government he created had been in fact accepted as a bountiful mother by the nation—but then the mother died, and otherwise refused to satisfy all needs, or revealed herself as incapable of doing so.

This license had been issued by the highest, most responsible authorities in the country, and it continued in effect until *they* revoked it. In the first instance, the license had been issued by Senator Taft, as a convenience in his forthcoming election as President of the United States. Taft personally is said to have had great contempt for McCarthy, and I am fully prepared to believe that he did; and also that he thought he could turn the man off when that might also suit his convenience. But what had been prepared by Taft was then utilized by Eisenhower. And the General experienced considerable difficulty in turning Joe McCarthy off: it happened to be a very rough course, especially the first nine holes.

McCarthy himself *couldn't* stop. That was inherent in the cards he was playing. Besides, he was basically a nasty bum devoted to fun and games. So he started to attack the new administration: he was helplessly, irretrievably anti-government, and so was his clientele. For a period, while McCarthy was charging that the new administration still coddled Communists, the new administration was still trying very hard to coddle him. But finally it just wouldn't work any longer. The issue was joined at a level of absolute absurdity, with McCarthy attempting to prove that the American army was dominated by Communists—and threatening to demonstrate that the secret intelligence agency as well had been infiltrated—while the army offered a magnificently principled defense to the effect that McCarthy had tried to get a commission and special treatment for a friend of his chief counsel. Only in America. The television camera was unleashed, a clever old gentleman from Boston goaded the bullyboy into self-destruction—"*Have you no sense of decency, sir, at long last?*"—and the evil genie rather abruptly disappeared into the bourbon bottle from which it had emerged.

8 But the experience is still with us: *he taught us so much about ourselves.* Most of all, he demonstrated that the lack of American government-in-depth, our failure to create a class or establishment or any group of people with a minimal moral commitment to running the country in a responsible fashion, was a deeply lodged national Doomsday machine.

The effect of McCarthy is to be read in relation to these persisting revelations:

1. He exposed a glaring weakness in the sense of rulership of our leading privileged groups, the people who should be running the society in addition to exploiting it.

2. The liberals are still suffering from the McCarthy-effect. The ADA, as an example, was necessary and effective for its time, but it constituted an ideological retreat of serious proportions. The Roosevelt experience should have been analyzed and projected forward upon a larger historical screen. Instead, it was canonized as a complete ideology. That the *ad hoc* wiggles of the Gay Maneuverer should have been accepted as a coherent approach to policy problems was so silly on the face of it, but then so fully achieved, that one hardly knows how to express the ineluctable fact. Anyway, we are only now beginning to emerge from FDR's patchwork of policy notions; and the politics of our day remains quite minimal.

3. McCarthy hit the liberal middlebrow where it hurts. He wore dark-rimmed reading glasses, carried a full briefcase, and waved impressive-looking papers on the slightest provocation: his parody of the professional expert was an act of genius.* In addition, he attacked them with the threat of exposure where they truly live, in their job tenure. And for the right-wingers, he offered—for the first time—an opportunity for active destruction *along with a sense of popular relevance*.

4. Previously, one might have thought that the great significance of the Eisenhower period was that the New Deal had not been repealed. Now, I am not so sure. Eisenhower encouraged McCarthy by "allowing" him. This was a deeply reactionary act, even though executed by a deeply moderate nobody. Also, toward the end of his career, Eisenhower became a genuinely tense hysteric on fiscal matters. We are still suffering from both of these Eisenhower doings. In this sense, he did not allow the New Deal to remain unrepealed. He put the stamp of his authority on the primary idiocy of the day—fiscal responsibility—and he allowed McCarthy to grow big enough to remain an indelible memory with incalculable effect.

5. The temporary success of McCarthyism still encourages the right-wingers, still inhibits the liberals. Indeed, I think it may be true that McCarthy-fear has become institutionalized in this country. Which would account for the exceptional regard still displayed in favor of the ridiculous right-wingers. No, we are not done with Mc-

---

* This was set forth beautifully by Richard Rovere in his excellent book, *Senator Joe McCarthy*.

Carthy. He has become a "presence" in the mystical sense: like the effect of someone who, say, was going to kill us or make us rich, but who then dies abruptly in the middle of the transaction. He haunts this nation.

In summary, please note the anti-majoritarian bias of traditional Individualism: we will return to this matter in Chapter Nine, but here we should at least realize that the puristic conception of democracy—anti-machine, anti-bloc, anti-charisma, and anti-all other Unclean Things—is not genuinely a *historical* conception of democracy at all. It is a pure image, referable to nice clean material surroundings—*not* to the actual environment of any feasibly desirable majority of living Americans.

Also note that it is not possible to admit one's helplessness, in the existential condition, without trying to do something about it—without, that is, acting in terms of power. The continuing hold of Individualism is that it is still a way of not admitting, for those who wouldn't know what to do about it if they did. But community is so necessary, and we so lack it, that we must consciously go about creating some. This means organizing; it means conscious coalition-building; it even means intentional brotherhood. And this is impossible under the myth of Individualism, with its foundations of fantasied omnipotence and us-them moralism. I say we are spiritually desperate. We must even have as-if communities—and even if they begin with the standard organizational ones. *Any* beginning. Only agony without community.

Out of the native anarchism of American life, we have jelled this destructive myth. The more we insist on it, the more authoritarian becomes our overorganized world. Now, with the prudent anarchy of the Goldwater organization men, it has turned so nasty that it will leave nothing green in the wake of its devastation. Their hatred is directed primarily toward the legal American government—not toward all American government, and not toward all organization. *Their hatred is of law when it is powerful, and of power when it is legal.* They would do away with law itself. Indeed, their hypocrisy alone is capable of accomplishing that. (See Chapter Ten for their Southern sources.)

I remind you that Thomas Jefferson was eighteen years old before he saw his first town. Repeat, *town.*

Particularly, I remind young Americans of this. The larger-than-life ideas involved in Individualism are compelling—and useful, if at all—for *new* individuals. As a way of growing up, yes; as a way of refusing to grow up, no. Also, learn a little, and don't be afraid of being shrewd. In this sense, Individualism is very much like nationalism: it is the willfully assertive mood in political discourse. But beware of that special point when nationalism, beginning as patriotism, finally exfoliates as xenophobia. Listen sometime to Sibelius' *Finlandia:* that grandiosity is one thing for some late beginners against great odds; but what if, after a late beginning, you *win* something? Then it becomes Hitler's own hearing of Wagner.

The major American myth is still that of Individualism—even though now it has lost its simple charm and has already turned vicious, as adumbrated in this chapter. Clearly, it provides the underpinnings of the New Fascism. *It represents an emotional paralysis far more profound than the post-New Deal political paralysis which President Johnson now seems to have resolved.* McCarthyism revealed and then bequeathed this profundity to us: he revealed, if it needed revealing, the terrifying emotionality underlying the ordinary images involved in our politics. (With the Negro movement since his time, and the McCarthyist revival involved in the Goldwater takeover, the deepening emotionality of our political life is further underlined.) The myths embedded in our national cultural fabric are not, then, mere museum pieces. They are frighteningly vital. They are, indeed, the religions we live by: they have that status.

Why these instead of the traditional religions? What happened to the traditional patterns of emotion, and their regular relations to political expression? Something happened; something replaced these. Our politics cannot be understood without developing at least a general sense of where religion went, and even a little bit of why. So now we turn to that.

SIX

Where
Religion
Went

1 At one time, it was inconceivable not to believe in God. Even if conceivable, there would hardly have been a serious point in going to the trouble. Only negative and destructive persons would have uncovered the hidden point at some period in their short, brutal lives. Now all that is changed. Today, polite belief accompanied by scarcely any shared discussion is the usual thing in the advantaged section of world society. This posture consists more of a strenuous lack of argument than of anything genuinely to be called belief. Thus, having no gods, we misuse God to forestall the sensitive monologue of the inner mind. The cause? The triumph of rational consciousness achieved daily by the cumulative successes of science. The result? Fugitive religious emotion.

It is time now to put the rationality of science in its place, by reviving the primacy of non-rational history and politics; and to do this it will be necessary to reopen the long-closed discussion—so as to overcome the restricted expression—of the ultimate and the eternal in human affairs. The time has come: the insidious and devastating *spread of the absurd,* abetted by scientific rationalism, now threatens the essential balance of human existence.

The thought of science is too much, the emotions of religion too little, and so man is misconceived. But the cure is clearly not more willed effort to make belief in God, and one or another of His dogmas. The cure is to move with some haste toward a theory of *secular* theology, if only as a stopgap. We must recognize that theology—the forms of consciousness for dealing with emotions occasionally called "religious"—is not dispensable because of the victories of other forms of consciousness, but also that any revived theology cannot readily be divine. God is perhaps dead, but we are certainly not. And to deal with this situation we require something rather more original than inventing Him all over again.

Murray Kempton once quoted G. K. Chesterton to the effect that "the problem with ceasing to believe in God was not that, thereafter, you would believe in nothing but rather that you would believe in *anything*." Chesterton, a converted Catholic, probably presented this thought as a reason not to cease believing in God; about Kempton, I do not know; for us, I will say that it indicates where religion went. It went every which way.

2   It is a simple enough rationalistic exercise to demonstrate the essential childishness of traditional religion. Indeed, the great virtue of religion—when it works—is that it concentrates the surviving child in each of us on harmless irrelevancies, thus freeing the remainder of our selves for occasional maturity. Unfortunately, formal religion doesn't work for many people —it no longer cages enough dependency to be worth the effort: I believe it always took a great effort. Being much threatened by the surviving child, I am in my need as religious as anybody can be, without God.* And while I have at times felt the necessity even of the inevitability of God, I have never been able to believe in His existence. I can believe in my own surviving childishness; I can recognize my religious nature, that is, my yearning for community; but I cannot bring myself—I long ago stopped trying—to believe that God is anything other than that part of the father that one never managed to incorporate into oneself, because that part never existed in the first place.

The solution to this quandary is not to take the mythical part into

---

* The "I" in this book is here for the purpose of convenient exposition: this "I" is not necessarily "me."

oneself anyway, to become as God. Anyone who insists in adulthood
on being as powerful and independent as he imagined himself to be
in his better moments as a child, is a mess. Let me suggest that like
the idea of property, the image of God has both obscured and distorted the truths of power. The existence of the very idea of an all-
powerful God—insofar as it has any real reference—contradicts one
of the first principles of power, namely, that no one person has or
can have enough. If God is the power none of us can have, then all
right; but then, very obviously, His nature is by definition emergent
and unknowable—indeed, no more than a reservoir of the unknown.

The confusion of self and God, however, sustains the myth of Individualism; and it offers no community. It does not even offer "security"—which we all want, even those of us who no longer dare to
hope for community. Because security is the state of feeling which
results from a balance struck with the surviving child: it is the relative quiescence (*not* mastery; there is none except true community)
of the conflict between one's childhood and one's adulthood. When
he still existed, the Devil, you must know, was in each of us: after
we stopped creating him in an image so much larger than life, it
turned out that "he" was simply that little animal-child in us enlarged with that same child's fear. The great devil of Christian history was only the impulse to repeat what the child wanted when the
child was no longer a child. Frightening enough; but the pointed
ears and the tail were our own doing.

Finally, the religious symbols became an emotional trap rather
than a means of elaborating, so as to manage, our involvements. But
the emotions did not disappear: it was simply that the *language*
wore out. Not for everyone, of course: mostly for those benefiting
from the new scientific civilization. For others, the language is still
fluid; note the following from the August 16, 1963, issue of *Muhammad Speaks,* which appeared under the heading "What the Muslims
Believe":

> 5. We believe in the resurrection of the dead—not in physical
> resurrection—but in mental resurrection. We believe that the so-
> called Negroes are most in need of mental resurrection; there-
> fore, they will be resurrected first.

I always try to respect another man's language, certainly as long
as I remain interested in listening to him. But I always translate. I
think it is correct to say that my language is based on his, but is not

the same as his. And occasionally I publish my translations—even to him. That depends: I want to talk a common language, but I will not in my eagerness rush toward incoherence or the non-language of violence.

An American woman once said to me: "I am not interested in politics—but I *am* interested in democracy." What would you have done? In abject gratitude, I kissed her. It would have taken me weeks to work out so perfect a formulation.

3 The heart of our problem takes us back to the science-religion argument of the nineteenth century—Huxley's defense of Darwinism, etc. The success of science occurred, after all, in a Christian civilization. Indeed, one could spell out the sources of it in the bifurcated nature of a Christian culture. But whether it was thus deeply derived or was an alien entry, it transformed that civilization and challenged it decisively. Science triumphed in the encounter; its triumph has increased with each succeeding decade. In the literal fact, religion—and the complex of emotion over which it had reigned—was thrown away. What survived as a religion was an increasingly incredible dogma. The choice was finally posed as being between belief and mind itself, and anyone with a real option naturally chose mind. The basic error was to have conceived the choice in these terms. All that really came to an end was the viability of a historical language.

Taking "religion" to mean the ineradicable human emotions expressed therein or thereby, rather than any historical means of expression, we ask: What happened to religion when science, defined as mind itself, won out? It became fugitive and illegitimate, emerging later as individual eccentricity and mass neurosis. Also, a great deal of the fugitive emotion attached itself adoringly to the winner, science. All in all, the emotions entered into a multitude of institutions, and new gods were raised everywhere, new ritual expiations of death-fear invented and instituted, and bits and pieces of security-dogma embraced on all possible occasions. Faced with the triumph of rationality in the guise of science, the human race did not give up; it went underground.

So the human being does not quite disappear in an age of science and administration; but large areas of his nature and circumstance are ignored, because science and administration are not yet ready to concern themselves with these. Their effect persists, however; and just what they are is not all that difficult to discover. It is just impossible to discover—or rediscover—what they are from the standpoint of scientific method. But the demand for rationality is so compelling in a technological society that we have been forced to presume that the data are at fault, not the method. This is absurd; it is not even "scientific." The human animal cannot and the human being should not have to wait as much as science seems to require. Indeed, he will not, which is called *politics*.

The historical success of science discredited theology proper, as we all know. I happen not to have taken Pascal's wager, so I go along with that whole general development. But the historical success of science has also been taken to discredit the *subject* of theology, that congeries of intense existential emotion which half-defines the human. This is not only unpleasant and unfriendly, it is wrong. *The data are never at fault.* For men less than gods, the method must always be adapted to the data: for instance, I can imagine a situation in which the first step in a scientific study of language would be the simple self-awareness of a scream of pain—of the scientist's *own* scream of pain.

What we call scientific method, that monumental success story, seems to me to be compounded of two or three primary elements: 1) the way very smart people think within a continuing tradition based on experimental verification; 2) the elaborate application of mathematics, through new and refined symbol-languages, to an ever wider range of instrumental problems; and 3) a consequential accumulation of instrumentation. This is wonderful, for what it is. What it is not, is the Whole Truth. But the scientific observer too often believes it is the Only Truth and that there is no Whole Truth. He has consequently been swallowed up in what he has been observing: he has identified himself with it so completely that he has become it. His commitment to one limited language is such that what cannot be expressed in it does not exist. Since much of this is *him,* he has also been excluding much of himself from existence. Thus science has been allowed to prosper as a form of spiritual suicide.

What cannot be expressed in a given language, because the language contains no words for it or the words are inadequate to express it, still seeks and finds some expression somewhere else. In this sense, anything that exists creates its own language. The emotions once expressed in the language of theology have not truly disappeared. Life is just as religious as it always was—it is only that the language is not so well known, and the expression not so well organized, as formerly. It is our responsibility now to rediscover or to create the usable language; we must begin by compiling a primitive dictionary and grammar; we must create a theory of secular theology. And clearly this requires an all-out contest with the tyranny of scientific method.

Whether this is called a sociology of knowledge, or the social-psychological approach to institutions, or perhaps the rediscovery of the existential human being in the organized technological society, is not so important. What is very important is that the poetic subjectivity of the human being be preserved as a datum; otherwise we end up allowing the method not to explicate but to create the object of study. This is the bureaucratic distortion *par excellence,* and it is itself a primary component of the unanalyzed secular theology of our present society.

4   What leads one toward a theory of secular theology is that people need and always manage to have and to hold the necessary *summarizing ideas.* It is humanly difficult or perhaps even impossible to think or to live very long without them. They make coherent consciousness possible, because at any random moment that must be a potential representation of the *whole* world, including the inner world of the human being: otherwise consciousness lacks a basic validity. An idea or an image can only be exchanged for another one, it cannot be exchanged for nothing. And all aspects of the human being and the human condition achieve some kind of symbolic expression in consciousness, no matter how wrong or distorted that expression may be. So the main difference between ideas is not just that some are true and some are false, and we need only discover the one and destroy the other, but that some are "better" than others for this purpose of expression and coherence. The intellectual difference between people is not merely that some rely on mythical elements of consciousness, and some do not; the difference is that some myths are better than others for the functioning of human beings in given circumstances. Therefore, the cultural critic has the responsibility not only to "destroy" myths by

noting that they are myths, but to replace the poorer ones with better ones. Or, more pointedly today, to exert himself to provide a grammar for a discussion of the myriad of existing mythical notions, in the hope that such awareness will induce better natural choices by the individual himself. Even in the law, that majesty of majesties, where power and justice are supposed to meet unmythically, Thurman Arnold has remarked with great kindness and wisdom that "the function of law is not so much to guide society as to comfort it."

Put another way: the free-market production of goods was not enough for our kind of society, and by one means or other a minimal organized synthesis has had to be achieved. So also, the free-market production of a "natural" culture is no longer good enough, and a synthesis is again required (and with our commercial culture, has even been somewhat achieved). This keystone sustaining culture was formerly provided by religion. Under the Communists, and other authoritarians relying on more traditional elements, it is again provided by something like old-time religion; thus Communism, in part, is a theocracy. We must do a lot better than either of these; but "better" cannot any longer be conceived as doing nothing. And these mythical meanings are not only sometimes enforced from above, they are also continuously generated from below. They may not safely be ignored. No cultural view or method which permits this continued ignorance can be countenanced. (And it will not survive.)

We are not going to restore the cultural coherence of the Middle Ages based on classic Christian theology; we are not going to accept the culture of Communism based on Marxist dogma; we cannot persist forever with the currently disorganized free-market notion of culture, which leads to cheapened administrative compulsion and existential despair beyond bearing: therefore, we must pursue a method of poetic synthesis in order to reclaim for man what is left of the unwritten world, including our inwardness. Moreover, we begin with a notion that secular theologies already exist in abundance, and that the problem is not to fight these data but to bring them into such awareness that they may be subjected to critical evaluation and be made coherent with other contents or our national consciousness.

All this suggests that dreams and other irrationalities are not to be overcome merely by some further assertion of rational will. Perhaps they are not to be overcome at all—certainly not if that implies "overcoming" the dreaming human as well. If indeed not, then in some special sense they must be "accepted." But nothing can be accepted without change: that is not acceptance but enforcement. What do we do with the vagaries of dreams, and the legions of marching items of irrationality, now known as neurotic and psychotic symptoms as well as by other names, and no longer implying "objective" references to magic? Shall we continue to detest them, and leave them all to other, crazier persons? Why not?

But what if all this is, now that humanity has the opportunity, simply the first true emptying of the unconscious mind into the care of self-consciousness? What if, were we more casual in our resistance, the junk of unconsciousness does not remain eternally damaging, or even engaging? As the fuller typography of the unconscious is revealed—and accepted in the sense that our prime efforts are not devoted so ferociously to its denial—it may come about that aspects of it are less interesting than formerly: *that the interest was in the act of repression, not in what was repressed;* that even some of the content was created by repression. Then form will be defined as health, and vice versa, and we can move forward a little.

5   The proper end-in-view of a modern "religion," put together as best may be out of existing secular mythologies, is the achievement of as much heaven on earth as the place can hold. This is also the proper end-in-view of political activity. The reason the two are not, even so, the same, is that the latter tends to become excessively historical and manipulative, while the former too often remains poetically locked in the head. However this nice conflict may finally resolve itself in the post-Christian and post-socialist worlds, the accompanying cultural proposition (our main interest is cultural) is simplicity itself to state: the critical reference of ideals is to action, and that of action is to ideals.

It seems tenable to suggest that religious beliefs throughout history have often enough sought a political and a military as well as a spiritual expression. In this sense, the Jews were a defeated army continuing a guerrilla campaign for several thousand years; the historically eccentric Church of Rome is obviously a political body, the oldest corporation in the world; and the Protestants created business. To buttress this historical assumption, one could also point to a number of theocracies, and to the even more common circumstance that few governing groups or even fully constituted states have ever conceived of ruling without the active concurrence of priests, of one kind and another. This might be summed up in the proposition: religion sanctifies power, and power very much requires to be sanctified. It is only in its initial revolutionary stage that religion is without compromise and overwhelmingly "otherworldly." Later, its other-worldliness—in the institutionalized phase—serves as a spiritual apology for revolutionary failure, for the political despair ascribed to the insufficiently altered order of this world, which order meanwhile has successfully been sanctified by the new religion. Religion was always very "practical."

From which I deduce that the basis of power, in the first instance, is the fear of death. That is why we have never been able to *wait* for success, or recognize a strenuously achieved failure.

I want to suggest also that these quasi-religious propositions are true with great relevance for our time. It is a common thing to speak of the Communists as constituting a religious movement. This is meant to be insulting to them; and whenever the analogy of religiosity is applied to their behavior or pronouncements, it is expected that all Western men and other freedom-lovers will immediately understand the meaning involved—that Communists are not rational, that they are dogmatic, that they cannot leave well enough alone, and that they *have* to conquer the world just as Mohammed or the Crusaders or Philip II of Spain felt the same godly compulsion.

The world was indeed meant to be heaven; or, at the very least, sacrificed to an idea of heaven. However, Americans are not all that more rational than Russians—they are not altogether without dogmatism, etc. Our ideas of Freedom and Individualism are singularly religious in nature; the difference between ourselves and the Russians does not lie so much in the degree of politically relevant religiosity as in the fact that *our* religion is aroused by an opportunity to "stop Hitler" or "contain Communism"—in other words, by a negative assertion.

But the essence of the Communist religion is not merely dogmatism—it is the scientific rationality which its dogmatism presumes to express once and for all. The disease has spread farther there than here. Neither of us lacks dogmatism; theirs is simply more scientific.

Among other things in the course of the science-religion show-down, modern man decided that religious feeling was too important to be left to the priests—they were not expert enough in handling it, under modern conditions. I would add that politics is also too important to be left to priests of any kind, or to be managed without religious feeling. A difficulty in pursuing this line of thought is that moderns have been so disappointed by religion that they wince at the very mention of the word. Well, my advice is, wince—wince once or wince twice, but wince and get over it. Because religious feeling is not an invention of the priests or the politicians, and it cannot be laid off on them; it is a condition of human existence.

To help things along, I will come halfway toward the reluctant reader.* I agree that formal religion is no longer believable, and that most of us who are having the difficulty should perhaps give up trying to believe in it. Even the half-hearted attempt to do so misdirects too much energy and emotion which is required elsewhere. I will also maneuver in your direction by admitting that politics has achieved very little success so far in replacing religion. The Communists have been very effective, as we all know; but I think it would be stretching the point unconscionably to call their effectiveness "success." They have much to learn about what human beings are like, and how they are to be organized "successfully" in great aggregates (and they seem strangely uninterested in allowing for the organization of the elements of the separate human being into a genuine individual).

6   One mentions "religion" and most people immediately think of God and the afterlife, and of memorizing a very limited number of basic propositions about life-and-death which are then believed in strenuously—and just as strenuously defended against all friends, enemies, doubts, and other evidence. There are a great number of emotional patternings concerning authority, death, and dogma, however, which are accepted—and without discussion—perhaps for no better reason than that they are *not* called "religion."

* Note that I am addressing myself not to people who profess traditional beliefs, but to those who (no matter what social posture they assume) are so bored with regular religion that they resent being reminded even of the emotions once involved therein. As to the former, I only ask them to ask themselves whether they in fact still speak the language.

The least of these problems is God;* and the most enduring one is the desire to memorize and repeat—to simplify. God as the old man with the long white beard who lives in the sky, indeed God as anything more than a fundamental force or principle in the universe which science will finally explain to us one day, is hardly credited by anybody who has passed through even an American college. And more important (this applies to a great mass of uneducated people as well), the God of formal religion is mostly not required because there are so many available substitute objects for the real emotions which once created God: so much in modern society is unfortunately Godlike. Also, life is much easier and you therefore do not have to grow up so much; and society has been organized on principles whereby it is not convenient to the administrators of these principles that you should grow up very much. In short, indulged children don't need a big father so much; and besides, there are plenty of substitute symbols.

But this matter of human beings' desiring so deeply to live by a few clear-cut principles which cover all aspects of life-and-death is profoundly extended into the recesses of our problem. It will not be fully overcome until human beings have been rather fully freed from fear and anxiety. Mark the day on your calendar. Meanwhile, we have to deal with the matter if only in order to survive a while longer. Please note the following about memorizing-and-repeating, simplicity and dogma: this rigidity is first of all a reflection in consciousness of recurrent patterns in behavior, and some very nice people suffer from this form alone. The larger problem arises when there is no habit and no clearly indicated course of behavior, and the human being is dependent upon ideas and images of merely possible courses of behavior—or even worse, when there are none of these, and he must build a mental home for eternal fear and trembling. The quality that has so discredited religious thought is, I think, *the fear of moving between one idea or attitude and another.*

Wasn't this matter of transit recognized in Christian theology? I am thinking of the role of the Holy Ghost in the Trinity. The Holy Ghost, in a gross sense, would seem to be the mystical manner of moving from father to son or son to father—that is, from the origi-

* That is, the issue of "the existence" of God; as an image, I find Him both unavoidable and indispensable: in simple fact, a key piece of our language.

nal idea to the new and necessary one. But the fluidity of this Christian transit gave out, for one reason or another—several reasons perhaps being that the Greek sense of tragedy had not been incorporated into the "whole view" with sufficient stature; that too much Hebrew morality had been joined with too little political savvy; and that, generally speaking, the whole project was extremely ambitious. In any event, it was clearly designed for the short course in terrestrial living. One reason why traditional religious ideas are no longer of much interest or clear use to us is that we live too long nowadays, and the consequent strain of trying to believe in all of that over so many decades, while at the same time living more and more in the milieu of consciousness, is too much for most of us.

7 The idea of the afterlife consists, rather obviously, of a Reason-For one's native determination not to (not to have to) think about the fact of death in the first place. If I say, *of course* there is an afterlife, and I can describe it—my friends and serious enemies will remember me, nobody else can live my history, my chemicals and my children remain—nobody believing in the "afterlife" would be interested. Belief in a Later Gathering Place is bound up with the notion that you don't really die at all. But you do.

Which raises a very unpleasant subject to be dragged into a discussion of politics.

Indeed, death is such a painful subject that one probably has to be a fool even to try to initiate a reasonable discussion of it. It is thought that doing so only stimulates fear, or even panic. But without a conception of death, there is little possibility of a clear view of the human being in history; and it is unavoidably a central if unspoken subject in politics. *We can hardly imagine what power would be like, unsupported by the fear of death.* Therefore, even though I join in the general revulsion toward the subject, and believe, with everyone else, that the best answer to the issue is not to think about it at all; still, to join completely in this common feeling would make it impossible to discuss politics—certainly to do the marvelous subject full justice. Also, while thinking about it too much can stimulate fear, etc. (I hope to be brief), not thinking about it does not precisely confront the matter either. Not thinking about it should be considered an everyday answer to this monumental fact of the human condition: on occasional intellectual Sundays, we might all just as well grit our teeth and face up.

Apart from silence, and decent rituals yet to be created for our kind of society, the human answer to death can only be God-in-heaven or Life-here-and-now. I myself would almost prefer the former after having taken a look at the latter; but it is just not possible. Formal religion ruined itself by overexploiting the fear of death (in favor of the imagined moral community), and avoiding excessively the actual facts of the matter. So that piece of pie no longer rests in the sky. Heaven is down here or nowhere. The answer to death is life here and now, whether in the head (myth, fantasy, poetry); or in history (love and actual community); or in the more general mythical and exploitative confusion between the head and history; or, at the bottom of the pit, in the death of the Other—Auschwitz. We are stuck with the religious feeling, because we are stuck with death.

Then, once again, where did religion go? Back into life, where it very possibly belongs. What has happened is that the usual identifying symbols for religion are no longer generally attached to the actual emotions of the matter, since these have been spread out among all the concerns of living; which means that nobody knows what is any longer religious, and what is not. It is entirely wrong to believe that the ideas of God and an afterlife are the essence of religion. They are not the essence, they are merely two ancient ways of expressing the essence. Today, they seem to have very little to do with actual religious emotions. They are dated conventions of thought about these emotions.

If this view strikes you as strange, note that one does not think about death and eternity in order to *solve* the problem, but rather to understand better the ways in which our feelings about these matters may corrupt or create an individual, a marriage, a friendship, a group, a nation.

The practical ways to deal with death are to prolong life and to make it better while we have it. Still, after a long and rewarding life, we die. Then what? Then nothing. But who ever heard of nothing? Why, every man born knows of nothing, because that is what he came out of. If we took the difference between the median age of all three billion people now alive and their life expectancy, we would find that the majority of them will be dead in something like twenty years, say. We would *also* find that a majority used to be the same as dead about twenty years ago, say. Generally speaking, death (or non-being) is not so unfamiliar a state as we like to believe. The intended and artificial unfamiliarity which we all indulge has an obvious purpose; but it also has a not so obvious consequence, namely, that a term is missing from our conscious equations. Really two terms, since our denial of the first death, which is completed, in order to blank out the second one, still to come, does as much damage to the past as our non-attitude to the second does to the future. (The myth of recurrent lives in Eastern religious thought had the virtue, at least, of spreading the burden of distortion.) In any event, the relegating of death to the institutional care of conventional religion, where it might hopefully never be heard from again, was too ambitious a project: the nut has escaped and is roaming all the neighborhoods of our conscious equations.

To get back to the more "practical" ways of dealing with death: these are political. Exaggerated ways of handling death-fear are involved (we noted at the beginning of this book) in the pursuit of power for its own sake and morality for its own sake; also, I suppose, excessive lovers practice their own forms of exaggeration. Besides these, making-life-better as a way of confronting death is so clear a choice as to require no elaboration—and since this is almost equal to "politics," we have had and will have sufficient thereof herein; just note that while the future may be as much of a fantasy as Heaven or Hell ever was, it is nevertheless a much more useful fantasy, certainly to our children (and certainly if handled with sophistication).

Worldwide, we prolong life with medical care and with food. Our meager effort in doing so has already created a revolution, worldwide, in the poorer areas of the planet. Every which kind of nobody now wants to live longer. I'm for it, but I have nothing to add to the Rx beyond what so many others have said. I do, however, want to emphasize a new-something having to do with the prolongation of life in the no-longer-poor-areas of the planet. It is a horror story, and it goes like this:

Because Joseph Stalin wanted to add the ultimate ruby to his crown and live forever, Russian medicine underwent a forced march in the matter of organ transplants. Post-Stalin, this idiotically derived technology made some impression and created some interest in the West. Now there has been real achievement, and probably a good deal more to come. The AMA, editorializing in its *Journal,* stated at the end of 1963: "It is now technically possible to transplant virtually all organs including the heart." In Sweden, a kidney transplant operation (unsuccessful) from a "100 per cent dying patient" led the Royal Medical Board in February 1965 to prohibit such operations without written permission from the dying donor. In this country, it has already been necessary to establish a citizen's committee connected with a hospital in Seattle to determine which applicants will be accepted for hemodialysis by use of an artficial kidney machine: in 1963 only ten of thirty were accepted—they lived, and several of the rejected twenty died within a few months.*

High-level research biologists (perhaps remembering the spiritual agony of atomic physicists some decades ago) have already begun to worry seriously about the social implications. It would not be too much to guess that in five or ten years the technology of organ transplants will have reached that level of immediate reality where people find sufficient reason to trample each other. Imagine the bidding and maneuvering for a certified QA106 kidney, or an ST15 liver (especially the latter, which is so intimately connected with high-living: well-to-do individuals may soon be able to drink themselves to death more than once). There couldn't possibly be enough to go around, unless mass production were adopted. So we may be saved from the terrors of the approaching world of abundance by commercializing the one absolute fundament of scarcity—extended life, or what may come to be called "fungible non-death."

Death? Death is also a very "practical" matter.

* The hospital in Seattle was one of the few offering the expensive (and unending) treatment other than with the prospect of a kidney replacement experiment. Doctors estimate that from 2 to 20 per cent of the 100,000 annual victims of kidney disease could be kept alive by the machine. Some transplanters, however, have objected to an adequate machine treatment program as a diversion from work on transplantation. And in fact most of the existing machines were not used at all, or regularly, because of the cost and the lack of technicians. Kidney technology seems to be at the forefront, but other organs have been "successfully" transplanted. To date, success refers to surgery only; the frontier of this technology has to do with the bodily mechanism which rejects all foreign substances, including second organs intended to be helpful. But chemical suppression of this misguided effort of the body has already produced results which the AMA calls "encouraging." In June 1964, a patient functioning with a cadaver kidney had survived twenty-eight months.

8 Death is the worst part of the subject matter of religion: it is every priest's ace-in-the-hole. The fear of unbelieving derives mostly from the fear of death, so if you can imagine the absence of death you can also conjecture a race of humans undogmatic and daring, for whom the question of the existence of God would become one of a number of interesting speculations (if He were for once not presented as the governor-general of the afterlife and all admission thereto). But as to both the fact and the fear of death, traditional religion offers only a demonstrable delusion—and one, moreover, that requires the strenuous sacrificial participation of the victim to preserve the possible non-thought benefit. It's an impossible myth for educated people. When these indulge it, the result is often ugly: it may undermine the utility of their education, and can become a vicious manipulative device: the most effective priests are not believers. We really do not need any more educated dogmatists.

Tunneling forward into our subject, I will be succinct about the reason we require a secular rather than a divine theology. It is simply that now we live too long to make believe we live in any heaven-in-the head; and also because now there are too many opportunities down here for us to ignore or sacrifice in favor of heavenly notions. Thus we cannot do *with* a divine theology; the remainder of this chapter is devoted to the reasons why we cannot do *without* a secular one (and the next chapter is addressed to why it cannot be "scientific").*

I think the main point that will move us toward a theory of secular theology is that science did not in fact legislate irrational need out of existence. What it accomplished, in this connection, was the conversion of irrationality from symbolic religious expression to symbolic political and social expression. (In this, its direct forerunner was "business," which was also a mutative form of social politics derived from religion.)

So now history displaces God, heaven lies in a temporal future—

---

* The writer apologizes for not being able to present a new and adequate and understandable and relevant theology; but have patience, it will be forthcoming in the next generation or so.

and this congeries of occurrences must be comprehended fluidly, poetically, and without the aid of memorized dogma. Our afterlife has been returned to our children, and to our effort for them, where it very likely always belonged. (As to this theological presumption, nothing could be clearer in the present direction and quality of American life.) But somehow the net result of Western Christianity, at least in its active Protestant phase, has been science and administrative rationality. If an abandonment of religion means giving up God, the afterlife, and sanctified dogma, well enough; but if it means giving up the human being, or (the same thing) giving him over to administrative rationality, then a loud "*No!*" must be entered on the record. The not-exactly-rational human being will not concur.

This assertion of the Existential Me is the beginning of a revival of religious feeling, of the amelioration and correction of our current unrecognized secular theologies, and of the long, hard effort to overcome the effect of science and to up-end its disastrous tyranny.

A valid triumph of rationality will be achieved when irrationality is no longer required by human beings. Not before. Science, I am sorry to say, takes a snobbish attitude toward human irrationality. (Even Freud, with his great scientific pretensions, was a bit of a snob in this way.) The proposition here is that the nineteenth century, with its great religious crisis, posed the problem acutely as it suffered the breakdown of the traditional order of the West. Although it was much anguished about the problem of the relation of religion and science, it did not in fact solve it—and perhaps it presumptively mis-solved it in a manner that still troubles us today: by elevating the dissociative conflict *above* any common image of the human.

Freud helped a great deal, but he was not able to save the nineteenth century from the burden of its breakdown. For one thing, he was too much of a scientist himself; for another, he was too strong and too isolated to conceive a truly modern man—he revived an ancient individualism, compounded of the stoicism of the Romans and what might be called classical Hebrew endurance. His snobbery came out as magnificent Jewish fatalism, which he thought was scientific because it was so necessary. Or take Marx, that other great pretender, who was so thorough in his scientific rationality that he ended up creating a newer, bigger, more idiotic religion than the one he thought he was overcoming. He joined science with the apocalyptic vision—with Prometheus, rather than with Freud's Job. But the emotional, the irrational, the religious in the human being has proved to be indispensable and ineradicable. It must be accepted in order to be dealt with. Scientifically? Perhaps: but not exclusively, and not in any event just yet.

There is more for modern man in D. H. Lawrence's courageous continuation of the spiritual destruction of the nineteenth century. The poetic method of Lawrence, his profound assertion of the existential me, may well be our root creative source for the twentieth century: Lawrence more than Freud gave us a remembrance of animal beauty. There is no question that his method is dangerous, much more so than Freud's (which is nerve-racking enough). But after all, the nineteenth century led to Nazism, with or without any help from Nietzsche and Lawrence: they simply saw it coming, and tried to confront it.

As Lawrence recognized, the problem of the relation of religion and science, and especially the lack in our present lives of what religion (perhaps also the absence of science) once gave us, is pertinently an issue of communication—of oversized and unrefined but emotionally effective symbols, as compared to the precise definitions which science and other rationality presume. One is even tempted, with Lawrence, to enter upon a murky speculation to the effect that there is something ultimate in human existence that requires ambivalent symbol rather than explicit consciousness: clarity, too, can lie. Whatever the difficulty, man cannot safely avoid himself and try to live by technique alone.

Science cannot serve as a "whole view"; but at any particular moment, a "whole view" is necessary. So it is supplied. It should not always be unconscious and remain *ad hoc*, an intellectual TV dinner. The critical intelligence has a very important role in this act of supply—and without the necessity of masquerading as science. The source of supply is called "culture," and it is superior to science.

Neither science nor religion, but rather this more human thing called culture, more broadly conceived than usual, is what we require to rely on. By "culture" I mean communal consciousness—with the immediate understanding, however, that consciousness is not just thinking; that it is certainly not any *one* way of thinking; that it is more a dependent result than an independent cause; and most important (with Freud) that, in whatever distorted form, it always does in fact express human condition and behavior. In this latter sense, the meaning perhaps rejoins the anthropologist's definition, which is tied to institutional patterns of behavior—to technique and ritual.

Culture is from the beginning and throughout involved with symbol, myth, fantasy and dream, and other expressions of human desire. So that when we look at the behavior of Americans in offices, for example, we look for the dreams on the wall and the fantasies stuffed in the lower-right desk drawer—we are not simply expert management consultants or time-study men. If the office has any function, we are concerned with that—but never just with that. Because a human being is never purely a functional animal: the mere suggestion is anathema; there cannot be a completely functional analysis of human behavior. The human being will not allow it; it is not in his nature to allow it.

Culture is all of what we are able to recall and use of the represented and imagined part of the human experience. It is man's big basket, bigger even than anything an American can carry away from a supermarket. It is all books, for instance, but it also exists in any one book—even a very bad one. It is unspeakably human. It is right There staring out at you from the television screen; it resides in the fascinatingly false prose of *Time* magazine and the New York *Times,* as well as the Chicago *Tribune;* its results are seen in the last office bull session, formal or otherwise; and its character is evident even in the way you explain your day to your wife. Culture in this sense is the source—*other than experience itself*—of all our means of awareness of ourselves, even in this over-organized, over-rational, over-implemented society in which the human being is at last satisfying himself materially, and experiencing a growing spiritual terror in the process.

9

Now it is very important that culture, this wonderful grab-bag, does not stand by itself: it rests on experience. Most nicely conceived, it is the balancing gyroscope of experience. But this culture of ours, the endless and even hilarious project of creating and criticizing consciousness, standing thus on the quicksand of experience, must "form" itself in terms either of religion or of politics—by way of a Holy Ghost or some other means of reordering and reentering experience. For its own coherence, culture cannot remain merely the receptacle of experience: it is not a storage closet. It requires as well a road back. There must be a Holy Ghost.

An image of the future, requiring an assumption of politics at least to maintain its formal validity, can serve for culture the role formerly played by religion. *A consequence of this formulation is that political thought must be big; and the political action, though small, must occur.** The alternative is not a cynical withdrawal from politics because it is "impossible"; the alternative is life-hatred—and, at last, a disastrous politics born of exactly this blackness and blindness.

So politics is formally necessary, because God is formally impossible. Most important, the use of the God mythology to sustain culture has not proven itself capable of maintaining a fluidly effective relation between culture and historical change. (T. S. Eliot "demonstrated" this while attempting to prove the opposite.) The Holy Ghost was too weak. Culture, all the way from a recent sense of oneself to the whole history of the human past, must retain a more creative relation to historical experience: there must be a secular reentry. This is the problem. This is the problem that is *not* solved by traditional religion. And science has dealt with the matter only in a piecemeal and clearly inadequate fashion.

Is all this obvious, even though impossibly abstract? I would hope so—I believe we all know it in our bones. The only thing "new" here is a cry for candor, the plea to admit that we lost too much when we lost religion, that we gained too little when we gained science. And while admitting this, to determine that we will not continue to mesmerize ourselves with the metronome of that conflict, but will require something more, namely, a full symbolic language for our emotion—"almost" a religion—which also allows us to be as rational as our instrumental science genuinely requires and our animal capacity genuinely allows. A religion without make-believe dogma, in other words. Nothing less will do.

As noted, the true underlying danger of Communism is that it identifies human consciousness—that is, continuing culture—with scientific method as applied to history. It would thus redefine the human being disastrously (and perhaps once and for all). The virtue of the West is that no matter how hard it has tried, it has not yet managed to accomplish this. The Communists, thinking to emphasize science, have actually perpetuated the worst aspects of the old

* This is the essential proposition in the argument of this book.

religion of the West. Christianity and Protestantism somehow eventuated in science and rationality—*especially* in Russia.

The ordinary idea that culture and politics, the high and the low, are properly separate is derived from the Christian presumption that action and idea are properly dissociated; and from classic capitalist notions that business and other similar "private" activity is not political. Here we notice just how science eventuates from Christianity—it is method abstractly dissociated from the flushed-out existence of human beings, and it accepts and even memorializes this dissociation. It presumes to be justified in this because of its successful relation to experience via experimental verification (as business is justified by successfully accumulating capital). But it still arrogates to itself an ideational "purity" it has in fact abandoned. Protestantism began the long trek back from pure dissociation with its creation of "business." Business and science have this in common, that they are both dissociated from the human context, but both have a compulsive relation back to actual experience of special kinds.

Now, however, we are due to go beyond business and I would think beyond science as well. The future as history beckons to the Christian as well as his heirs, for we are beginning to understand that dissociative rationality is probably the most dangerously irrational capacity of the species. And while the conversation about the eventualities of Christian culture continues, so does history. The meaning of an idea changes with or without effort; to be wrong, one need only stand still long enough. Devotion to a safely irrelevant religion or ideology can introduce a major element of dynamic irrationality into the finally resulting politics. When not this kind of disaster, *politics is a learning process*, which is a basic reason why it is so essential to the cultural endeavor. It is that particular assertive connection with historical experience whereby one's ideas about one's world come to have some true or at least more realistic connection with that world. In this sense, if you like, it is even scientific—an experiment leading to verification. But it is not scientific in prescribing the problems which may be suited to the method or otherwise domineering over the data. It is so only in the sense that through it we may exercise elements of rationality, and we may learn from experience.

But in politics so conceived, the emphasis shifts from the method of science to the "scientist" himself: it is man in history, whatever his method or lack of one, who is both the subject and the object of the "experiment." The scientist himself is the instrument, and no new microscope will uncover anything quite so important. Half of what one is purportedly rational *about,* is the emotion of the rationalistic observer; the other half is the even more irrational "order" in the outside world. How then to avoid myth through rigorous deduction? . . . All myths, indeed all stories which people tell themselves (like all dreams, as a matter of fact), are based on history. They are unconscionable elaborations of something that really happened: therefore important.

Thus we approach what it means to live in history; and this turns out to be not at all what traditional religion or triumphant science told us. Instead, we are beginning to learn what it means to hunger for and to try to create a proper ultimate form—a theology—for this inevitable living-in-history of ours.

SEVEN

Scientism—
The Stultifying
Style

1 If any one new god has been elevated to the vacant pedestal, it is the god of science. By overdenying the subject matter of religion, science ended up inheriting some of its worst qualities—authoritarian godliness, dogmatic prescription, and lately (with Herman Kahn and company) perhaps also a New Unreality concerning death in the guise of a post-nuclear afterlife.

This spiritual exaggeration of science, its method and manner, is called "scientism." It is the great cultural disease of our day. No other intellectual method, unaccountably neglected, will quickly make everybody intelligent; but the current virulence of this "scientific" view of Everything has already demonstrated its capacity to make otherwise intelligent people quite stupid.

How to characterize this scientism? It is the illegitimate appearance of science, science overextended and overasserted in its social role—a form of cultural imperialism. And it includes the stylistic presumption whereby one must be scientific in order to be right, proper, useful, or even (God help us) interesting.

The root cause of this prevalence of scientism is the social embarrassment—the downright body-shame—experienced by intellectuals as they now move out into society. This occurs simply because they are "only" intellectuals, and seem to have no independent class basis other than their airy intellectual status. This hastily gathered and tightly worn clothing is treasured once these trained people have moved out into society because, out there, their jobs depend not on their true culture but on their apparent intellectual posture. To term an inane remark, or an appropriate grunt of professionalism, "scientific," is to sprinkle modern holy water on the concurrent activity. Scientism has become the rhetoric of the timid intellectual jobholder.

Personally, I am a devout admirer of science and the achievements of scientists. Science is surely the core of the modern world; most of the social and cultural problems that concern us proceed from its successes. Modern science, through its application in technology, is perhaps the greatest achievement of the rational human mind to make itself evident as such to the mass of humanity. It has made non-priestly intellect respectable—widely valued, I would guess, for the first time. But in doing so it has more or less preempted the field, and has displaced and even dishonored intellect and sensibility which do not call themselves "scientific." It has, by its successes, become a conformist uniform for the intellectual—and at just the moment when, exactly because of its success, intellect other than the truly scientific is most urgently needed. An exasperating paradox which many of the atomic physicists feel quite deeply, I am sure: holding naïve notions of community, they "counted on" intelligence like their own operating in other areas.

We are concerned here not directly with the real thing, but with a popular image of science: with the ideology of science which is popular and even dominant among certain educated groups, including some lesser practicing scientists—but not merely "popular" in the sense that such-and-so is the way truck drivers characteristically misunderstand it. When this kind of image presumes to be a "total view," we are in the thick of the mess. And for many working intellectuals, it presumes to be exactly that.

Whatever else it is, science—popular or otherwise—is also a rhetoric. By rhetoric I mean *the way in which* one says something, whether or not it is otherwise true or useful, in order to convince the person to whom one says it. Science as rhetoric is based on authority quite as much as the priestly rhetoric of the past was. Since science at its best is both highly particularistic and thoroughly involved in an on-going tradition (the only successful practical permanent revolution, the truest tradition of the new), it requires very imaginative rhetorical aid to achieve its own purposes in the larger social context which is not so constituted. Paradoxically, the more successful it becomes, the less it is itself a valid rhetoric in its own terms, and the more it requires one that is so in other, broader terms. What happens instead is that it is undermined by the success of its own mannerisms. To be brief about it, this is a cultural disaster. It inhibits imagination just when and where it is most needed; and everybody, instead of doing his best at what he does best, ends up posing in some inappropriate "scientific" obscurity or other.

There are many possible rhetorics for us, and some of them are superior to that of science even at its best and at home with its own; moreover, this one tends quite willfully to curtail spontaneous thought and perception in favor of the idolatry of method. (It is also, incidentally, helping to destroy the language, the root resource.) Science is purportedly a development of the practical side of our traditional body-mind dualism: thus very Christian in its origin. It is premised on a severe compartmentalizing of the mind, between the facts or the truth or whatever it is you get when you properly apply scientific method, and our values or dreams or whatever it is that remains when you have not applied or cannot or will not apply scientific method: just as, in the past, it was required for salvation to think the Right Thoughts. The great heresy here is that scientific method has been identified as *thinking* itself, or even as a total human response, whereas in truth it is merely a rhetoric which requires for completion a discourse with actual controlled experience. The assumption of the true and good rhetoric of science is that any individual can "talk to experience" and therefore avoid the unpleasantness of persuading other persons: they will persuade themselves, also by "talking to experience." It is a rhetoric, then, that properly requires an *answer*.

But science is by the stretch of no one's imagination co-equal with good thinking. Giving it all that it is entitled to (either as a method of verification or as an accumulation of effective technique), it is still no more than all the technology we have, and the more or less well-mapped road to its reattainment. Science is not really entitled even to all of this credit, in the grand sweep of things, because technology must exist in a social context; it must be prepared for and assimilated institutionally and politically. The full effect of technology in the United States, for example, would never have been achieved without the "unscientific" creation of the social techniques represented by the corporation, the military, the academy—to mention only three. The total human activity of, say, building a bridge is not limited to the engineering-scientific knowledge now on hand; there is also the financing, the social maneuvering, the political decision as to where to build it, and to build that bridge rather than another one or something else, and the motivations of the persons actually building it under "scientific" direction, even including the supporting mythology of these motivations. (This may seem so obvious as to be silly, but I warn you that it is the obvious which is ignored in the wake of a successful rhetoric.) Moreover, our confidence and our capacity relating to the engineering aspects have had the effect of making us rhetorically imitative of the "scientific" part of the project when we come to all of the other parts. This monkey imitation of science in a large range of inappropriate areas of human life—*this frequent inappropriateness of science*—has escalated to the point of substantial idiocy.

So science represents the greatest triumph of the human intellect in history. But human intellect very obviously has not quite *fully* triumphed; thus one can hardly resist the suggestion that the current extreme exaggeration of scientific method beyond its utility is the concoction of partially triumphant intellectuals.

2

Perhaps the heart of the matter is *rationalism as the wrong rhetoric:* it simply is not and should not be considered all that persuasive. It may be that "we" are terribly rational; but that is not a proper occasion for ignoring the irrationality of the rest of the world. The definitional, decided-once-and-for-all-in-the-head kind of intellectual method is, I suggest, more truly irrational than any other. Rationality should always have the quality of appropriateness, and it should never become purely technical. There simply are *no* areas in human life to be dealt with solely by technique. Any intellectual method, indeed any thinking, is supposed to help one live, it is not supposed to be a substitute for the whole game. This substitution is an ugly personal indulgence to which intellectuals have always—even in the pre-scientific age—been exceptionally prone, and it half-accounts for their traditional isolation from the rest of mankind.

The beauty of science (deriving, it is true, from this propensity of intellectuals) is that it imagines a perfect community of truth, and then it demonstrates the potentiality of this extreme ideal. That is perfectly acceptable to any idealist, and it is acceptable to me. What is not acceptable is the usual assertion by a rigid idealist that his ideal way is the only way, and that the state of grace derived therefrom may be substituted for most other contingencies in life. Thus science—like other ideal endeavors—is extremely presumptuous morally. And then social scientists, imitating their betters and being caught up in awful contradictions thereby, have vulgarized the underlying idea of this ideal community. Scientific method is not a way of thinking; it is an ideal rhetoric of experience and a way of verifying a proposition, not of deciding in the first place whether a proposition is true or interesting or even worth pursuing. But the ignorance of this truth has proceeded to a far point where the adjective "scientific" has taken on a revolting and even exclusive identity with clear thought—indeed, with an undogmatic approach to anything. This is, all by itself, a new and awful dogma.

We have all been involved in conversations in which the issue was between something described as "scientific" and something that can only be described as simple perception. *How dare anyone!* Don't you see the corruption that has set in?

In the work of the physical sciences, the idea was set forth of the priority of controlled experience, beginning with simple acts and simple perceptions. This was so successful that it was greatly elaborated, which again increased its success. Upon reflection it was noted that a community of truth was created by allowing this priority to the kind of event which anyone could see for himself. *The community was constructed initially on no other new elements than this.* Naturally, certain aspects of procedure were noted which had this-or-that relation to proposed and possible experimentation. But all this came under the heading of clear thinking, with the special object of devising a clever or significant or convincing experiment. Apart from this end-in-view, no one was told how to think in any special new way (except for the sanguine injunction of Socrates not to believe anything for merely conventional reasons). But when applied to those areas where controlled experience can hardly be imagined, much less carried through, an ideal community of truth was subtly corrupted into a rhetorical community of monkey imitation; and in the absence of possible subsequent experimentation, *the prior thinking itself became defined as scientific or unscientific.**

Scientific method concentrates on soluble problems; and inappropriate scientism presumes to ignore any other kind. But since all problems "solve" themselves whether or not we help in the process, this kind of "scientific" attitude thus excepts any current help in dealing with insoluble problems. It is thus conservative, since it reinforces unexamined traditions. And all the while that it is not able to solve, even properly to state or properly to confront, these "other problems," it presumes out of some esoteric communication with a semi-divine priesthood of methodology to denigrate and despise any and all lowly efforts of others to do so. To the point where, in the hands of the positivistic epigones, what has not been subjected to the scientific rhetoric simply does not exist. How convenient for the established powers!

In the social sciences, statistics—and the IBM machine their cornucopia—have been assimilated to the rhetorical method of scientism, whereby the obvious does not exist until there is a statistical series to demonstrate it. Meanwhile, other thought and perception are inhibited and otherwise stand in disgrace waiting for the magical output of the IBM machine: and now the computer, the golden egghead-goose itself. And around on the other side, the convention provides that if enough statistical studies are referred to in footnotes, the body of a text may properly contain any dull or outlandish statement an author may have in his inventory. As an example, Professor Lipset in *Political Man,* pursuing his strenuous Marxist exodus (by means of an unspeakable number of graduate-student footnotes): "To Marx, social constraints did not fulfill socially necessary functions but rather supported class rule." What does he mean by "but rather"? Indeed, what or where is the important difference between social constraints and class rule, whether or not they fulfill socially necessary functions? And, as a matter of fact, Marx made it very clear that class rule itself fulfilled such functions. . . . The point is that sociology may be usefully entitled to vulgarize ideas in order to count things, but it is not entitled to nor is it useful to ele-

---

* The earlier rhetorical community of religious belief was corrupted similarly, and very likely by the same deep human weakness—the desire for fuller community at any price.

vate the process of counting things in this way to a level where it substitutes for ideas, and even causes a license to be issued for the exercise of *free-floating* vulgarity.

Sociology will make its greatest cultural advance, I am convinced, by studying the sociologist: subject and object are certainly primed. And then, further to relieve the tension, it may go forward and study some less notorious victims of scientism.

Of these, none is to be viewed more in awe than the economist, who has been kept in the business of being scientific by the great wealth of statistics he has been given to play around with. This is all well and good; it does not succeed, however, in making his efforts "scientific." Traditional economics is mostly an elaboration of the logic of scarcity; this logic weaves in and around the wealth of statistical series provided for the entertainment of economists, and obscures its increasing irrelevance in this setting of neat precision. For a more compelling example of learned unclarity of thought, one would have to go back to the medieval schoolmen. The statistics are useful, and so is the logic of scarcity. Neither is a science of economics; and even together they do not inevitably add up to good economic thought. Scarcity was never the single compelling factor in the complex of economic fact: it is now less and less so as each day passes. But in order to be scientific, in order to elevate the statistical windfall into a body of scientific knowledge, the beautiful and psychologically compelling logic of scarcity is retained against all reason, and retained in its original exclusivity.*

The abstract models of the traditional and neo-classical economists have resulted equally from a desire to imitate science and from the fact that these people were not seriously involved in policy-making (i.e., doing something with their knowledge). A great deal of the impetus toward abstract-model elaboration proceeded from the unfortunate circumstance that economists who should have been constructing and administering economic programs were not allowed to do so. They were subservient to the businessmen who did,

---

* One is identified as a heretic simply to attempt, however haltingly, to develop a logic of power or a logic of behavior more appropriate to the understanding of a technological society such as ours. The reason lawyers (yes, like myself) can make out somewhat in analyzing economic activity, and in other intellectual areas suffering from an excess of academic tradition, is that they have *not* been trained in the discipline and so have less to unlearn—and they *have* been trained always to consider the actual power relationships which are apt to occur in a business civilization.

and so were redundant—that is, priestly. They were allowed in the conference room at all only because of the professional mystique of scientism, and because to sustain that they were willing, sad to say, to make a private matter out of their values, their politics, their actual full comprehension of policy issues.

But this is not an unimportant role. As the kindly J. K. Galbraith says in *American Capitalism* (1956):

> Man cannot live without an economic theology—without some rationalization of the abstract and seemingly inchoate arrangements which provide him with his livelihood. For this purpose the competitive or classical model had many advantages.

(What a delightful understatement!)

3 To put this issue of emotion and style in a somewhat broader perspective, let us briefly back up and start over again: Western man has moved from the religious society to the economic society, and now is entering more fully into a political society. From God to property to power. The present dominance of science (and business) should be understood as a camouflaged way station on the road out of the economic society into the political one. If, in fact, we are moving from an economic society into a scientific one, then I say, with full confidence in the assertion, we are finished. A scientific society is not livable: it would be humanly incompetent. A society must be—all past ones were—built around an image of the human being: this image is the true interior burden of the complex of emotional form which has been called "religion." There is none in science. There is only a catalogue of the human being's knowledge of technique, including the technique for manipulating himself.

The ideological or emotional part of science proceeded from a deep reaction against the intellectual backwardness of historical religion. That was surely, then, the fault of religion; but just as surely, now, that is no longer the point.

The economic society was organized around property and money. Ours is centered around power and consumption. That's a big change. The proper way of dealing with a society changed as ours has been is political, e.g.: How are the power and the consumables to be distributed, and for what purposes? In this, science achieves nothing more than tinsel rhetoric when it presumes to be anything more than technique. And under press of this technical emphasis, we come in a society like ours to the absurdity of absurdities—American advertising culture in which product-use is assimilated to religious devotion. Savor, if you will, the infinite silliness of being "saved" by a deodorant or a hair cream!

Worse yet, scientism has in fact been grafted onto the pre-existing methods of academicism (or it has grown fat ingesting these). Academicism, like scientism, *is a compulsive substitute for a traditional cultural order;* or, the desperately willed preservation of the putative community of rationality at all costs. I agree that a comprehensive cultural order is a necessity; the human being will always achieve one of some kind, if only in the head: and if he has only one idea, why then he will make that one serve all his purposes. The notion that he doesn't need comprehensiveness, or that intellect is irrelevant to the creation of it, or that it is an impossible task in the first place, is nonsense—an abdication on the part of intellect to the established social reality. But with academicism/scientism we have, once again, a willed and artificial community: the ideal is right, but that particular high road to it leads to a stinking Eskimo village—the fancy part of New York City lies in the other direction.

Primary thought is speculative, is not exclusively rational, is not primarily scientific. In the absence of a dedication to the human part of us, science is a waste of time even as mere thought. As an example of waste, of how the "non-scientific" part of life must be "rediscovered" and then invited to sneak its way back to assertion through the interstices of the dogma, notice the current use by the scientific community of the horrible term "feedback." This represents a rediscovery of self-consciousness as a part of intellectual method. But notice that this puerile self-consciousness was allowed to enter the scientific intellectual community only on the analogy of the computer. Moreover, its users presume to have *discovered* something by inventing this awkward use of the word.

We have here more than merely a question of the conflict between an application of scientific method as against a statement and an urging of one's values (although the term appearing out of this ethos —"value-judgment"—is a dreary, dispiriting one). It is more profoundly a question of one's reasonable expectation of rationality itself. Rationality is not the big red tomato some have thought it to be.

This is one of the ancient insights of religious thought to which we must return. When religion was dominant in the minds of men, it happened that technique was very primitively developed. Then something else happened in Europe whereby this great capacity of humanity was unleashed. That is all well and good. But the pendulum swung too far, and rather than having once and for all overcome the religious-dogmatic frame of mind, mankind unconsciously thrust the same basic forms upon the deceived mind which resulted from the enlarged technique. Having assumed, in the course of the nineteenth century reaction, that since we had science we did not need or could not countenance religion, we allowed science itself to become religious—and, because it was unconscious, in the worst way.*

Given the dominance of the overriding political requirement, and the necessary irrationality of politics—*it being action as a substitute for education*—one begins solidly to approach the limitation on the uses of rationality, and therefore of pure methods of arriving at the truth. For instance, politics without lying is impossible (which horrendous statement will be elaborated in the next chapter): Are we then to have a "science" of the right lie to tell, or how to tell it? If we are going to lie, then surely we must rely on our full, innate, animal deviousness rather than merely on the "right" technique.

---

* The same order of mistake, incidentally, was repeated in American governmental history: it was thought that if we did not have a national central government, we would escape having any concentrated power at all; instead, by denying ourselves a legal federal government, we created private constituencies of power not graced by legality—or even by national interest. In line with this indigenous illegality of ours—this nearly continental tropism—the modern American has concerned himself more with validity than with authority. The latter proceeds from outside demands, while the former involves inner turmoil. One requires incessant questioning; the other exists by virtue of the absence of any questioning. If we had chosen one rather than the other for our aptitude in carrying it on, we probably would have stayed with authority, but that was not the way the wheel turned. There was not enough of it on this continent. And now we are left with unending inner validation, a kind of permanent revolution of the psyche, until the shallows of our society are filled in with the accretions of these endless efforts. Perhaps this validating need is the source of our excessive affection for science (as it most certainly is the source of the reception afforded Freud and his followers in this country).

4 A secular theology—encompassing the general content while excluding the specific form of divine theology—will be created both by and for the New Class. Hopefully, the culture of this dominant formation will contain the capacity to criticize such theologies as may be created or may be found to exist. This does not now exist; and it will not, until science is properly "placed" and scientism overcome.

Mostly I have been trying to reserve a fuller discussion of this phenomenon of the New Class for a later chapter; but this commitment has been difficult to live up to. For one thing, the New Class is the creature of organization, which is power, and will be the class that must master it for humanity's benefit, if any group can; so it is hardly irrelevant to any aspect of our subject. Moreover, its emotionality and style are, at this special historical moment, even more significant than its potential dominance of our social order some maybe-future day.

To be brief*: the New Class is propertyless and educated—its training substitutes for property as it inhabits the good positions and pursues the better ones in the organizational jungle of an a-borning world. It is coming on strong, but it has not yet arrived: the class that will rule the new world is *here* no more than, but just about as much as, that world itself. When both fully arrive, we will all know it. It will not have to be advertised on television (although it undoubtedly will be).

Meanwhile, we confront the educated class in an organized society which knows little of the proper relation between expertise and generalism. The generalist must often today be a make-believe expert, even a charismatic fraud, in order to function at all. This problem results in good part from the dominance of the ideology of scientism among the members of the New Class.

The raging epidemic of scientism among the general members of the New Class (more so in Russia, presumably, but also here: in government, the academy, the corporate order) is a threat to the real scientists as well as to the rest of us. We now have the scientific

* See Chapter Eleven for more detailed treatment.

uniform as a rationalization for jobs, for academicism, for lack of imagination, for dull conformism, for one spiritual rascality after another. Well, the real scientists—as well as the rest of us able to face up—have a social responsibility to speak out against this process. To do so, they require a humanist cultural platform.

People of my persuasion are not against science, scientists are not against a humanist culture; where does this so-called "two cultures" issue come from? Wherever it comes from (and whatever it really is: I suggest that Mr. Snow didn't know), it nags us. It is here because of the monumental failure of traditional religion—and all that stood for; and the just as monumental success of modern science—and all that threatens to stand for. This peculiar conjunction has simply unbalanced the human race. The redress requires emotional/rational daring, existential passion—and a much less sanguine view of science. Its successes could destroy us, and I mean in many more subtle ways than the use of The Bomb.

The matter is urgent, for now the intellectual has finally entered upon the historical stage as a technician-participant rather than as a mere priest: as a doer instead of as an attendant to ritual. In order not to turn doing into ritual, the intellectual must become aware of this profound change in his position of power. As he characteristically thinks grand thoughts, and indulges the free inner movement of his mind, the intellectual develops a very nice sense of himself as an extremely rational and even interesting fellow, very capable and charming—if only people would listen to him. In fact, however, he is tradition-bound, and by nature hell-bent for ritual. He yearns deeply for a traditional order of meaning, and if none acceptable is around, he will invent one. Freedom of the mind is a very terrifying phenomenon. The metaphysical explorers are equally heroic with the great navigators, the builders of industry, and all the other daringly expansive types ensconced in textbooks: and all these great captains of this-and-that have had their battalions of boobs, too.

Academicism, for instance: it is not the minor matter of irrelevant priestliness that it once was. Because the academies are now in charge of training the new elites of our society. (Indeed, *all* of the older intellectuals will finally be drafted to teach the New Class.) Important future battles will be fought on the campuses and in the bureaus—cultural and political battles of the first importance. Whereas the earlier businessman, the property-holder, was very difficult to talk to because he began with a deep conviction as to the irrelevance of the culture of the intellect, the current academic and his spawn, the administrative intellectual, is extremely difficult to talk to just because he has been led to believe that he has mastered this despised culture—that it is his personal bailiwick. Most important, he lacks awareness of how his own patterns of thought are determined by his institutional relations and commitments: he too often fails to comprehend his sources or his circumstance, the effects of his given social position.

Especially in the area of human behavior, the academic separation of disciplines is currently achieving a rampaging order of high nonsense. One should begin with a problem, not a discipline: the latter is merely a crude pedantic method. It is proper that some intellectual workers, perhaps most, should busy themselves with small areas of detail. Since it is necessary work, they ought to be honored for doing it: they are not, however, to be denominated ruling high priests for this effort. If their work is valuable, it is such because it provides material for reflective synthesis by other *non*-experts. The chairman of the department of English should not be the expert in Shakespearean commas: he should be the man who is creatively capable of using the work of all the experts, all the way from Shakespearean commas to Lawrencean images. Otherwise, the intellectual endeavor is stood on its head. We are now standing on our heads.*

Previously, mind entered history mostly in the care of a priestly class. With the superabundant success of the physical sciences, the independent power of the human mind is now involved in history as a mutatively new factor. But the physical scientist is followed by a host of imitators and administrators, all suitably "educated." We will be spending a great deal of history from here on in shaping and being shaped by this New Class.

To distinguish them from historically less significant types, we may call them "administrative" intellectuals. They believe that ideas are to be used directly to get and hold jobs, to arrange people and things, to accomplish bureaucratic actions. In other words, the first thing you do with an idea is to make a program out of it and get financing. I don't mean to compliment them so much as to suggest that they are always practical and efficient. But their ballets express

* Also, unlike the lawyers and doctors, many of the current educated professionals do not seem to be aware at all of the extent to which they operate by means of *professional mystique*. Thus it operates on them as well as on the "client" (which makes for a dangerous priest).

these values even when, as job-holders dancing around the office, they are not accomplishing anything much. I am sure there is such a thing as "creative administration," and we may hope to see much more of it in the near future; but mostly their work is not that, but the administration of creativity (or at least work and vitality). Let me give an example, one that recurs frequently, I believe, as a basic pattern of power in our administered society:

In a university (which, being the chrysalis, may well become the unconscious model of many new bureaus), the important administrative positions do not go to the most accomplished, or even necessarily to the most representative members of the faculty. They don't want them. Administration is not so interesting to such people as their own research and other creative work. Administration would very likely be interesting, however, to people who begin with a taste for it, or who develop such a taste after playing around (unsuccessfully or without enough motivation) with regular university work. And the faculty, having finessed administrative responsiblility when such people appear, can then pursue its own interests. There is an added advantage to this standard system, based on the apathy of the New Class: namely, the faculty remains pure and above it all and can gripe to its heart's content about "power-hungry" fools who do not understand the first thing about what a university *really* is. The principle underlying this pattern is quite extensive: the fanatic troglodytes who have dominated the bureaucratic machinery of the American Medical Association, for example, do not represent the views or sentiments of many of the doctors in this country (perhaps most). They do not even have their respect. But those who do have it are much too busy practicing medicine, which thoroughly engages their attention. They don't have time for the annoying details of "politics." Leon Trotsky, as another example, was much too busy making the speeches he made so brilliantly, and leading the Red Army he led so well, to be bothered diverting his attention from these major concerns to the low, dull infighting that Stalin so enjoyed. Besides, in that worthless arena, he would have been outclassed.

Now that there are so many intellectuals and so many jobs for them, there are also many more routes of escape for the serious ones. What difference does the AMA and its clientele of buck-hungry suburban practitioners (dredged up from the petty bourgeoisie by reason of a back-breaking peonage called "medical training") make to bright young doctors who are going into well-financed research anyway? If you are good, there are lots of jobs—and soon everybody, without exception, can get a job teaching. I know a computer programmer who could not bear any longer to continue to work for the RAND Corporation—he couldn't stand the insane over-kill discussions at lunchtime—so he went to work for the Department of Health, Education, and Welfare. A great number of people who are well trained can "choose out" of the military-industrial complex, even that monster. Then they go into a non-military corporate, governmental, or foundation bureau, or they teach. That's about the size of it. Meanwhile, they are developing disgruntled ideologies to account for their upgraded, increasingly comfortable powerlessness.

But whatever they do, they are the audience and the actors—the great new ones of our time. We should not be confused because the upper classes, who should have been cultured enough to rule this country somewhat better (and somewhat before now), are lately attempting to take their opportunities and their culture more seriously, as history ironically accrues their irrelevance. They may very well provide a distinguished leavening, nonetheless welcome though so late in coming. But they are an old class, and mostly used now for ceremonial purposes. The profounder power lies elsewhere. Just as the traditional images of man we have developed over the ages must now be altered because men live so much longer, so our entire traditional culture must be readapted to the uses and purposes of the New Class, the educated masses now active in history. If this effort to educate the putatively educated is not undertaken with great seriousness, these new people are perfectly capable of destroying our inherited culture—the *real* culture—for which countless great spirits have undertaken infinite lifetime chores throughout recorded history.

Clearly it is not enough to feel superior to them (whoever you may be or think yourself to be). They must be truly educated—into a kind of consciousness whereby their living can be better comprehended, criticized, and realized. Into *culture,* that is; not just jobs.

I think it might be appropriate at this moment to apologize for—but certainly not to retract—the preceding diatribe. The stultifying style of scientism now dominates the New Class, and right-thinking literary persons like myself (who are convinced of the importance of this new formation) can do no less than mobilize their available ruthlessness to undermine the vile style on all possible occasions.

But enough: even justified venom must finally uncover its own marginal utility.

While suffering from a moderately contrite mood, I might as well also apologize for—or at least compliment the hardy reader on persevering through—the calculated morass of emotional speculation in which we have been involved ever since we moved beyond the more sanguine subject of President Johnson's political magic. The compelling reason for which I embarked us on an investigation of the underlying stuff is the very simple one that it is there; and as to it, the President's magic only reaches to exploit, does not comprehend in the large, and cannot adequately ennoble. He may, genius-like, bring us up to date; he cannot be expected as well to save us from the necessity of politics in the future. This future politics of ours—and I am very clear on this point—will more and more involve the underlying emotionality.

The third (and final) apology: We are not yet finished with this effort. Since I am a suggestive rather than an authoritative commentator, I am going to attempt, in the next peculiar chapter, to convince the American liberal—maybe even the whole book-buying sector of the New Class—that (suggestively rather than authoritatively, of course) we ought to get closer to political lying. I don't mean spend all day at it: but cozy-up a little. This unauthoritative suggestion is so awful, all things considered, that I had best introduce it by presenting an intellectual *mea culpa*.

So what follows is something like a few pages of my personal philosophy.

5 Man is an irrational animal— the only one. Other animals make mistakes, or fail to adapt, and the lemmings of course are crazy; but man is the only one who, knowing better, imagines the world differently from what it is (and can do so for purely personal reasons). He can live in two worlds, swiftly back and forth, at the same time. His capacity for this eccentric *two-mindedness* is phenomenal.

—Which reminds me that I was never a very good student of Aristotle because, after dutifully accepting his infamous proposition that man is a rational animal and later squirming to get out of that box, I was thereafter never able to trust him as a student must trust a teacher. He held me for a while with the thunderous Man-is-mortal; but then I was told by a graduate student that this was only part of the illustration as to how a syllogism worked—disappointment was added to suspicion, and I never recovered my early enthusiasm for mankind's greatest mind.

I grant that if man were not capable of rationality, the significance that may lie in terming him "irrational" would be reduced substantially. Still, I remain more impressed with the one than with the other. I am most impressed of all with the least-remarked term in these several propositions, namely, that man is an animal. Did you "discover" this fact in college, as I did? Isn't that fabulous? Moreover, having "discovered" it—and establishing it once and for all to my full and complete and even scientific satisfaction—it turned out that it was a very interesting and useful fact. Often I would entertain and instruct myself by remembering this fact I had learned in school and applying it to unusual circumstances outside the classroom, as, for instance, in my home, on the street, at social gatherings, etc. Very instructive—but then I was excessively intellectual as a young man, much prone to abstract philosophizing.

Back to the jungle? We would never find our way—all the maps are out of date. At which point in the discussion many people say, Well, to hell with it. And after a while, they begin to enjoy the footlight variety of acting the non-animal part; certain tense types even begin to find the game desperately necessary—belches are finally outlawed, ties and belts are invented to sever the body from the darling de-animalized head at two crucial junctions, and the objective correlative of laundry starch at last appears to seal our fate. What began as lack of direction ends as a rigid passion.

Even thus demonstrating his irrationality, man remains an animal. He is an animal, but not just an animal; he is a conscious-social animal—barred from the jungle, and doomed to a not-exactly-jungle irrationality which is nicely brought into focus for him periodically by the strenuous exercise of his rational (non-jungle) capacity. Moreover, man's dubious condition does not allow for much standing still: either backward or forward, but movement nevertheless, is his animal fate. Lacking earnestness, or suffering too much despair as a result of his conscious-social nature, man becomes a dangerously half-civilized animal who, with Olympian ambivalence, tries to race back to the lost jungle via rationally organized operations like Auschwitz. To "live like an animal" means to live without the intervention of consciousness between perception and action; to live (again, like an animal) "close to nature," implies sufficient projective landscape to dispense with consciousness: really, to trade it in for revery. But the phrase "live like an animal" no longer implies a cleansing closeness to Nature—it means to live low and evil, and only that. Interesting how these meanings change: in the heyday of rational revolution, natural law, mechanical science, and Deism, the meaning was quite otherwise. But the Noble Savage is now a reservation drunk.

The highest level of pure and true and complete rationality about social affairs is that of our recent nuclear warriors. Herman Kahn certainly would have been incapable even of considering the application of his considerable intellect to Hitler's evil concerns: he is not a German. He is an American, and our basic rational problem, requiring the devotion of our greatest talents, is how many people and livable square miles will survive in merchantable condition this, that, and the other kind of nuclear experiment. To the solution of which the best of our rationalists are devoted. And if, as at the time of the Cuba confrontation, rationality throughout the world may be temporarily in short supply, why then one of these rationality practitioners will—quickly to make up the then-observed deficit—write a letter, for instance, to the New York *Times* announcing to the intensely assembled universe the necessity of conceiving the situation rationally, that is, as the Hudson Institute did before it occurred.*

No, we have to think. *Toujours penser.* But, after much of that, to hell with the absurdly elevated status of the noble rationality of mere ideals. The human animal is sufficiently in touch with useful ideals of rich variety when he is just in touch with his own undistorted animal nature. And if he has not the latter, no amount of the former can save him or much serve his neglected humanity. To be human is to remain animal. To be animal, in society, is to aspire to the human. That is the conjunction that avoids both the stale Authority of God and the new Devil's work at Auschwitz. None other will.

Let's state it as a formal abstraction: There is the context in which a thing is observed, and there is the observer. Religious and other sincerely primitive thought fails most often by loss of context; the new administrative or scientific thought regularly collapses by oversight of the observer, whom it mostly ignores. So it must be an extremely delicate trail that leads to an appropriate use of any par-

* *This happened,* God help us.

ticular abstraction. But the forced idea that more and more, and then even *more*, rationality will turn the delicate trick is so willed a distortion that it is not even rational. I cannot accomplish everything I desire: I am not omnipotent; I cannot be satisfactorily moral in every situation (if that includes *doing*); and I also have limited choice as to the exercise of my rationality. All depend on a community and its gestures—that is, something more than me.

How can anyone insist over and over again that he is "rational" simply by virtue of not making *some* of the obvious mistakes that masses of his brethren persist in making, generation after generation? That is a mis-definition of the problem in order to be superior to it: like two dead birds with the same un-animal stone. It is, besides, merely a prescriptive assertion—that is, we would all be better off if everybody were rational—and that's all it is. (There would also be less nighttime crime if everybody went to bed after the eleven P.M. newscast.)

Is the irrelevance of ideas treasured for its own sake? Or is there some devious but decisive connection between the current situation and the specific bit of cultural debris that survives? I think the latter; if you like, this is my personal myth. I have an example, however, that warms me: Law was, before science, the great rationalistic presumption. Now the better lawyers, while still operating the gears and pistons of their symbol-machine, know better. The moralists will say, *Phooey!* I say it is a great advance. Any new lie, as well as any new truth, may be an advance.

6 In all this emotional discussion of the emotionality of politics, I am relying most heavily on George Herbert Mead's work. Mead, the "lost" co-worker of John Dewey, devised a naturalistic epistemological theory which presumed to resolve the classical body-mind problem. He put the farthest reaches of the human mind and imagination *in* history and *in* society. To accomplish this, he defined mind as *social* rather than individual. (His sources were catholic, not to say pagan—as disparate as Watson's behaviorism and Berkeley's subjectivism.)

Mead presumed to solve the perennial body-mind dualism problem by finding a source of consciousness in natural and obvious animal activity. This was the exchange of gestures between two animals each capable of making the gestures exchanged, therefore of "understanding" them—that is, each animal being capable of seeing himself as the other doing what he himself might do. In this context, he defined meaning: Meaning, he said, was based on comprehended gestures— *and a gesture is a part of an act, not the whole act.* We communicate with parts of acts: consciousness consists of the reflection of parts of acts, ours-and-others. Therefore, the most distinctive factor about human animals—ultimate consciousness—is derived from acts, which is not a distinctive factor: the difference between a stone and an animal is that an animal acts; we are thus no longer embarrassed, analytically, by the differences between stones and amoebae and poetry. Everything about man can be included in one world, and the second (ideal) one is no longer necessary to *explain* anything about us—although it may remain appositionally necessary for the purpose of bearable living in an un-ideal world.*

But with meaning explained in this naturalistic and animal way, one is stuck with nature thereafter in dealing with and evaluating this and that "meaning." And if meaning is shared gesture, then *any* shared gesture is meaningful among any who share it. Also, it must be respected as such—until invidious "moral" distinctions between gesturing animals are established and enforced (which is apt to be both difficult and ugly). So meaning and consciousness and mind are social. And therefore my mind is not exactly mine, in the complete animal sense of me. A certain part of the animal-me has been given over to consciousness, which is social and which is never fully me. This "mind" we are talking about requires an animal like me to make it exist; but it uses me, as I try desperately to use it (for my own animal diagonal human purposes). This relation is always— whatever else it may be—an uneasy coalition, never a secure and final marriage.

If meaning, the fundament of consciousness and of mind, is social, then so is truth—a merely occasional quality of meaning. (We can join, even consciously, in efforts to mean untruths, as everybody knows.) So "truth" is a social definition, a given. Thus defined, it obviously is not true—especially to non-traditional moderns. This is the next problem Mead dealt with.

And here was his most fruitful brilliance. He said that truth was not just truth, it was shared truth; or, there had to be two truths

---

* I am personally convinced both of the validity of the explanation and of the fact that it was a major intellectual event, sublimely neglected.

from the point of view of any one observer, the shared truth and the real truth. And with this understanding, he defined the basic categories of "objective" and "subjective." Men do not live in a real world to be defined by a discovery of truth: they live in a world of social reality, because their very minds are social, and this world presents itself in a naturally mis-defined form. It is not less important—not less meaningful—thereby. Meaning and truth are not the same thing: a falsehood is not, then and thereby, meaningless. Mead does not for one moment suggest that the real truth is useless, or not worth suffering and struggling for; he says it has use and worth as some animal gives it such (an existentialist point), and this use and worth extends itself as that animal convinces other animals, by appropriate gestures, that it is what he says it is and not what the previous social reality said it was. So truth has two qualities, or else it is not "true": to be true a statement must be true and accepted by others as true. (Practically, it must be truer than other similar statements and recognized as such by others.*)

On the other hand, the ordinary subjective statement can be less true than the accepted (objective) truth of the social reality. This is not likely, but it can happen. And besides, insanity, in a sense, is always truer than sanity—but anyone who values sanity doesn't give a damn about the truth of that situation. Anyway, with Mead, truth is not so all-important as it once was: it is no longer the golden fleece. It is as important as the accompanying capacity to overcome impulses to untruth which it confronts in the maelstrom of animal gestures which is its natural and inevitable habitat, *amen*.

The fact that complete truth is not individual, but is social—as are mind and consciousness—does not make the individual less important; it merely makes his importance more difficult to establish among others (which we all knew anyway).

Everything human exists in community: elsewhere, it is merely potential. That we are so little human, and so much potentially so, is painful, even tragic; but there it is.

If I may rush quickly to the conclusion (as promised): The point for intellectual method is that one begins more-than-indulgent thought and investigation with the given situation in front of one,

---

* Note that the distinctive point about the highest order of scientific truth is not that it is unshared, but that it is shared among a specially qualified and limited elite: as such, the objective status and the subjective status are beautifully merged.

*including the crazy and mistaken ideal/ideological factors em-
bedded in the social reality* in which all human beings live, and do
their thinking. These elements of the social reality, no matter how
absurd, are "objective." Their spurious objectivity is corrected (indeed, it is discovered or known) only by *my* more genuine subjectivity. In this sense, all intellectual method is social and cultural criticism. Notice also that this leads to a major revision of rhetorical
method, in that the expression of one's fresh perception of reality
must confront the accepted views of the society; otherwise, it is
"selfish" or elitist. A very effective example of the application of
this rhetoric/morality was Galbraith's *The Affluent Society*, wherein
the entire dialectic was a dramatic interplay between what he
called the received wisdom and what he thought to be the obvious
facts of the matter. Appropriately, this was accomplished without
much direct assistance from IBM machines.

It is also implicit in Mead that both action and language are structured around the same rhetoric or—the same thing—gesturing style.
For him, the two are no longer so bleakly separate as they once
were: this would be a necessary consequence of the theoretical resolution of the body-mind dualism. The more we live in consciousness,
then the more it is true that pieces of acts dominate, and the less are
we to be saved by *full* acts. The relation between action and knowledge is thus "resolved" by philosophical and historical redefinition.
As true action becomes rare and even impossible (animal violence
being outlawed, for instance), and knowledge, the reflective thing,
becomes vaguer despite precision (lacking full action as proof), the
distinction dissolves. Knowledge is action, action is knowledge—and
everything beyond event tends to be a symbol: many action/events
are nothing but symbols.

Once conscious of this logic of the relation of the subjective to the
objective, the road forward becomes somewhat more discernible.
Truth is a social convention—whether or not it is truly "truth." We
learn a great deal from science if we learn to respect the facts as
much as the best scientists do in their process of sharingly defining
truth; but that is very different from a monkey imitation of the rational mechanics of the machine, or men acting like machines,
which characterizes scientism. Machines, if they are any good, are
"just" rational; men, however, with the animal source of their social
minds, have other capacities.

EIGHT

An Essay in Defense of Lying by a Compulsive Truth-Teller

1 A persuasive reason people have found for lying to themselves, and then learning to accept the lies of others, has been their fear of death and the other ambiguities touched upon in the immediately preceding chapters. Now to conclude our quick investigation of the perplexing complex of emotions underlying politics, we enter upon another distasteful subject—because of a simple but devastating proposition that cannot be side-stepped: Politics is inconceivable when not accompanied by the activity of lying. The two are not the same; but they *are* inseparable.

Politics conceived as the fervent pursuit of the truth by means of the truth, is . . . well, whatever it is, it obviously is not politics. One could maintain, of course, that this pursuit, etc., should displace politics as the proper activity for superior human beings. Here and there, certainly; but this could not possibly hold, as a general prescription. We have by now (I hope) fastened with finality around our necks the albatross-proposition that politics is necessary, not only to improve life but to sustain culture. All truth-tellers should now feel themselves to be tightly boxed in:

Politics is necessary.

Politics is impossible without lying.

This being such a weird subject, some personal credentials may be in order. I am a compulsive truth-teller, and find lying to be a tremendous effort: if I were rich, I would hire someone to do it for me—and before I would hire a valet or a cook. It has been all I could manage, in the course of my uneven existence, to unravel enough of the fabrications of my lady friends and business associates to keep my head above water—often months and years after I had drowned without even recognizing the event. Luckily, I was trained as a lawyer by a man of deep suspicions, carefully ordered and expressed; his gestures were gross and obvious enough even to me (thus, an excellent teacher), and so I was able to imitate him almost at the level of a child learning to walk. If not for this great good fortune, I don't think I could ever have made a living in the law, which can be described in part as the art of speculative and preventive deception. (In drafting an agreement, one strains to imagine the thinking of the other thief who will sign it, and then wraps him tightly in a precautionary verbal package—while the attorney on the other side, of course, is going through the same mental and literary processes.)

On the other hand, in the course of psychoanalyzing myself endlessly, the wistful conclusion has been forced upon me that I am one awful liar. It must be that I helplessly tell so many out-of-place truths in expiation for one or two whopping lies that I absolutely cannot do without. If I speculate on what these might be (don't be frightened, I am certainly not going to reveal them here in my own book), the general area of investigation is clear enough and can be safely mentioned: My big lies, for the preservation of which I have sold myself to the devil of occasional truth, concern the several intimately personal failings and frustrations I can never hope to overcome: as to these, I am doomed to make believe forever.

The foregoing implies that I could expect to become an ever more comprehensive liar with age, as my failings and frustrations accumulate. I find it very interesting that the opposite is the fact. As I grow older, I become so accustomed to my basic lies that (on choice occasions) I can playfully admit them to myself—which, of course, transforms them into truths. We will now loosely investigate this paradox. The key can be revealed ahead of time—and without loss of dramatic interest, since I haven't the foggiest idea of where the lock is. The key, for what little it is worth, is that the difference between public and private truth is nearly absolute. So the alteration between age and youth ends up merely as an increased willingness to accept the difference. I think that is a reasonable statement. As I remember my youth, I accepted the difference hardly at all. Then my youthful energy gave out, and I accepted it—once, twice, a hundred times. But beware: I may (anyone may) at any moment feel another surge, and that might well be the end of yet one more Public Truth.

2 To the private individual, all public truths are lies—unless they are his own. And then? Well, *then*, they are at least a different kind of lie.

The self intervenes between private truth and public lie. Indeed, the self nearly exists for purposes of handling this ambiguity. I may possibly survive in a world populated by strangers, without moment-by-moment control over my own death; but if my discretion to choose between truth and falsehood is denied, I am immediately done and finished with. No human being can make it from Here to There without a minimum amount of this power. Humanity has not achieved that level of togetherness; or our advanced section of it has lost it. I may travel the city and get through the day without the capacity for effective violence, but if I cannot lie to myself at will, the chances of getting to sleep tonight—or getting up tomorrow morning to face another such day—are slight. To do all of these things I need an ego. An ego is merely necessary; it is not thereby true. Indeed, an ego is so obviously and completely necessary that I cannot see how it could possibly be true as well. According to legend, Christ's ego was true. Which is why He died the way He did; why no one has managed to live His life again; why no one can or will—and that is the prototype of Western ideality, which derives from this deficiency of perfection.

How can any ego be true for anyone other than its possessor? It can, even viewed from the outside, be effective, secure, justified in the circumstances, enviable, perhaps admirable, etc.—but *true*?

Stated this way, the point may be too murky to grasp. To restate it, let's assume that an ego is neither true nor false; but clearly it will consist of or be involved with ideas, images, perceptions, beliefs, suppositions, etc., which can and ought to be denominated as true or false. And let's further, for the moment, bypass the insoluble problem of truly knowing the truth concerning all of the relevant matters, and instead define truth by reference to sincerity, that is, truth as my best idea of truth. Go even farther into the recesses of the problem and assume that I have been as thoroughly psychoanalyzed as anyone can be, and that my sincerity, consequently, is dearly purchased day-by-day: I am aware of aspects of my personal history far beyond the ordinary, and also am more than ordinarily aware of the immense complexity of the continuing invasion of my present by my past. So, in relation to myself, I am a really exceptionally hot tomato when it comes to truth (or, more reasonably, an avoidance of avoidable falsehood). My point is that I would, then and thereby, become inevitably an unconscionable liar in relation to everyone else.

"The insane do not lie," a psychoanalyst tells us.* Then how do they manage? Ah, but of course—they *don't*. The writer certainly intended to say that the insane do not lie to others; being insane, the question of whether they lie to themselves is a lost issue. They do and they don't: they do, but they do not any longer have the capacity not to, so maybe therefore they don't. Anyway, they do not lie to others—and that is a personal progress terrible enough to contemplate.

Having no vital present but only an uncontrollable past, they have also lost the need as well as the capacity to lie.

The uninhibited pursuit of truth is the road to madness: you can never achieve enough of it for yourself, and you can easily achieve too much of it for others. So the First Lie—designed to save yourself while sparing others—has to do with the prudent adjustment, called "ego," between the conscious and the unconscious mind of the individual. And all other lies, it is suggested, are derived from, at least in being excused by, this one.

To tie down this unfortunately but inevitably obscure point, let us for a paragraph compare the compulsive truth-teller with the clinically more established compulsive liar.† The reason a person tells the truth, uncomfortably and against his will, is that he suffers from the delusion that, having confessed Everything, it is then up to the Other to tell him what to do. We may call this the Ancient Mariner syndrome. The compulsive liar, on the other hand, is an inverted Ancient Mariner: he represents the manic stage of the disease. Like so many emotional problems, this one also is contracted in childhood—

* Philip Q. Roche, in *The Criminal Mind*.
† The compulsive truth-teller is not so well established clinically because the going morality forbids anything of the kind. Being one, however, I would very much like to get established clinically: as things stand now, I can secure neither sympathy nor other medicine for my affliction.

where the truth can come to be defined as the one final way of beseeching salvation of one's parents (or of God, if they are not listening or you have meanwhile become an adult), usually because of their insincere invitation, whereby a weapon is put in the hands of the child which is too powerful to be either used or denied.

We noted in a recent chapter that truth is like morality, being a very stupid game—after the mere love in it is exhausted—unless both play it. Indeed, truth is merely one gambit of morality, and subject therefore to all of the applicable rules and considerations. Most pointedly, it is not to be overdone, for the reason that it readily tends to become a substitute world of its own, like the more familiar one of high moral righteousness. One's own truth is then seen more and more frequently in opposition to "that mess out there." But the mess is never really and only "out there." Also, this kind of relation between subject and object leads to a unilinear logic, whereas the more creative relation between truth and falsehood is dialectical. The quickest way to expose a lie is to assume it to be true; the simplest way to pervert the truth is to embrace it rigidly—in effect, to lie about its exclusivity.

Truth is a very sharp sword; but the trouble with it is that it has no handle—it is all blade. The truth can kill, especially when it is not part of and exercised in support of a shared morality. Then, the blade can cut both ways: it can kill the life in those you would help; and it can kill your loving desire to help them. The truth is too pure, too powerful; it has a good deal in common with the simple solution of homicide—and people protect themselves against it as they would against the threat of an assault. One of the more dramatic moments in a courtroom trial is the bailiff's invitation to tell "the truth, the whole truth, and nothing but the truth": everyone tenses with the pregnancy of danger.

It is duration, the time factor, that finally requires a dialectical rather than a unilinear logic in dealing with truth and falsehood when these are *in*, not above, existence (and even if truth is the sole end-in-view). Lies exist inextricably in the web of society as well as in the myths of the ego. Still, from lying and repression can come transcendence as well as illusion and symptom. There is, for an obvious instance, the Glorious Lie whereby Oedipal love for the mother can concoct its own creative future as love for an outsider female. But not under the burden of exclusive concentration on the truth of Oedipal love. (And if a man, old, forgets his wife and finally remembers his mother, nevertheless a life has been lived in the meantime.)

Being a compulsive truth-teller, therefore, with an ego founded upon a few Really Important lies, I am now and again enticed into thinking that the key to every man's life is what he decides to hide from himself, and how well he succeeds. The choice once made, the commitment after a while becomes overwhelming and the "success" of it would seem to be irrelevant. Schlesinger quotes Tugwell as saying of Roosevelt: "The serious student . . . is forced to conclude that this man deliberately concealed the processes of his mind." Schlesinger's own view of FDR is summed up as follows: "He was complicated everywhere except in his heart of hearts. There he perceived things with elementary, almost childlike, faith." So, relying on some monumental falsehood or other, he preserved the inner simplicity of a child and, with that as his personal anchor, managed to be exceptionally receptive and maneuverable with respect to a wide range of outside factors.

He was an actor. After his personal disaster I think he literally *became* an idea—the idea of his "due" place in American history, which he could achieve only imaginatively because of the intervening imperfection of his body. It turned out that, thus disembodied, his political technique was substantially more relevant than it would have been had he succeeded, according to his first intention, merely as a smarter, bigger, more handsome TR. He was a greater President for imagining the role rather than being it.

3 The search for truth, certainly in politics, properly begins with the going public lie. Generally speaking, one has to be fairly slow not to outdistance the going lie with ease (but in the more advanced areas of science, one may have to be a genius). The purpose of the attack, the mode, the extent— these are not to be taken as simple deductions from the fact that it is a lie you are going after. That would be both too simple and too unkind. The principal considerations of strategy are often: Who will be hurt? And how much? And is it necessary? (For example, to seduce a woman without lying would be an act of untoward cruelty.)

It is the limited but decisive number of private lies we *must* institute in our own psychic economy, in order to retain control over ourselves, plus that part of the established public lies which *cannot* be contested fruitfully without undergoing a measure of destructive social alienation whereby too much of both the audience and the common language are lost—it is these two danger zones, where even heroes travel with fear, that ensure the two-mindedness of man. Our traditional dualism, the result of accepting these inner and outer lies, is thus *enforced* dualism. Our two-mindedness, traditional or eccentric, is the way we ordinarily lie to ourselves; it is the very structure, the logic, of our necessary lying. The one sure context of man's two-mindedness, the real source of its persistence, is the *historical* (not metaphysical) disjunction between the public and the private.* It can be resolved, or further brought into more convenient relation, only through forward movement within the historical context. As this occurs, and until it is completed (which may never finally happen), certain acts of deception and other lying will be indispensable. And, therefore, justified. The moral issue is not whether to lie, but which lie to tell and how to tell it.

For needed clarity, let's go back to the Basic Situation of pragmatism: Life is going on, there is no reason to think as distinct from doing; then a snag develops, a barrier is confronted, and instead of "going on," Life presents a problem which requires thought before any more doing occurs. Then, according to the prescription of pragmatism, the actor thinks hard, solves the problem, and Life continues its forward movement. And the latter is the proof of the former. I agree that this is what happens. But I do not agree that it happens without lying to oneself, or accepting the given lies of others: the fact that some lies are dissolved in the process of problem-solving does not disprove the fact that other lies are retained and even utilized in the same process. (Indeed, a problem may be "solved" by creating a new and better lie.)

Here we have the rudimentary lie—the fresh commitment, exactly by virtue of the Problem Solved, to a pre-existing lie; the secure basis of historical two-mindedness, as to which the abstract elaborations of traditional dualism are a mere exercise in lily-gilding—as if a personal choice and not an inevitably human error had to be justified eternally. This mess was resolved by William James through the

---

* This was discussed briefly, in the previous chapter, in connection with G. H. Mead, whose work is based on this public/private definition of the subjective and the objective.

rhetorical assertion of a will to believe. All right: this will exists, and it requires some recognition. But this will of resolution also requires a great deal of analytic understanding, which was forthcoming not from James but from Mead. And besides the will to believe, there is the willingness to know—also requiring some status. When the lies are too thick—like locusts as far as the horizon—it may become necessary *not* to solve the problem: consequently, *not* to believe. That would depend on an evaluation, at least an orienting sense, of the web of pre-existing lies. (We will return to this terrible problem of the occasional utility of truth.)

Further, the very process of human thought appears to condemn us to a fate of two-mindedness. Abstraction, leading to propositional truth, produces a simplicity and clarity which is in itself unreal, not lifelike. Properly, abstraction does not dispense with the flotsam of perception and memory, even in the same mind and nearly at the same moment. But in the keeping of enthusiasts, literalists, or other innocents, abstract truth can become a favored mode of fabrication. It is better to understand the inevitability of our native two-mindedness, retain an awareness of the interplay, and consciously lie to enhance the coziness of the duality. We live our lives and think our thoughts in conflict: nothing has one side only; a clearly stated proposition derives its usable meaning also from its absent opposite —and even from the ambiguity of the general and merely sensed context.

An excellent example of this process is the growth of the law. The special genius of the common law has time and again been said to be its content of yes/no corollary propositions affording a greatly desired freedom to judges and practitioners, with the result that experience rather than theory is the teacher of law, which thus can grow while seeming to stand still. Another means to this end, encompassing a further creative duplicity, has been the role of "legal fictions"— first described, I believe, by Sir Henry Maine in *Ancient Law,* as follows:

> The earliest and most extensively employed of legal fictions was that which permitted family relations to be created artificially, and there is none to which I conceive mankind to be more deeply indebted. If it had never existed, I do not see how any one of the primitive groups, whatever were their nature, could have absorbed another, or on what terms any two of them could have

combined, except those of absolute superiority on one side and absolute subjection on the other.

Legal fictions have gained rather than lost utility as mankind has moved from ancient to modern primitivism. The corporation, for example, has been welcomed into the American legal order as a "person"—and this is not merely amusing, but is also the basis for some of the minuscule amount of law that has been applied to corporate behavior.

The summary specification of our two-mindedness, before it is elaborated into ideology or religion, is, *First,* practical directions to achieve changes in self or the social order, and *Second,* a magical view of same which more or less assumes that the changes have already been effected, or soon or inevitably will be, by guaranty of willed belief.

Perhaps the main distinction between myths is whether they are, in their distortion, devoted to outgoing desire or inward defense, whether they are designed to induce action or *in*action thus indicating the qualities of desire or fear involved in a particular concoction. The man who fabricates only as an interim device, to allay his fear of not achieving the object of his desire, is my favorite among liars. But then even this good-hearted fellow may be trapped into adding another lie, and then another one, as the existential difficulties appear one after the other like a line of marching soldiers defending the world against his potential satisfaction; and finally, at some obscure moment, the object of his frustrated desire loses its original qualities and takes on those derived from his lies. For the purposes of human action, lying is no more certain than truth. Still, I like that fellow better than the one who holds to an idea rigidly—the major form of lying to oneself—and thereby elevates the past to unassailable heights.

All myth involves some falsehood in the subjectivity of the individual. But the myth of a desiring human, even when it fails by perversion, is of a different order of life than the private myth duplicated or reinforced by official public myths which are designed to sustain an established public distortion. We should try to lie for ourselves, and out of love, not at the direction of statelike powers. And lie to act, not to defend inaction: because motor-action is closest to emotion, which in turn is closer to needful images necessarily involving mythful lies (unless one acts as an automaton, at the direction of an outside power, in which case the lie is merely a minor part of the larger surrender preceding it). So choose; and choosing, realize that we may have to lie, or find ourselves unable not to lie, in order to induce the anti-automaton action of politics, the private becoming public by the joinder of passion and intellect to create, alter, and on occasion even to preserve the superior public reality.

4 After physical force and dexterity, silence is the next great form of natural power. Silence, and other brute failures of communication, should be seen as simple forms of the power of ambiguity—posing difficult answers to the basic questions of perception: What is the nature of the object? What does the subject intend? Next come natural camouflage and other physical indirection; then, civilized fraud and deception, whether or not buttressed by physical force and dexterity. (As men move on to higher forms of power, they do not necessarily abandon the occasional utility of the lower ones.)

Deception is so natural as to be biological. Animals that are not strong, armored, or fast, will survive best when they appear to be something other than they are. The chameleon, I suppose, is the champion deceiver; but many other animals have their more pedestrian physiological camouflage—and even the mighty polar bear, not to forgo an obvious advantage, is white. Natural deception is the exploitation, for survival or triumph, of the other animal's equally natural difficulties of perception. So the capacity to perceive (to ascertain truth) can also be said to be a natural power of sorts.

In a civilized order, lying becomes as well a means of defense against one's own animal nature: that is the practice of lying to oneself. The extent of this capacity that a particular social order may engender, and then require, is a profound index of its basic destructiveness. The Germans under Hitler, the Soviets under Stalin, the racist South in America, or racist South Africa—these daring societies have been nearly suicidal in their abuse of the privilege (just as some ancient social orders indulged promiscuous mayhem by armed men).

The state traditionally has been defined and measured according to the effective monopoly of force achieved. Under modern advanced

conditions, we are moving beyond this tradition to the creative departure of the totalitarian state, which asserts as well a monopoly of
deception—where no one may lie to the state about anything, and
the state may at its discretion lie to anyone about everything as a
normal exercise of its power. Analogies to the medieval order in Europe could be drawn—but not too meaningfully, because of the great
disparity in technique. In the United States, luckily, the technical advances in widespread deception have had to be shared by the state
with the corporate order, which, year in and year out, tells many more
lies even than the federal government. But the basic federal jurisdiction is maintained (as in many other areas) under the war powers
clause of the Constitution: commenting reflectively on certain official
deception during the Cuban missile crisis, Mr. Arthur Sylvester, Assistant Secretary of Defense for Public Affairs, maintained that the
government had an inherent right "to lie to save itself." The point was
well taken, of course, even though Mr. Sylvester did not, with respect
to salvation, say *from what.* But just as the ghetto police defend the
use of their killer-dogs as preferable to a bullet, surely a lie is more
acceptable than either.

It is the alliance of force and deception, in order to perfect the
monopoly-effect of each, that particularly characterizes modern totalitarianism. Himmler's actions were worse than Goebbels' lies, although the latter prepared the way for the former, and neither would
have fared as well without the other. With the mixed situation in the
United States, the major fabricating power is in the hands of the
industrial government, which rules by means of its advertising culture. On occasion, the federal establishment will exert state power to
limit somewhat the private monopoly of lying—as in disclosure statutes: for instance, those administered by the SEC or the Internal
Revenue Service. The totalitarian joining of the two powers is probably the most fearsome conjunction; but an absolute separation or
contradiction would create a very unstable social order. Veblen com-
ments on this in *The Theory of Business Enterprise:*

> Systematic insincerity on the part of the ostensible purveyors of
> information and leaders of opinion may be deplored by persons
> who stickle for truth and pin their hopes of social salvation on
> the spread of accurate information. But the ulterior cultural
> effect of the insincerity which is in this way required by the busi-
> ness situation may [be] . . . favorable to the maintenance of
> the established order. . . .

The Shah of Iran in his book, *Mission for My Country,* writes that the lack of honesty throughout his realm "still ranks among our formidable problems." He suggests that Persians learned to exaggerate the utility of lying by finding it to be "the price of personal survival" under Mongol rule: and now they are cursed with the talent.

So many patterns of fabrication: a catalogue would be even lengthier than the complementary list of weapons and military groupings since, say, the beginning of the Christian epoch. An enumeration of both, printed *en face,* might be a useful reference work. The second volume, I suggest, could appropriately begin with the Moscow Trials, which constituted perhaps the greatest *organized* lie in history. Legal proceedings in societies without law are a peculiarly apt forum in which to have a great lie solemnly sworn to. There have been numerous precedents, most pertinently the Reichstag Fire Trial —which may well have been the occasion of Stalin's inspiration. But the Moscow Trials exist on a plane apart, being the attempted lobotomy of an entire nation and a far-flung international movement. They involved the coherent fabrication of thousands of historical details, were supported by the rewriting of history books, accompanied by the slaughter of thousands of uncooperative witnesses, and then sworn to in public by leading elements among the accused. The final grandiose embellishment was the confession of Yagoda, the man who had been in charge of engineering the initial mechanism—a thrust of genius worthy only of a Shakespeare who thought like a Dostoievski.

But the Moscow Trials were too big a lie for the country to support, just as an oversized military establishment can drain the strength of a nation. A few years later in the Ukraine, the Nazis were welcomed with flowers; and a few years after Stalin's death, his henchmen placed his spirit next to Yagoda's.

5 That was at one theoretical extreme of lying; at another, it is difficult to imagine what the process of benign education would be like without a teacher's thoughtful and judicious suppression of the truth.

One learns in steps or stages, and some students learn better than others. Also, true teaching of the truth would often enough consist mostly of an attack on the student's prior "knowledge." And apart from that sort of thing—prior mis-education—there is prior non-education, being structures of myth naturally or socially generated by non-school education and ordinary growth. Not all of these can be attacked right then and there; some must be indulged for a few weeks or months, and others even for a lifetime; if not, effective education could become a process of destroying the previously existing person. For the sake of truth, of course; but no less destroyed thereby. And whence the simple Rx that there are no problems of living (involving the content of the mind) that cannot be treated best by massive and immediate doses of somebody else's truth?

The first truth that the humane teacher must sacrifice is his own most dearly held. If, for instance, he has devoted his life to studying and appreciating the qualities of literature, his pedagogic approach —to those who, unfortunately, know much less than nothing about the object of his strenuously pursued passion—should be shrewdly plotted: it cannot then avoid conscious dissembling on his part. The less of his own truth he offers, the better off his students will be—and the better chance one or more of them will have of later imitating him in the essentials of the matter rather than in the mere snobbery of it. One or another form of untruthfulness is indispensable in that central human project of the less ignorant instructing the more ignorant. Properly undertaken, this is the warmest, friendliest form of inducing change. And if it were not for lying somewhere along the line, all such change would be revolutionary: one generation would suffice to transform the human race, or kill it off.

But the teacher, having suppressed his own personal truth, somehow then feels freer to become "professional" and devote himself to inculcating official myths. This eventuality, I believe, is the result of moral confusion compounded of frustration and hostility: the truth, the whole truth, and nothing but the truth—and if not that, then any crap will do. But what if the teacher were not so helplessly the victim of the categorical imperative to tell the truth? Why then he would have entered the modern arena of morality, which is not based on Christian devotion to powerlessness—helplessness before God as the final proof of virtue and the only means of salvation. He would accept his own superiority in the context; and he would know that if he is in fact superior, then he in fact has a power that must be used according to its obvious terms and can certainly be misused—and will be, or will not be, only as he decides. In order to be moral in this modern mode, he would—on the road to grace—accept his power rather than deny it: and thereafter, of course, be responsible for its exercise.

It is not such a simple matter, every time, to uncover the relevant differences between conning somebody for your advantage and giving them hope and help for their own advantage. This difficulty—with the moral chanciness involved—may be the larger part of the reason why the modern mode is not more often indulged.

Note the advantage of tradition over individual discretion as the source of difficult truths and/or lies: presumptively, with the former, the decision has already been made for you by some ancestor or other. In the law, that impossible pseudo-moral realm where issues of power are somehow actually resolved in a pious atmosphere, argument by analogy from precedent is ranked absurdly high.* The deep feeling for tradition—the embalmer's myth of authority—has always struck me as being like a deep fear of forgetting some half-remembered lesson from the past; as if you once had the truth securely in hand, but then lost hold of it by becoming too involved in experience and too distracted by its pace and variety. Tradition strikes me as an ineptly ordinary way of trying to recapture innocence.

Stupid people, of course, find it much easier to be sincere (and vice versa). Candidate Goldwater, for example, seemed to strain less than many others in his entourage in presenting, with considerable sincerity, the evil combination of racism, internal xenophobia, and moral purity which characterized his campaign.

But if to a sensitive intelligence is added a genuine feeling for the truth—let us say, even a talent for it—then we have a real problem when it comes to politics. This unfortunate conjunction has ensured the political irrelevance (or pained absenteeism) of many intellectuals; and for many who nevertheless engage on the necessary terms, it has required that the initiating condition of engagement be a personal lie, usually ideal. Nobody else begins with this handicap. Nor is it once-and-done-with: the resulting strain and guilt invite exploitation and early surrender, or more lies to avoid same.

Deception is a basic personal power, like physical strength; and

---

* Freedom from this tyranny may come soon, not from a revolutionary abandonment of the role of precedent, but by turning that aspect of legal work over to the computer, thus affording the legal mind something like a housewife's freedom from drudgery.

with it—just as with the other power—one can hurt or help. But we believe it to be more awful and effective than it really is, probably because we outgrow more easily our child's fear of physical force than we do the child's helpless horror at being lied to. Also, most civilized middle-class people feel they can control their impulse to dominate physically; but they are guilty about their capacity to dominate by deception, and so utilize it compulsively (and masochistically, by lying to themselves first). The simple power-fact is obvious, however: that is the worst way to lie. Without reasonable deceptiveness, moreover, one's own power quickly becomes pure destructiveness—or it ceases, at the last moment, to be even that, and becomes someone else's power.

The power to deceive, based on superior knowledge or similar facility, is a power like all others—it can be used to dominate or exploit those without the power; and it is needed by the latter to achieve like power of their own. We would show a more generous morality in our use of this power if we were less moral to begin with, and admitted its existence and deployment. If we so frequently assert our single-minded devotion to the truth, we make it much more difficult to acknowledge our use of deception. That is true of all power: if our moral presumptions do not allow us to admit its existence, there is nothing to be responsible about.* But active morality *is* the responsible use of power.

So I would like to see the application here of the simple American street-morality which prescribes that a big guy does not pick on a little guy. In a street brawl, the big guy wins nothing but the label of "bully." Why not the same thing when it comes to lying? Why, in matters of skilled deception, do we not have this kind of useful, honorable conception of a "fair fight"? Because we don't admit that lying is a power that we use—and the small guys we lie to do not have the lying or other power to force us to own up. In a bar or on the street, everybody can *see* which guy is bigger.

Also, lying has erroneously been thought to be the weapon of the "smaller" man, as with the Persians.†

---

* Note the similarity to money, which is nothing in itself but stands for nearly everything; with the result that anything it doesn't easily or obviously stand for, hardly exists.

† Here, we may note a neglected aspect of the stupidity of American men, who were once in charge of the streets and the morality developed there. Young males in America are so narrow-mindedly manly that their crucial, unsupervised, adolescent street-training has been traditionally devoted

6 "Lying" is such an unpleasant word. Even in the blandest context it carries a twinge of guilt—more so, I suggested, than the notion of "violence." The latter is feared as something somebody else may do to *you;* but with lying, *you* are more often the actor, not so often the recipient. Also, violence is more satisfying, being an immediately completed act, whereas lying is a more civilized avenue to the achievement of more complex ends.

Lying, however, involves a considerable physical strain. This fact is the basis of the device for measuring physiological reactions known as the lie detector. When we lie, the pace of breathing is affected, also pulse, blood pressure, temperature, salivation, etc. Men work harder at lying than women do—their reactions under a lie-detector test are more noticeable. An expert in these matters, John Edward Reid, believes that the reason for the difference is that women self-justify more effectively and thereby in fact feel less guilt. J. K. Galbraith, the lie-detecting economist, has remarked: "One of the uses

to the development of gross physical prowess (with much more emphasis on chivalry than on bullying, incidentally). The result is that female and other older shrewdness arrives a few years later as a shocking cold bath—and some of our post-puberty street-heroes never recover from the startling loss of hard-earned status. Meanwhile, the girls and early male losers have given up on Power One and have retreated to Power Two, which then turns out to be the useful one for later living. A neglected basis of the American—or perhaps "industrial"—matriarchy is that women are better trained, from an early age, in the arts of deception: a form of power much more useful in modern organized living than the more primary strength and agility which boys so admire and yearn after. In an office, it is no-contest (at age twenty-five to thirty) between a former athlete and a girl trained on *Mademoiselle*. Also, with so much ethnic mix on the streets of America, the boys never learn the depth of brotherhood, even developed out of physical prowess, which might sustain them in later, subtler encounters. And from their mothers, of course, they learn chivalry; while the matriarchs instruct their daughters, at least by example, that some tyrannies are to be overthrown by any available ruthlessness. The father-to-daughter passage is altogether characterized by the old man's yearning for another chance to be even sweeter; and to the son he insists, in the manly fashion of the streets—*Son,* she never laid a glove on me (and on bad days, Don't bother me—can't you see I'm sick?).

When American men abandoned culture to women in favor of money in the nineteenth century, how could they have known that the women would end up beating them over the head with both in the twentieth?

of women is that their motivations, though often similar, are less elaborately disguised than those of men." I think women lie more easily and less elaborately than men because they are more repressed to begin with, are devoted to creating a world of Appearance close around themselves (elaborately designed to "present" themselves), and are not compelled to seek so far and so wide as men for the Reality they think they want to live in.

Men have a readier sense of physical violence; so they feel more strongly the necessity of facing up to the reality which, if put out of mind, may sneak up on one in a relaxed moment. They therefore find it somewhat harder to deny-and-deny merely by reason of clear convenience. Women, I think, are greater fantasists than men (because of their deeper repression): they will have more nightmares of violence upon themselves, but also more daydreams of obvious wish-fulfillment. All this is a matter of degree, however; and in a maturing matriarchy like America, the differences may even be reversed one day.

Women are not the only Persians. In his pursuit of liars, Mr. Reid uses a questionnaire he constructed. Only one "student" ever got a perfect score, which was so suspicious that the event was followed up by an imaginative interrogation in which the subject was finally revealed as a professional confidence man. Among criminals, as you may know, there is an inverse relation between status and the use of violence. The lowest order of criminal is a hold-up man who would, for psychological reasons, rather shoot than steal successfully: these slum types used to be called "cowboys." At the apex of the criminal profession is the con man, who would rather go to jail than demean himself by the use of violence. There are certain areas of life which are simple laboratories of the various human adjustments to issues of power: that is, *where an* ad hoc *power-relevant morality is created*. Crime is one of the more noticeable of these.

According to legend, American con men had their heyday when the cities and mining camps were filled with farmers and fresh immigrants. They were artists of deception, concocting custom-made delusions out of native environmental materials which they understood better than most of the recent natives. They are somewhat admired by Americans, along with the fast guns of the West; and soon we will have many more Westerns in which they figure prominently as bad-boy heroes. But note that their work and place in history concerns the individualistic artistry of intentional distortion. Not yet the org men of American advertising, nor even the cosmonauts of the Moscow Trials.

In a way, we are all con men of the West—all of us Rugged Individualists who are not mere Cowboys. But to see ourselves in this blinding light, we must engender an awareness of the fatal human continuum that stretches all the way from a helpless lack of essential knowing, and rather ordinary mistaken perception, to the unspeakably evil (and organized) invitation to take a shower in Zyklon-B. This new awareness cannot be achieved simply with the ancient moral admonition to "tell the truth, the whole truth, and nothing but the truth." That would only make unconscious liars of us all.

We cannot be concerned merely with the question of intentional lying, the personal kind that is universally condemned. Lying, like violence, spreads itself across the full range of the human condition. The word is wrong? I withdraw it. Let's speak of inevitable anti-truth, or pedestrian non-truth—of friendly dissembling, white lies, polite distortions, pleasant Appearances, and gratefully hidden Realities. *Let us speak of the deviously constructed reality we all live in.*

The specific subject of lying is useful in a general discussion of power because the guilt is so indigenously *there*. But the matter is complicated in such a way that, with an irresistible *non sequitur*, we may lie more freely *just because* we are so certain that we would never hit a little man over the head with a bottle. Therefore, one must clearly insist that restraint of violence is not really probative as to lying.

Is rhetoric a lie? I say it is—and I am a compulsive truth-teller, self-confessed, *and* a rhetorician. Are reputation and accomplishment somewhat different? Yes, they are. And if you go to a bank for credit, it will be better to have the former than the latter; indeed, you will have to translate accomplishment into reputation in order to get any money. Is that because the banker is stupid or evil? No, it is because he deals with a *public*.

The world sees form and style; and finally the world-actor sees mostly with the eyes of the world, in order to act better. Since the public so requires it, style is a personal gift to the world: it is a lie better than the truth, or at least necessary in addition to it. The truth is not enough: people are not strong enough for that strong stuff. And while style or form is not true, it *is* essential, being an action rhetoric, an imagined con, that has much more effect than the truth of propositions (which may comprise pieces of it). I know of a very successful and talented man who denied his talent in order to achieve his success. Later, it became a compulsion with him. I sympathize, and I do not condemn—although I am convinced that his life has been a mistake of sorts. Though all of his lying gestures were learned without talent, and in derogation of his real talent, he is now a *powerful man*. He has thus competed successfully with his lesser contemporaries. It has been a great triumph. He will die without regret, only wishing he had lived in Edwardian England, or in the eighteenth century, or among the Maccabees. He will die in the shadow of something much deeper than regret.

The master of the problem of lying is Pirandello, the great Italian dramatist. As Pirandello states it, the issue is the world's insistence that we live up to its convenient lies. The truth, for him, is a wild assault upon reality. Especially in love, the conflict is poignant to an unbearable degree, as follows: to insist on the truth is selfish, in disappointing the loved one's expectations; to satisfy these expectations is exploitative and unloving. Then the horror: she doesn't love me, she loves the image of her own lying need of what she insists is me. In this situation, what is truth? (Indeed, what is love?)

If we were all merely individuals, we would have none of these problems.

7   Having established the inevitability of lying, we may now inquire as to the occasional use of truth, in politics. Frankly, we need an excuse for public honesty—on special occasions and for specially qualified eccentrics.

Except for the fear of retaliation, one would always be free to blow the whistle on opponents. The fear alone is highly effective, however. Besides, the truth about the personal lives of politicians, while interesting, is mostly irrelevant. There was a time in New York City, I recall, when there must have been a hundred thousand people who were "in" enough to know the name of Wendell Willkie's girlfriend. Big deal. And in the God-fearing countryside, a warm innuendo will do as well as a cold fact. Senator George Smathers is quoted on this point by Victor Lasky in the latter's tribute to the late President Kennedy, *JFK: The Man and the Myth,* as follows:

Are you aware that Claude Pepper is known all over Washington as a shameless extrovert? Not only that, but this man is reliably reported to practice nepotism with his sister-in-law, and he has a sister who was once a Thespian in Greenwich Village. Worst of all, it is an established fact that Mr. Pepper, before his marriage, practiced celibacy.

A more serious utility of public truth is the heroic one that occurs when the web of lies by which men ordinarily and preferably live has become so impossibly complicated that even the born liars cannot safely thread their way through it even to their own evil ends: then, telling the truth is like yelling "*Fire!*" so everybody can get out before the roof falls in. Of course, the truth-tellers are always at-the-ready for just this heroism: but noticing a fire when there is none is somewhat illegal, under Justice Holmes's interpretation of the First Amendment. Anyway, to give the angels their due, there are some things which, to do them, would so violate yourself that neither the utility nor the justification can avail the act.

But the basic consideration, for me, is that in the course of a functional or benign participation in necessary lies, the capacity to recognize or remember what the truth looks like may be lost. Truth is a great commodity (with no serious problem of overproduction) and, just as we are pleased to have a few people around who still remember how to take care of horses, a few truth-professionals certainly should be subsidized. Also, the autonomous advance of science, with all the immeasurable political consequences thereof, has left a very strong impression on the popular mind of the commodity-nature of truth. This is potentially so unfortunate that the sagging utility of old-style truth-mongers has, as a consequence, been revived. The vogue of science, spiritually, is based on the unwillingness of human beings to try any longer to speak the truth to each other in a simple manner: you have to "prove" it, even if it is obvious. So science becomes a way of "not making mistakes." Anybody in *that* business should have somebody else, even a compulsive truth-teller, watching him around the clock.

Obviously, truth is important. Obviously, it is not—without action —determinative of Everything, except when that is taken to be a mental state of grace.

We Americans just have no adequate talent for discussing power and morals in conjunction. That is primarily a cultural failing; but its effect, also pointedly political, is that the world of truth

—the world of the mind at its best—still requires a passport and a visa even for a short visit to the other world of practical affairs. Despite the power-success of science; despite the new rampage of educational imperialism; despite our best feelings, even, of friendliness and brotherhood among the educated and uneducated alike. Despite everything, mind (and truth, its occasional product) do not readily mix in the practical world.

Eventually, falsehood and deception may be brought under adequate institutional control—reduced to a level, so to say, of police power in a disarmed world. Thereafter, only little, well-behaved lies. Along with the control over violence, mankind has already made some progress on this subtler front, as with disclosure statutes and some slight control over the various magnifications of our advertising culture.

Meanwhile, and awaiting further advance in this area, morality is either a convention enforced by conformity, or an unenforced act of love—at least of fellow-feeling. I believe in it: I do not believe in parading it. With no parade, the initial subject introducing any love is power. And unparaded truth has, of course, a vital relation to this subject. Thus, each according to his own capacity—and, one day, without compulsion. It is pacifism I object to, not the occasional nonviolence of truth.*

Morality is for the powerful, not the powerless. So the relevant morality of our day applies to our Leading Persons, and it is this: Do not deny understanding to anyone capable of it; do not require it of anyone our society has created without the capacity to absorb it. With or without understanding, hurt no one unnecessarily, simply because they are *there,* more or less waiting to be hurt.

Power is not the only thing in life that may be misused: almost anything can be, especially including moral posture. Therefore, a genuinely moral position can no more be founded on an absolute prohibition of lying than on a revealed injunction against violence.

There can be no moral position that does not also propose power over power. And whatever else that may come to include, it must contain the will to dissemble generously for the benefit of others, and to tell yourself the best truths of which you are capable.

* I may add that my objection to moral belief held in the head primarily for the comfort of it, which common practice I have been railing against throughout these chapters, is not absolute. My point has not been to attack comfort as such, but only to insist that such morality is immoral unless based on decisive failure-in-action.

(In my notes for this chapter, I was amused to come across the following two stimulants to further thought: "Truth is stranger than fiction—and it is also less believable." And: "In the end, the truth is always obvious." The first effect of these stimulants was the further thought that I must be something of a fool. Then the fool thought a step farther: Why couldn't both of them be "true"?)

8 In the modern world we live on the edge, not of existence any longer, but of the meaning of existence. For the social animal, meaning is social. The content of mind is social, and this is no less so if I spend all of my time talking to myself—right up to the point where I become insane, and my mind surrenders so much to the Other that the animal-I no longer has much relation to it. Jungle animals live on the edge of existence; human beings, imitating them, can imagine they live some parts of their lives this way. For this purpose, the idea of scarcity is extremely useful, perhaps a necessity. As scarcity recedes in fact, however, life tends to lose meaning—we edge over—unless we deepen and otherwise enlarge the social dimension. That is, unless we get together and share more meanings. This enlarging is variously called "love" and "community." After a long destructive hiatus, there is nothing to do with a wealth of anything except to be somewhat generous with it.

The main thing about either love or community is whether it is genuine. I don't mean to suggest that authenticity is the only issue: a false community, for example, may be acceptable, depending on the alternatives and the desperation of the individual choosing it. But the necessity of an artificial community occurs very much like the onset of insanity, in that the social part of the social mind overwhelms the animal individual trapped within it. And, we noted a chapter ago, if he then attempts to race back to the jungle, he will never find his way: that part of him is, so to speak, already dead. False love or an artificial community represents a failure of social mind to encompass the vitality of the animal—as form to content— just about as much as insanity is, so obviously, a social educative failure. To race back to the barred jungle, to collapse forward into the arms of a false community—each is what it obviously is, a failure. This is why, since there is so little genuine love and community, life is tragic. This is not our doing; but we should be clear that life can proceed beyond its native tragic quality to convincing worthlessness only with our active participation.

True community can be created only by, and out of respect for, natural animal vitality, and a necessarily "strange" combination of this with forbearance toward the existence and needs of the Other; the need of the Other (to be read as a *double entendre*) is both the means and the substance of community. The existential basis of newer and more valid community is the mutual recognition of the need for it; a sure male sense of the inadequacy of existing artificial ones; a female feeling for small beginnings; and more than anything else, calling a halt to mutual hostility as a way of life. It is a lousy way of life; and it is what it obviously is, a failure. (The decisive "created community," of course, is marriage—the birthplace of public subjectivity, and the final resting place of deadly hostility resulting from the failure thereof.)

The routes to new community are as varied as insistent truth, abject surrender, and calculated coalition. Individualism, the spiritual structure of an isolated life, should be a programmatic way station, even if lifelong: individualism should never be more than the best means for searching a way out. And once in, subjectivity or individualism remains programmatic, in presumption at least, but becomes collectively so. That's it: always the animal in society, never in a jungle; and always the effort to make society less of a jungle for us, the special animals—and for our children, the *very* special animals.

Community is one's expectation of and willingness toward the Other: its essence is mutuality. The genuineness of community depends upon the facts of mutuality. To the extent that my offering or initiative creates a response in the Other, the fact of mutuality begins in my imagining—and not to have imagined it is "unrealistic." This is the arena of the basically important judgments of life: no wonder life is so difficult.

When a moral position is not shared by all those whom it will affect if acted upon; and if your insistence does not persuade, and your action does not induce; then it is not, properly speaking, any longer a moral position—at least that use of the term, for the sake of the substance, should be abandoned. *Morality as failed initiative,* when it is retained but not integral with community, is no more than defensive self-righteousness. As such, it is for you alone, and not for them at all. Shockingly, the same proposition applies as well to rationality. And truth itself.

I often speak the truth in public (I have already admitted) for no better reason than a little boy has for whistling in a graveyard.

This suggests the proper relation between community and myth. Myths are properly indulged, even when the truth concerning them is known to some few persons, because they are a community's chosen means of representing and educating itself. It is easy to feel contempt or even hatred for people bound by myths other than your own. It is harder, and more worthwhile, to understand that you lie, too, and that their lies are a piece of their language which it is loving of you to understand if you wish to speak to them.

And we wish, finally, to speak to everyone. That is the largest point about community-building: it should be open-ended. All human beings are accepted: later, additional species may be welcomed. In exclusion, one defines the Other in order to define oneself —and then certifies the definition by carrying out the exclusion. I personally may want to escape the fate of an African native, but I do not want to be defined by the fact of that desire. So I am selfish and I am certainly arrogant, but I am not a snob. Indeed, I have difficulty understanding snobs: Who in his right mind would want to be *defined* as that fellow over there who never got syphilis, never starved, wasn't drafted, went to Harvard, etc.? To avoid the unfortunate conditions, yes. But to revel in defining oneself by their absence? I can see that only if you imagine somewhere inside that you deserved these and escaped them only by virtue of some exquisite talent-x. In other words, community-by-exclusion is a vulgar rebellion against the need for community.

In this slight reprise, I might have talked about love as well as community, the private as well as the public part. But we are much too hesitant concerning love to make rousing speeches about it. Also, love is mostly for doing. Also, this is after all America—and here we don't exactly love and get married so much as we decide, upon careful reflection or desperate need, to go steady for life.

Natural coalition-builders, all of us, except the paralyzed Individualists *trembling behind their righteous moral screens.*

9 After we have pushed some of the rationalistic presumptions of science out of the way, and a new politics replaces the old religion, we will still have a few problems remaining. Mainly to achieve a deeper education-for-community; a continuously refined sense of ourselves and the movement of history; and, most important, new means and methods for resignation—because we are not going to win all the battles, or live to see all the tomorrows, just because we are wealthy and think more clearly and act more effectively. We need something that will do everything religion used to do, minus a few distortions. But any such new secular theology (that's an impossible phrase, isn't it—but what to do?)* will amount to no more candy-and-cake than the older divine ones did, when taken seriously. The Future is almost as far away as Heaven ever was.

Young people are not interested in resignation, and I agree wholeheartedly that they shouldn't be. I also agree that no one should stop being young any sooner than necessary. But finally everyone wakes up on a certain morning more tired, for no apparent reason, than he was when he went to sleep: the experience is repeated once too often, and that's that. There must then be available a spiritual view, a sense of the community *between* generations, which allows for the event of aging without turning the victim vicious: everyone finally a Moses. Once we allow (and help) our children to grow up somewhat more than we managed, and into their imagined world rather than ours, we—the human race—will have burst our chains. We are on the edge of this, with our child-centered culture and other opportunities here in America.

Isn't that what religion, at its best, intended? If the generations ever managed to accept each other, on the basis of each other's inevitable differences, the resulting culture founded neither on ancestor worship nor on youth sentimentality would have incorporated the essential Holy Ghost, the transit from father to son, the required

---

* What is meant by "secular theology" is the fully extended emotional pattern for living-in-history which has been (and continues to be) elaborately explained and argued and justified in intellectual discourse, with whatever symbology.

principle of change. And no principle of change not so founded can ever be quite adequate. But this requires, of the fathers, that they digest and transcend their own experience sufficiently to apply the lessons thereof to the building of human houses they will not live in. This would be creative resignation as important as the son's proper lack of it. The relation of the generations was perhaps the center of religion, and must be as well the center of a political culture that is more than mere business. Protestantism taught us to accumulate wealth, and science has now shown us how to accumulate technique, for later generations; next we must accumulate and pass on the coherent cultural elements of the capacity to be human. For our sons.

And as for them, with whatever beneficent inheritance or lack of it, their creative and expansive youth is nevertheless limited. It may even be that each generation has the capacity for only one major experience—the Depression, the War, etc. Schlesinger quotes a remark Wilson once made to FDR, which expresses this view in Wilson's usual idealistic way: "It is only once in a generation that people can be lifted above material things. That is why conservative government is in the saddle two-thirds of the time." With our affluence, we "can be lifted above material things" as a regular matter, if that's what we want. But we will still use up the capacity for experience, become decisively tired. This problem is exaggerated by the fact which I have been emphasizing throughout this section, that most people in America have been given an extra thirty years or so to live, and most of them haven't the slightest idea what to do with it.

One thing they can do with it is to digest and shape it for the use of their sons, or, failing that, just ruminate quietly out of the way. We needn't conscript individual experience; but we must be concerned with what the experience of a generation adds up to: because that is "culture"—models and deep directions for the next generation. Where the ages of men differ, culture *is* law: culture is the law of generational succession—the enforcement of which (often called "education") involves as many difficulties, and as much simple failure of justice, as does the administration of our other laws.

So to the fathers, I conclude: Life is like a split-frame range finder. The clear and fascinating focus is not what people think they are doing, but what they are actually doing while they are thinking it. To understand what you are doing while you are doing it is the best chance we get to have understanding affect doing. The true opportunity of subjectivity and individualism. That's the best we have to give: and even if we have to manage some of it projectively, by noticing the faults and foibles of others, I think that's all right, considering how important the over-all activity is. So, with the deeper participation of consciousness, history may become more the education of the human race and less its nightmare, and each individual education a kind of recapitulation of phylogeny. Finally we will have a theory of education/history, with politics as the center of our curriculum, which may guide us as religion once presumed to do.

The coalition between the generations is the main one.

THE SOLUTION

Existential
Coalition

NINE

Apportionment
and
Majoritarianism

1 We now enter an area in which that special American institution, the Supreme Court, has accomplished so much in the past few years that one is truly left breathless. There is something quite magnificent in the fact that a handful of men, having scratched their way to the top, could and would do so much so quickly to set us back on the right path. The startling series of reapportionment decisions, beginning with *Baker v. Carr* in 1962, has reintroduced the nation to the idea of majority rule. It has been almost as if God coughed, apologized for an oversight on Mount Sinai, and spoke again.

Is it too much to say that the law has now recognized that in the majority lies the law? In any event, we may, if we choose, now recognize that in the majority lies the ultimate historical legitimacy of power. And here we also witness one of the more fortunate aspects of our national character—the love for law: indeed, the desperate need for law. In the past decade, this passion for absent law has been revealed in the daring role assumed by the one ideality the most cynical lawyer never quite overcomes: the utterances of the majority of the nine men who, we all agree, are closest to the mind of God, if God is both American and rational. Never was there such an institution; and never has the mere majority of this institution reached out so long and strong to remind this nation of its heritage. Beginning with *Brown v. Board of Education* in 1954, they have literally given us a second chance at American history. That could never have happened in Europe, because only in America, the revivalist nation, is the Second Chance—without destructive revolution—a valid and continuing part of the national effort.

It would take too long to prove the point, but the Supreme Court is not exactly a court. It is more than that, in the hindsight of our history: *it has been the nation that never was.* John Marshall fastened upon the Court the post-Federalist burden of maintaining the dream, the formal possibility of nationhood. He did this by exploiting the most obvious weakness in the original constitutional system —that is, the lack of effectively prescribed articulation between the several branches. Just as Hamilton presumed to approach Congress as the Minister of the Exchequer, in proper parliamentary fashion, so Marshall construed the founding document, with its ink still wet, as a definite road map to serious, coherent, and responsible national power—as if there were a sovereign, although there was none. It seems to me that this view of the eccentricity of the Court as an institution holds well enough even through its illiberal periods, as when it succumbed to the overwhelming force of business power after the Civil War (indeed, until the late Thirties) and made of the Due Process Clause a cleared highway to the ascendancy of that irresistible power. The alternative would have been to tempt big business, in its nascent illegality, to ignore or overturn the fledgling national power and the attendant dream of mature continental law. Similarly, the disgrace of *Plessy v. Ferguson:* what could nine old men do—even nine *other* old men—in the depths of the counter-Reconstruction occasioned by Northern indifference?

In the American context, this practicality does not disgrace the Court—I would go all the way and say it ennobles it. The Supreme Court is our *historical* institution, sometimes our institution as a substitute for the achieved accretions of history; and only secondarily is it our fair-and-square summit of rational balance. Of course, a court is always the softened point of application of the sovereign imperative: law itself is the attempt to give power a rational appearance. But *this* Court had—and handled—a very special problem in this respect, because ours has been a very special society. Perhaps what equity jurisdiction was to the building of England, the Supreme Court has been to the more hurried construction of the United States: it encouraged history to happen even when confronted with an impossible requirement of legitimacy, and yet not to happen in too distorted a manner; it preserved a continuity, at least of discourse, but not at the cost of inhibiting too much necessary history. All in all, this sanctified repository of the illusion of national government has done marvelously with a nearly insurmountable situation, namely, enunciating and administering law often enough before there was a government at all, and most often thereafter before there was an adequate one. (The Supreme Court has been our *only* aristocratic institution; and I think it would rate as a very good one anywhere.) Usually, law follows the advent of government. But not in America—not if one is thinking of *official* government.

And certainly not today, with our immense crisis of urban helplessness. Must the nasty facts be repeated again? The American people have moved from the farms to the cities. The governments of the people have not "moved" along with them, which is called malapportionment. This lack of movement includes ideological "governments": we still live mentally under the ideas of the farmers, although in fact we have become city-dwellers. Both indubitably. Too bad. We should have stayed on the farms if we intended to come to the cities quite this unprepared.

I misspoke: we used to live in the cities, now we live in the noncity concentrated areas quite near the cities called suburbs. But the significance of this difference is not very clear. The clearest part of the difference, at the moment, is that the suburbs are white, the cities are colored; the suburbs are new, the cities are old; the suburbs are for families and sleeping, the cities for working and other exotic occupation; and, generally speaking, we have to live in one and are delighted to visit the other. But all this is transitory: the suburbs are simply new cities—with the incalculable addition that pretty soon there will only be cities, which is unheard of.

Meanwhile, the suburbs (which will benefit most from reapportionment) have become a special, juvenile, willed effort at community: as if a brand-new playing field would change the nature of the game. Perhaps it will; but probably not for the coming weekend. Indeed, without the deeper joys of Consumption As a Way of Life, I think even the present suburban-frontiers would be substantially otherwise. In a decade or two, many of them could become ghost-towns. Having discovered the limits of the experiment, we might even force the niggers (whoever they might be at the time) to live there so that we could get back closer to where the action is.

2 Numerical majorities—*merely* numerical—are important in most of our cities and suburbs, where, and because, there are hardly any communities. Granted the existence of a real community, the exact size of each voting district might occasionally fail to become a primary consideration, even to the members of each. But if the problem is community-building, or the inhibition thereof, then power on the basis of numbers is so exquisitely and exclusively appropriate that one begins to doubt the intellectual capacity, educability, and/or good faith of the consistent objectors thereto. Which we shall now proceed to do.

First, we may characterize the political structure that the Supreme Court has begun so dramatically to disrupt. The quickest, most horrendous picture of the state legislatures is provided by imagining what technical percentage of the total population could amend the Constitution—and therefore wield absolute national legal power—if amendment could be effected by the state legislatures alone, without the compliance of Congress: the nearly unbelievable figure just prior to the first of the reapportionment decisions in 1962 was 15 per cent. The figuring goes like this: the Constitution can be amended by thirty-eight states; the thirty-eight least populous states have 40 per cent of the population; on the average, 38 per cent of the voters—because of intrastate malapportionment—could select a majority of a state legislature; 38 per cent of 40 per cent is 15 per cent of the whole. To appreciate these figures fully, one must recall that the amendment power is superior to all others, and that the Framers consequently provided the requirement of excess-majorities as occasions for its exercise—two-thirds of both House and Senate, and three-quarters of the states acting through both houses of their legislatures (if bicameral). The requirement of the affirmative vote of two-thirds of the House was clearly intended to imply two-thirds of the total population of the country, whatever the population differences among the states might be. So the 15 per cent figure should be read against 66⅔ per cent, thus indicating a theoretical disfranchisement of a mite more than 50 per cent of the population.

The foregoing is not a "real" horror story—but it was real enough in the minds of those who would benefit from it if it were, for them to try to bring it about. The effort began in Biloxi, Mississippi, a few months after the first Supreme Court thunderbolt in 1962; about a year later, twelve states had endorsed the proposal to provide for amendment by the states alone.

By June of 1964, when the third and decisive stroke of fearful lightning was loos'd, half of the states could elect a majority of their Senates with 38.4 per cent or less of the vote (down to 8 per cent in Nevada); and half could accomplish the same disgrace in their Houses with 39.9 per cent or less (down to 11.9 per cent in Vermont). In fifteen states, one house or the other (it takes only one, of course) was controlled by less than 20 per cent; nine more came in under the 30 per cent line. Only eleven states (plus Nebraska with one house only) had apportioned to provide for the election of a majority of both houses by at least 40 per cent of the total vote; three others were close. And some of these had risen to this level of propriety as the result of lawsuits—including Tennessee, which had been the defendant in the first case, *Baker v. Carr.* Moreover, New Hampshire, which qualified as a "good" state, contained the rottenest borough in the country: eight persons elected a member of the House to over-represent them. Among the numerous other parodies of democratic representation, California's Senate was the most hilarious for a big, grown-up state—with the smallest district containing 14,294 persons and the largest somewhat crowded with 6,038,771.

As for congressional districts in February 1964, the date of the decision affecting these, nineteen states had a disparity between the largest and smallest districts of about 2 to 1 or more, while in ten states the disparity was itself about equal to the national apportionment factor of around 400,000, based on 435 seats and the 1960 Census figures. Texas, Michigan, and Georgia were the biggest offenders, with Texas leading by un-virtue of a 4½ to 1 disparity; Georgia was, however, the defendant in the deciding case.

The disruption produced by the apportionment decisions has been enormous. By September 1962, five months after the initial decision by the Supreme Court in *Baker v. Carr,* which was handed down on March 26, litigation had been started in at least thirty-one states.

Within a week following the third great decision on June 15, 1964, redistricting suits of greater variety were under way in forty-one states. It is expected that not more than two or three jurisdictions will remain safe from challenge. These lawsuits are mentioned merely to indicate the geographical breadth of the disruption: it takes an imaginative effort to appreciate the social and political depth of the ensuing earthquake. The august fact of the matter is that the new rulings on the voting-apportionment of power constitute a sudden-death challenge to the existing political system in nearly all of the states.

The revolution now occurring, if carried to completion, will raise the cities and the suburbs, and decisively reduce the rural and small-town sections to a proper minority status. But since the suburbs are unformed politically, and certainly are not captives of the cities, they will in many instances constitute the decisive new swing-group. In any event, neither the issue nor the likely outcome can be seen as a simple city/farm affair.

But the old system of "downstate" minority obstructionist rule in the state legislatures is finished, unless the current development is reversed. The greatest blow has fallen on *traditional* party power-and-policy—Republican in the North and Democratic in the South, generally speaking. Insofar as the struggle for the suburbs is seriously undertaken, a substantial blow has also been delivered to traditional Democratic city organizations. In the South, the "downstate" power has been used against the urban areas even more unfairly than in the North, although both sections have been nominally Democratic. So the shift, especially along with the additional factor of Negro enfranchisement, will accelerate the rise of New Democrats as well as the already notorious rise of New Republicans in that area. All in all, a revolution of staggering proportions, which well could mean the beginning of effective local government in the United States, is occurring.

As a result of the Supreme Court decisions, a house of cards is tumbling: many states had not reapportioned seriously in a half-century or more (even though state constitutions required periodic redistricting, as in the Tennessee case), that is, during the full period in which the American population shifted overwhelmingly to the cities. The facts are that gross. So it would hardly do to attempt a factual survey of the events in process. Also, pasteboard cards tumble quickly, and only a newspaper can even try to keep score. The overriding consideration, already an established fact, is that the situation is being *shaken up*—as if, with each swift movement of the arm, a toy kaleidoscope reveals to the amazed eye another rearranged image of the political world. This continued disruption of the established web of power relations was *exactly* what was needed.

There will of course be massive and frantic re-gerrymandering: whatever the outcome, this must mean that *all* groups will be forced to re-form and reestablish relations to each other. *Everyone will be creating new coalitions.* This fact has two immediately useful consequences: a) the true power bases of the conservative or governing coalitions in the re-forming districts will be revealed as they are being revoked—the power advantage derived from secrecy or even conventional obscurity will for a moment be lost; and b) for the same reason, the possible elements and purposes and opportunities of new coalitions will likewise be more apparent to all concerned. Which should provide much needed political education: as "City Hall" crumbles, or at least squirms, more people will be emboldened to go fight it.

3 *Baker v. Carr* was one of the reasons I started to write this book. The potential of that decision to tip the scales of gross injustice impressed me greatly, coming as it did after the second legislative year of the Kennedy administration had begun, and after the Rules Committee fight of the previous year (positively) and subsequent congressional votes (negatively) had established the narrow margin of the administration's domestic frustration. I was thinking about the significance of the decision for congressional districting, while looking for a shift of twenty to forty votes from the conservative coalition in the House to the national urban majority which seemed already to be in existence everywhere else. Also, following the spread of the sit-ins and the Freedom Rides, the Negro movement was gaining momentum in 1962 (although it did not crest until a year later in Birmingham); again, with my amateur accountant's mind, I was thinking of the potential increase in Negro registration, especially in the South. Finally, the Reform Democratic movement in New York City (where I was living) had begun to show some success along with its moxie, and it came to me (late) that this sort of new activism had been going on for some

time—had really started in California with the Stevenson candidacies and was now threatening to become a national big-city phenomenon. All three, it seemed, should certainly prove capable of shifting a mere twenty to forty votes in the House, thus establishing a "liberal" working majority in that den of obstructionism.

And thus it is with mice and men and writers. The rapidity of American politics since the *Baker* decision has carried us quite beyond those tempting few votes in the House. Writing after the decisive national response to Native Unreality, one may *assume* the New Deal and reasonably effective federal government. (See Chapter Four for details.) What, then, is the remaining problem, if any? To begin with, it is certainly the need to ensure and improve our new national majoritarianism, its structure and its effects. In the light of this somewhat new purpose, one might still begin to write a political book because of *Baker v. Carr.*

This case did more than *Brown v. Board of Education,* because *Brown* simply signified a reversal of the indecent trend of decision since the Civil War amendments had been abandoned—which course of abdication was confirmed in *Plessy v. Ferguson. Brown* overruled *Plessy.* But *Baker* overruled even more of American history. *Baker* said that whatever our beginnings may have been, and however fumblingly we may have tried to deal with these, now—today, in this world—our Original Social Contract unalterably specified "democracy." It added: Now we begin to try to define this term, even if against convenience, before any group induces us to abandon it altogether, for the sake of convenience. The courage of this decision—clearly, it placed the institution itself in jeopardy, thus majestically redefining it as only Marshall previously had dared to do—will resound throughout the annals of American history. Along with *Brown, Baker* more or less revives the Constitution as a seriously arguable document. In 1937 (or perhaps the later day before *Brown* or the even later one before *Baker*) no one in his right mind would have taken any of this as conceivable. Thus our dangerously magnificent institution—which had devoted nearly a century to the unabashed defense of raw property interests—has picked up the administrative torch of American history and said, like Chekhov, No, my friends, *this* is the way. As Kennedy's death was the serious beginning of Death in American popular culture, so this decision was the beginning of a thoughtfully active intervention with the arguable part of our cultural history. On March 26, 1962, there was returned to us the opportunity to redefine American citizenship—because we had done so badly with all our previous opportunities. The Court said: Well, what does it all come to, this great experiment on this great continent; and what lie or truth do we *really* mean by "Democracy"?

Baker v. Carr held that the Supreme Court would undertake to review the institutional weight of one man's vote in relation to that of any other. The Court thus set out to carry the responsibility of refereeing the terms and counters of a basic distribution of power in a seriously voting society. The Court said that it was the ultimate authority in determining when any state had made or enforced any law denying "within its jurisdiction the equal protection of the laws" with respect to voting. A monumental presumption, previously denied to the Court by a long line of misguided decisions reaching way back and down, like an oil well, to the rich black fears of initiating a constitutional collision.

The view before *Baker* had been that legislatures should reapportion themselves. That they had not, did not, and would not, for rather obvious reasons, was considered an unfortunate "political" question.* "Courts ought not to enter this political thicket," Mr. Justice Frankfurter had said in the leading case, *Colegrove v. Green,* decided by an exceptionally divided Court in 1946. Dissenting in the *Baker* case, he warned ominously that the assumption of jurisdiction over the political issue of population and representation "may well impair the Court's position" and authority in an ultimate sense. Mr. Justice Harlan, the other dissenter in *Baker* (who has carried the major burden of judicial opposition since Frankfurter's retirement and later death), took a less majestic and harder line—he simply denied the applicability of the Equal Protection Clause.

Somewhat more impressively, he also denied the ground of decision in *Wesberry v. Sanders,* the second major apportionment case, handed down February 17, 1964, which applied the doctrine of equal proportions of population to congressional districting. Mr. Justice Black, writing for seven members of the Court, reached high and far in securing the dominance of the doctrine in House elections:

* With current hindsight, it is exquisitely ironic that legislators in one state after another, attempting to redistrict under a judicial gun, have been unable to do so and have, in the end, passed the buck back to the courts to do it for them. In effect, redistricting is so superbly a "political" question that only a court or a commission can deal with it, as if the effort were a "little" constitutional convention each time.

We hold that, construed in its historical context, the command of Art. I, §2, that Representatives be chosen "by the People of the several States" means that as nearly as is practicable one man's vote in a congressional election is to be worth as much as another's.

The applicability of the Fourteenth Amendment was specifically left to one side. The significance of the difference is very likely that, as long as the decision stands and short of a constitutional amendment, Congress itself will be more constricted in the scope of future apportionment legislation relating to itself. The Equal Protection Clause has been and will be the subject of a great deal of complex interpretation; it applies to a multitude of circumstances; and has been generally taken to preclude "invidious discrimination," not any and all discrimination. The Art. I, §2 ground in *Wesberry* of course has no general applicability, and opens argument only as to the meaning of "the People" and as to historical context (referring primarily to the Constitutional Convention and subsequent ratification debates in the original thirteen states). In his dissent, Justice Harlan put together a rather good argument derived from this historical context. But he set out with horroristic bombast, intoning that "today's decision impugns the validity of the election of 398 Representatives," meaning that the current House hardly existed, constitutionally. He might as well have said that the decision revised the legality of much of American history, *nunc pro tunc*. In fact, however, history can be changed without being rewritten, even in the law, which presumes to join history and rationality in tight wedlock.

The third great decision day was June 15, 1964. Six cases on state legislative apportionment were entered in the books (a week later, districting in nine more states was overturned with summary orders). An Alabama case led the others, and *Baker v. Carr*—which had merely found the issue of apportionment "justiciable"—was extended therein with a force and effect its warmest supporters had hardly dared to hope for. The hurdle of the Alabama case was a notion called "the federal analogy," to the effect that one house—the upper, Senate-type house—of a bicameral state legislature could be apportioned geographically and without warm regard for equal proportions of the population. Roughly, this would have provided one veto each to urban and small-town interests, with the possibility of positive enactments thereafter forever entwined on newer and shrewder levels of horse-trading. But if you don't ride horses, you don't have to trade for them—and mostly only the urban side requires a positive-acting government in the first place. The other fellows already have their system of "government," as to which the state legislature is mostly a fifth wheel to be restrained from running over anything important or expensive.

So much for fifth wheels and horse-trading: now to the unmixed metaphor of the Alabama decision, which was the steam-roller of them all . . .

Reynolds v. Sims found "the so-called Federal analogy inapposite" and held that "the Equal Protection Clause requires that the seats in both houses of a bicameral state legislature must be apportioned on a population basis." With these words the Supreme Court deployed the entire federal judiciary in the ensuring of majority rule in state government. Considering the size and complexity of the continent, and the established absence of majority rule in nearly all of the fifty states, this act—by a court, not a sovereign—must rank with the grandest lawgiving in history. Writing for the majority of six, the Chief Justice said: "Our constitutional system amply provides for the protection of minorities by means other than giving them majority control of State Legislatures." As a matter of American political philosophy, this statement—containing a current denial and a future presumption—is the center of the whole apportionment issue.

For a lawyer (and former member of the board of editors of the precisely produced *Yale Law Journal*), I have been unforgivably cavalier in the foregoing treatment of legal issues and arguments. My defense, shockingly, is that I am not any longer in that business. Lawyers have to talk the way they do; I don't. And law *is* mostly a special language—with rationalization as its grammar, and historicity for syntax, whereby every legal "sentence" has Reason for the subject and History as the predicate, which is why lawyers alone can make sense out of the paragraphs. Law, to be law, must change while it seems to stand still; and it is hardly ever permitted the simple human statements—"I am sorry: you were right, and I was wrong"; or, "Yes, but things have changed." The most engrossing complexities in the law are derived from the avoidance of these simplicities.

Justice Harlan's increasing ferocity in his *Baker, Wesberry,* and *Reynolds* dissents would appeal to me, if I were still in that business. He showed a close appreciation of syntax, and a strong feeling for the predicate; he did not, however, end up with very many full sen tences. His main point in *Reynolds,* probably well taken, was that the Fourteenth Amendment was not adopted in order to deal with reapportionment in 1964. Throughout his argumentation, he stuck to the legal and the historical points—to begin with. Then the enormity of what the majority was doing in spite of his careful legal handiwork threatened to overwhelm him, and he would add six unimpressive arguments. When (very rarely) he daintily touched on the non-legal substance, he said (as in *Reynolds*) things like: ". . . I believe that the vitality of our political system, on which in the last analysis all else depends, is weakened by reliance on the judiciary for political reform; in time a complacent body politic may result." The complacency, not to say the disastrous apathy, enforced by the existing situation did not concern him—it was not "justiciable," did not state a cause of action, was not meet for federal decision, etc. *Baker v. Carr* he characterized as "an experiment in venturesome constitutionalism." Which it certainly was. But when he spoke to the non-legal issue, he relied piously on the myth of Individualism.

By and large, there were the nightmare facts of history on one side and the equally true daydream of rational justice on the other; and not at all surprisingly, neither faction dealt fairly with the other's arguments. How could they?

4 The issue is majority rule—whether we can achieve it, what it might look like, and whether we can live with it once achieved, whatever it looks like.

Somewhere between the close legal reasoning of the constitutional lawyers and the desperate rationalizations of, say, the "Pork Chop Gang" which has controlled the steeply malapportioned Florida legislature, lies a serious question as to the role of the Supreme Court. But Justices Frankfurter and Harlan have not so much argued this question as asserted their answers to it. This involves very complex theory—much of it only implicitly available in their writing—as to the nature of the law itself, along with one's most sincere guesses as to the best way of nurturing its growth here in America. That's another story; indeed a very interesting one, but having little to do directly with apportionment and majoritarianism. Not all of us need be concerned to prognosticate the institutional future of the Court. Let us recognize that the Court extended itself severely on our behalf, and be grateful.

As a lawyer, however, I suggest that this extension is in the Great Tradition of English-speaking law: the enlargement of Due Process to contain the post-Civil War business revolution, of the Commerce Clause in order to allow the New Deal to occur, and now of the Equal Protection Clause to revive majority political action as our last best hope; each amounts to imperative expansions of "equity" jurisdicion as centuries ago the Crown first created that jurisdiction itself. There is nothing wrong with—certainly nothing new in—judge-made law if it works. Besides, we can always amend the Constitution to do away with the Marshall-type Court, whenever we so desire. It happens, however, that because of our minimal nationalism, non-rule peculiarities, rationalistic beginnings, and moral presumptions, this particular refereeing institution is nearly the core-slice of American Apple Pie. I believe that the current Supreme Court majority has made a precise as well as a courageous judgment balancing realizations as to how much is needed of it, and how much it is needed, in America. Subsequent historians will applaud this post-New Deal Court for reviving the relevance of our major eccentric institution.

But the issue is not the role of the Court: the issue is majority rule.

Is there, or is there not, something *sacred* about the majority? Is there, or is there not, something supremely *useful* about the concept? I say that if we live together, and if there is need of some kind of rule over this living, then the more it is determined or limited by majoritarianism, the more legitimate it is. Legitimacy does not begin with truth: it begins with numbers, the more so the more fairly ascertained. Law is not truth: law is law, which is both less and more than truth; law is actually historical as well as presumptively true. To quote a fine writer, Oscar Gass: "American democracy is an inheritance, not a philosophy." If we turn it into a philosophy, we may destroy it; at least we stop its development, thus denying the next inheriting generation its birthright. In America, we have taken law with us on vigilante raids, and into the sewer of the San Francisco waterfront; wherever we went, it was buckled around our waist. My point is that a gun was never enough; our deep need to legitimate our history, often enough while it was occurring, is perhaps our special genius. The English were empirical, but we invented pragmatism—which made truth itself a practical matter; and law, therefore, an even deeper necessity.

All of the conservative conversation directed against equal proportions assumes a political advantage to one group over another which must be achieved in the *structure* of the political system itself rather than in the voting or other political process. Once the web of complexity has been brushed away, all of these arguments are at bottom absurd—because there neither *is* nor can there be a legitimate structure apart from function (unless legitimacy is identified with the sanctifying force of duration). First of all, the minority group is never identified, nor is there ever a reasonably clear statement made as to why it must have an advantage at the expense of some other. If we were to talk about which group should have an advantage, then, for instance, I would assert that the Negro should be over-represented in all legislatures, particularly in the South. The Southern whites would very likely have another point of view. The notion that this essentially political process should be prejudged in the structure of the political system itself means that one intends to use structure in order to keep politics from occurring. Obviously this can only work to enthrone a particular existing political advantage; obviously, also, it could only be brought about by an existing superior power. It always comes down to the statement that politics, to the given extent of the structural distortion, is not necessary, or should be avoided anyway.

But the appeal to equal representation must be ideal rather than historical: we have a deep background of upholding inequality in this country. The justificatory arguments therefor were at one time quite candid. The early constitutional debates in New York, for instance, were clear that the purpose in the distribution of power was to ensure that the propertyless masses of New York City would not be so advantaged that they might constitute a threat to the property-holding of upright upstate citizens. It must remain ideal also in that it cannot be fully achieved: bicameralism, which has been enthroned irretrievably in the national system, has the effect of making a truly majoritarian order impossible. At the very root of the idea of a Senate, an Upper Chamber, is the assumption of the existence of an aristocracy—a better class of people—in the society: that, and regionalism (also called "federalism" by political science professors). But the equality of votes in the Senate as between states, and irrespective of the population of the states, is the one provision of the Constitution not subject to amendment. This aspect of the original deal between the original thirteen states is thus a curse upon the generations—and a fairly ironical one, in that the subsequent thirty-seven states (being an amendment-majority, incidentally) were created by the government created by the initial thirteen. But there you are.

The idea that one man, one vote is equal to one fully inclusive unit of power is of course nonsense; but the one man, one vote ideal—or prejudice—is not. Because it sustains majoritarianism, which sustains law in this particular democracy. If our lesser brothers are a burden or an embarrassment to us, why must they be made powerless *before* we raise them? And if we do not intend to exert ourselves to raise them, where do we come off justifying a repressive system by calling it "democracy"? A little power on the part of a student can ensure, for instance, that the teacher does his duty.

I, too, could dream up a better ideal world than the one a current American majority would be apt to institute or tolerate. So what? Law reflects power, which means it reflects the given distribution of power. Only the majority—or self-appointed "superiority"—can determine the propriety of any particular distribution, or correct it. And who is initially to determine superiority? (The beneficiaries of any power distribution may claim superiority, of course, as an afterthought.) No, the majority must be the lawgiver.

It is not hard to imagine a situation some decades from now where all men of good will would regret a majoritarian system, were one established now when it is so desperately needed. Yet there is no alternative to it: it is too obviously the democratic way of ruling. And non-rule is too potent a weapon to be tolerated against all present reason as a defense against some frightfully unreasonable future. It is a sad fact of the species that each generation must discover its own reasonableness—using, of course, the heritage the preceding generation leaves in its passing. Under continuing non-rule today, we will bequeath nothing but disaster to our children.

Since there is no "natural" majority in America, the overriding issue becomes the composition of the coalitions constituting the desired or achieved majority. And this is the predominant subject of the remainder of the book.

5 There is a purportedly sophisticated anti-majoritarian point of view somewhat current, which we might notice, to the effect that either things aren't so bad as all this or they're inevitable, take your choice; everybody knows democracy isn't real anyway, and who could bear it if it were; and therefore the equal proportions principle is not important or will not solve all problems of representation—again, take your choice.

One of the more interesting exponents of this position is Professor Alexander M. Bickel of the Yale Law School. Mr. Bickel is a contributing editor of *The New Republic*, therefore a "liberal," which is one part of what makes his point of view so interesting. The other sources of interest are that he is a highly trained legal reasoner in the Frankfurter tradition; and he appears to speak also from within the traditions of "modern political science," as, for instance, "the equal-vote premise ignores all that we have learned in a generation of fresh inquiry and reflection." What Mr. Bickel ignores, it should be said immediately, is not quite that extensive, but still significant.

Indeed, he makes a point of ignoring almost nothing, except the practical heart of the matter, in his careful evaluation of the apportionment problem. A year after the *Baker* decision in *Commentary* ("Reapportionment & Liberal Myths," June 1963), Mr. Bickel's balanced appraisal of the situation led him to the judgment that "we cannot look for any enduring result from this particular enterprise in judicially-directed reform." This, he said, was most specifically so because the Court in *Baker* established the "meaningless" test of "rationality" as the standard for applying the Equal Protection Clause in apportionment cases. A less careful analyst would have been more impressed with the fact that the Court had held the Clause applicable than with the fact that it had also mentioned the most obvious and unexceptionable criterion for its newly determined applicability. In the course of beating the dead horse of the rationality test with precision, Mr. Bickel noted—probably one of the achievements of "a generation of fresh insight and inquiry"—that legislative acts must be good as well as rational. It turns out, upon further mature reflection, that equal proportions is no-good because it is too simple—life is more complicated than "that."

Caught between the proprieties of the Frankfurter view of the Court and perception of the complexities of actual political life, Mr. Bickel manages without any ill will at all (I think) to miss the point of *Baker* and of the whole apportionment issue. Alfred de Grazia (for whose views, see below) does not manage this feat without ill will. Bickel succeeds because he, unlike de Grazia, is simply an overly sophisticated lawyer who, in the established Frankfurter tradition, is determinedly engaged in confusing rationality and history by distorting the role of the Court. In this effort, the Court is so burdened with supra-historical rationality that it is reduced to a very narrow focus of actual historical intervention. In this way, enough rationality is secured in the keystone of the lawyer's house so that he may live in it with reduced dread of its imminent collapse (upon his comfort and his conscience*).

As a necessary corollary, of course, we must wistfully say to hell with the peasants who might have benefited from a different conception of the role of the Court and a broader use of its power.

To avoid the unpleasantness of stating this corollary explicitly, "a generation of fresh insight" from political science comes to the rescue. As, for example: governing "institutions must not merely represent a numerical majority—which is a shifting and uncertain quantity anyway—but must reflect the people in all their diversity," etc. So democratic representation is "reflection," and this is so complicated that counting doesn't help much; and maybe it's altogether too complicated to talk about to any real effect—that is, the *status quo* is smarter than we are (the conservative's ultimate argument). Although I can think of a very short answer to this, the position is so silly in its seeming shrewdness that I will take a whole paragraph.

Professor Bickel says "the legislature carries the burden of reflecting the diversities of population, and . . . it could not under any circumstances perform this function if it were built strictly on the one-person-one-vote principle." I suggest that this is exactly wrong, that a legislature can reflect diversity only insofar as it approaches the equality principle, whether or not "strictly." Otherwise, the representation reflects inequality, which is not democratic—even in reflection. Were a mirror to reflect two apples and one orange as being

* *To the lawyers:* This is the particular impasse achieved by the paralysis of legal realism—and none of us have achieved much beyond legal realism and this particular impasse. What is disturbing to me, is that the impasse is so monumentally *current*.

one of each, it would present a distorted reflection of apple-and-orange diversity. If there are 400,000 idiots in the country, and the apportionment factor is 1 to 400,000, on what theory of reflecting diversity are the idiots entitled to more than one representative? If there are twenty million Negroes in the country, in what sense does a national legislature reflect diversity except as it contains nearly fifty Negro representatives—or is structured on the possibility of such occurrence, if every Negro voted as every rationalist thinks? And if the process cannot be accomplished perfectly, then exactly what exists now is just about all right? And if the Supreme Court does not demand perfection in so many words, then it should leave the situation just as it is? And what are we going to call this kind of thinking, which so blandly confuses the provision of a *voice* for an interest group with its *weight* in a representative body?

Our native aversion to democracy is so profound that it often enough occurs as an unspoken *assumption* in the arguments of very intelligent and otherwise well-intentioned people. The reason, I think, is that, through both the remnants of classical education as well as the ordinary civics course, democracy is "justified" on the Athenian or town-meeting model. Which means that modern mass democracy cannot be "justified" at all, and so is, at best, tolerated—with elite loathing. But it is exactly the great unwashed and uneducated for whom democracy was intended and is still important: the well-educated and well-placed do not want it, and never practice it in their own lives. People in the middle who have something to defend are not natural democrats—they exclude their inferiors, aspire to associate with those above them, and with these purposes mingle carefully with their peers. But people at the bottom cannot exclude, nor can they aspire very much—they can only mingle, and they do not have the time or the resource to be careful about it. Therefore, a modern well-washed (middle-class) democrat, when true to both the commitment and the circumstance, is not primarily somebody who is benign toward inferiors and even likes New York cab drivers—he is someone who favors the relative representational strengthening of the Negro bloc, the urban bloc, the labor bloc, and any other under-represented blocs, which might help the country forward with their power and their votes. He does this whether or not he looks forward

to sipping sherry and discussing Proust with the leaders of any of
these blocs. And he uses his good taste publicly, if at all, to refrain
from applauding the going undemocratic show.

6 Throughout the writing on ap-
portionment, one notices a consistently reappearing confusion between numerical apportionment and the political gerrymander.
There are some other frequent arguments not derived from overt
anti-democratic sentiment—for instance, the naïve non-rule assertion that the Executive is majoritarian and that should be enough to
satisfy any reasonable, well-behaved majority. And similar nonsense
which overlooks the need for government in its devotion to "reflection." As another instance, the impossibility of mathematical exacti-
tude is again and again noted. (Generally, I have been struck by the
overfull basket, or kitchen-sink, character of the objecting side in the
apportionment argumentation: they tend toward a kind of hysteria
of detail, or compulsive cataloguing, which lowers the whole tone.)
But the argument worth pursuing, the revealing one, concerns the
gerrymander.

In his dissent in *Wesberry,* Justice Harlan stated that

> by focusing exclusively on numbers in disregard of the area and
> shape of a congressional district as well as party affiliations
> within the district, the Court deals in abstractions which will be
> recognized even by the politically unsophisticated to have little
> relevance to the realities of political life.

But the "exclusive focus" of the Court was certainly more the result
of judicial savvy than of political naïveté, and Justice Harlan must
have known this. (When the purpose of a gerrymander is demon-
strably racial, the Court has held it to be unconstitutional.) If anything, the Court has been overly acute politically, in its great effort to
administer electoral and representational fairness nationally and as
a matter of ultimate law. The practical point which is the main underlying point of all the recent apportionment action—which has
been missed by so many rationalists, and taken advantage of by so
many anti-democrats—is that numerical apportionment *can* be administered by the federal judiciary under the Fourteenth Amend-

ment, and it is a difficult, outstanding question whether this is true of any other aspect of districting. Contrary to Professor Bickel's supposition (noted below), numerical apportionment will prove to be infinitely easier to administer than school desegregation (once the Northern school cases start rolling in, certainly).

Number is as obvious as color: ultimate justice, of course, will never be obvious. If only the rationalists had the courage to be practical about ideals—if only they could better conceive the coexistence of ideals and practicality— history might lose some little area of its agony, and also occur somewhat more readily. But, no—a proper all-or-nothing, even for the smart ones. (Especially for the smart ones?) And thus the unrelieved agony of history.

But with all of the Court's best effort, it will remain extremely difficult to hold back the dawn of serious efforts to deal with the insidious gerrymander. Especially since, as the numerical doctrine succeeds, the next problem more clearly emerges (there is always a "next problem")—and this is certainly the next-most-gross misuse of districting power by interested parties—that is, the gerrymander. Like the first, it is crudely political. Still, I stay with the conviction that welcomes anything to shake up the situation—and even to keep it shook. In this, I make a political, not a merely legal, judgment.

Since the *Reynolds* decision in June 1964, when no one could any longer in sanguine doubt delay as to the over-all intention of the Court, guilty state legislatures around the country began to devise reapportionment schemes in swelling, devious quantities. The issue being who would be dumped, rural-controlled bodies discovered some of the "reflective," traditional, and community-type groupings to be less than organically steadfast facing the unrelieved onslaught of Grecian tragedy. So much so, indeed, that rather than embark on uncharted seas of sacrificial gerrymander for the greater good of the party—or even of the rest of the Traditional Community in the next county—many of them, as we noted earlier, seem to have said, To hell with it; let the courts do it. Which is what happens, one imagines, to any unmastered ship of state whereof the barnacles have not been scraped lo this last half-century.

In an advisory portion of the great *Reynolds* decision, the Chief Justice ominously mused aloud concerning the wriggling gerrymander. Bowing this way and that with respect to the numerous arguments which have been advanced to justify departures from the equal proportions doctrine, he suggested with an oblique inflection: "Indiscriminate districting, without any regard for political subdivision or natural or historical boundary lines, may be little more than an open invitation to partisan gerrymandering." Always holding to the overriding equal proportions criterion, he added: "And a state may legitimately desire to construct districts along political subdivision lines to deter the possibilities of gerrymandering." The initial paragraph on the issue reads as follows: "A state may legitimately desire to maintain the integrity of various political subdivisions, insofar as possible, and provide for compact districts of contiguous territory in designing a legislative apportionment scheme."

On reflection and rereading, this is seen to be very pregnant *musant* indeed. Especially when one recalls that the traditional prescription for hamstringing the indigenous gerrymander has been to require that districts be contiguous, compact, and of equal size. In one form or another, one or more of these requirements has (for instance) been a part of congressional apportionment statutes since the first was enacted in 1842. (Before that date, there was no national requirement for congressional districts and, many Representatives being elected at large, the party taking the state took all the House seats as part of the booty.) The 1842 law enthroned "contiguous"; in 1872 districts were required to contain "as nearly as practicable an equal number of inhabitants"; in 1901 "compact" came in; the 1911 statute repeated the foregoing criteria; there was no reapportionment following the 1920 Census; the 1929 statute enacted automatic apportionment without the three criteria; and besides, whether on the books or off, none of the principles in the statutes from 1842 on has ever been enforced—no Representative has ever been denied a seat for any of these occasionally statutory reasons.

Anyway, the Court has—as lawyers put it—retained jurisdiction over the question of gerrymandering, i.e., has not foreclosed the possibility of a future decision on the issue. Which means that the Justices are *really* serious: there is no question in my mind that a majority of the 1964 Court fully intends to oversee voting/representation practices with the same absolute devotion to the austere commands of the Fourteenth Amendment that it has shown it will follow with regard to race. Neither issue, as to principle, is any longer "negotiable." All nuance hereafter lies in application, and in timing.

In a country without enough "natural" communities, the question of proper "districting" presents nearly unmanageable philosophical depths. Which nevertheless must be managed. But we may hope to avoid overmanaging by, say, focusing-in on *artificial* gerrymanders while avoiding the too-deeply-philosophical issues involved in reordering *natural* gerrymanders. (This bit of prudence may even be applied to school districts as well as legislative districts, although the pressure is much greater on the former.) Since the issue will grow in importance, we may pause to note the following:

There are two contrary principles of party-vote gerrymandering: one is to crowd as many of the opposition party's voters as possible into a single district, so that one's opponent achieves 90 per cent majorities in electing a candidate that he could not in any event be prevented from electing. The alternative principle is to "waste" as many of the opposition party's votes as possible by distributing them throughout districts in which your own party maintains an adequate majority. The comprehensive principle is essentially that of making a *de facto* approach to proportional representation on your own behalf only, namely, that you distribute your voting power among as many different candidates or districts as possible, and do not try to get more advantage than you are capable of digesting. It is significant that the Republicans have an extreme gerrymandering advantage in the North because Democrats tend to be concentrated in particular areas much more than are Republicans. This makes it easier for the Republicans to gain an advantage from the excess-votes-in-a-single-district gerrymander.

A possible technique to inhibit the gerrymandering process would be to create districts on the basis of past voting records, which then would be as nearly as possible equal in Democratic and Republican votes. This would be a kind of political Sherman Act, constituting an official gerrymander in favor of competitive districts. But short of proportional representation, which is objected to because it furthers fragmentation (although being a superbly "reflective" mechanism), all that one can do is to circumscribe the area of discretion of a politically-intended gerrymander. And that is why equal numerical apportionment is important—not because it enacts an ideal, but because it is the obvious first step along the path of making it more difficult to effect a grossly political gerrymander. The same is true of the standard phrasing of an anti-gerrymander law, that districts must be compact and contiguous, as well as equal in population.

Professor Bickel believes that "it is possible to achieve all the malapportionment in the world by careful gerrymandering of perfectly equal districts." This strikes me as a wild and woolly presumption; but if it turns out to be true, the Supreme Court will have to move through the door it left open in *Reynolds,* and further constrict the districting discretion of state legislatures.

Or perhaps we can just give up on the issue of majority rule in favor of Proper Proportions in the world of legal doctrine—yes, Mr. Bickel?

7 Neither Professor Bickel nor Justice Frankfurter can with certainty be said to have favored the rural edge in the current malapportionment. Their concern seems to have been with the method of reform, and the complexity of the whole legal/political process. I have argued that this line of thought suffers from the fallacy of misplaced delicacy, that democracy unavoidably involves majority rule, that it has raw substance as well as formal refinements, and so on. Although much exasperation is experienced on both sides, something like a reasonable argument can take place with thinkers in this camp.

Not so with Professor Alfred de Grazia. His opposition to equal proportions leaves nothing to the imagination; but even so, his opposition to it is only one item in a broad range of notions supporting the current system of malapportionment. If his contempt for the doctrine has been placed up front, that is because it is now in fact displacing his own worked-over web of rationalizations. He is not concerned with the method of reform—he is against any reform at all.

In 1963 he issued an all-out attack on *Baker v. Carr* and the whole doctrine of equal apportionment, called *Apportionment and Representative Government.* It was published by a right-wing think-group in Washington with the definitive name—American Enterprise Institute for Public Policy Research. In this book, his vilification of the proponents of the liberal doctrine discovers absolutely no bounds. We witness awesome scholarly rage against the knaves and fools who can propound so simple a doctrine. Apart from vilification, his chief method of argument is to complicate the issue of apportionment by referring to *all other* elements of the full political representation system, legal and otherwise. He proves conclusively, more than a few times, that equal apportionment will not introduce nirvana, even for liberals.

Professor de Grazia's hatred is intense, with the consequence that he sputters inordinately: his arguments assume one conclusion after another as he lays low the on-marching infantry of straw men. In the totally re-created world of the scholar, this kind of scholar, everything must be put in its proper place—and by *him*. Otherwise one will get a mess, namely, history. In this wild attack on the simplistic equality doctrine, he marshals all the countervailing notions and gimmicks—based on history, theory, and bad digestion—but never once makes anything like a fair analysis of the effect of equal apportionment itself. Apparently the notion is just too misconceived to be entitled to that kind of attention.

We get to page 63 in this volume of 180 pages before it is revealed to us that equal apportionment is disproved, finally and at last, because it leads to majority rule. Majority rule, this theoretician tells us, is unacceptable because it creates "inequality"—that is, the minority becomes "unequal" to the majority. Besides, any majority that *really* wants to act like a majority can always manage to do so against *any* contrary institutional arrangements (whether with guns or not, he fails to reveal; nor does he explain why such energetic "inequality" on the part of the majority is acceptable). So, for instance, he justifies the New York legislative malapportionment because it provides against overcentralization of power in New York City. Exactly. The power that should reside in New York City, where it is needed, is transferred instead to the upstate regions, where it is neither needed nor entitled to be used. Isn't that wonderfully democratic?

In making the usual sophisticated argument that communities, rather than merely numerical populations, should be represented, he fails even to try to demonstrate that there is any such thing as a community actually represented in or by the present system of malapportionment. And never does he approach the problem that such representation, in any event, would be representation *against* the over-all population. A serious argument on this matter would note the unfairness while insisting on the necessity: I've yet to hear it. Even if one were to establish that an actual community of a kind did exist, this would not mean that it was thereby entitled to outvote another community or even another non-community. (Are we going to *penalize* people because they suffer alienation?) This line of argument merely takes advantage of the lack of community in cities to justify depriving them of power. And this was, in fact, a basic argument in favor of unequal suffrage advanced straightforwardly 150 years ago.

Throughout the arguments of those who oppose equal apportionment, we noted, there runs a particular and probably purposeful misuse of the word "representation." It is frequently taken to mean that a certain group, community, or interest should have a "voice" in the legislative assembly. Of course. But obviously not a voice strong enough to outshout two other voices, because that reduces the "voice" of the majority. But this simple fact is too simple for this big theorist and his friends. So his answer to it is a continuing flow of insults, a great massing of anti-democratic historical precedents (which are quite true and prove nothing other than the known injustices of history), mixed with statements that majoritarianism leads to dictatorship, anything new is disruptive, and profound assurances that life is very complicated. Also, the look-you-got-a-hole-in-your-pants type of argument which reveals—with a great flourish—that the proponents of equal apportionment really and truly favor the doctrine in order to achieve some increase in power for particular urban or liberal groups. Who would have suspected anything like that! (The primitivism of this kind of overeducated "discussion" of power is really appalling.)

As far as I have been able to determine, there are only two really good conservative arguments about anything: 1) that nothing helps and nobody can be trusted anyway; and 2) a Burkean view of "good" history as a kind of well-gardened organic growth. The first idea may be true, but is just too black a gruel to eat regularly. As for Burkeanism, it should be noted that it is exceedingly English, even as a fantasy. H. Trevor-Roper, writing in the *New Statesman* for May 24, 1963, said of the history of the landed interests in England: "As so often in English life, continuity of form concealed continual change of substance." One has to be born to English hypocrisy; it differs from other national forms. When it works, it works well; it doesn't always work. More important for us, America as originally constituted was so exceedingly rationalistic that Burkeanism is nearly irrelevant to our messy condition: having "interfered" excessively with Slow Growth History from the beginning, we are stuck with rational reforms as a way of doing business. Besides, the Burkean way works best over a long period of fully contested history. Short of this (and really it is the development of a national character, not merely a so-called form of government), a Burkean type of growth does not necessarily create true form; it may merely conceal the not exceptionally elevated proposition, "What happens, happens." This is nicely illustrated, in the present instance, by the fact that the mal-apportionment existing today is based on vanished farm communities, not existing ones. The historical growth here did not create an integral or even a useful form: it merely shifted power disfunctionally to windfall parties. Meanwhile, the cities and the suburbs are denied the power to govern themselves properly. (The malapportionment is often enough not a *positive* help even to the few remaining farmers.)

Probably the real significance of writers like de Grazia is that the unfortunately backward position they take is a perverse result of their particular type of intellectuality. It is elitist, by inadvertence if not by intention. These writers just do not understand that clear thought is not a substitute for reality, but is only one among a number of means of reentering it usefully. As an aspiring purveyor of clear thought and a scholar's orderliness, de Grazia, for instance, has a totally unacceptable notion of constitutional law and the role of the Supreme Court. He says he favors "the objectivity of law" which he defines as

> that idealized condition when informed and reasonable persons agree that the application of a law to a case does not deviate from previous applications to similar cases except by the rules of empirical and deductive logic. The objectivity of the law is the ultimate condition served by the operating principle: "a judge does not make the law; he only applies it."

One begins by thinking that this is a naïve view of the relation of power and law, and ends up convinced that it is a dishonest one. It is law conceived as an utterly *willful* rationalization of existing power. If law preserved its rational consistency against all history, we would end up having no law at all or (the same thing) a system of law irrelevant to our *actual* history. What could be more obvious?

Putting the matter most generously: Professor de Grazia is perhaps against equal apportionment primarily because it is too simple for a political science scholar. But what sophistry, in pursuit of that assumption, is he not capable of! No argument is too low to be used

—including the lulu that reapportionment is so easy that the courts need not intervene. And he will employ mysticism, too; he does not refrain from referring to "the will of the people" in defense of the existing mess.

The following is a statement of his position providing the full flavor of the book (it appears on pages 130-131):

> The equal-populations numerology . . . is a dangerous flirtation with mass neurosis. Man loses standing as a citizen—without regard to slogans of "one man, one vote"—when he is reduced to a naked, abstract number. He has a faceless equality with other numbered citizens. They become equally devoid of group ties and human responsibilities until they become the mass. The "mass" in fact cannot be said to exist until citizenship has been destroyed through individuals being torn loose from their social relations and reduced to separate items, helplessly confronting the central state. That philosophical considerations such as these have weighed not at all against the numerology of so many courts and commentators should serve to warn Americans all the more of the ultimate issues involved in the events of these days. The astonishing swiftness with which even the most facile presentations of this image of man as number have been seized and acted upon in the present apportionment controversy suggest an appalling readiness to accept such an image of man as compelling and final, as axiomatic.

This, friends, is the kind of elevated and perverse use of elitist ideals that leads at last to fascism.

If de Grazia, or any other scholar, could content himself with pointing out what equal apportionment will not accomplish, what problems will remain after it accomplishes what it can, his contribution—with or without medium animus—would be welcome. But he does not limit himself to such work. By no means. In a disguised, disgusting, and undistinguished way, he simply revives the ancient arguments against democracy—that some people are better than others, that a mass of equal units is not a particularly attractive view of humanity, and so on.

But ideals are to be achieved in, not plastered on, a nation's history. Equality for the unequal and inferior is our highest ideal and safeguard—*still*. As an ideal, democracy is inevitable. As a fact, it does not exist; and it would annul itself by achievement. One of our difficulties is that we have confused it, present ideal and future fact, with bourgeois aggressiveness. A true democracy will forgive and will provide for inferiority: in the end, no one will be forced to be equal. But Professor de Grazia says *today:* "To make votes count best, they cannot be made equal." That puts the ideal before the fact, and is exactly backward: Votes must be equal today, in order for achieved excellence *ever* to count best.

8 This great matter of reapportionment, viewed very practically, washes out as follows: While the American population was shifting massively to the urban centers, the basic structure of the distribution of legislative power was not altered in any degree commensurately. This factor told most heavily in the state legislatures. For the future, the expected great increase in population will make whatever home it can in and around the cities. Numerical apportionment alone is capable of accounting for this fluid and basic movement.

Writing in 1961, Paul T. David and Ralph Eisenberg (in *Devaluation of the Urban and Suburban Vote*) stated that, taking the country as a whole, the average rural vote was worth more than twice the average urban vote. In 1910 a city ballot was worth 72 per cent of a country ballot; but in 1960 it was worth only 44 per cent. "The rate and scale of population movements involved in the urbanization of the country have been sufficient to throw the whole political system out of joint," says Professor E. E. Schattschneider, a former president of the American Political Science Association. And he quotes the late V. O. Key, another leading political scientist, to the effect that the political consequences of the population shift have been "cataclysmic." Moreover, the shift continues: "One-fifth of the people now move every year."

So much for "organic" communities seeking "reflective" representation.

If numerical or quantitative malapportionment had been overcome a decade or so ago with respect to the House of Representatives, the redistribution of power would have been almost entirely from farmers to city-dwellers and, other things being equal (they never are), might well have made the difference as to large portions of the "liberal" program in Congress. Today, such fair apportionment, according to a *Congressional Quarterly* study, would benefit Southern cities, leave the other urban centers about where they are, and add a decisive twenty seats or so to new suburban constituencies. Andrew Hacker, in a careful appraisal of congressional districting just prior to *Wesberry*, stated: "The conflict, therefore, is essentially between two groups of Americans. On the one side are those living in small towns and rural areas; on the other are those inhabiting the fringes of large cities." Both groups are minorities, however: the 1960 Census counted thirty-six million as rural and twenty-nine million as suburban.

Most importantly, this means that the city proper has been *by*-passed historically, and *sur*passed politically as well as socially, by the suburbs. Another point: the political character and direction evidenced by suburban communities when these finally jell will be even more important than everyone already suspected. So that great new mass of more or less educated people, primary beneficiaries of the postwar "income revolution," devoted worshipers of the children-and-automobile culture, has become the decisive swing-group to mediate, and perhaps finally to resolve, the classic American conflict of the city-dweller and the small-town agrarian, the immigrant and the WASP, and at last to dispel the effects of agrarian ideology.

The classic opposition between the big-city vote and the upstate or downstate group has been cast since New Deal days as a Democratic/Republican opposition. Note that the Republican suburbs, however, have been captives not only of the malapportioned state legislatures but of the consequently unbalanced power situation within the Republican Party as well. Also, the new suburbs are not really as Republican as advertised—this view perhaps derives from the Eisenhower victories, which were definitive neither for the suburbs nor for the Republicans. Anyway, the great disruption following upon the apportionment decisions—along with the shattering electoral defeat in 1964—is changing this situation substantially. Hereafter, a special appeal must be made to the growing suburban constituency, and a special program constructed for it, by Republicans and Democrats alike.*

---

* On the question of business support for, or opposition to, the rural-suburban disproportion, Professor Hacker suggests that privately owned local business interests find rural legislators more amenable to their programs requiring state legislative endorsement—examples would be local banks, utilities, etc. The large national corporations, however, do not require such amenable legislatures and indeed experience some difficulty in working with them (since the latter are perhaps accustomed to "immediate personal money"—no longer a national political currency). A politi-

It is a very melancholy fact, to this city boy here, that all the wonderful dreaming nervousness of my generation and my father's generation, and even the generations of some earlier immigrants, was not able to generate the political what-with to carry our beloved country somewhat decisively farther into its Beginning Dream. But there you are. The sons and daughters of the suburbs will make the big decisions, for the next generation. Now, if we had *known* we were an urban civilization, and had not been quite so *fanatic* about making so much money . . . well, who knows?

9 You will have noticed, of course, that the fear of the majority now joins with the fear of positive government to round out the general American attitude toward power being depicted in this book. As elsewhere, the result of this fear, too, is not less power, better power, or more legitimate power, but merely unacknowledged power with a severe negative twist.

Until we develop better institutional habits for dealing with power —whatever quantity of it the necessities of our history may at the time require—we have an important hedge against majoritarian abuse which may be duly noted and appreciated. It is not so good a hedge against central power as countervailing paralysis, but neither is it so discouraging or dangerous as that traditional barrier. It is the simple fact, previously noted, that there is no "natural" majority in the United States and that, therefore, any working majority must be coalitional and must satisfy its components in order to be allowed to continue to work. This is different from class-rule government, as classically practiced in England (and attempted in France). We are moving, I think, toward a system of rule by institutional elites based on, and more or less responsive to, coalitions of surviving classes and newer social formations emerging out of the conditions of the maturing technological society.

For moral men of good will, the American purpose can no longer be to preserve the crumbling traditions of non-rule, but must be to join in building and furthering the interests of the best majority co-

---

cal factor to be added to this one would be whether a particular national corporation still fears city-based labor power, or has worked out means of dealing with it.

alition of which the country may be capable. (What this may be, and how it may be accomplished, is pursued hereinafter.)

The problem of coalitions, and therefore of American power, is perhaps most simply posed by the questions, Who is to be teacher, and who is to be taught? How does one teach, and how does one learn? The first question answers itself: Those who have, give; those who need, get. The second question is nearly unanswerable—but we may derive hope from the fact that learning seems to happen anyway, and some direction is given to the process from the continually reborn opportunity not to repeat past errors.

But the primary principle of choice I want to suggest for all serious men in America, who have time or resource or inclination to think of more than their selves and other aspects of their own indeterminate stay down here with the rest of us, is to begin at the beginning, which is to begin at the bottom. And I make this suggestion for what is nearly a selfish reason: the alternative will become an ever more vicious and self-corruptive "administration of surplus population." Unless we put the *dividing line* at the biological/social bottom, where it belongs, it will rise inexorably as the problem of technological living grows. Now that we really do have the time and the resource, most of us will not survive the imperatives of such administration if it is not founded on some gross notion of responsible brotherhood. By "not surviving" I mean that we will not recognize ourselves in the end; and the sons will not know their fathers: *we must now absolutely cease to identify images of our personal death with other social failure.*

If we are going to do something about this now, the *entrée* is psychological. Our traditional notions of Individualism, as they confront the actual facts of our lives, must be abandoned now; if nevertheless maintained, they will serve the imperative presumptions of the administration which we will not survive. No-choice is the choice of drift; and the drift is clearly totalitarian. The significance of the McCarthy-and-Goldwater phenomena—that bubbling, burbling level of idiocy raised to national prominence—is that in our profoundly unconscious commitment to Individualism we have been proven vulnerable to the dissociative and immensely irrelevant ideality which is the one true fundament of totalitarianism in the new technological age. Only when the power of the individual mind is thus decisively misdirected can the monster of rational inhumanity rise from out of the phoenix of the old cultures.

I know that saying this contradicts our traditional notions so much that the very opportunity of communication is startled nearly into insensibility—but the truth is that for most of us who are not at an institutional apex, the *idea* of individual omnipotence and the *facts* of organizational power are not simply different, they are antithetical. This was *not* true for Wm. J. Bryan; it *is* true for us. Our power is coalitional, if at all: otherwise it is merely the positional power at the apex of the institution—and that is so unlike past notions of personal power that we may soon need a new word for it.

Whatever we want, we can now get only through and with others. *That* is the New Frontier for our society, whether or not it achieves its "greatness." (I wonder if President Kennedy had something like this in mind? He might have: whatever his faults, and they were not inconsiderable, he was modern, he was intelligent, and he wasn't in it for a fast buck. Although it was mostly his special death that brought him to the heights of modern relevance, it is only fair to say that the way he lived some of his life did initiate that fascinating eventuality.)

We must begin with gross and bottom issues and persons (like Negroes and numerical apportionment) because the active affluent elite must *assume* these as an effect if it is not willing to *present* them as a problem. In this sense, social life is becoming more "logical": the conclusion either follows from the premise, or requires a greater and ever more subtle effort *not* to. If "we" are going to be so smart, we must educate "them" or destroy them. In either case, "we," too, will be changed.

Power through coalition. Peace, bread, and land. Liberty, equality, fraternity. Come ye as little children. And Jehovah said unto them . . .

The main problem in urban America is the explosive accretion of unsolved urban problems—this is where technology has taken and will take its greatest toll, because this is where we live. So, then, here is the problem: As for people, there is most pertinently the Negro revolt, being a concerted demand, both practical and spiritual, for admission to the national system, which to accomplish will necessarily modify that system itself (therefore including us, snugly within it), and which speaks or prepares methods and programs for all future Outsiders and other Surplus Persons. And then there is the upward drive of the propertyless educated masses who must administer the national system. So there is mostly the Under Class and the New Class.

I do not mention the institutional Over Class, or the *rentier* Old Class, or the persistent Possessory Property Class, because they are not apt to be major participants in the new best-majority coalition. The Over Class is the *object* of the power of the New Coalition; the Old Class is with us frequently on an individual basis; the Possessory Class is against us, with individuals taking our part for eccentric reasons. If we threaten to destroy or dispossess none of them, we get more members of each (eccentrically or otherwise). I'm for that approach.

But the heart of the New Coalition is the joining in interest of the under-dogs and the new and rising middle-dogs. In and around the cities, the two make a majority. (And I would hate to imagine any other one.)

So we will now look at these; and in this way we answer a persistent question of this book: What Is Power?

It is the Reader, affirmatively joined with the Non-Reader.

TEN

<hr>

Negroes
in the
Streets

1 Reporting the Birmingham dem-
onstrations in 1963, the New York *Times* published a picture of
several Negroes striding through a current working-class suburb.
There were three prominent figures. One was a youth: disheveled in
an ill-fitting T-shirt, loose-jointed, his features showed emotion
barely controlled—anger, fear, hysterical challenge. Behind him,
moving forward firmly, was a more mature man dressed in a
worker's jacket and cap, an impressive look of determination—close-
jawed, certain, and almost calm—on his face. Standing off the pave-
ment on the grass, and only half-facing in the direction of the line of
march, was a small, thin, agéd Negro woman: she presented herself
in an all-out hallelujah posture, with one arm pointed rigidly toward
the sky, her head at a sharp right angle, her body unreasonably
twisted. The men were moving, but the woman was next to glory.

In the South, the Negro has marched out of his churches and into
the streets, headed toward City Hall. The churches, dominated by
the women, infused with their purpose and need, have been the
backbone of the Negro community in the South. They constitute
what community the Negroes actually have in that forlorn area: and

the emotional patterns cooked in that atmosphere could only have been the work of the women—including the travail of beckoning to the men.

Thus it was a self-contemptuous set of slave-holders who viewed their religion alone as cultural material appropriate for their wards, who were, in the more practical areas, even forbidden to read and write.

What urges me to this view about the role of the women and their use of the masters' religion in creating the Negro community is that, upon reflection, it is obvious that our great oppression of the Negroes fell most heavily upon the men. It is the man who suffers most deeply from not being allowed to grow up. And it is the man who was injured at the bottom-base of his identity by the sexuality of the Southern racial system. This latter point is apparent, as follows: the American Negro today is not a pure, black, African strain. There has been a great deal of mixture with white blood, and it all took place in the United States. There has been practically no marriage of any consequence between white women and black men, or black women and white men. There has been only very special illicit sex, one would imagine, between the women of the dominant race and the men of the inferior race. Almost all of that white blood in the biology of the Negro group resulted from the rape or seduction-from-superiority or purchase of Negro women by white men. *The Negro male has been burdened with our bastards for three centuries.* The system, note well, did not allow him to disown the child—he was required to raise it. This is intolerable for a man. All the Negro male could do was to run away or, sitting-put in fact, to retreat socially through an abandonment of responsibility. To grow up was to grow up into his rage against the white men. This was impossible because it would have cost him his life. Comprehending this Negro rage, the white men made a point of killing a Negro male every once in a while after he, the guilty white man, had taken a Negro woman.*

* This complex event goes so deep that it must be imagined, not merely stated. In effect, the white man stole the love out of Negro life. The black lynch victim (only symbolically, not in fact, the displaced lover) was killed to keep the white man from being haunted by the theft, and thus perhaps himself becoming black. The whole crime, from commission through psychic "punishment," was one of identification: the Real Crime of the white man had been against the tight religious order of the White South, and it was to imagine—but to stop short at merely and momentarily imagining—himself as black enough to be primitively sexual. The

The Southern churches turned activist with the Montgomery boycott in 1956 and the resulting organization of The Alabama Christian Movement for Human Rights, which occurred June 5, 1956, in the Sardis Baptist Church in Birmingham. (The immediate occasion was the enjoining of the NAACP from operating in Alabama.) Writing about Birmingham, Martin Luther King later said, "it is not an uncommon occurrence for Negro women being accosted by city police, forced to submit to criminal assault, and their lips sealed under the threat of death to the members of their family." (This statement was made to show why it was "almost foolhardy" to choose Birmingham for the 1963 demonstration.)

If Protestantism can kill the body, in the South it killed the male and deviously fertilized the female. And if jazz was the Negro male-body's revenge on Protestantism, then this new Negro Protestantism has something to do with the Negro woman's courageous revenge on herself. . . . If only one were able to map the minds of Martin Luther King, Malcolm X, James Baldwin, and Bessie Smith, the mother of them all, one would then perhaps have the basic prototypical characteristics in this sexual drama which took place in the white man's backyard.

The Muslims in the Northern ghettos are anti-Christian in their male emphasis, achieved by a kind of negative religiosity. Other than this, the basic movement among the Negroes is in the South, and it is Christian-religious, and it derives from the female. That is perhaps why James Baldwin, with his intense interest in homosexuality, has played such an exquisitely revealing role in the movement, even though for a long time he had little practical contact with it. (He entered the army as a five-star general, retiring from the Other Wars in France.)

It is even more profoundly a religious movement in that the aim of the Negro struggle is to reform *us*, the whites. They cannot really achieve their purpose unless they make us better, since not until we are thus improved will we allow them to redefine blackness or will we accept their redefinition of it, which consequentially requires a redefinition of whiteness. But even if a white man sincerely goes up to a Negro and says, "Black is all right," and really means it, he will only have begun the effort. Because he will still have to define white

---

black women, note, were at least loved in a way; and then they found the rapist's religion, the same one he had transgressed in taking them, to be useful in their new circumstance. It was a strange form of proselytizing.

so that the Negro will one day come up to him and say, "White is all right, too."

The movement is further religious in being a new and practical application of Christianity, by way of Thoreau and Gandhi, on behalf of the male. This consists of the nonviolent "confrontation" executed by young men in the South. It is heroic, and for the participants it has amounted to a "transcendence in the streets" equal to the great acts of spiritual conversion recorded in history. The spirituality leading to this youthful heroism derives from the Southern church-community, and that community is immensely enheartened by its young heroes; but religion completed in the streets is not exactly religion traditionally conceived and executed. Since most of these martyrs are apt to survive (nonviolence two thousand years later benefits from choice of environment), the religion that is their source will never be the same thereafter. Most lose their pristine Christianity in gaining their spiritual manhood, which is a cultural achievement of great potential consequence to America, not merely to the Negroes (Northern whites have already begun to imitate the young Southern heroes).

The Negro male also became a man of a kind by moving out of the South, whether or not taking his woman with him. Until Bessie Smith sang, and until the women of the church went out into the streets, the desperate migratory impulse of the Negro male constituted the basic protest-ant stirring in the body of the American Negro community. When it became clear that slave rebellions could not succeed, the hero-slaves ran away to the North (some smart ones managed to stay South through buying their freedom). The great mass migrations were the result of two wars—voluntary industrial travel and the involuntary migration called "conscription." Soldiering, as well as riding the rails, is a road to manhood of a kind. Whether the "soldiers" returned, stayed North, or "remained in" Paris (like Richard Wright and James Baldwin—or even, half-time, Adam Clayton Powell), the basic Negro-event of manhood of a kind had occurred. Also, to be fair, let us note the achievements of the much-maligned ambassadorial Toms throughout the land: the Negroes must learn the Jewish lesson of male cunning, and honor it in their community.

But in the North, the rage became a disease. Naturally. What else could it become? The white man did not, could not, change enough, thus undermining the migratory triumph. (Even jazz didn't work—

and turned "cool.") And what are statistically-better-jobs to men seeking their manhood? The last migrant is bottom dog—that is the American Way. And the Negro, physically resident longer than all others except the Indians and equal therein to the Daughters of the American Revolution, is the Last American Migrant.

Then four young men sat down in the wrong place and asked for a lousy hamburger and Coke in Greensboro, North Carolina. The lions roared, as did Caesar.

2 This time, the Negroes are their own Abolitionists. This time, they are seizing an identity rather than accepting it as a gift from the Good White Man. But in the South it is Abolitionism still, and it proceeds from out of something like the same religion. As Richard Hofstadter has pointed out, "abolitionism was a religious movement . . . its agencies the church congregations of the towns." And Wendell Phillips, like the practitioners of civil disobedience today, said (stating a Protestant rather than a Catholic view of "natural law"): "Immoral laws are doubtless void, and should not be obeyed." But the Abolitionists at first favored secession. According to Hofstadter, they held that: "The Union had been a moral failure; only the money interest wanted to save it." Not so the new Black Abolitionists, at least not in the South: they want in—and on the original ideal terms.

The Negroes, with their black skin as a battle flag, may save this nation yet (I say "nation" because they insist on it). It is they who suffer most from the American Dream—they are the only true believers left. The Negro movement seems almost powerful enough to sweep the country along with it to a new spiritual level. It is spiritual and religious, we noted, because it requires for its own fulfillment that whites become better people—the Negroes are not really interested in greasy hamburgers, white toilets, and another Ralph Bunche. This is the persuasive underlying truth that the Muslims rely on (by denying the possibility) and that so agitates the immense talent of James Baldwin, who was and remains a greatly gifted preacher nicely poised above the emotional eddies of black and white. The Negroes are a small part of the population, however, and I feel their gift will always be primarily a cultural, or catalytic, one. Their skin makes them spiritual witnesses to the current state of the white man's belief and practice. Their skin can change only in the white man's eye, just as it was created in his beholding. Being thus doomed, and carrying an incommensurate historical hatred, they can allow us peace only when we have allowed them to escape into middle-class comfort. Before that happens, the nation will have been transformed. The poor will have been raised, the unemployed hired, and practical justice of a kind proffered to many city and country victims.

With the new movement of the Negroes, this nation reverses its entire history. We do this—if we continue the Second Reconstruction—because the Negro no longer acquiesces, and because the effort toward his further suppression would be intolerable to *us*. We would like to go as slow as possible, and we undoubtedly will; but now the Negro participates in the decision as to how slow is "possible." Moreover, we created the Negro in our history in order to make ourselves white. The Negro has more "right" rather than less because of this created inferiority: we owe him our whiteness, and now he asks for some payment.

The race issue was first used to divide this country in favor of local self-interests: it is now being used to unite the country against such interests. It would seem that the fate of the Negro minority is always to be "used" by American history. Among other things, the Negroes will now prove to the rest of us the general and inescapable utility of federal power to accomplish necessary human purposes. Then others will learn the lesson, and will use it for their own purposes—just as the Negroes learned something of this lesson from the Populists, and from the unions.

Whenever there was a turning point in American history, the Negro was there with his awful problem—and evil opportunity—for the white man. The lack of plantation labor, when it turned out there were not enough convicts and that the American Indian did not prosper in servitude; the fatal structural flaw in the system of government established at Philadelphia, produced by bludgeoned compromise with the plantation owners; the irrepressible conflict, when the West was being taken into the fold, as to whether there would be slave labor in the new states; and so on. And then there were the Abolitionists, with their effort to rejuvenate white Protestant society by taking the Negro as an example of their questionable love of God —and the use of the Abolitionists by Northern business interests to lead their crusade into the Southern colony, and to secure the exploitation of the Western farmer for themselves. Next, the profound corruption of American political parties made possible by the post-Civil War mess in the South: the basic anti-democratic quality of the system established after the Civil War by business and finance was again made possible by the general utility of the sacrificial Negro. The New Deal, based in part on the Negro migration in the First World War having placed a swing-group of coalition votes in the Northern cities, finally took the North away from the Republicans. And the Negro today, threatening to revive the National Dream and attendant constitutional ideals. The Negro, with his well-earned hatred, will test each and every premise of our society over the next century.

And if we jail him, we jail ourselves along with him.

It is difficult to say whether one should emphasize that history in America which *did* happen because of the Negro—or that even greater history which did *not* happen because of the Negro. The race issue is a deadly one; but in the most serious sense it is not a "real" issue. It serves as a symbolic substitute for other issues, which are indeed real. The race issue is one of those pseudo-issues which greatly facilitate distortion on the part of (and for the special purposes of) that body of opinion which does not care for a candid confrontation of real issues, which must survive by stealth. (This relates in an obvious way to the larger matters, previously discussed, of myth and lying in politics.) Race especially shows the extent to which a distortion can become institutionalized because of its great effectiveness, and in this way more real than reality itself. I rather think that this is true of many more issues than the racial one. But there is no question that at this stage of our history it is the racial one which will haunt us into the indeterminate future. The great utility of the race issue is that it "seems like" a real issue so long as you do not assume the general equality and right of existence in all members of the human species, either as a mode of historical procedure or as an end-in-view. The Negro, as the Jew and others before him, has thus suffered from the unfair distribution of human cruelty. Humanity prefers not to kill its friends; if all were friends, it might have given up killing long ago.

In early January 1964, Hindus and Moslems were destroying each other in Calcutta because of the theft of *one* of Mohammed's supposed hairs. Primitive religious conflict appears to have been an even more pronounced reason than race for murder in human history. Up until today, that is. For even after men forgive each other for believing in different gods, and then for believing in the same god differently, they can still unite in revulsion toward members of the human race who are even more obviously different from them— any surviving gods notwithstanding.

However that may be, the two great symbols of the American experience were a continent of empty land and the Negro slave. As this sweeping statement is uttered, one is immediately made aware of two necessary equivocations: 1) the land was not empty, but populated —however sparsely—by Indians; and 2) the Negro slave was not the only immigrant, but he was the only immigrant who remained such for three hundred years—the Perpetual Immigrant. And startlingly enough, there appears to be a compelling connection between these two exceptions, namely, that the Negro thereby replaced the Indian as the basic indigenous presence on this continent—and therefore, also, as the living reminder of the successful American immigrant's obligation to history.

3   If race can be everything, it can also be—in the ecstasy of embracing the *fact*—merely a few physical differences. So before one reaches the complicated question of social identity, there is the threshold question of appearance, or even beauty—i.e., physical identity: this is the only quality of race which may have any *independent* objective significance. Therefore, the essential beginning to the discussion of this point is to emphasize that any decently fair-minded person can say that he has seen many beautiful Negroes and many ugly white people.

But the very existence of the Negro has been an assault upon the ordinary American's notion of billboard images. The abidingly terrible thing that happened to the Negro in America, finally, is that all the ugly white people (especially in the North) decided that Negroes were even uglier, and the good-looking white people everywhere graciously acquiesced in this additional applause. It is an evil "created fact" that a cultural decision was made that black skin is not attractive. It obviously is, from a natural aesthetic point of view. But there are simply not enough natural beauties in the world for the natural aesthetic point of view to triumph. It is the ugly people who create our images of beauty, more out of an inversion of self-distaste than out of a natural perception of beauty. And the Negroes must come to understand that even under the best circumstances there is a deeply *popular* selection for beauty and other talent. Many attractive whites lose out in this cruel process, too.

So there is a cultural advance to be awaited as to our received notions of beauty. Meanwhile, to be hopeful for a moment, natural beauty is undoubtedly one of the most compelling events in the world—especially for young people. And many American Negroes are beautiful *even* in the American mode. This whole complex of matters is enlarged by the fact that the American Negro is not a pure strain, and neither is the American white. Therefore, each can discern physical similarities in the other—beyond the fact merely that both are human, which they so regularly find it so easy and convenient to ignore.

For the Negro, black skin is an immense issue. A friend of mine, traveling through the South, talked to a girl who had become active in the Negro youth movement. She had been somewhat dissolute before joining up, but now exhibited that beautiful controlled forwardness toward life which the Southern Negro activists live by. She told my friend that when she joined the movement, she gave up hair straighteners and wasted no more time on skin creams. He asked her what exactly was it about a young Negro that qualified him for the movement, or that led him into it. She had no hesitation in answering: "We are black and glad."

This is the heart of the matter, *because blackness is something the Negro can accept without the white man's permission.* The Negro achieves an immense increase in human capacity by this single act (the more so, the more deeply attained). So I find myself forced to accept the validity of the Muslim movement for its achieved effort in urging the black man to accept his blackness, even though Muslims do this by celebrating it, which reveals an inner weakness. Nevertheless, any advance must be welcomed. It is the white man who made black skin the sign of all. The Negro must accept it as a physical fact forever, and as a social and cultural problem until solved. But he can at least keep the infection of meaning from spreading within himself, even if he cannot dominate the society's "establishment of meanings."

If it were not for the fact that "white" means "non-Negro," it wouldn't be all that wonderful to be white, even for the simple act of

looking at oneself in the mirror. And by excluding the Negro from
our culture on these grounds, we will never know how many lies told
on other grounds are thereby included in that culture; at least we
can never be sure; and the longer excluded, the greater their capacity to reveal to us these other lies. They have already done so in
a major fashion in the creation of jazz, which has dominated the national popular culture. As a literary matter, so to speak, they are entitled to the sexual presumption of jazz. But note what a demanding
and vulnerable position this puts them in: they must maintain a
higher order of sexuality than the whites, although living in a similar
technological and overorganized environment: and they are shaken
in this element of identity by any achieved white sexuality. (No
wonder the Negro male is so ostentatiously sexual: no wonder jazz
was so hot; and no wonder it cooled down so much.)

On a distorted matter of this kind, with this sort of inter-identity,
the effective meanings flow back and forth in considerable disarray.
As an example, note the conjunction during the Twenties between
two important events—that loudly free sexuality was expressed for
the first time as a cultural style in America, and that also for the first
time it was broadly felt to be a mark of beauty to achieve a sun tan.
It poses no difficulties to imagine meanings for the darkness of a
man. But why dark women, just when sporting sex came to America? By inversion, perhaps: the pale whiteness of the delicate blond
girl denotes great available passivity, suitable for fantasies. But
when the time comes to get down to business, a measure of cooperation is welcome, especially for the novice. Since the Twenties, even
the All-American Blond Beauty has been an athlete, at least in the
ads.

This matter of racial difference leads through beauty to sex, and
then on to larger questions of identity. Somewhere in and around the
sexual passage, the racial factor becomes an excuse rather than a
reason. It is important here that the white has exploited the Negro
spiritually as well as materially. Perhaps more the former than the
latter on the part of the middle- and upper-class white, since these
never lacked for a variety of human objects of material exploitation.
On the lower level, "white" has a sharp, immediate, material meaning, in both the North and the South. White men took the jobs of
Negroes in the South after the Civil War; and later in the North and
throughout the country at all times, in that the Negroes are favored
for the menial jobs, thus deprived of the better ones. They are of

course the last hired and the first fired, the greatest victims of unemployment of whatever kind, from whatever source.

Then again, at the bottom of the bottom—in certain ragged rural counties in the South where no one has much of a job—"white" once more takes on a ferocious ideal meaning. But elsewhere the spiritual exploitation has had importance independent of the material factor, has been subtle and devious, following the lines of the classic patterns of prejudice—as with forcing upon the Negro the human value-burdens of sexuality, animal grace, and laziness.

On black/white identity, James Baldwin was not only the self-appointed ringmaster of white guilt. His great talent, before it was immobilized by the problems of his success, enabled him to record a clear scream of import to us all. He made primarily one point—that what it means to be white is determined by what the white man has made black skin mean. He insisted repeatedly on the mutuality of self-identity involved in the race issue, especially in this country. Long before Baldwin's effort, a white Southerner, W. J. Cash, had written: "Negro entered into white man as profoundly as white man entered into Negro—subtly influencing every gesture, every word, every emotion and idea, every attitude." But Baldwin is a Negro, his thought has benefited from sophisticated French existentialist notions about authenticity, and he has an unmatched talent. Also, he has cunningly complicated the whole endeavor by injecting the distorting but not irrelevant matter of homosexuality into an issue of identity which does, in fact, involve the bases of manhood.

Baldwin is perfectly correct in asserting that "the Negro problem" is as much an issue of *white* identity as it is of anything else. But as one reads him with care, an undertone of despair as to his own blackness appears. He is often magnificent, as well as occasionally hysterical, in his efforts to bestow humanity on his color. But because of a lover's need, or something of the sort, he persists somewhere in himself in seeing blackness as ugliness. In the end, he confuses color with homosexuality. There may be great cunning in this, for his own purposes; but the solution for the Negro's identity-in-blackness is not the basic ambiguity of homosexuality.

Where he has failed is in imagining a white man as a man. After all, the white color on the other side of inter-identity reveals a human being beyond color—just as black may, on a closer look. But not yet to James Baldwin.

4 The Muslims claim that God is black. Their slogan is: "White man's heaven is black man's hell." They refer to the Bible as the "poison book," and to white men as "white devils." Another group, the Nationalists, enjoin the Negro to "think black, act black, buy black, and not trust the white man."

Elijah Muhammad has said: "If the master accepts him as an equal in words and deeds, he will be degrading himself to the level of his slave." This is the view that Baldwin shares with the Muslims. But Muhammad emphasizes Negro inferiority as the reason that integration is impossible. It is also impossible because: "The white men . . . have a profound hatred for the Negroes. We are in a terrible position. We live among a terrible people and we know it."

The Muslim movement has been very effective among the prison population: freedom for all believers now held in federal prisons is a part of their program. The movement has been credited with reformative successes among former criminals, dope addicts, and so on. As with Alcoholics Anonymous, personal reform is achieved by adherence to rigid belief, and a trimmed-sail concentration on The Problem. The degradation of the black man is The Problem for the Muslims. The pattern of reform is to give up on white society and especially its religion, and to emphasize black strength-for-survival. The Muslims expect only the worst from white men, and they "ask" white society neither for love nor for friendship but only for their due. It is, for instance, a part of their program that black people be exempted from taxation.

A quick look at their newspaper, *Muhammad Speaks*, reveals some of the quality of their thought. The issue of August 16, 1963, includes a glorious and gory retelling of the Nat Turner slave revolt in Virginia in 1831—an Elizabethan story of primitive violence, the stage covered with the blood of the principals at the final curtain. In an article called "Georgia's Harvest of Rape and Poverty," the following statement is made: "As it was in slavery and as it has been ever since, the wanton rape of Negro women by white men continues without a pause in remote, rural areas." But the most revealing statement in the paper was an impressive testimonial of the worth of conversion by a female nurse:

Islam has done what some would call a miracle for our men. Husbands are desiring and learning how to work and take care of their families, and how to respect their women—and are willing to die for them.

Never has a so-called Negro man really stood up for his woman and held her in such high esteem until his hearing and accepting the teaching of our beloved teacher. To the lost-found nation (so-called Negroes) Islam is a blessing. I am forever thankful. All praise is due to Allah.

The admiration of the Muslims for the more forceful efforts of the integrationists is scarcely hidden. But their revised emotional organization is built upon the indulgence of fantasies of violence and separateness—which to them means that they don't believe they can win, that they don't have to win in order to get along, and that the main point after all is that black is good (whether or not victorious in the world of the "white devils"). Muhammad himself has told them: "The white man is a two-legged rattlesnake." They cannot afford to *expect* anything good from the white man. They must be self-reliant; and clearly their self-reliance, given the vulnerable situation in which they live, requires an elaborate fantasy-structure of violent rejection.

The Christian-oriented Negroes rely on revivalistic images of redemption: they want to forgive and be forgiven. Theologically, despite their disastrous weakness, they insist on the brotherhood of man. Muhammad, however, has called Christianity a slave religion; he, instead, wants an eye for an eye—which is somewhat more Hebraic than Mohammedan. (It occurs to a political Jew that the Muslims served something of a similar purpose to that of the Irgun in Palestine; and SNCC, CORE, and the SCLC were elements of the Haganah.)

When the Negro comes North, his rage surfaces. The Muslim movement is a Northern ghetto movement. And it is most deeply anti-Christian. This development of feeling, I am sure, is not limited to the Muslims and the Black Nationalists. Sammy Davis, Jr., for instance, converted to Judaism because he could not bring himself any longer to forgive the white man, to turn the other cheek and to confess his hatred and ask forgiveness, as he felt his mother's Catholicism required. He preferred what he considered to be the unmitigated justice of the Jews. An eccentric figure in the Southern movement is the Reverend James Bevel, a young Baptist minister from

Mississippi and a field secretary for SCLC. He appears in overalls and a dungaree jacket, along with a *yarmulke*. He wears the skull cap, he says, because: "I'm very Jewish in my thinking. Christ was a Jew, and all of my heroes who stood for decency, equality, justice and human dignity in the past were the Jewish prophets." The Reverend James Bevel was also quoted by Claude Sitton, in the New York *Times* Magazine, June 9, 1963, to this effect: "Some punk who calls himself the President has the audacity to tell people to go slow. I'm not prepared to be humiliated by white trash the rest of my life, including Mr. Kennedy." This amount of expressed hostility was unusual, I believe, for Southern workers.

The commitment to Christian forgiveness, and even to the nonviolent tactic which derives in part from that source, is thinning out. It is profoundly painful to the Negro spirit to persist in an appeal to the white conscience. In a real sense, the act of doing so constitutes a Christian martyrdom for each Negro so engaged. This process cannot continue indefinitely. (If nonviolence were not so aggressive a technique, its use would have thinned out even sooner in the North.) The Negro must achieve some actual power for which he is not beholden to the white man, and this must happen before his immense effort at Christian love turns rancid. For a growing elite this will mean education, status, and appropriate employment; for the mass of the Negroes it can only mean the bloc vote as a road to basic jobs and welfare supplement of one kind or another. Note that a tenet of Muslim belief is the following:

> We do not believe that America will ever be able to furnish enough jobs for her own millions of unemployed, in addition to jobs for the 20,000,000 black people as well.

The actual power change must occur before the Negro mass in the North (or the desegregated black Southerner once "Northernized") decides out of spiritual exhaustion that Christianity is an impossible emotional pattern unsupported by prejudice, and that the American Negro will forever be the final chosen "object" of the continuing possibility of Christianity on this continent. A deprived and primitive anti-Christian core-group in our society would be an incalculable disaster. For people without other cultural resources, Christianity is to be transcended, not relinquished.

5 The recent struggle of the Negroes is the most exhilarating since the labor push of the Thirties. It is also much more extensive than many of us at first realized. For example, the issue of poverty—the deeply disgusting issue of poverty in this wealthy nation—has been a live one politically almost only as it was a subsumed part of the general Negro movement. Likewise, the mounting question of technological unemployment. Moreover, the positive bid of one-tenth of the population to overcome deprivation which ranges from the most brutal material factors to the spiritual heights of mis-identity with a white God, must inevitably affect the whole white culture.

With hindsight, the chief advantage of Emancipation was the opportunity it afforded for migration—with the substantial push of two and a half major wars. Taking this interior route, the Negro had a second chance as an American immigrant. One million Negroes abandoned Southern farming in the four years following 1940, for example; and from "1950 to 1954, the number of Negro farmers in the South declined 17.1 per cent," according to the New York *Times,* although white mobility in general has outdistanced that of the Negroes since 1950 (reversing a long-time trend). Still, more than two-fifths of Negro heads of household born in the Confederate South no longer live there. But the Negroes have experienced considerable disappointment in the Northern promised land. And whether because they had been slaves for two hundred years and more, or because their color did not change in the Northern light, or for the reason that they were the Last Immigrants, they have not yet settled in.

From the terror of Southern segregation to the alienated despair of the Northern ghetto—the main advance has been that the rage has surfaced. And they started to vote. From having been worth three-fifths of a vote each to his master, the Negro in the Northern cities is now worth almost one vote each to himself. As long ago as 1956 the *Congressional Quarterly* estimated that the Negroes held the balance of power in sixty-one congressional districts in the North; year by year, this factor increases. But they are overconcentrated and suffer from a "natural" racial gerrymander, which creates very tough machine-control; and, being at the bottom of the ladder, the Negroes like older immigrants are interested in low-level patronage jobs, which further enhances the position of old-style machinery. This will be true *a fortiorari* in the South, as the vote is afforded them there.

Given little of any worthwhile tradition, the Negro is forced to be too creative: in the South, he (more properly, she) represents perhaps the last burst of Protestant revivalism; in the North, Negro spirituality becomes excessively "modern." His very life begins with a spiritual failure in the North: the Northern rage is almost as much of a burden as the Southern terror was, so that at times it must seem as if the trip North was not worth the bus fare. He must live in the unlivable sections of decaying cities; he is barely wanted, even for the most menial jobs—and his male children, it would seem, are wanted even less; the most dangerous temptations can be found, hardly avoided, right around the corner; and if he gets into the rest of the city at all, on the job or otherwise, he sees the clean ease of television come alive before his eyes (especially when viewed briefly from outside). The whole weight of The City has fallen on the Negro's back: he is the one who carries the burden—totes the water and lifts the bales—of urbanism.

Indeed, whether or not believing, the Negroes carry the cross of the lack of community of all of us, our isolation and our negativism. Imagine the truth of our condition in these absurd cities if we had not even our whiteness to join us in brotherhood.

And for the North, we now have a "war on poverty." The fighters on the other side of this war are juvenile delinquents (kids who gave up on growing up long ago), irresponsible shoeshine men, absentee house servants whoring around the neighborhood, junkies and booze hounds without the patriotism to kick the habit, and kids of all ages who are transfixed with the vision of a shiv or a zip gun pointing the way to a manly resolution of one's circumstantial annoyances. All of them no-try slum-losers who would rather break a window or a jaw or go crazy than take a mail-order course in mushroom growing. Why we even bother with thirty-year-old kids who refuse to dance for pennies—and the tune is The Battle Hymn of the Republic!—*is quite beyond me.*

On our side of the war are serious, dedicated, well-educated, thoroughly qualified experts in the administration of Something Difficult —and a substantial part of their qualification is that they have not been and never could be corrupted, or even affected, by It. But we will win. Troops of this kind, with fervor from these sources, and considering all of the Lever Bros. products which are at stake, cannot fail of final victory.

But we should all know that it is a real war that we are in. Buy Bonds! (*And if you happen to have some real money, buy stocks.*)

6 What is wrong with the North, is wrong with urban America (a problem of infinite scope). But the white South constitutes a Thing almost beyond descriptive comprehension. Russell Baker in his column of June 10, 1963, in the New York *Times,* made the sly point that there is no such thing as a "Northerner." "The Northerner is a creature of Southern fabrication," he said. I think this is true: the Southerner has a sense of identity as such, but the Northerner does not unless he is thinking of the South.

Which he seldom does, in any realistic fashion. The white man in the North understands the South mostly in moral terms, as did the Abolitionists; and, as if the Civil War were still in progress, he responds most deeply to emanations of the Southern system when a white Northerner is killed—as in Mississippi in the summer of 1964, and Selma, Alabama, in the spring of 1965. Drawing himself up to his full Christian height, he then demands an immediate end to the outrage and, to underline his determination, he passes another federal law. This activity is often accompanied by a further demand that the President proceed immediately to the diseased area so that the mana from his person will excise the poison recently discovered there. And if the President is chicken or short on mana, send troops.

But the historical relations between North and South, just as the current understanding or lack thereof between white and black in all parts of the country, runs a bit deeper than these popular-culture events are able to reveal. Given the true corrupt depth of the racial issue on this continent from the beginning, *nobody* comes out smelling like a rose—not white nor black, neither North nor South. Of course, the white man with a weapon is the worst. But innocent white skin itself is a weapon throughout the black land. And a black man with a knife can cut through all kinds of white and black skin. Also, since we Good Guys are obviously so awfully sorry about the whole thing and say so all the time, why don't the Negroes stop being so resentful and get better grades in school? And what's wrong with those crazy white Southerners? We passed a law, didn't we? We have the troops, don't we? (And just between you and me, if the colored race had a stronger instinct toward cleanliness and used more soap, I bet they could wash some of that dirt off their faces.)

Still, the white South is the worst of the problem, no matter how many New Englanders made money out of the slave trade. And once the needle was in, even the best of the white Southerners would say, as Jonathan Daniels did— "We know out of our past that the worst carpetbaggers were the ones who came down here to improve us." The cultured fatuousness of that remark, with its stale insight into the unpleasant quality of piety, which is then taken illogically as a permission to overlook the obvious and rather more important fact that the worst carpetbaggers were the ones who got there first, before the Civil War, and after that the ones who stole indiscriminately from black and white both, using a gun as well as a cash register in doing so.

Since I want to concentrate now on this incredible Southern white, I may properly take a final moment to kiss off the Northerner, as follows:

If you will not comprehend the Southern system except occasionally in hot headlines, you will never understand the Negro immigrant in your cities. And no sweet old word like "poverty" will save you from the consequences of your incomprehension. For example, our statisticians of social failure tell us that at the very base of the poverty pyramid is found the broken family: a high-correlation poverty-linked characteristic (you should excuse the sociological expression) is the absence of a male figure in the family. The absence of a male figure in the Negro family was caused long ago, in a Southern backyard—and then exported to Harlem. (And read James Baldwin to discover what it may have cost a Negro father, and his children after him, that he clenched his soul and stayed on.)

The Northern liberals never understood the depth of the distorted problem in the South; they tended to think in "reasonable" political terms, with only the flimsiest use of psychological categories, except the fantasy-ridden literary categories of the Southern school of fiction (the greatly talented William Faulkner has much to answer for in a later historical hearing). The Negro government-in-exile in the

North listened too attentively, I suspect, to their liberal mentors because they wanted desperately to forget the human disaster they had escaped, the one the Northern whites had difficulty even imagining. The vitality of the Negro movement today is concentrated in the South; in the North there is mostly the impotent hatred and underlying violence released by an approach to "winning" in a merely legal way. Eventually, of course, the spearhead will move to the North, as the Negro himself has—and sooner rather than later, to judge from the "black power" noise that dominated the summer of 1966 and declared the current agony of the Mississippi heroes.

Having avoided the racial quality of the race issue in the North by joining it with the general problem of the Under Class, the affluent white Northerner chances the re-creation of the underlying issues of inter-identity, the core of racism, on a new basis. The city poor are, after all, unsuccessful in *our* terms, in *our* social order, and thus they define and bless (in that dark fashion) *our* success and *our* superiority. If something of this kind were to happen while (and because?) the racial conscience of the Northerner was directed toward the merely *legal* reform of the South, we would have lanced a boil and suffered the metastasis of the basic cancer.

We in the North had best exert ourselves to understand the South, not leisurely as an exotic enterprise rich in Cultural Values, but urgently as an existential need, in order to avoid establishing the racially induced *general lawlessness* which, more than Northern bayonets or Morgan's money, in fact destroyed the South—and made Liederkranz-destruction "so interesting" to the North.

. . . But of course this will not happen, in the enlightened North. Things are bound to get better—probably soon, perhaps easily. It is most likely, for example, that Negro-white conciliation-preaching will be a profession within a few years, as labor conciliation became a profession some time back.

One of the principles to be preached to Negroes—the whites are in for a great deal of well-deserved preaching in any event—is that signing the nonviolence pledge is not to be taken as a certified license to vent their historical fury as they please, on allies, potential allies, and enemies alike. Nonviolence must proceed to nonhostility, if one's intention is not merely to undermine the Southerner with the conscience of a Northern culture. It is not so easy to explain what color means, when the meaning cannot be stated simply by repealing a bad law and passing a good one. When both men are colored, even if differently, mutual hostility will only confirm the worst color of each.

But forgive me: it is perhaps too soon to begin to preach to the Northerners, black or white.

7 It is traditional, Greek, and unfortunate that one can and must say of our most accomplished President, Thomas Jefferson, as the historian Richard Hofstadter did—"the leisure that made possible his great writings on human liberty was supported by the labors of three generations of slaves." But these slaves perhaps had the satisfaction of knowing, in Another World, that they helped to create Thomas Jefferson. Not so some later generations of slaves, somewhat farther west in Mississippi.

Senator James O. Eastland was quoted by Barbara Carter in *The Reporter* as saying: "All who are qualified to vote, both black and white, exercise the right of suffrage in my state, as I am sure they do in Louisiana and other Southern States."

Exercise yourself, for a moment, to imagine the character of mind of the white man making this incredible statement. (Senator Eastland, Democrat of Mississippi, is of course the immovable chairman of the Senate *Judiciary* Committee.)

Hypocrisy in the South constitutes a different spiritual order; it stands by itself alone. It is hypocrisy without limit, derived from the fabricating hunger of desperate men. The Southern racial system requires the telling and retelling of thousands upon thousands of unblinking lies any one of which, although known to be a lie, is welcomed as cool water in the desert (so long as it is a closed Southern desert). It is simply not possible to face the racial truth in the South: it is nearly impossible for the Negro and literally so for the white—not merely the redneck. For those who cannot bear the lies any longer, no matter what depths they hold in place, federal law comes as a blessing. They are dying to submit to superior force. Anything to end the long nightmare of vigilante law enforced indiscriminately by the lowest elements in the community. In the end, when the South is nearly assimilated into the national legal system and the final fear of abandoning the fear of redneck terror must be faced, they will welcome federal bayonets as well as federal law.

*Who can destroy the ready potential of the nightriders will initiate
the Southern march to freedom, and perhaps even to long-imagined
greatness.*

Everyone in the South is a member of the racial system; until
recently, only a handful of heroes have fought it; but not everyone
benefits from it or needs it equally. It is a tyranny for many whites
as well as, differently, for almost all Negroes.

Racial words are knives in the South, which recall the backsliders
in the community to the hidden personal horror, the original sin of
indecent unbrotherhood, with as much effect as the never-forgotten
violence which lies behind the words.* But not only the vile words of
the hysterical redneck: by no means. Most particularly there are the
fine, degenerate words of the lawyers, the high priests of Southern
racism. As an example, return a moment to Jefferson's Virginia:

A pamphlet called "Civil Rights and Legal Wrongs," distributed by
the Virginia Commission on Constitutional Government, attacked
President Kennedy's civil rights proposals, as follows:

> We do not believe the intensely personal problems of racial feel-
> ing can be solved by any Federal law; the roots go deeper than
> Congress can reach. In any event, we believe that whatever
> might be gained by this particular Federal law, if anything, the
> positive harm that would be done to constitutional government
> would far outweigh the hypothetical good.

The high-minded deviousness of this kind of reasoning is capsulated
in the following quote:

> At this point in our argument the Virginia Commission would
> beg the closest attention: We do not propose to defend racial
> discrimination. We do defend, with all the power at our com-
> mand, the citizen's right to discriminate.

And later, several times: "We take no position here on the merits of
these proposals as such." The members of the Virginia Commission
on Constitutional Government included the Governor and many distinguished attorneys, editors, businessmen, and members of the Vir-

---

* According to both W. J. Cash and C. Vann Woodward, violence was
traditional in the South long before it became predominantly racial
violence. Woodward says: "The South seems to have been one of the most
violent communities of comparable size of all Christendom." (This statement was made in comparison with Italy, which had the highest homicide
rate in Europe.)

ginia House of Delegates. There, at the apex of the social order, we uncover the final degradation of the Southern system, because this and similar nonsense passes for *law* in the South.

Between the various efforts of the rednecks and the lawyers, the nightriders and the daytalkers, a simple fact was obscured—that the Negroes were participants in human existence. A wise old Jew I know in Mississippi ascribes the critical cause of the Southern system to Christianity, on the theory that the white man, because of his religion, could not countenance slavery *except* on the assumption that the Negro was subhuman. Dean Erwin Griswold of the Harvard Law School points more specifically to the unfortunate heritage of the English common law which, unlike Latin law deriving from Rome, contained no developed concept of slavery and so assimilated the slave to a "chattel"—i.e., a *thing*. And that is the root-source of all the Southern lies: any time you cross-examine a white Southerner, you will again discover that innate Negro inferiority is the one and only point that concerns him. Everything else is expendable. Grant him this point, and he will even try to be sympathetic about the difficult plight of the Nigra. Deny it, and he will talk you to death during the day—or ride over you at night.

The South is a lawless land. Even though people there seem just like Americans and even wear Northern clothing, do not be fooled. The primary postulate of the South is that there is no law for the Negro because he does not need or deserve any: he is not human. Ignore this point, and Southerners can seem very reasonable. Remember it, and that it is incorrect, and nothing they say makes sense.

In point of fact, the Negro in that area is now basically superior to the white because of the limited character of his participation in the corrupt Southern system—despite the deep, corroding fear at the core of his personality. And sometimes I think that at least a substantial part of his violence and sullen childishness, when it surfaces in the Northern ghettos, derives from the fact that for a long time he had only the Southern white to imitate, *that he is really a Southerner*—under the skin, so to speak.

8 Along with the traditional violence to mind and body, the South has also been poor. The post-Civil War poverty of the South was such that the whites took over some better jobs which had previously been known as "Negro jobs," such as carpentering, thus enforcing a genuine *decline* in the position of the former slaves. In *Origins of the New South,* a superb book published in 1951, C. Vann Woodward illustrates the economic problem dramatically in terms of cotton:

> The farmer got less for the 23,687,950 acres he planted in cotton in 1894 than for the 9,350,000 acres of 1873. . . . In plain words, under the new system he had to work more than twice as long for the same pay.

Woodward's careful view of Southern development after the Civil War, leading to the disfranchisement atrocities of the period 1890-1910, is based mostly on the thesis of colonialism. His point is that the North first exercised a missionary enthusiasm for the colonial South, and following Reconstruction turned to economic exploitation. "Profit motive and missionary motive have often gone hand-in-hand in the development of 'backward people,' " he points out. The major instrument of colonial domination was the railroad, and he offers a marvelous description of railroad politics in the South after the Great Compromise of 1876, ending with the consolidation of the Southern Railway in Morgan's control.

But in portraying the large sweep of railroad history, he does not lose sight of the poignant social effects that prepared the way for the ultimate racial degradation. For instance, he tells us: "Membership in the Southern Methodist Church, lower in 1866 than in 1854, doubled in the fifteen years following the war." This recrudescence of revivalism in the South was comparable to that in England in the early days of the Industrial Revolution, which suggests that the reasons, too, were similar. And further inducing the colonial poverty of the area, to sustain its fundamentalist revivalism so appropriate emotionally to the victims of primitive accumulation, there is the example of the development of sulphur in Texas and Louisiana—

which could have been a great boon to the Southern farmer, as fertilizer, but instead was developed as a colonial export. Annual profits of the Union Sulphur Company "varied between 150 and 400 per cent of its total investment."

Also, there is good reason to believe that an important part of the problem of the South was that so many of the leading elite, and young candidates for elite-status, were killed off in the Civil War; and many of those who were not, came back to discover that they were no longer an elite or would remain so only by strenuous money-grubbing—and, moreover, money-grubbing as colonial agents of the North. The quality and cohesion of the ruling groups were destroyed not merely by Emancipation. So instead of reasonable rule, there was the creation of the myth of the Lost Cause, about which Woodward says: "The deeper the involvements in commitments to the New Order, the louder the protests of loyalty to the Old."

It is Professor Woodward's political history, however, that is particularly instructive in our effort to comprehend Southern lawlessness. He begins the story by pointing out that the Whigs—who had by then become pure business-inspired obstructionists—did not disappear in the South, but entered the Democratic Party more or less *en masse*.

Woodward's next main point is that the carpetbaggers were in power in the South for a very short period indeed. He says:

> Apart from South Carolina, Louisiana, and Florida, where the Radicals did manage to prolong a troubled and contested authority for nearly that long [a decade], the Radical regime in the average state—from the time it was recognized by Congress until it was overthrown—lasted less than three and a half years. . . . For it was not the Radicals nor the Confederates but the Redeemers who laid the lasting foundations in matters of race, politics, and law for the modern South.

The point is that neither the Confederacy nor its opponents, the Radicals and the carpetbaggers, were able to determine the character of the South we know. This was accomplished by the survivors in the postwar mess, known as the Redeemers—and their opportunity occurred in the disputed presidential election of 1876 between Tilden and Hayes. No wonder the myth of the Lost Cause was needed so much and lasted so long! And if the North fought the war for both an ideal and a material purpose, it decided in 1876 to sacrifice the former to the further securing of the latter. (So much for Northern myths.) Finally, Woodward sums up this 1876 period as follows:

> And while the Northern Whigs were taking over leadership of the Republican party from Free-Soilers and Radicals, Southern Whigs and conservative Democrats had to a considerable extent replaced Jacksonians as leaders of the Democracy of their region.*

Jacksonianism reemerged for its denouement as Populism toward the end of the century. In this struggle of the poor white farmer against the large landowners, railroads, and other colonial agents, the truly towering tragedy of the South was consummated.

Throughout the formative period of the post-Civil War South— after political initiative had been restored to the area—the great recurrent issue was whether that section should make an alliance with the West or the East. The farmers were naturally impelled to look to the West; the Redeemers, business interests, and representatives of the absentee colonialists of course turned to the East. With Populism, the farmers, on their own, made an alliance with the West. But they did not succeed, despite some genuine effort by radical elements at the beginning, in making an alliance with the indigenous Negroes. And that was the final doom of the South: it was, note well, the worst of all American failures—non-achievement of the next necessary coalition.

The racial issue is everywhere and always used to achieve non-racial ends. *It has no other use.* It is a form, not a content. The postwar political struggle in the South was directed by leading property elements against the white farmers as much as against, perhaps even more than against, the Negroes (as illustrated by the deep corruption in the election process).

The non-racial conflict in the South had always been between the planter in the Black Belt and the white farmer in the uplands. The former had at all times a decisive malapportionment working in his favor—first, the three-fifths of a ballot for every slave, and after the Emancipation Proclamation and Reconstruction, five-fifths for every freed man. And apparently the planter controlled the Negro vote—or

---

* Note the similarity between total surviving Whiggery and the conservative coalition in Congress. Perhaps the historical losers win the major negative victories in America.

non-vote, as the case may be—after the Civil War as much as he had before. This gives some greater substance to the poor white's hatred of the Negro in the South. As to why the Negroes voted for the planter's white supremacy parties so consistently in this post-Reconstruction period, Woodward suggests that it was planter paternalism which made the difference. That is hard to believe—there must have been a good deal of intimate intimidation as well; and perhaps the planters promised "protection" for the Negro against the poor white.

Woodward notes: "It took a lot of ritual and Jim Crow to bolster the creed of white supremacy in the bosom of a white man working for a black man's wages." It may be that the Negroes understood this, and, for this reason as well, made their alliance with the reactionary political whites. Woodward characterizes the unhappy results as follows:

In fact, an increase of Jim Crow laws upon the statute books of the state is almost an accurate index of the decline of the reactionary regimes of the Redeemers and triumph of white democratic movements.

Whether misdirected by their enemies or betrayed by their leaders and their indigenous Southern disease, the popular forces participated in their own destruction. The florid nigger-baiting in Southern political rhetoric owes much to the Watsons and the Vardamans, the low leaders of Southern Populism in its later degenerate stage.

In any event, the Negro disfranchisement movement, carried through in constitutional conventions in many Southern states beginning in 1890, drew its sustenance by leeching the moral fiber of the community. The white Southerners of the ruling group consciously went about sacrificing the morality of their society to the immediate end of securing their own political control. They knew they were doing this, and some undoubtedly suffered consciously from both the evil event and their knowledge of it. Opposing the publication of the proceedings of one convention, a delegate said:

We will say things down here *in our Southern way,* and in the great old commonwealth of Alabama . . . that we do not want read and criticised day after day as we deliberate in this body. (Emphasis added.)

The ostensible purposes of the disfranchisement movement were to get rid of the Negro vote which had occasioned corrupt elections in the South; to allow white men to disagree vigorously by removing the possibility of the Negro as a swing-group; and to establish more firmly the local apartheid system by depriving the Negro of any hope of political power. The net historical result, however, was more or less to destroy the political participating system altogether. The development in Virginia, for example: "In 1940, fewer than 10 in every 1,000 of population were voting, as against 147 in 1900."

Roy Wilkins, head of the NAACP, was arrested in Jackson, Mississippi, while picketing the Woolworth Company. As reported in the New York *Times* of June 2, 1963: " . . . the charge against Mr. Wilkins and the two other Negroes was conspiring to combine to restrain trade or hinder competition." Thus the final utility of the Populist-inspired laws against the trusts in Mississippi.

9   The conclusion of the 1963 report of the Mississippi Advisory Committee to the United States Commission on Civil Rights:

> We find that terror hangs over the Negro in Mississippi and is an expectancy of those who refuse to accept their color as a badge of inferiority; and terrorism has no proper place in the American form of government.

The report also stated:

> This Committee finds that the Federal Government has not provided the citizens of Mississippi the protection due them as American citizens.

And Ralph McGill, editor of the Atlanta *Constitution*, has stated out of more than adequate experience:

> There has been no progress in the South that I know of except under pressure from the Federal Government—the courts or Congress or the President.

At present, law in the South is partly in the courts, partly in the streets, and partly in Washington. It is being born. The end-point of all the Negro action in the South will be to teach the meaning of law, beginning with federal law, to Southerners both black and white. As it is, the white Southerner has abandoned to the black Southerner both the burden and the benefit of law. But it is an illusion to believe that the Negro can achieve the realization of law by himself. He requires federal power—and he must have as much as he requires, including a second military occupation, if necessary. (One should not forget that the first occupation was corrupt: it did not have Negro rights or the protection of Negroes as its focus, and it did have too much of a vindictive and profiteering motive.)

Law derives from power. There is no law without power behind it. Law is power that is both enforced *and* accepted. In the South, there is no effective law covering race relations that is consistent with the national charter. There is no power-source in the Southern community adequate to establish such law by itself. So there must be an exercise of federal power, to bring federal racial law to the South. This can be done, or at least begun, by allowing the Negroes to express themselves as they have been doing, and protecting them in this expression. It will, one hopes, be furthered as well by a growing body of white Southern opinion which realizes that there is no real law where they want law if there is no real law in race. But with all this, it is still federal law and power that are required. It is simply asking too much of a people to expect them to accept and live up to an alien law, one that contradicts premises of their social system, except as a consequence of an exercise of "foreign" power. People respect power, whether they admit it or not, because power is very real. Maybe that's all that power really is—*the forced reality one respects.*

I am suggesting that there are limits to the quantum of hypocrisy and distortion a social order can sustain, and remain legal, that is, retain an operating system of law. What happens when the limit is passed is that law itself becomes a pure façade. This may be something of a natural-law notion, but note that the "nature" involved is a matter of social psychology rather than of Catholic metaphysics. Law too far distant from the nature of the humans it governs is no longer law, but merely a duplicitous excuse for its absence. I further suggest that the South is defined in its soul by the fact that it has lived under such a system for three-quarters of a century or more. It is not one or two federal statutes that are required in that area: it is the introduction of the root idea of the rule of law to a people who have forgotten what it means, while living under a culture resourcefully devoted to obscuring what it means. A new Southern culture must be created, and by the Southerners, in order to free the South both black and white. It will take more than one generation. Meanwhile, the impulse to "go slow," in view of the magnitude of the problem, is ubiquitous—and the radicals are absolutely correct in their distrust of officialdom on this score. But there is also a "too fast." And how slow is too slow, and how fast is too fast, is an issue, not a subterfuge. A federal military dictatorship administered by SNCC activists, even if conceivable, would be "too fast." But last year's pace—*any* last year's pace—would be "too slow."

I repeat: A *culture* must be changed—just "changing" individuals will not do. Let me illustrate the tradition-depth of this culture with an anecdote: One *learns* the kind of lawlessness first permitted and then required by the Southern "order." When I went to law school at Yale, there was a noticeable contingent of Southerners who were, at first glance, preparing for no known career. That is, they obviously were not dashing around in pursuit of the money-side of the law, and even more obviously they were not about to become scholars. Along the way, I misunderstood them as regional variants of the upper-class Northerners who were casually getting a good degree to complete their qualifications and not, like the urban Jews who were my friends, to compensate for their disqualifications. But finally an occasion arrived that brought these sleepy characters (one was an eight-hour-a-day bridge-player) to life: An issue they wanted to suppress came up in a student association meeting, and a handful of them brilliantly made a parliamentary shambles of the gathering. They had an amazingly creative relation to *Robert's Rules*. Then I got it: they were preparing to become "intellectual" leaders of the next generation of Southern politicians. (I even imagined that some county political organizations had provided them with scholarships.)

These bright young men were not individually delinquent: their delinquency was professional, and qualified them for leading careers in their communities. George Wallace could well have been one of them; I would give odds that one or more of them have actually worked for him.

To change a culture: "foreign" power, including federal bayonets, will make a difference, but cannot directly accomplish the purpose. Law is based on power—and where there is no law, it must find its beginning in an expression of power—but it is a failure if it is limited to force. Crudely, power is the threat of force; and law, also crudely, is the threat of power expressed conceptually—with the force of reason, so to speak. Putting the matter briefly, to bring law to a lawless land, especially to a land with a developed culture nurturing lawlessness, power must be educational; destruction of aspects of the culture of the people, not the people themselves, is the purpose.

The people who cannot be educated to law, and who express their failure violently, must be killed or isolated. Exactly as an incorrigible criminal with a gun in his hand is killed. And this is the only justified killing to survive in a civilized, lawful society. To kill an incorrigible lawbreaker once he is captured and disarmed is indecent; to isolate him irretrievably before his incorrigibility is established is uncivilized. To make believe he cannot exist, however, is fatuous.

Some Southern whites alive today will never learn racial law, and will never abandon the gun. They must be killed if armed, or isolated when disarmed. Because their criminal potentiality has been an integral part of the Southern system that was established, long ago, to substitute for law. To use a modern analogy, the Klan was Maoist (as was the Mafia). Communal law enforced by a self-chosen minority—illegal law—survives in a highly organized society because the organized society is not yet a community. Illegal law of this kind must be fought, even by means that risk the centralizing of police power, because it contains too great a totalitarian potential to be permitted to continue its course uncontested. Power is not mere force; but, given the terms of the encounter, it is readily reduced to mere force. Street revolution of the 1848 variety—the source of Marxist violentism—has become nonviolent: replacing it in the violent mode, we now have Maoist community-style subversion. It is violent, and it is violence peculiarly appropriate to a nuclear age. Apart from spontaneous riot, it is the last form of available non-state violence.

Wiley A. Branton, former director of the Southern Regional Council's voter education project, has said:

> I know from experience in representing clients across the South that many Negroes feel that the local F.B.I. agents are not too much different in their attitudes from the local police in the communities in which they live.

The issue of the FBI is crucial in civil rights action in the South, particularly when and after some real racial progress is achieved, because at that time the white reaction will take the nightrider form of armed guerrilla resistance derived clandestinely from the community in which it operates: the Maoist mode. The only way to fight that sort of thing is with espionage. The good faith of future federal enforcement can at any time be judged by reference to the effort of the FBI.*

But while power *can* be reduced to force, mostly it remains elevatedly social and complex. Barbara Carter suggested in *The Reporter* that the racist friend of Senator Eastland who was appointed to the Federal District Court in one of the Mississippi districts by President Kennedy—Judge W. Harold Cox—was given the job in exchange for Thurgood Marshall's confirmation as a federal judge in New York. If this is so, Marshall should have refused the job. Having the awareness of what to do, and the integrity to do it, is an issue not only for the FBI.

10

In Baker County in Georgia, one of the Black Belt counties, Negroes outnumbered whites by 1,000 persons in 1960—but not a single Negro was registered. One Negro compared the attempt to robbing a bank. He said: "You might get in but you might not get out." Baker County was described by Claude Sitton of the New York *Times* as follows:

> Three plantations cover much of its area. Two are owned by Northerners—Richard K. Mellon of New York, and Hill Blackett, a retired Chicago advertising executive. The third and largest, Ichauway, is the property of R. W. Woodruff of Atlanta, board chairman of the Coca-Cola Company.

And Birmingham, of course, is an absentee-owned steel town. Thus colonialism continues in a more leisurely fashion.

The first effort of Negro voting in the South will be to make it unprofitable for *both* contestants in an election, whether primary or general, to engage in racist rabble-rousing. This would mean that at long last the leaders of the Southern community, including the loud-

---

* This effort cannot—easily and immediately and all by itself—be sufficient: the Southern jury system is such that even the *coup* of an espionage agent as an eyewitness to murder is not enough for a conviction, as in the incredible and indecent Liuzzo case. When Southern juries convict —*that* is the truest of all barometers measuring the spiritual success of the Second Reconstruction.

mouth political leaders, would no longer divide and rule by means of racism. It is obvious that many of the lower-class whites will, in the first instance, take this changed situation very badly. But if they could accept their own social and economic degradation, they may be able to take this, too. They might even begin to see their own situation in its proper aspect, once the racial veil has been lifted. What federal power is required for, and can accomplish, is to stop the *easy* exploitation of that rotten colonial order which has gone into our history under the heading: "South."

There are dangers all around, of course, in disrupting any rooted situation, even one of degradation. In *The Mind of the South*, Cash says significantly of Huey Long: "In any case, he was the first Southern demagogue largely to leave aside nigger-baiting and address himself mainly to the irritations bred in the common white by his economic and social status." Doing so, he attacked the established power of the Democratic Party, and substituted his own machine for the previous one. Was it really worse? I suppose so. But note what was involved for the poor white victims of either Long's tyranny or the usual party oppression. Cash writes a beautiful paragraph characterizing the role of the latter in the collapse of the Gastonia strikers:

> And when, in addition, they found themselves set down for Communists, for atheists and "Negro equality citizens," it became simply intolerable. Under the cold and dangerous glance of their old captains, economic and political, under the stern and accusing glance of their ministers, they wilted much as the Populists had once wilted, turned shamefaced, shuffled, and, as the first joy in battle and in expressing their will to defiance died down, felt despairingly that they probably would be read out of the Democratic Party in this world and out of paradise in the next.

So the strikes failed.*

The creation of a Negro voting bloc in the South will have *two* broad power effects. It will give a new form of power to the Negroes,

* This passage suggests yet another aspect of the revolutionary importance—for the whole political future of the South—attending the Republican invasion of the ruling groups à la Goldwater. With defection among the rulers, it cannot remain a religious issue for the poor whites to be the kind of True Democrats—subject to vicious demagoguery—which has been the pattern of the "New" South.

and not less significantly will deny an old form of power to the whites. I rather think that the latter will be more important for the future of the area. The kind of tight organization the Negroes will have to accept to get the greatest mileage out of their vote is apt to concentrate power in the hands of the leaders, not all of whom can possibly be saints. The Southern Negroes are so poor (including their leaders) that any low-level patronage or other bribe is certain to be welcome, and understandably so, to many. On this factor in Mississippi, Barbara Carter reported:

> Yet of the 3,800 post-office employees in the state only 134 were Negro, and of these only three, who worked in all-Negro post offices, earned more than $4,600 a year.

It seems obvious to me that people this poor must inevitably cash in their new political power for immediate economic benefit, as soon as it has been used to put a halt to the worst of the daily humiliations and terrors of segregation. No matter how crudely used, of course, power to the powerless Negro of the South is the *sine qua non* of any advance in that benighted area.

But note what an immense advantage will just as inevitably accrue to the white simply by denying him reliance on the foul techniques of power which so obviously damage perpetrator as well as victim. The Mississippi Advisory Committee report stated:

> In 1962, the Mississippi Legislature enacted a new law requiring the publication of the names and addresses of all new voting registrants for two weeks in a newspaper of general circulation. This law is ostensibly designed to facilitate challenges of registrants on moral grounds. In fact, it can be used to facilitate reprisals against Negroes who seek to register.

Not only will issuing invitations to assault and murder no longer be the function of the state, but a whole cornucopia of fraudulent devices may be abandoned. As just one example: In an effort to keep the Civil Rights Commission from examining records of registration, Alabama in 1959 passed a law authorizing registration boards to destroy records after a very limited period. So the poor white housewife who takes a stinking registrar's job for peanuts, and must engage in daily criminal acts to earn her pay, will also be set free.

When the big push of the Negroes began, the situation was

summed up (by Anthony Lewis in the New York *Times* of April 2, 1961) as follows:

> Only 25 per cent of voting-age Negroes in the South are registered, as against 60 per cent of the whites, and in rural areas the percentage of qualified Negro voters sinks to zero.

In 1960, only 1,200,000 Negroes were registered in the South. Just prior to passage of the 1965 voting rights act, Negro registration in the South had reached 1,900,000 ranging from 69.5 per cent of the eligible voters in Tennessee, to an indecent 6.7 per cent in Mississippi. Shortly before that date, a white Memphis politician had said of the Negroes: "They don't have the votes to elect a candidate yet, but they sure can defeat one." The reason for the emphasis on voting during the Sixties was concisely stated by a Negro from Charlotte, North Carolina: "We can gain more in one day at the ballot box than we can gain in one year in the courts." Another virtue of the registration drive—as compared to educational integration—is that tokenism is very obviously tokenism, and is worth nothing, even symbolically.

Not everyone is aware that the Southern counterattack following the desegregation decision in 1954 was directed against voting rights from the beginning. Indeed, the "beginning" is dated pre-1954. According to Anthony Lewis, "Fewer than 100,000 Negroes in the South are estimated to have voted in the general election of 1940." Then, in 1944, the Supreme Court abolished the white primary system. There was a great increase in Negro registration from 1947 until about 1952, when it leveled off. This must have been the result of the Court's decisions and of the assertiveness of returning servicemen. But the registration movement finally met an official white resistance. Between 1956 and 1958 there was an actual *decrease* in registration in such states as Arkansas, Florida, Georgia, Louisiana, and South Carolina.

In the first six months following passage of the 1965 act, 200,000 Negroes were registered by local officials, and an additional 100,000 by federal registrars. After one year of the act, the percentage of eligible Negroes actually registered in Alabama, Mississippi, Louisiana, South Carolina, Georgia, and Virginia increased from 30 to 46 per cent: *32.9 per cent in Mississippi.*

11 The Negroes can be expected to provide a radical leavening for some time to come, until new comfort joins with old discouragement, and a generation settles. But if before they burn out they manage with federal assistance to register enough voters in the South, as they seem to be doing, they may well have given us a decisive turn in our political life. No matter how few Negro congressmen and other officials they actually elect, the time will come when statewide candidates will have to deal with Negro blocs in Southern states. The cities are even more deeply at odds with rural districts in the South than elsewhere in the country; eventually, then, the urban and Negro blocs will together elect governors and senators. Moreover, as Southern diehards are isolated by the continued application of federal pressure, the ordinary Southern whites will be freed from the extremist political tyranny of the nightriding kind, and will themselves have an opportunity to develop more normal brokerage-politics on the regular American model. It will be important at that time for the Negroes to have something to trade—namely, registered and deliverable voters. (It was Negro voting in the North, following the war migrations, which prepared the basis for the present movement.)

And one day, Negroes in Black Belt counties will regularly elect their own sheriffs. At a later date, white men will be convicted by local juries of violence against black men—and women. Then, for the first time in three hundred years, there will be law for both races in the South.

Culturally, the heart of the matter lies in the Black Belt counties. But in the raw political sense, including the serious intervention of a state in bringing fair law to the government of a county, the power of the Negroes will first be felt in the larger cities and in statewide elections. It must be kept in mind, however, that the Negroes are an absolute minority statewide, even in Mississippi. Which means they require an alliance with whites even in the South. Most rosily, one would hope for a second chance at Populism—a coalition including poor farmers and workers, led by elements of the liberal middle class. But it is the poorest white in the South who values the distinction of race more than anyone else in the country. I imagine he can.

be brought into such a coalition, in significant numbers, only by means of expert leadership pointing directly to immediate economic benefit; he is not apt to be brought in by virtue merely of a rousing speech.

Here, the new conservatism and dynamism of the Republicans in the South can only be described as a great, glowing bonanza. Because this new move divides the rulers, not the ruled. The Democratic Party was the sharpest instrument of Southern segregation. It strikes me as quite late in the day to change scalpels. It took a long time, and a good number of historical struggles, to trap the popular white masses in the party of the Confederate captains. Assume that these masses, out of bad habit alone, followed their new captains into the racist Republican Party. What could that party do for them economically? How long could they resist the blandishments of the "moderates" with useful federal connections? And notice that it will no longer be necessary to attract and hold an overwhelming and monolithic white majority, once the Negro votes—and votes in a bloc. Substantially less than a majority of the whites could, along with bloc-voting Negroes, put together governing coalitions throughout the Old South. (The ordinary Negroes, note well, will be double captives—of their own leaders and those of the coalitional white minority.) The whole point of lawless segregation and disfranchisement in the postwar South was to create and maintain a political unity based on white skin. And now at last the whites will be divided: thus, non-racial politics comes to the South in a fundamental way.

At a press conference in 1956, President Eisenhower relieved himself of some reflections on race. "I don't believe you can change the hearts of men with laws or decisions," he said. Those Southerners with the presence of mind to know that they had been otherwise occupied in the womb than in hating Negroes, were undoubtedly insulted by the General's remark: they knew full well, deeply and desperately, just exactly in what way and how much state laws—and the power behind them—had extorted intimate changes of heart in them. Inhibit the use of state force in confirming segregation, by an exercise of federal power, and the heart will change back rather naturally—in the emotional free market, so to speak. (It surprises me that the General, with his known devotion to free enterprise, failed to grasp this point.)

In Chapter Nine, we discussed the case of *Wesberry v. Sanders,* the second of the three great apportionment decisions. This case was brought by qualified voters of Georgia's Fifth Congressional District —that is, the city of Atlanta, where Negroes vote. Since the Fifth District contains 823,680 people, according to the 1960 Census, it will one day soon elect *two* Representatives. Meanwhile, it has been represented since 1962 by Congressman Weltner, who voted for the Civil Rights Act of 1964. During his successful reelection campaign, Charles Longstreet Weltner said, "Come with us, and the verdict of history shall be ours." Probably.

And thus the burden of American racism shifts awesomely to the white suburbs of the North, there to be re-formed once again in the crucible of ghetto-containment politics.

ELEVEN

The
New
Class

1 As stated in Chapter One, this book represents an appeal and an explanation to the members of the New Class. This was also admitted, earlier, to be shrewder than it sounds, since the great majority of the book-buying public is included in this new, educated group. Neither the workers nor the intellectuals, but the new mass of *working intellectuals,* now constitute the decisive class of the future. It is you, my likely reader, who is both subject and object of this book; and to you I apologize again for Chapter Five (and some other passages) and for what follows. My continuing excuse remains simple and direct: you need some critical self-consciousness, it will do you good, and should prove a useful abrasive to grow on.

To begin with a slight reprise, we may note that major historical phenomena tend to sneak up on us. The Big Events are simply too big readily to be seen for what they are. Further, I would imagine this to be especially true of class movements, which are among the more significant and multiformed of all historical phenomena. The *last* thing we notice are basic changes in the basic conditions of people's lives, especially our own.

The deepest event of the century in the United States has been the growth-to-dominance of the corporate order. The core-meaning of corporations is that they have become our chosen form for the social/political control of technology. So you may presume that the growth of technology itself is the dominant force; but as we are all now aware, the *human* point concerning the advent of technology has occasioned the shifting of our emphasis from the thing itself to the desperately sought means of controlling it. What is wrong with Russia, for instance, is not that it has steel mills, but that it has commissariats of a particular social and political nature to control these steel mills—and, therefore, the lives of the people producing and consuming the steel. The chief effect of the creation of the corporate order, apart from the fact that it has worked so devastatingly well, is that it has also fairly fully undermined the previously existing system of private property. In doing so, it has seriously undercut the class of property-holders, and has created a New Class of non-property-holding individuals whose life conditions are determined by their position within or in relation to the corporate order. The essence of the matter is that they are unpropertied in their primary career-line. Most significantly, they do not look forward to the personal accumulation of capital. They desire and they achieve a privileged standard of living; and they may, indeed, gather in some "property" for personal security or general economic sweetening. But they are job-holders, not capitalists: as to property, they begin and end as minor *rentiers*.

The propertyless New Class is most broadly defined as that group of people gaining status and income through organizational position. They achieve their positions—or at least they enter the race to achieve them—mostly by virtue of educational status. There are some exceptions: one would think immediately of those with special organizational experience in lieu of academic training; and marginal brokerage persons not at the center of the new development—an indigenous group in any system, new or old, including any right Reginald who dresses well and talks nicely (someone who is invited to Any Party). But the New Class, pointedly, is a growing group of similarly situated people, with distinctly similar purposes, who entrepreneur their way through society by means of an educational qualification rather than by property ownership, and who take as the object of their efforts not the accumulation of personally held property, but a higher and more secure organizational tenure.

This big change has so effectively sneaked up on us, we are so many of us so completely involved in it, that we do not recognize it for the major historical transformation it in fact is. We are part of a great revolutionary alteration, but we have not seen the forest for the watering of our own little trees. Most of us thought we were just getting and holding "good jobs": actually, we were (for better or for worse) changing the whole world.

Let us restate the proposition: Under the duress of modern technology, productive property has of necessity been organized in larger and larger aggregates. Thus, the corporate revolution. Control of the major property held by the corporations is in the hands of non-owners. And, as technology gallops forward, its processes require more technologists, and ever more refined patternings of sophisticated men and sophisticated machines. As technology becomes more involved with accumulating know-how, and less dependent on the gross division of labor which characterized industrialism, the central factor in production again becomes people, their particular qualities and capacities: humans thus a second time become more important than machines (even though they may persist inordinately in "acting like" machines). The truly productive "property," then, is the utility of the person. Moreover, this skill is not merely individual; it is social and political in that it requires not just that the individual can do something, but that he can relate what he does to what others do (and he learned what he does from others). This is the *entrée* for a great deal of *purely* organizational or administrative effort. And consequently the opening for a great number of people who mostly organize and administer, and criticize and comment on, the activities of others. (These people are required either to administer others or ceremoniously to adorn such administration, take your pick: I think, both.)

So without much argument, to begin with, we have technologists and administrative intellectuals as primary elements of the New Class.

2 In helping to appreciate the scope and character of this major phenomenon of the New Class, one may properly recollect the previous rise to power of the bourgeoisie, the property-owning class. That long event revealed various means of achieving the initial accumulation of property; meanwhile,

pockets of stagnation would exist alongside spurts of growth; at one time, a particular area might be the liveliest, then a little bit of business across the street would grow faster; there were important national and geographic differences; it did not happen all at once, and the people responsible for carrying it out were not, at the time, all that easy to identify; the whole process in duration was loose and rough, real rather than apparent; and the dominance of bourgeois power was achieved over a very long period of time—the final step was a small one, because of the lengthy precedent development. The currently occurring changeover in emphasis from money-capital to education-capital—to be invested in the status-play of organizational life rather than directly and personally in the production of commodities for a market economy—is not apt to be simpler, clearer, or in any way less complicatedly "historical."

Isn't it fairly clear that the present scramble for educational advantage, and the struggle to translate achieved educational status into organizational advantage, has much in common with a gold rush, or the fierce competition of early business growth? It was front-page news in the spring of 1965 when the letters were sent out from the admissions offices of the major Eastern schools. Even the initial edge of family or propertied background is similar to the advantage enjoyed, say, by a seventeenth century aristocrat with a house full of gold plate, in an earlier entrepreneurial age. The important fact here is that, to become fully effective, a particular old class-based advantage must be translated into terms appropriate to the *new* class: from aristocratic status and tenure to entrepreneurial use of property, from a property edge to educational and organizational use thereof. In the nineteenth century, the education of the upper classes was an occasional adornment: today, it is a functional necessity. This being so, the capacity to scramble forward in the environment of the elite academy (often called "talent," in the lily-gilding mood) is competitive with the wealth and family background which formerly governed admission all by itself. Writing in the New York *Times* for March 14, 1964, Robert Trumbull reported that Harvard, Yale, and Princeton—the Big Three for men—were shifting, although glacially, from wealth to ability. He cited a study of the New York Social Register for 1963 by Gene R. Hawes to the effect that "while nearly two-thirds of the men listed went to Harvard, Yale, or Princeton, fewer than half of their sons" have done so.

Some distance from these exotic happenings, but still pointedly illustrating the same class-movement principles, the heir of Tough Tony Anastasia, former boss of the Brooklyn docks, is Anthony M. Scotto, his son-in-law, who has a degree in political science from Brooklyn College. According to John P. Callahan in the *Times* (April 13, 1963), Not-So-Tough Tony Scotto began as a longshoreman at age sixteen, and eight years later was organizational director (second man) behind Tough Tony, who served the working class as business manager of Local 1814, the biggest in the ILA. The younger Tony dresses well, and has been observed entering union headquarters "with a book on the philosophy and practice of political science under his arm." (Why Tony Anastasia's son-in-law would find it useful to read a book on political science is quite beyond me: he might *write* one to pass the time of day—but *read* one during working hours?)

Is the New Class merely a "new style"? I don't think so. I think the "new style" is nothing but one loud emanation from the New Class; and the bigger significance of this style is that it has even affected other and older classes. No, I go back to the key Marxist prescription: the fundament for hungry animals (all animals are hungry for something) in jungle societies is the relation to the means of production—or, in surplus-societies, to the products produced by these means, that is, to income and its what-for and because. Thereafter, if we still think in causal terms, style and much else derive from these deeper relations.

Education is now a manipulable and alienable property. Capital in the past was a quantity alienated from the person by virtue of duration: one "saved." This constituted a personal cost, a thingification of life-capacity. Likewise, education today, except that one intermediate step has been eliminated: the duration creating the capital no longer passes through the commodity stage—*the person himself is the product.* With capital alienated from the capitalist by the system of corporate ownership, and investment out of retained earnings, the distinction between capitalist and *educated* proletarian fades into something less profound than it used to be. Indeed, the latter has the more significant and dynamic relation to the means of production in that the system doesn't work without him; whereas the capital that *works*—machines and buildings rather than bank deposits and stock certificates—hardly needs the alienated capitalist at all. More and more he becomes a mere *rentier,* and his best defense is tradition.

How big is the New Class? Perhaps not yet as big as the small-property class or the still-uneducated working class, in mere numbers—but these latter are declining, in significance as well as in quantity, while the New Class grows greatly both numerically and in strategic position. In 1960 or thereabouts, 2,000 institutions of higher learning cared for 3.2 million persons. The figure is increasing rapidly: various Bureau of the Census projections estimate that college enrollment will be two to three times as great by 1980. Persons twenty-five years of age or older in the 1960 population who had completed four years or more of college numbered 7.6 million: the farthest-out projection to 1980 puts the figure at 14.4 million, nearly double. These people—two million college graduates a year—capitalize four years or more of their lives not for cultural adornment or use, but for career reasons. *It's a business*: 10,000 doctorates bestowed each year, 10,000 LL.B.'s, 7,000 M.D.'s—and numerous other qualifying certificates from animal husbandry to social work.

Another way of getting at least a kinesthetic sense of the gross size of the New Class would be to view the flow of the material product ordinarily accompanying their work—paper. Better than sixteen million tons of paper are produced annually in the United States; but this includes newspaper and toilet paper. Trying to assess the cost of "paperwork" (not merely the cost of the physical stuff), a congressman has suggested that business spends as much as $111 billion thereon each year. The federal government spends $110 million on the material part alone. The Stanford Research Institute says that it costs business $4 billion just to file the paper properly. (All this heavy communication has been seriously compounded in recent years by the installation of 400,000 copying machines turning out ten billion sheets annually.) The New Class writes memos and letters and reports in considerable quantity. What else can you do if you are just educated, and relying on same as if your life depended on it, which it does?

But the situation *can* get out of hand. A couple of years ago, the Superintendent of Schools in New York City declared a "moratorium on reports" by his staff. He thought the quantity of the stuff was "beyond belief" and that it was (a minor problem, but irritating) hindering "almost everyone here who has a job to do." That's right: fun is fun, but don't block the fire exit.

3 In his thorough work on the New Deal, Arthur Schlesinger says that the idea of the "brain trust" had its beginning in a conversation that occurred in March 1932 between Sam Rosenman and Candidate Roosevelt concerning the general lack of ideas as to what to do about the Depression—and especially the fact that businessmen and politicians did not have anything much to offer. Rosenman suggested going to the universities. The first ambassador from the academy to the future New Deal was Raymond Moley of Columbia. Moley then recruited Tugwell, Berle, etc. Thus began the revolutionary, non-priestly, and ultimately successful onslaught of the New Class upon the heights of national power.

Roosevelt, however, had been primed for the event—as for much else—by his tour of duty under Woodrow Wilson. In a speech in 1920 he had said:

> Wilson's administration would not have been successful in the War if he had not adopted the policy of calling in the experts of the Nation, without regard to party affiliations, in order to create and send across the seas that great Army in record-breaking time.

I wonder if the First World War was the first time "the experts of the Nation" had been called to the centers of power? Let's say, the first *industrial* time wherein the front issue was effective organization.

A qualifying digression may be in order here: We are not discussing the first appearance of cultured individuals around the centers of American power. But if we go back to the Adamses and others—necessarily beyond the Civil War and the resulting business surge—we are left with the colonial imitators. These were second-class even if upper-class English-type carriers of culture to power, expatriate aspirants to the status of the liberal arts amateurs who have in fact ruled England so decisively. *The New Class has not invented culture, nor has it devised an initial application of culture to power: it has simply established both of these on a mass basis, and with an income-gathering emphasis.*

The breakthrough-event was the New Deal: but the New Deal it-

self had roots, and the sturdiest of these was the Progressive movement (after having been fertilized by Mugwump worry). Hofstadter
expresses this matter concisely:

> The development of regulative and humane legislation required
> the skills of lawyers and economists, sociologists and political
> scientists, in the writing of laws and in the staffing of adminis-
> trative and regulative bodies. . . . Reform brought with it the
> brain trust.

Hofstadter (we have noted) sees the Progressive movement as a revolt against organization, and especially against its spiritual consequences. The Progressives differ from the New Class—although in
many social ways similar—in that the latter are not WASP, and
many of them know that they live in and through organizations.
This much at least has been accomplished. But for both, "expertise"
has been terribly important—the validating stamp on the status-
passport. Also fundamentally altered is the definition of a key term
for both, "opportunity": for the Progressives it meant "competition,"
but for the New Class it means "education," whether or not competitive: anyway, differently competitive. On this difference, one may
reasonably base a new politics.

There is too much to say on this general subject: the New Deal
was almost literally the creation of the universe for *working intellectuals* in America. But their universe (with a sensitivity to their powerless beginnings) was never more than half-born. Schlesinger says:

> Tugwell found Roosevelt's readiness to pick one idea from Lewis
> Douglas, another from Frankfurter, another from himself as
> reasonable as "to use part of a cotton picker, part of a rolling
> mill, and perhaps part of a bottle filling machine, all together
> and all with the intent to produce automobiles."

But I think that when all the history is in the book, Roosevelt
emerges as the greatest administrator of intellectuals who ever lived.
And this is a rare, new, worthy talent truly needed for the building of
the new world.

And I certainly recognize that intellectuals are painfully difficult
to administer. They are so pure, so utterly devoted to just exactly
what they and no one else has: that is, ideas. The front quotation in
The Crisis of the Old Order is this one from Emerson—"Every revolution was first a thought in one man's mind." Which is very much
like the famous Keynes quote (very much like it in being so reveal-

ingly untrue, and thus so revealing of the people who take it as truth) which is cited again and again by the *working intellectuals*. Being the last paragraph of *The General Theory*, it explains and predicts the future success of that book. It reads to the effect that

> the ideas of economists and political philosophers, both when they are right and when they are wrong, are more powerful than is commonly understood. Indeed the world is ruled by little else. Practical men, who believe themselves to be quite exempt from any intellectual influences, are usually the slaves of some defunct economist. Madmen in authority, who hear voices in the air, are distilling their frenzy from some academic scribbler of a few years back. I am sure that the power of vested interests is vastly exaggerated compared with the gradual encroachment of ideas.

Keynes is, of course, the John Locke of the New Class.

As an aspect of the New Class adventure, note that both Donald Richberg and Raymond Moley, who were important early New Dealers, used that experience to go over to the big interests somewhat later. Lippmann had done the same thing before them; Dos Passos and his crew more recently. These intellectuals represent the rise of a class which, as it rises, makes necessary deals in order to "amalgamate" with previously existing classes. The same phenomenon is to be noted as between those members of the New Class who rise solely within the corporate structure, and then make their deals with the *rentier*. There is no good reason for this process to produce the unease in the Nice Observer that it does. It is perfectly ordinary and, in the human scope of things, even desirable. What is unsettling, I think, is that these people are *intellectuals*. But that is exactly what is upsetting about the whole New Class phenomenon. This sort of thing, not a hero's lonely endeavor, is the pattern for the future of active thought in history. Can it ruin culture altogether?

If so, then mostly because what we have known as "culture" was born as dry fruit, with a seed of genetic powerlessness. We may have to tuck in our tummies and stand for some quite unpleasant early operations, while ideas and actions come into a better working relation by reason of the involvement of the intellectual in effective (not merely prescriptive) history.

In an early Newspaper Guild case under the NRA labor boards, a jurisdictional conflict in the government set-up occurred which Schlesinger describes as follows: "So Biddle, the former counsel for the Pennsylvania Railroad, contended for labor organization against Richberg, the former counsel for the railroad brotherhoods." Lawyers, of course, have always been awful whores. But also they are the intellectuals who mainly have dealt with genuine issues of power—in that long period when the rest of us were living in the academic desert. So, I think the lawyer's mode will be a functional model for a large part of the cultural future. (Also, from another, less sanguine aspect, all bureaucrats—with their endless rules and regulations and precedents—are "little lawyers.")

But there are also social aspects of the New Class advance. Writing about FDR's tour of the European front during the First World War as Assistant Secretary of the Navy, Schlesinger mentions that Roosevelt "ran into" Robert A. Lovett, Fiorello H. LaGuardia, and Charles E. Merriam (including information as to their rank and service at that time). This social coziness is specially characteristic of Schlesinger's writing. It reveals a very club-like view of history: history almost as the conjoint action of talented classmates. Since historians do not merely collect facts but also dream the dream of a better story, I think Schlesinger here reveals *his* idea of the better story—namely, that America really almost does have that ruling elite group, if not ruling class, that it so noticeably has lacked since the Civil War. He finds this needed clubbiness in the Progressives and the "liberals" and just in the people who "made it" (and many didn't have to go far to make it, being of upper-class lineage).

Schlesinger is our first historian of the New Class—for its great New Deal victory; spokesman for it as a creator of the ADA interregnum; and a prime representative of the impressive return to Washington of its elite elements under the managerial style-baron, John F. Kennedy.

4 Following along with the basic cleavage in American society, the first great division noticeable among the members of the New Class is that between private and public bureaucracies: perhaps, with more meaning, between profit and non-profit institutions. In each, the important matter for the New Class individual is his job, and the educational status that has afforded him his hold on the job. But most of the basic productive property in the country is under the control and direction of private corporations; apart from military considerations, the public govern-

ments—national, state, local, and recently devised—are decidedly junior to the power of private bureaucracies. For example, the income from taxes (the primary source of our public power) is passively received by public governments: the pattern of taxation is the result of private pressures and influence much more than it is the creation of public bureaucratic assertion—or coherent public policy, certainly. Private business is less passive about both its prices and its policies.

So the first proposition here is a traditional one, that the primary division among the members of the New Class is to be understood by deduction from the quality of directness or indirectness in relation to the basic means of production, determined by organizational position rather than by property ownership. Thus, industrial power is more important than financial power, and financial power is more important than governmental power (absent the military).

The difference of the distinction, for the particular purveyor of a certificate, is that he partakes of the inferior income and status of the public organization with personal impact. Also, he suffers or benefits (according to his nature) from the absence of the profit ideology as an organizing principle of purpose in his life. Most nonprofit activities have been confirmed in this country as aimless, halfserious, and time-serving. But this is changing: education, for instance, is becoming a big business; and the larger corporations take care of a great number of people who are not, I think, realistically and passionately concerned with profit-making. The distinction is continuously reduced as time goes on.

In the first instance, I think it is fair to say that the technological revolution is a revolution being pursued by technologists. But technology and technologists have always been controlled politically—in this country, by the political organization of production we call a corporation. The corporations were first controlled or at least articulated by financial power; but the Twenties saw the end of that period, and the shifting of the balance of power from financial centers to industrial ones. In addition, a considerable amount of the former power of finance was transferred to the national government by reason of the failure of the financiers in the Great Depression.

So first you have technology and technologists, and then you have all the people who control and exploit technology and technologists. But both groups are members of the New Class. The New Class is the non-owning class; and they non-own everything important, eventually. But the technologist, through his work with things and tools rather than with people—even his concepts refer more often and more easily to nonhuman matters—has an escape-route from the complications of New Class dynamics: *he can concentrate on his work.* Often he prefers to do so; and mostly he needs only to be left alone in order to do so. But in bureaucratic life, this may be asking too much: the irascible Admiral Rickover, speaking some years ago before a professional group, blamed it all on democratic egalitarianism in the face of IQ excellence. He said:

> The work of professional persons in bureaucracies is severely hampered by administrative interference. We have such interference because we do not draw clear lines between the respective role of the professional man and the administrator and because, of the two, the administrator enjoys the higher prestige and position. He is in fact king.

Concentration on work, especially non-people work, in effect delivers the power of the organization to the people-oriented nonconcentrators. Sometimes this power is delivered ahead of schedule: writing about the New Deal experience, Schlesinger refers to a certain Hugh Hammond Bennett, an early crusader against the evil of soil erosion. An important issue at the time was whether the problem was to be approached through the social and economic structure which induced soil erosion, or whether it was to be gone at directly in a physical way. "Bennett no doubt felt that one bureau could not do everything, and that the engineering approach, by avoiding the politically sensitive problem of rural poverty, could gain conservation a broader support." Everybody ends up playing politics, and it is not really the height of scientific insight to do so *after* surrendering power—and, incidentally, distorting the solution of the technical problem in favor of crudely imagined political obstacles. But this is typical, I fear, of the technical wing of the New Class. They are much too "rational" ever to become effective politicians—or, what is the same thing, non-concentrating administrators. (For further indignation on this subject, look back to Chapter Six.)*

---

* Al Smith's comment on the technocracy craze in 1932 is amusing: "As for substituting engineers for political leaders in running the country, I cannot refrain from mentioning the fact that we have finished an era of government by engineers in Washington." Hoover's devotion to politics-as-morality, and his very rational ideology of Individualism, certainly overwhelmed his technical comprehension of the course of events during

5   We can also sense some of the quality of the New Class from its characteristic habitat—the suburbs.

What is a suburb? It is most obviously the new place where the new people live. The growth of these areas constitutes the big postwar change in America: they are where the new money has been spent, where the much-discussed "income revolution" erected its shopping-center barricades. One out of four Americans now resides, or at least sleeps, in one; they grow three times as fast as central city and rural areas. Two suburban counties adjacent to Washington, D.C., were expected to increase by one-quarter during the four years ending in 1968. The suburbs are affluent frontier towns. Writing long ago in 1925, a commentator named Harlan Douglas said of them: "It is the city trying to escape the consequences of being a city. . . ." (That's not so bad, if only the suburbs don't end up being the place to which Americans retreat in trying too hard to escape the consequences of being Americans.)

Having become frontiers mostly during the postwar period—new bedrooms shaken out of old cities—many of them present an aspect of apparent homogeneity which is frightening even to the residents. An astute sociologist, William M. Dobriner, argues in *Class in Suburbia* that the awful homogeneity is a passing phase. He comes to this view as follows: "Life in the small town and in the suburb is far more open, and thus more visible, than life in the city." So, underneath, the suburbs are not so middle-class as they seem: the factor of visibility has too pointedly refracted middle-class behavior and made it more apparent. This, he suggests, has been confused with the suburbs themselves as new institutional arrangements.

The true and demonstrable differences he details as follows:

> To summarize, when compared with central cities, suburbs have higher fertility ratios, higher percentages of married persons, lower percentages separated, higher percentages in primary families, high socioeconomic status in the labor force, higher

the Depression: *the man who fed Europe out of technical enthusiasm, allowed America to starve out of moral commitment.*

median income, lower median age, a higher percentage of mobile families, and a higher level of educational achievement.

Youthful people in youthful places.*

If the suburb is a small town inhabited by at least one big-city person per family, the issue may be which ideology will come to govern—that of place of family or place of work. At the moment, the job is primary for its income and perhaps status, but secondary in all other respects: the wife doesn't come to visit the husband, he comes to visit her—despite the demands of his job. However, when the man dates his wife on the weekend—suburban weekends are ferocious—he participates seriously in The Celebration of The Income. A welfare worker has stated: "I know some kids who have to make an appointment to see their own fathers and mothers in between golf dates and bridge parties." Failing to make an appointment, the kids hold their own cocktail parties, borrow other people's cars indiscriminately, and otherwise participate in the joys of abundant consumption.

It just won't work to sacrifice Everything to a standard of living that is less than a full way of life. Perhaps the current consumption impulse is merely responsive to production despair. Anyway, it can't last. Every town in America was at one time—and not so long ago—a frontier town. The only thing new here is the upholstery and the purpose. There is still a great deal of milling around and fumbling, as to location, for instance: in Nassau County, the average turnover on mortgages has been six and one-half years. The society and the culture of the New Class are being created: naturally, it takes time. First, the appeal of gadgets must be overcome; then, the true human scope of the job must be measured and accepted, without unalterable despair; finally, you actually read some of the books you bought. Meanwhile, there is PTA, fluoridation (anti-fluoridation is merely anti-New Class), Nice Negroes, and in the end the really illicitly exciting thought of electing a councilman, or even—we *have* made it, haven't we?—a congressman.

And he should look and act like us. And more and more, they do: with a high class *rentier,* they even look and act like we would like to

---

* The whole project of modern urbanism is new, Professor Dobriner says: "Although cities, as a distinguishable community form, have existed for over five thousand years, the city in its metropolitan guise is scarcely one hundred years old."

look and act like, which is even more democratic in the American mode. Some of this action goes to the right-wingers; but most of it goes, inevitably, to our New Progressives, the enlarged group of status protest-ants called Reformers—the people who yelled *"Adlai!"* and meant it. Anyway, the style is clear. Also, the national power-significance: in 1964, the *Congressional Quarterly* identified fifty congressional districts as predominantly suburban. *CQ* has also predicted that with adequate arithmetical redistricting under the new Supreme Court rulings, the suburbs would gain something like twenty seats. Seventy congressmen is a heavy swing-group: it almost equals the hard-core Southern contingent. And it is growing, while the latter is declining. James MacGregor Burns divides "political" issues into style-of-life and economic ones; and he suggests that the new swing-group of voters in the new suburbs can be appealed to, and given a political character, through style-of-life issues. Yes. And probably through no others. Which indicates a very substantial change in American politics—based on the New Class, and involving matters that go somewhat deeper than ideological liberalism. In Nassau County, Trotsky could beat Halleck—if only for the accent and the beard.

The new suburbs seemed to be all-out Republican at the beginning only because of their newness, the fact that the earlier suburbs were unrelentingly wealthy, and because of Eisenhower with his soda-pop magic. But President Johnson—no cherubic doll-baby, certainly— did just about as well as the General had done (except for the South): and if you think the reason was a "revolt of indigenous intelligence" *contra* Goldwater, note that Kennedy—with style and intelligence to spare—did not quite split the suburbs with Nixon, taking 47 per cent in 1960. The fifty suburban seats in the House were split almost evenly between Democrats and Republicans in 1964.

Political power to the suburbs will heighten the conflict, and induce adjustments, between the different and as yet undeveloped elements of the New Class which live there. Through this kind of political worry and hustle they will come to know themselves better: their style will jell. With redistricting—state legislative as well as congressional—the increased importance of the suburbs will provide an ideal atmosphere for the increased participation of New Class people in politics. And note that political participation, wherever and however it begins, is a learning process—not a stand-still thing. I tend to trust the American people, especially that portion which has benefited so much from the new affluence, to learn how to operate their own society, once (and if) they seriously begin to try.

The regular "downstate" Republican leaders have been no fairer to the new people in the under-represented suburbs than have the city Democratic bosses. In this sense, the suburbs are truly in the middle —and it is a question of which old-line force sends the most effective ambassadors, and does so first; or makes and accepts the surer alliance sooner with indigenous "style" representatives. Charles Percy in Illinois, for example, understands the necessity—and appears to have the capacity—to appeal to the Chicago suburbs. The old guard Republicans do not—cannot—accept the new order of doing business, and seem to be splitting the party in an effort to hold on to the past. In Maryland, the Democratic bosses of Baltimore have allied themselves with the Southern-type ruralists of the Eastern shore against the Washington suburban counties—and moderate Republicans in that area survived the Johnson sweep in 1964. And John Lindsay—despite the disaster of having been elected Mayor of New York—is still the absolutely perfect suburban candidate (as well as the most adventurous scavenger among the ruins of the Republican Party). It will go back and forth like that, according to which old machine adjusts sooner or better to the city or country leanings-and-alliances of the suburbs, which were definitely *not* Goldwater in '64, whatever their attitude toward central-city Negroes may be in '68.

I find it of long-term significance that the Reformers, even where they were weakest in Chicago, did well in the former heavily Republican suburbs.* The Reformers are dealing with their own class in the suburbs, even if not with their own liberal ideological grouping. And the class factor, the style factor, is the more important one. Also— explaining the Chicago failure—they are just not as good as the professionals in organizing lower-class groups. In New York City, the machine was over the hill; and lower-middle-class residents were, I think, rather complimented to be paid court by such nice young people who obviously bathed on schedule. But the Reformers, even there, have not done so well with the Negro and Puerto Rican masses, due to become numerically dominant before long. Anyway, the point

* With the Democrats, it is a question of rising to the imitation-WASP style; with the Republicans, it is a matter of rising to a suburban issue or two—and keeping the Hallecks out of sight, which of course was begun when Ford replaced him in the House after the 1964 fiasco.

that the Reformers, being middle class in style, do better in Republican areas, augurs well, etc. In the new society of the suburbs, almost everything will be developing toward this kind of future—and rapidly.

When you stop to think about it, the suburbs are strangely like the immigrant neighborhoods of an earlier day—newcomers of another kind (second time around), disfranchised by other means. But these new areas are really just neighborhoods for the sons and daughters of the immigrants to grow up in (even more, for the grandchildren to grow up in).

6 Potentially the most important, perhaps the major, contradiction or division in the New Class involves neither the work nor the bedroom, but specifically the "education" which is its historical *entrée*. To go at an understanding of this in a proper way, however, requires some subtlety. The advent of the New Class concerns not only a change in the property and power structure, but also brings about a considerable diffusion of what we may begin by calling "culture." Educational status does not function simply as a substitute for property, but also unavoidably provides a basis for awareness. One way or another, these new people *are* educated. With an excess neither of hope nor of despair, it would seem reasonable to explore the possibility that this increase in "culture" will itself amount to a political factor of independent significance.

All classes, of course, develop their own culture—indeed, the class is finally defined by it. The New Class, according to its segmentation, naturally has and develops a culture of this kind. But it also becomes involved in realizing itself by means of for-real culture, meaning some serious reading of some serious books. People whose passports to organizational position and class tenure were derived from education would seem to be under a continual threat of becoming "intellectuals," or something futuristically similar. That is, they can be influenced by more than a few ideas on a narrow range, and they may more readily intellectualize their frustrations—and their ideals. If this is so, some great political battles of the future may well be fought over curricula in the schools—not simply repetitions of the current battles as to who gets in what schools and how many places there are in all of them. The importance of curricula, and the attitude or method of the teachers, would take on a heightened political significance on the assumption that what you teach them *there* determines what they listen to *afterwards*. That would certainly be a newly contested power factor.

Also, education induces ideals. It does so by making people read more than otherwise, and by delaying the process of growing up, of gaining any experience: the person in process of being educated spends so much effort trying to decide *which* experience to have that he ends up nearly having none. So education produces frustration— it very possibly produces a personality based on continuing, unrelieved frustration. I would suggest that this is already a political factor in the accommodation of the New Class (or lack thereof) in the total American setting. At this stage in its unfulfilled development, it may even be that the distinctive elements of the New Class are nearly defined—after the more decisive matter of allies—by their specific frustrations (which probably, come to think of it, would even influence the choice of allies).

This factor of frustration has already led to a number of significant status-revolts and will undoubtedly lead to many more (both within and outside the ambit of the new student/university disruption). On the right wing, Goldwater's appeal to New Class tension was patent.

This factor is particularly acute because of the manner in which the educated member of the New Class has been accepted into American society. He has been given a job, period. Intellect in America is still substantially ghetto-ized, but now it resides in a much more comfortable (and promising) ghetto. The intellectual in America is more and more frequently a necessary adornment in and around power centers. But it is important both that he is an adornment *and* that more and more power centers require this particular chandelier.

However, additional frustration certainly results, on a major scale, when a person is trained to do something and then is either not allowed to do it or is encouraged to do it meaninglessly. This is the condition today of many educated individuals. Because more and more people have had to be educated—what else could you do with them?—there are more and more educated people around for whom jobs must be provided. So the jobs are in fact provided. But "just jobs." In this sense, the ancient trained irrelevance of the academic has become a model applied with great extension throughout society in dealing with this New Class for whom jobs must be provided, but whose irrelevance must meanwhile be maintained. This could not have been clearer than it was in Washington, certainly before the 89th Congress, where thousands upon thousands of educated people occupied jobs in the federal bureaucracy in which they were supposed to analyze a wide range of social problems and provide programs to deal with them—which programs were hardly ever enacted by Congress. This is called staff policy research, and it is an infinitely frustrating way of life. A friend told me about a group in one of the Cabinet departments (this was during the Kennedy days) who had devised and revised a piece of legislation, with accompanying Executive message, and had sent it over to Congress so many times that they finally quit out of perfected boredom (having been worked over so much, the documents were gems). In effect, they had simply handed in that term-paper once too often.

(At the spring meeting of the American Psychoanalytic Association in 1964, the incoming president disclosed the results of a survey of analysands. According to the report in the New York *Times*, May 2, 1964, 1,100 analysts with M.D.'s treat 11,000 patients a year: "Almost all are college-educated. Many have graduate degrees." This high educational level was the main factor identifying these private patients. That, of course, and their frustrations.)

Members of the New Class can be distinguished from each other by noting not only the extent of their frustration but their manner of dealing with it. Some become utopians; others are compulsively realistic; almost all go through a more or less extended period of undertaking personal consumption as a form of idolatry; many create and concentrate on a rigid aura of professionalism; most, at one time or another, retreat from their actual condition and over-identify with some more traditional grouping, as the right-wing intellectuals identify with small-property ownership, or the urban Jews with problems of social justice, and many serious Protestants with the Negroes, and so on.

My overriding point is that the "new men" are newer than they know. Meanwhile, we cannot answer the main question—what the effects may be of achieved class-awareness. We cannot know just what the effects may be, but we know there will be some—and we cannot guess otherwise than that they will be important. (As their power matures, they may even, one day, in a paroxysm of class-awareness, choose their own barons.)

7 One of the first things the youthful New Class will do, in advanced countries, is to change their teachers. That's all right with me: the academics are an old class—the "reading class." The old scholarly mode, in our present moiling context, is substantially fraudulent: and some of the academics may even welcome the enforced change, as the Nice White Southerners will welcome their own dose of inevitable change (see Chapter Ten). Anyway, when training and jobs come together, so will knowledge and action; and as that happens, priestliness of all kinds may contract somewhat in scope.

Speculating—again rather broadly—I would say that there are already too many educated people in our society. What are we going to do with all of them, and their monstrous frustrations? Note that if one of them is frustrated because not allowed to do seriously what he was trained to do, which may be what he still thinks he wants to do, then the job itself is probably functionally unnecessary. Again, the Washington example: the numerous people at work in the Executive, devising programs that Congress will not enact, are quite inutile. They could become somewhat necessary if Congress became a different organization, in which case the same people on the same jobs would be something else again; but if programs were being actually enacted and tested, the training of long-time mere Devisers might well be irrelevant. It is always difficult to decide just what part of an activity is ritualistic and what part functional. Meanwhile, it is certainly "functional" to provide jobs for educated people: without them, they could be dangerous as well as hungry.

One way the New Class typically deals with its frustration is to develop "professionalism." This allows a person to view a job as independent from his personality, even though carrying out the work requires a deep personal involvement. Professionalism consists of doing a job well irrespective of its purpose. I first apprehended the depth of "professionalism" when Red Barber, of noble Dodger fame, abandoned the sinking local ship and began broadcasting for the Yankees. Everything thereafter was anticlimactic. Part of the anticlimax, for me personally, was practicing as a lawyer. Professionalism came so easily, or at least was so inevitable, that I hardly knew it had happened until I became bored with it. (Imagine having to decide each uninteresting "case" twice—once at the altar of your conscience and once as a telephone or courtroom advocate: the impulse not to bother is overwhelming.)

As another miscellaneous example of New Class adjustment, note that the activity of the foundations represents a significant redistribution of income to unpropertied intellectuals—in effect, the *rentiers* buying off the New Class. I don't mean to use the phrase "buying off" altogether invidiously, but only to suggest that this source of income helps to pacify the intellectuals. It is often more significant for this social effect than for the ostensible work-product.

As the former style of politics was based on patronage involving low-level jobs in big cities, there is now a new style of patronage derived from the distribution of New Class jobs. This exists in both the private and the public spheres. In the Fifties, professional and technical jobs grew by 2.4 million, gaining three points as a per cent of the total labor force, up to 11.3 per cent. Much of this was in defense; but also 796,000 in education, and 111,000 in welfare, religious, and other non-profit activities. Most of the growth was in the public sector and in industries connected with government efforts. (Also, nonproduction workers not academically trained increased more than 1.5 million in manufacturing.) The provision of such jobs constitutes a good deal of the story of the New Deal and the New Frontier—and apparently Modern Republicanism was not able or did not try too hard to slow down the process appreciably.

The growth of the New Class in England (for just one foreign example) is both clearer and more disruptive than it is here. Because the old classes so thoroughly dominated education and the upper ranks of almost all major institutions, and because the education was not scientific or technical in emphasis, the New Class there has been made up of recognizably new people—with the wrong accents, for instance. Also, being a *mis*-developed country for the modern world, England must change radically to survive—and the obvious direction is that taken some time ago by Sweden, toward high-quality technical performance. In this very special political conjunction, the Labour Party has undertaken to represent the clamor for New Class jobs based, of course, on technical education which will be both of a higher standard and more generally available to the whole population. Harold Wilson's keynote speech to the party's annual conference in the fall of 1963 (like an American pre-election convention) concentrated on this undertaking; and Richard Crossman at that time called for "a revolution against educational privilege." The revolution will be politely English, however; what is happening is that new schools are being built—Oxford and Cambridge are not being "nationalized." * (In Sweden, with a population of 7.5 million and not growing, the plan announced in 1963—perhaps anticipating English competition—was to double the capacity of the four state-supported universities by 1970.)

In America, we are creating a culture, not overcoming one. But still, in favor of the New Class. While we are discussing class generally, it may be useful to mention the relation between personal interest and class interest, especially since both involve "culture." Note that one can more easily rebel against class interest than one can in a genuinely effective way overcome it. But rebellion too often has the psychological quality of mere denial. Especially when one rebels intellectually, one will (as a consequence) become too dependent on intellectuality itself. Since this is emotionally inadequate, it produces hostility and even projective hatred. The more stable approach is the more devious one, containing more of James Joyce's "cunning" in it. To live with a class situation, and to satisfy oneself within it, may be the better part of valor. Too big a struggle can be ruinous; if one can stand the contradiction, it is frequently more effective to give in to a certain extent, and to use the remaining extent to contradict that part one has given in to. It is not possible to be human all at once and altogether: not from our modern beginnings. In this, the lower classes are right—one has to "give in" to the structure of authority (or the authority of structure), and then sneak up on it in a human-animal way. I would like to see more of the educated people comprehend this wisdom, and consequently abandon all-or-nothing postures.

Certainly both the myth of Individualism and the more realistic struggle for majoritarian democracy will be altered under these fresh and special pressures. We are going to need fully as much democratic mechanism as possible in *all* social areas, since it is perfectly obvious that this society will be managed by qualified elites—

---

* My feeling about the explosive Profumo scandal was that it served as a culminating symbolic episode in the larger social impulse of the "underallowed" class of experts, and nominees for expertise, to find fault with the Establishment system of government by amateurs. It is significant that they do not content themselves with referring to the old ruling caste, but now refer to these people as "amateurs": this was the major burden of the cartoons dealing with Lord Home.

win-out segments of the New Class. We are surely moving farther into a period in which formal democracy will become ever more a cover for authoritarian bureaucratic structure—as previously it was a cover for property-power. On this score, the unionized workers, for instance, can still offer a great deal toward the shaping of our society. Their irascibility in relations with foremen and other immediate management should be welcomed—and further allowed-for organizationally, even as a matter of constitution.

In happy conclusion, note that the more an educated person is frustrated in his life aims (even if these are grossly material or simply concerned with status), the more he is apt to retreat into a reliance upon what he imagines his education to be, in order to *compensate* for the lacks in his actual life. If education is all he has, he will exaggerate it. In this sense education is still dangerous. Although the education of these new people is not all that we would want it to be, to say the least, we still should not discount it too severely. It will be no cure-all for the world's ills, any more than the earlier spread of general literacy turned out to be a cure-all, even though it had previously been advertised as such. In any event (and in all fairness), the true educational process is endless. If you have been "had" by the genuineness of your education, then let us say that Dostoievski is really important to you. And if Dostoievski is really important to you, you are never finished reading him or thinking about what he wrote.

8

In looking for understanding of the New Class phenomenon, one must not expect pure typologies; even if one found them, they might well be misleading as to the overall course of events. No matter how serious and determinative one's propertied or propertyless relation to the means of production may be, man does not live by property alone. Especially in periods of great change. And again, especially in America, with its raw national style, its inherent regionalism unto anarchy, constituency-brokerage politics, and its conflicts between a national popular culture and the more mature elite varieties.

Also, all classes have antecedents in history. The first of the bourgeoisie were not the first traders or property-accumulators; but the bourgeoisie were the first to make trading and property-accumulation the dominant tone, and then the dominant activity, in their particular social orders. In doing so, they undoubtedly took in and assimilated previously existing social elements, items, and forms. Something like this is happening in the development of the New Class. Thus, doctors and lawyers and teachers, as well as technologists and other bureaucratic specialists, are incorporated into this ongoing (and eventually overwhelming) development. Indeed lawyers, as usual, are often the leading creative individuals in carrying it forward.

And a person is not "out of it" simply because he owns one piece of property or another. Take a fairly typical circumstance, such as that of a doctor whose career is obviously based on education and whose practice more and more involves him with large hospitals—that is, in big-organization activity. The doctor's basic style was long ago derived from that of the local small-property-owner. Today, he will very likely achieve excess income which may then be invested in local real estate (thus assimilating to the full-ownership group); during the Fifties he will have put some of his excess income into the stock market (involving him in *rentier* property); this latter may have been based on income from real estate or from his practice or from inheritance; he may also be actively involved in AMA organizational politics; and he will certainly be concerned with other community groups, bringing him into close touch with additional class interests. So it will be all mixed up (and he, also being all mixed up as a consequence, may become rigid ideologically). And I will still assert that the previously existing profession of medicine is being assimilated into the New Class movement—is even a big part of it (because of the prestige and the technological significance).

This matter of excess income derived from an exploitation of educational status is an interesting one. Note the relation to (as well as the difference from) consumer financing: underlying the New Class phenomenon, which I have limited to the replacement of property by education, there is the even broader phenomenon in the modern Paper Economy of a generally more prosperous and more secure proletarianization—that is, the job itself, whether or not based on an academic certificate, is becoming a status-thing which can be utilized as a piece of property. The unionized worker, for example, can borrow against the property-security of his job—and he does—in order to finance his acquisition of consumption items. The well-to-do professional, who already has an adequate standard of living by direct reason of his income and may thereby (if he's careful) not require any particular financing for it, still has a related status and flow of income which can be capitalized. What he does, as distinct from the more poorly placed union worker, is to go to the bank and borrow money which he then "invests" in a real estate or stock market speculation. The proceeds of this may then be reinvested, or perhaps diverted to consumption, and more likely will be used further to secure his future and that of his family—that is, to extend his standard of living and educational-edge farther into the future, thus capitalizing the next generation by covering a large part of its initial operating expenses. But whether the result is $20,000, which will buy a college education for one's son, or $2,000, which will buy an automobile right now, the process is the same—namely, the capitalizing of the non-property income-and-status of the job.

The education of the New Class member—an electronics engineer or a systems-research analyst with a Ph.D. in sociology or a physicist working for the RAND Corporation or an economist dealing with manpower problems in the Department of Labor—is an application of training *to think ahead.* These people administer and they plan— indeed, it is impossible to administer without becoming engaged in some form of gross plan, at least a "plan" for resolving the conflicts among the interests you are administering. So it strikes me as distinctly possible that *all* the education of *all* the members of the New Class has a common denominator—namely, to plan something.

The whole theory of rule by property was that the accompanying Competition dispensed with the need to plan, and thus dispensed as well with "planners" (intellectuals) and the state (the primary planning agency). This was never an accurate representation of the old trading order, since no matter how hard a businessman might try not to think ahead, and cooperate with others in not doing so, he and they did in fact indulge. There was always communication beyond the market, beyond that provided for by an Adam Smith market-model where communication was not so much refrained from on principle as it was considered to be impossible in fact. Where it is possible, it occurs. The more important planning begins with the business unit, in the application of technology. But it is not limited to that; the business unit is a political as well as a technological organization. Moreover, the relations *between* business units can be exquisitely political, when they are not merely that of the impersonal market.

So, at the end of this brief analysis, we note that the New Class consists of the planners—the thinkers-ahead. Which explains why they are so frustrated when they are members of the non-military public division and not nearly so much so when members of the private division: planning is encouraged in the one area, nearly forbidden in the other. But planning is inherent in the educated person's activity—conceptualizing and thinking ahead, this is planning and this is what education comes to. Indeed, what is this terribly feared political planning—what is it, really, but a kind of mutual consciousness, an awareness of what you are doing in relation to what others are up to at the same time? In any event, the fact that educated people have been placed in and around the centers of power (as this is or may become a fact of usefulness and not of mere adornment) indicates power's need for planning.

It is a serious maladjustment of power in America which keeps this planning from going forward, and consequently frustrates the members of the New Class.

Their deeper sense of community *must* begin—however it may hopefully end—with the triumph of planning and its positive politics, as the dominant American style and purpose. It had better come peacefully: and any more exaggeration of adornment and redundancy—"just jobs"—may well lead at a not-so-later date to a convulsive reaction. They must have their due. We have invited it: now we must satisfy it.

TWELVE

The American Liberal

1 Perhaps the most significant division among the members of the New Class is determined by the individual's proximity to the class firing line: that is, how much time and effort he spends—the obvious or subtle burden he undertakes—in brokerage relations with members of the older classes. Especially this concerns relations to: 1) the smaller business organizations in which full possessory ownership is still important; and 2) the strategically placed and persistingly powerful *rentier* class. The point here is that the growth and rise to power of the unpropertied class, based on the need both to control and to clear the way "organizationally" for technology, has to date been achieved peacefully in the United States. It has occurred in the pattern typical of major historical developments in America: 1) it is not noticed; 2) it is denied; and 3) it is accomplished by delicate and devious brokerage, where fact and image are kept at a sanitary distance. However handled, class-brokerage will be more important than the previously mentioned public/ private bit, or the cakewalk of keeping the technicians in line.

First among these brokerage relations is that between the organizational heirs and the family heirs of the robber barons—between the top strata of industrial management and the remaining concentrations among the owning classes. This accounts, as an example, for the stunted character of managerial ideology: the top corporate executives are not free to assert the fullest expression of their own spiritual view of the world; they are still required to defer periodically to the spiritual presumptions of the old owning classes. Since the corporate people are the new fellows, they naturally defer to the *social* presumptions as well, and without any considerable urging: they have none of their own, and so borrow those of the previously dominant class (e.g., they tend to dress Ivy League). I think this is historically ordinary.

Bankers and Wall Street people who devote so much time to managing the *rentier* money are naturally called upon to appear as more unctuous dissemblers than are burly production executives or narrowly devoted technologists. (At least, I would *hope* so.) This division between production and finance is also repeated *within* the corporation. But even more firmly in the Uriah Heep tradition are the educational/foundation managers, which is accounted for by the fact that education and culture are considered to be less complicated than finance and, since they are non-profit-making activities as well, also less significant. (Even as they become in fact more functional, they remain burdened with a weighty tradition of insignificance.) This predisposes the *rentier* to intervene more frequently and with more disruptive effect. After all, culture and charity were always the private preserves of the rich: they still consider themselves "experts" in these amateur areas.

Because of some profound malapportionment in the American power structure, the still active small-property class appears to have its greatest effect on the educated managers wherever governmental politics is concerned, and especially so the more local the emanation thereof. This is mostly derived, I think, from the fact that, in the heyday of American capital accumulation, public governments were never considered to be very important. Now it is also a consequence of the immediate financial interest of small-property types (e.g., real estate taxes support primary education) and the accompanying character of campaign financing for locally representative offices, all the way up to congressman.

But it must immediately be added that this Goldwater-like puddle occurs in the context of a special American definition of "politics" (as we noted much earlier in this book). In America, politics is thought to consist of electing government officials and of the effort involved thereafter in gaining a favor or forestalling a penalty with respect to one of them. But if politics is defined, broadly and properly, as human interaction when and wherever there is an issue of power, then obviously much political energy is expended in this country which is not then and there known by its right name. Let us be very specific, even unpleasant: When moral-emphasis and power-obscurantism characterize a culture, the difficulty of defining politics cannot be laid to the commentator alone. Now "politics" is either the contest for control of the state, or it is any contest concerning power, or it is any such contest—somewhere between a *coup d'état* and your domination of a helpless infant—which *you* define as "public" or "social."

The lack of central state power; the early dominance, frequently denied, of overwhelming non-governmental power centers; and the moralistic perception of circumstances involving any issue of power —all these have helped to create an absurdly difficult set of American meanings to use in pointing out the obvious. Hacking my way through this underbrush, I would naturally prefer to go back to simple beginnings: Politics is concerned with issues of power; the more extensively social the context of such issues, the more our American concerns fit into traditional European or Greco-Roman images. In advanced countries with wealth, as an example, the number of illegitimate children an illiterate may have is—has become here—a matter of policy for the central state power: therefore, unless we are administering things instead of people, the original power aspects of the illiterate's decision, if any, to have the child illegitimately, are connected in a direct line of ascent with the congressionally approved content of the federal budget covering the Department of Health, Education, and Welfare. No?

A class is ordinarily known by the self-image of its asserted importance, its ideology. But not a *new* class. The contour of a new class must be guessed at; its content, style, and intent must be sensed rather than catalogued academically. So I have sensed a line of the contour, and now I assert that the "liberal," although an acute minority of the New Class, is the most fully achieved and self-conscious form of it, to date; and while this may be altogether bypassed in the long run, elements thereof will persist in a later, more successful style. So, now directly for our interest in the New Class phenomenon, we take another look at "the liberal." (Incidentally, because it is a dynamic class, because it is educated, because it is frustrated and tense, because it holds key positions throughout society and is growing, the New Class itself figures more heavily than its simple weight would indicate—therefore, also its most fully achieved representatives.)

2 The liberal is "purer" New Class for being less WASP, less *rentier*, educated for more (even if not much more) than the purpose of gaining and holding a job, less of a technician and more of an operator, also more resentful of the upper hierarchy than frightened of slipping back to one's origins, and so on: e.g., it is harder for Catholics than for Jews, for small-town than for big-city types, to move quickly into "uncontaminated" New Class identification. Those less alienated or modern hang on longer and tighter to previous or neighboring old-class identifications (often with an absurd effect). Also, and finally, the liberal is less buck-hungry, pound for pound, and more confident of maintaining and being satisfied with his New Class standard of living: he thinks more readily, therefore, of "surplus"—both of time and of money. He is combative rather than accumulative in the deployment of his tension. Do not misunderstand me—he is *not* a Saint Francis. He looks after himself first, but not infinitely. He acts not solely in his own self-interest: he acts as well for his idea—often half-baked—of some larger, newer community.

Just as one example of the liberal spearhead of New Class style, *in extenso:* Professor Wilson's major distinction (in *The Amateur Democrat*) between the California and New York Reform movements is that it was feasible for the emphasis to be on reform in New York since an "anti-boss campaign" was possible there, whereas in California there were no bosses and so the same people were required to emphasize liberal "issues" to stay in business. Thus, the California Democratic Council holds Issues Conferences. He points out a New Class factor in this involvement: "The emphasis on fact-finding, *expertise*, research, background papers, and 'resource persons' . . ." has been a feature of the issue-efforts of the CDC liberals. (A friend of mine who is an experienced New York Reformer spoke wistfully to me, after a visit out there, of the issue-atmosphere in California: he was somewhat bored with anti-bossism as a way of life.)

Wilson notes that the new approach in politics represented by the Reformers among the Democrats exists as well among the more conservative, and the younger, Republicans. The newness of the phenomenon consists in the style: both are New Class representatives. Placing the "style" in a general way, he uses Robert K. Merton's distinction between the "local" and the "cosmopolitan"—the professional politician being a local and the amateur Reformer being a cosmopolitan: that is, the one is more involved in the national corporate culture, less involved in the local community. Another New Class "common denominator" is that there seems to be little question that a primary source of the Reform movement is the need, even the necessity, of some form of activity supplemental to the affluent job-activity (including more than that of the "all-consuming" home). This need gives a form to the activity itself, so that some clubs are devoted to shouting, others to maneuvering or to whatever forms of self-expression first or mainly occur to the participants. Ideology is a means rather than an end. A West Side leader in New York said: "The only thing you can give the workers in reform politics is an object for their enthusiasm."

What is being discovered in this kind of politics (both right and left) is a form of activity which seems to the participants quite meaningful and which has no commercial object and no commercial source. So this may be the beginning of adjustment to the cybernated world, where the job and finally even the home are no longer adequate as the primary points of concentration. That the initial effort at adjustment may seem more like medium-level group therapy than a serious attack on City Hall strikes me as quite understandable, all things considered: as a New York leader said, "I think the reformer basically is a very neurotic kind of person." God knows the Goldwater enthusiasts also were (or should have been instead).

One gathers the distinct impression that the Reform movement in New York would not have succeeded so well or so much without the parental presence of Senator Lehman and Mrs. Roosevelt. Professor Wilson suggests an underlying envy or hostility in the attitude of the ordinary Reformer in New York toward the Lexington Club, and of his counterpart in California toward the Beverly Hills Club—each of which is the more well-heeled and fancier group. Yes, but they work together—advance guards in the meeting of the New Class and the Mugwump *rentier*. The enthusiasm of the one, salted with the dollars of the other, will mean more to each than the accompanying status-hostility of either. (After all, by whom would you rather be snubbed? And where can you get more action when you're "taken"?)

The Reformers succeeded beyond anyone's expectations in New York and California: they failed in Chicago.* Why? Well, the Daly machine remained too vital. Was it because Chicago has more impoverished and less assimilated lower-middle-class ethnic groups the members of which are still organized old-style with patronage, neighborhood loyalty, etc.? Or were there too few New Class types on the scene—more having moved to the suburbs? Might the Reformers have won anyway, had they persisted more: do they need easy pickings to prevail? Is Chicago more of a "Southern" Northern city, with displaced crackers and Appalachians as well as raw Negroes? I was raised in Chicago, but have no certain answers to these intriguing questions. Over the years, however, I did notice that Chicago was clearly five to ten years behind New York in one cultural issue after another. (The West Coast, of course, is *sui generis*.)

For a revealing peek at the New Class/liberal conjunction, *The New Republic* in the middle of 1963 presented a profile of its "typical" reader, based on a fairly substantial sample. The magazine reported that its statistically average reader "is 35 years old, has completed at least one year of graduate school, is married to a college graduate and has one child. His family income is over $10,000." A quarter of the wives worked; a quarter of the readers lived in the Northeast; a quarter read the *Wall Street Journal* (three-quarters read the Sunday New York *Times*); two-thirds were professionals, teachers, and students.

Many of the respondents feared that their stated response would lead to a "change"—in the editorial policy of the magazine, they said.

3   We have a distorted view in this country when we believe that intellectuals are usually and necessarily radical or even "liberal." They are not. The endemic disease of intellectuals is purism—the historic curse of Plato. Intellectuals are in truth radical only when and so long as radicalism is more exciting, more romantic, more stimulating, more assertive, and more

* Incidentally, they are not running the show anywhere.

"intellectual." And now I think it may be that America has at last begun to be sufficiently "cultured" so that the inevitable conservatism of cultured individuals is surfacing: which contradicts our recent past quite upendingly.

The radicalism of American intellectuals, for peculiar American reasons, had gone so far that no one need be surprised that many far wanderers discovered the exquisitely perverse joys of dull conservatism. In a sense, some of them sojourned elsewhere only as a training stint—exercising for the big meal, so to speak. (Eat, boys, eat: the devastating loss will be noted somewhat later.)

Besides, the intellectuals of the American right and left do not differ absolutely, underneath. They share a tropism for free-floating moralism as the high road to Achieved Irrelevance. And hostility— endless, aimless, insatiable hostility toward American existence. Where the beginning of intellect may well be a distaste for living, what else would you expect? Where unhired intellect is homeless, what else can you hope for? The negativism of the right-wingers, with their passionate rediscovery of the eighteenth century, hardly needs any emphasis.* New qualities on the left will bear another look, however.

Professor Wilson quotes a Northern California CDC vice-president as saying: "CDC people thrive on adversity." The hostility and negativism of the Reformers is emphasized by Wilson as a structural factor; he believes that the movement consequently will disappear before it will mature. (I think it will do neither, but just change.)

On the difference between conservative and liberal amateurs, he notes that

> conservative amateurs are perhaps not caught by the tension between Populism and Progressivism that afflicts so many amateur Democrats. They are more ready to accept an elitist view of government, deriving, perhaps, from their experience in business, as contrasted to the liberals' experience in the professions. The professions are characterized by a kind of commercial egalitarianism in which expertise is regarded as the determinant of success and reputation.

And later on he says: "A business-oriented civic organization rarely has 'members'; instead it has 'contributors.'" Conservatives have

---

* If we were bothering, we would bother with the mess of American education which could produce-and-allow such polysyllabic primitivism: but we are not bothering.

more money; they buy their way in. He correctly adds: "The liberal, lacking money, brings numbers and personal contributions of time and effort."

With this time and effort, the big-city Reform movement in the Democratic Party is huffing and puffing and blowing down the burned-out structures of the old neighborhood organizations based on immigrant illiteracy. It is doing this, so far, with little more than the impetuous hostility of disgruntled *arrivés:* the movement was so little prepared for its early success, in an emotional or ideological or organizational sense, that it may indeed only fly up the flue—a new version of the fate of the old municipal do-gooders. In New York City, for instance, the Reformers have suffered from hilarious forms of purism whereby they were rent from end to end on issues like the support of electable candidates and the ten-foot-pole approach to patronage.*

They don't yet want to win; in a distorted fashion, they have their own version of the traditional American power-negativism. But the point not to be missed is that their impetuous victories came so easily. In California they were an essential influence in the reshaping of that volatile state (including a professionally executed Democratic gerrymander). Understandably, their efforts did not result in the desired dictatorship of the educated consumer—but these efforts did make a great deal of difference. They are very important leavening: if the Reformers understood their role, they would be even more important. (Being halfway people culturally, understanding dampens their enthusiasm, which is all the fun.)

Despite the adolescent militancy of the Democratic Reformers, I want to reemphasize, again speculatively (as in Chapter Four), that the right-wingers are providing the more substantial impetus toward polarization or "party realignment" or other such political advance. In Congress, where it really counts, the parties had for some time been realigned *de facto*, thanks to the right-wingers. Even more important, they have the money—as limitless as Texas oil and local real estate. They are smarter than one might think in spending it, too: it has been reported that the Birchers concentrated on sparsely populated Western states where a dollar goes farther in buying a new Senator. Also, the pressure of events—once more, with the

---

* Imagine getting excited about being "for" or "against" Bob Wagner! Like saying you hate soggy Wheaties: who doesn't? and who cares?

Negro as catalyst—has been forcing the right-wingers together irrespective of formal party affiliation. They mostly end up isolating themselves, however, which is the beginning of political death; for while such isolation concentrates and purifies ideologically, it exposes practical weakness at the same time. Once the country discovers the depth of their weakness . . . remember, it happened with McCarthy. It is too early to chance saying whether this has already occurred as a result of the Goldwater episode.

Even if the right wing does not retain control of enough of the Republican Party organization to make a difference, it will never become so isolated and politically irrelevant as the radical left naturally tends to become. Very simply, the rightists and their allies have too much money. I think we will from now on have, as in some European countries, the continuing presence of a noisy, nasty, nationalist right wing that can cause trouble at any time, but can seriously threaten to take power only on a fascist wave.

4 Sharing native moralism and the underlying hostility, the rightists and the Reformers are both firm ideologues. And, interestingly, both are traditionalists. It is just that for one group, tradition ended in 1929-32—and for the other, that was when it began.

Since both are obviously wrong, we must ask: Whence this ideological need? Why these truncated traditions as vehicles?

My answer is that the active or leading elements in both political groupings are members of the New Class.

Because the New Class is now incompletely arrived and therefore vulnerable, it is subject to great tension—especially including the extreme tension of not knowing it is a New Class. This is not a matter of "quantity" of arrival: indeed, the bigger it gets, and thus the more committed it becomes to its New Class distinctions rather than to its sources, the more tense it becomes.* It is also tense for the character of its necessary allies. And this is where the New Class divides into left and right wings—according to its allies, for whose benefit it devotes its un-arrival tension to the concoction of artificial traditions, ideological images, and other transient baggage.

* This is the Upward-Mobililty Blues so often sung by the sociologists.

But before we proceed farther into this matter of allies (and before we choose up sides), a further look at the special case of the Reformers through Professor Wilson's *The Amateur Democrat:*

> Because of the way organizations such as the CDC or the Manhattan reform clubs must be maintained, they can (and must) generate a concern for issues without being able to assemble the power to realize them.

There is this factor, of course; but the professor is wrong in his flat statement of the eventuality. His book emphasizes a kind of free-market theory of politics, whereby mobilized self-interest on the model of standard city-machine politics is taken to be democracy itself—"realistically conceived." *

Perhaps the key line in the book occurs at page 357: "The ignorance of voters is what makes party government possible." This would seem to be based on the notion that politics is *either* quite reasonable and rational *or* it is the particular historical mess which the professors have devoted themselves to studying for such a long period of time. Obviously (to me), the ignorance of voters creates only one category of party government—and even that is not made up of complete and unadulterated ignorance. Of another kind of party government, one could as readily say that the intelligence of some voters makes it possible.

A couple of pages later, he sums up in what can only be described as an obnoxious fashion:

> In short, a politics of interest is made possible by the fact that the American party system occasionally collapses under the onslaught of a politics of principle. The former is the desirable norm and the latter, the undesirable but perhaps necessary exception.

* What is too often wrong with one set of political scientists, I find, is that they have such an investment in the previously existing system which they have set forth at great pains, and in great detail, that they cannot readily conceive of changes in that system: alterations in the objective historical system are the same thing to them as reductions in their professional investment. So they love either/or's. And the underlying anti-majoritarianism of the chastened rationalist is everywhere obvious. They sound as if they do not actually believe in democracy, but only that things could be worse under other systems—and they love to quote Winston Churchill to this effect.

And then he proceeds to some of the poli sci, free-market nonsense, namely, what is, is good—or at least it is the "system." If ignorance and interest always go together, then we are in fairly bad shape—especially if the occasional alternative is a preoccupation with principles which cannot be achieved. But if principles can be intelligently conceived as being in some kind of working/learning relation to interests, then the sky may brighten a bit. Such principles, and such use of principles, would require certain intellectual departures from rationalism, however. Professor Wilson, in the end, almost departs —but unfortunately only to state the issue, not to carry it forward into the disruption of the professional investment. But he does end on the issue of motivation, that is, the practical need of unrealistic ends in order to induce activity, which he then considers to be destructive of "the system" as well as just plain *dumb*. If it is destructive, then I say—not a moment too soon. Any social system that requires unrealistic ends to induce fresh activity is indefensible and unstable—and maybe that is exactly what the amateurs are proving.

Also, the "interests" enthroned in the system are not unrelievedly realistic. For example, the relation between professional politicians and reformers, from the days of the Mugwumps until the current Reform movement, has involved some underlying sexual fantasy. The Spoilsmen referred to themselves as manly, vigorous, virile, etc., and to the Mugwumps as effeminate, sterile, vainly impotent, etc. The extent to which ruthless selfishness has been identified as an essential element in the structure of the male personality in America, has been a disaster all around—for those who believe in it and pursue it at least as much as for those who risk iffy-ness by denying it; and certainly for the women who seize upon it as a weakness in male defense. (In this context a *culture* was supposed to develop!) So, recently we witnessed a backbracing, tummy-tucker of an Air Force Reserve General, who was graduated from a military prep school and nothing much else, parading laughable masculinity-of-the-mind— and nothing much else—before the American people.

On the other side, Professor Wilson quotes a Tammany man as suggesting that:

> The New York reform clubs are composed of frustrated, aggressive women who act out their hostility to males by attacking Carmine De Sapio, whom they unconsciously see as a handsome, sinister symbol of masculine virility.

I wouldn't be surprised. It may even have been significant for the power structure of the House that both Rayburn and Martin were bachelors. Who knows what may happen when the omnipotent core of the myth of Individualism decides or is given permission to assert itself?

5 The professional politicians are not willing allies of the New Class. This proposition holds whether one refers to the heart-warming hostility of the Village Independent Democrats to De Sapio and his ragged Tammany Tiger, or to John Grenier's new Southern phalanx with its assorted maneuvers against the old Democratic organizations in Dixie. Evans and Novak, in their column for August 23, 1964, quote one of the defending Southerners as follows:

> Those bright young Republican boys think they can shout nigger, nigger, nigger, and run all over us. Well, they're going to learn there are other things the South cares about.

Probably. But only after the South learns to remind itself more often of exactly what else it is that it cares about. Just as New Yorkers will certainly remember how boring it has been to listen to the chorus of boss, boss, boss—even in second- and third-generation accents. New Yorkers, I suppose, also care about other things.

Politicians, fully professional or merely ambitious, have a happy capacity to swim with the tide, roll with the punch, and generally to end up where the action is: pride is the least of what they are called upon to swallow in the course of an ordinary business day. They will not remain a major problem for either wing of the New Class. What will be determinative are relations with other classes and near-class social groupings. Indeed, these relations currently obscure both the identity and the massive movement of the New Class; and are also, as noted, largely responsible for the character of the two wings.

On the right, New Class elements are allied with new money and status in the newly expanding regions, and generally with local proprietorship whether fresh or fading. I believe very strongly (and I believe the point is very important, so I repeat it) that the two underlying factors in drawing a modern political map in this country are the density of population and the amount and significance of close, possessory property as opposed to alienated, organizational property: the two factors are of course correlated in that organizational-property forms accompany and create modern density of population. It seems to me easy to see that different circumstances in life, like these, will tend to generate different attitudes toward both situational power and alienable power (i.e., money). Also, the attitudes thus generated are susceptible to development over time, so that the older the circumstances (within reason), the more opportunity there is for sophisticated and flexible attitudes to develop. But the opportunity can be missed, and age can lead in a fairly straight line to rigidity and ritual: some attitudes, like some people, "develop" better than others. Finally, plain fear, initial lack of perception or limited capacity for it, help as well to determine who ends up where, and with what allies; also, especially, the intensity of *the mysterious personal need* for ideological coherence—involving as it does the capacity to entertain a complex ideology, or the lack thereof creating a greedy demand for a simple one.

To illustrate how these subtleties may enter into the final political character: I have the impression that the one truly radical aspect of the young right-winger is his underlying animus toward big national corporations and their godlike oligarchs. But many of these people are organization men themselves—they work for the corporations they hate. So they cannot (for what obscure cultural and personal reasons?) admit their hatred to themselves: they therefore feel great fury against Big Government, the effect of which on their actual lives they hardly notice at all, while never mentioning to themselves or anyone else the power-effect of the big corporation, which determines in fact almost everything about their immediate lives. Such existential "dis-reality" is a classic source of the fascist impulse. But however these subtleties achieve expression, the basic rule holds: As conditions of life differ, the mode of power (being a shifting conjunction of motivation derived from the two worlds of existence and idea) changes; power, we noted previously, is that close to life itself.

Could an adequate "power-map" of the United States be drawn? Well, you can imagine the difficulties. There have been efforts in the past—most recently, C. Wright Mills's *The Power Elite*. But Mills drew a rather primitive map. Even if grossly correct in outline, the constituencies were not sufficiently particularized; and worst of all, he assumed the main point—that is, the connecting links. At times he even seemed to be suggesting that the various constituencies were neatly organized at the top because the various gang leaders met regularly at the Stork Club, 21, and so on. A more mature power-map would require an identification of constituencies and subconstituencies in some detail; these would have to be properly "weighted" for power significance; there would then have to be a correction for duplication; most important, the cartographer would have to suggest finally the actual extent of organized coherence of and between the major constituencies; and last of all, some dynamic principles should be introduced further to establish the life-simulation of the map. Even good guesses would be useful, however, and terribly needed.

The purpose of a map, of course, is to help you find your way toward a chosen destination. In this instance, somehow to put this jigsaw country together, in power terms, in order to get the best out of it. To understand and identify discrete power elements, in order next to conceive the necessary and best possible majority coalition to be created out of same; and then, insisting that moral idealism is a personal fuel and *not* a social motor—that morality which is not merely a system of personal defense and consolation *requires* the protagonist to think and act in power terms—to go on and convince the elements of this imagined coalition that they exist, that they are what they are, no more and no less, and that they rise to a necessity by coming together. For some elements this would mean an expansion of ideal aspects and a contraction of situational ones (labor); for others it would mean the opposite (intellectuals). To paraphrase Marx, if power is organization, then freedom is either *dis*organization or it is the recognition of power (which is, in fact, a kind of social form of Necessity). Again, to paraphrase an earlier thinker, necessity may very well be the mother-in-law of prevention. Finally, without paraphrase, power-thinking leads to coalition, to the conscious construction of necessitous communities, to downright practical efforts at friendliness.

To achieve its inevitable ascendancy in society, and in the end to define itself in the grand historical sense in which bourgeois property-owners did, the New Class will make new coalitions. It will transcend its present allies (some of whom will not survive a great deal more history, in any event). But let us note the present basic alliances, even though they are being transcended as we write:

The right-wing elements of the New Class are—strictly as servants—allied with the oligarchs of the big corporations who still play an emotional right-wing game. More significantly, as initiating activists they make a specifically WASP appeal to the suburbs; sometimes as leaders, sometimes still as servants, they are allied with newer business and capital (enterprise and paper), smaller *b* and *c*, more localistic *b* and *c*, and business relying more decisively on possessory property; and they appeal to the WASP prejudice throughout all areas of *b* and *c*. They are sopping up, and they deserve to inherit, established racialism in the South. They also have, and deserve, the firmly mindless *rentier*, even in the East. Their power derives from quality rather than from quantity, more from money than from people; and in their hysterical efforts to appeal to a democratic majority against its own interests—that is, in the midst of a campaign—they must indulge every stray prejudice and evanescent fear, and they plumb the depths of mass ignorance in order to do so. In this, they manage to gather in even a little ethnic action— as with McCarthy and the Catholics some years back, the "white backlash" of the recent Goldwater campaign, and the dreary drivel about "Captive Nations" which has become an annual celebration of the absurd.*

The left wing, the so-called "liberals," are mostly big-city Democrats and mostly have the allies which make up the New Deal coalition. Some have managed to remain pure enough to have few allies at all; a significant group in New York City are simply beholden to the ILGWU; others, as is well known, have pushed the alliance with the Negro out of embarrassment with the South's presence in the party; and here on the left side, more and more members of the New Class have simply made an alliance among themselves—around personalities like Stevenson and issues like peace or civil rights or full employment. They inherited working relations with the ethnic blocs of the big-city machines. Courtesy of Roosevelt, they inherited the Jews. They are allies—more as consultants than as pure servants —with advanced or old or Eastern *b* and *c*. More so, happily, as time goes on. Most spectacularly, they are firm and enthusiastic allies of the Mugwump *rentier* (including not only a Harriman and a Leh-

---

* I don't want to make this sound too simple—the only thing really simple about America is that it is the shallow society: how we respond to what that means is far from simple, even when it seems to be clearly puerile. For puerile ethnic mess, surely only in America would the culturally degenerate grandson of a successful Jewish immigrant lead the first truly serious fascist movement—twenty years after the death of Hitler.

man, but even half-a-Rockefeller here and there), both in and out of the foundation/academic circle.

I am not cartographer enough to draw a real power-map of the United States. Still, like everyone else, I have to find my way to one destination or another. So I have a little piece of paper containing shorthand social directions which I look at every once in a while, when my mind goes blank. I suggest the reader draw his own—like those little Xerox scribbles people send you nowadays when they invite you to a party in their own strange suburb. Meanwhile, here is how you get to my house, which is situated four turns beyond a tumbledown church in a new underdevelopment beyond the city limits: *

1. Big national corporations—growing, declining; military, non-military;
2. hard-nose managerial—modified by Harvard Business School-type sector; regional emphasis; mark-up and hard-sell character; Eastern or port-city international;
3. financial/managerial—banking, corporate, trust dept., entrepreneurial;
4. big *rentier;*
5. local *rentier;*
6. proprietorship—note whether self-exploiting, which region, how long, business relation to national corps., quality of customers;
7. entrepreneurial daring—e.g., packaging, plastics, electronics, RAND-type, sociology, or displaced lawyer;
8. knowledge and administration—note whether close to cash register;
9. unionized—old socialist; had to join; grievance-expert; picnic and softball enthusiast; doesn't remember joining;
10. farming—big or little, old or new style;
11. sexual—esp. angry housewives; still waiting for revelation; hasn't heard; doesn't care;
12. age;
13. racial and ethnic—as in Negroes, Jews, Polish Catholics, Jersey Italians, Boston or Midwestern WASP, Bleecker Street Italians, out-of-town Puerto Ricans, college Italians, etc.;
14. veterans—career, occasional;

* Please note that one can coalesce with groups *or* around issues insistent enough to create groups.

15. local government—with or without college degree;

16. education—teaches or operates; writing book on side; semi-retired; will or will not move on;

17. military and foreign emphasis—with or without independent income;

18. cases—queer, alcoholic, misc. health problems, regularly institutionalized, really nutty;

19. intellectual—is; has to be; prefers it; good living; waiting for an opportunity;

20. fun-loving—beer; beach; charter flight to Europe; with or without girls; hobby or profession; cost per week;

21. emotional—a basically friendly American, or one of those tight-lipped bastards.

"Drinks at seven; dinner *absolutely* by nine."

6 The pervasive frustration of the New Class provides the potential basis for "a rebellion of the intellectuals." For one thing, there are simply too many of them, and their numbers must finally become heartening to themselves and frightening to others. Then again, their very existence is an "illegitimate" value in the American scheme of things, since intellectuality as such is not traditionally a money-exchangeable value. And they have been deeply snubbed by the power-men. As these latter recognize their mistake, and try to correct it, they will be confronted more precisely with their increased need of the intellectuals. What I mean to say is that the power-people, having accepted intellectuals as adornments, will be stuck with them as influences or even teachers. Also, they are status-thorns: an increase in the status-value of intellectuality necessarily decreases the inflated status-value of the more ordinary success.

But most important, the New Class will inevitably become conscious of its identity and its size. It does indeed have definite elements of community: the rudiments of a self-conscious ideology are present, and these are bound to emerge more clearly. The anti-war enthusiasm on the campuses during the period of the government's military build-up in Viet Nam may even have had this unconscious purpose, as it certainly is having this effect.

So it appears that the Negroes, by activating the elite white students in the North, will have been the force here, too, that made the difference. The students—not the aging liberals, nor the suburban consumers, nor even the commando squads of shrewd inter-class operators—have taken the lead. The youth of the New Class, beginning with fewer memories of older classes and other days, will fight to settle for less frustration. We must all wish them godspeed. (Being a mere observer myself, however, I can hardly wait for my first serious conversation with the first Youth Emeritae of the Sixties generation of activists.)

But the incredible idealism! How they manage to stay alive and find quiet, pedestrian time actually to read some books, much less have the social effect they are having, really leaves me with a large flabbergast. The young Negroes have a special condition to deal with; and the activists among them are not traditional students in the first place. But the white ones! *From panty raids to protest is one of the longest American miles ever.* The previous generation did not travel quite so far: of course, a Depression or a War can beat it out of you—also, to be candid, a parent with an accent, and a fierce and desperate look in his eye. Further, "we" crapped out to such an extent during the McCarthy-suburban-Eisenhower epoch that the kids became not only impatient but contemptuous waiting for some of the post-graduate students in their forties to indicate, even slightly, where the outer action might be. And then there was all that inhibiting gook about some silly phantasm called "Communism" which seemed always to be presented—not squatting on your haunch in a sharecropper's hut or in an Indian peasant's hovel, but relaxing, highball in hand, in nice American surroundings—with a holier-than-thou inflection, easily recognized as an *educated* parent's "No, Johnny."

But the incredible idealism (even so). Sometimes, talking to them, I feel like a ravaged parent insisting on dull prescriptions, like, No, you don't just flap your arms: you wait in line, pay real money for the ticket, sit patiently while the qualified pilot gets the thing off the ground, and then you peer out the window—*that's* how you fly. They look at you suspiciously, with a What-about-lynching-in-the-South? gleam in the eye. Still, they're young and I'm not; so, beyond peradventure, they are right. And when you stop to think about it, it *has* to be in part my fault that after two thousand years their best idea of political action is a Central High rendition of the Sermon on the Mount.

Not that (along with their solid knowledge of the difference between Right and Wrong) they are not organizational to the *nth* degree. It is all, thank God, a new form of basic American togetherness. The Great Events at Berkeley represented—at the outside—a revolt against a particular style of administration by a particular group of young administrators-in-training. The men in the middle were the delinquent post-graduate students (aging nifties from the Fifties) drawing excellent New Class salaries and thereby subject to considerable guilt. Having failed to lead the students, they naturally succumbed to the first serious effort of the students to lead them. Now, the nasty kids—feeling their power—keep them up all night on off-camera telethons called "teach-ins." Serves them right. (Where were *you* when McCarthy fried This-one or That-one?)

So now we have fall organizational riots, Christmas vacation think-sessions, Thanksgiving and spring demonstrations in Washington, and summer activities in Mississippi or—if the old man can afford it—in Calcutta. (*Gee, I wish the old bastard could put me in on just one Aldermaston march, before I drop-out, crawl-back-in, and graduate. Maybe I could get a three-month Fulbright beginning in January, before I put my neck on the block for Yale Law School . . . ?*)

My point is simple: they are "in" *before* they thumb their noses at us. It is a *new* kind of revolution. To the purists in the middle-aged ranks, I offer the following sop: The *old* kind didn't work. To the ranks of the young purists, I suggest: Don't be such a *chazer*. You think life is a bowl of berries? Berries, I'll give you. Cream you can beg for.

And then, after all is said and done, there is the Peace Corps—the absolutely individual solution to world problems—and Vista (or Whatsa) as its new domestic counterpart. This is the Protestant-missionary expression of the youthful New Class in America. I am probably prejudiced, but teach-ins appear to my sensibility as the newest maneuver of the Elders of Zion: a twenty-four-hour argument was a way of getting your feet comfortably wet, down by my grandfather's *shul*. As for Marches on Washington and similar ways of getting well into a spring vacation, I went to one in 1941—"Let God Save the King, the Yanks are *Not* Coming!": I carried a banner that read "Wyoming": Vito Marcantonio explained why. Summers, I read Dostoievski. (Where the hell was Mississippi in 1941?)

So the New Class tour-of-duty is becoming somewhat more formalized—drop out of Yale, drop in to London, Eng., or Jackson,

Miss.; join something non-monetary. Just as well. If education is going to be a mob scene—like, say, the '49 gold rush, also in California—better it should be organized. And it will, very likely, create some denser self-consciousness leading even toward class ideology. By the time this book comes out, tens of thousands of American students will have met in a Christmas-Easter-or-summer jamboree-demonstration, somewhere in this country, protesting something or other. And it will probably be important, certainly to them. And that *is* the main thing.

(At Tougaloo College in Mississippi, I met a twenty-year-old *zengakuren* who remembered proudly the day he marched into Tokyo—against Eisenhower, he thought; he wasn't sure—along with more than a million Japanese students. Ah, those were the days! What was he doing in Mississippi? Investigating the American racial problem, just for a while, before he went back to Japan and took the technical/administrative job that had been promised to him—threatened on him?—in the Mitsubishi plant near Nagasaki.)

I'm not against it. I was a kid once myself. Weren't you? Of course, we were worried about where the next suburb was coming from—worried, that is, from the day we were born. It's nice the kids don't have it so bad, ain't it?

7 Having noted the underlying similarity between the liberal and the rightist of the New Class, we may now distinguish them by defining the liberal—and noting our hardly hidden preference for same.

The moralism of the liberal is the *better* moralism, it is my moralism—I trust, in your better moments, it is *your* moralism. On the other hand, I don't care for moralism: I distrust it, even my own. But the Goldwater variety, for instance, was one of the more evil things I have witnessed in this country. Considering the wave of historically occasioned hysteria Joe McCarthy had working for him, he was a happy, lovable bum by comparison. So *that* Liederkranz brand of American moralism raises problems beyond anything I think I am talking about when I generally go around exerting myself to ridicule traditional American moralism. The Goldwater Thing is not traditional: it is the stupid, backward American scratching his way out of the ordinary national moral-box into the wild blue yonder of absolutely free and irresponsible righteousness—and without sacrificing one little bit of prejudice, prurience, or insulated ineptitude along the way.*

Morality like that peddled during the Goldwater campaign begins as garden-variety stupidity and finally exfoliates as cunning filth. Purveyors of this new Know-Nothing view actually become more intelligent as they pursue it—they have to, to hold the world together as seen through their chosen prism of distortion: in this sense, it is even "educational." But the merely implied references to experience —which are the substance of the mess—finally supply *all* the content to the initial moral vacuities. When one defines the major part of the real world as evil, and denies any individual connection with this evil or any personal responsibility for it (whether as solvable problem or as insoluble tragedy), the world thus defined "returns"—as with "the return of the repressed" in Freudian thought. And when it returns in this manner it is alien, unmanageable, and victorious. At this primitive moment, one either submits or kills—accommodation is no longer feasible. Since this denouement is implicitly "present" at the outset, practical means are properly irrelevant also from the beginning. That is why Goldwater could, from within the confines of the Know-Nothing view, quite naturally call for the dismantling of the federal government while at the same time insisting on moral action against the Communists and against "crime in the streets," each of which obviously required more rather than less central power.

With this attitude of mind, the point is not to solve a problem but to destroy it. Usually this is done by repressing or exorcising its manifestations, but on occasion one is "forced" to certain actions and attitudes which are neither. This latter is the route by which central power would in fact be greatly augmented under Goldwaterism—in order to seek military resolutions as to the Communists, and impose *de facto* martial law in containing the Negro and other ghettos. Finally, and most disgustingly, all-out moralism of this us-them variety —in which the preservation of righteous self-regard becomes the *summum bonum*—can produce a burst of truly creative hypocrisy. Goldwater personally struck me as too uninterested and too stupid to have participated in the creations of his cohorts: his personality

---

* For the total quality of the Goldwater campaign, I think of some well-known lines from a writer whose name I forget: *Try and get it! she screamed, crossing her legs so tightly that white welts appeared where the blood had been. Rod looked at her with loathing. I'll take this little baby back to Guffey's Reader, he snarled to himself.*

seemed to be that of a deeply violent adolescent surfaced over with sincere, even friendly fatuousness. But not the leaders of his organization. The men who developed the ploy of using "crime in the streets" as a metaphor covering the whole race issue are entitled to the Bollingen Award. As soon as I heard it, I was overcome with a technician's admiration.

The moralistic liberal middlebrows rose to great heights of both hypocrisy and fatuity in defending the Soviet Union during the Thirties and Forties—but they mumbled, they shifted their weight from one foot to the other, every once in a while one of them would burst into tears, and in general they really wanted you to agree with them. But not these cool ones around Goldwater. They couldn't care less. And they are not defending anything as real as Russia and its October Revolution (even in a degenerate form). Indeed, they offer a *positive* defense only of a Liederkranz frame of mind, a specific way of misconceiving events. As for the practical world, they are utterly negative—in an administration of theirs, they would simply destroy a problem occasionally, as its existence too insistently contradicted the True Ideology. They would repress and exorcise, periodically beheading a piece of historical reality as ritual sacrifice, until the full weight of the history that cannot be destroyed finally overwhelmed them, and they came to the decision of whether to submit or to kill.

But the liberal is not like that, no matter how moralistically inclined. He is capable of surviving in the interstices of the cracks in his ideology; he can stop lying to himself and even admit that he doesn't know what the hell he's doing, if necessary. And he submits before he kills. He is still confused, but his confusion—and especially his occasional ability to admit it to himself—turns out to be a social gold mine in the midst of the modern mess.

American liberals are, all in all, quite a grouping. Many of them do not even know that they *are* liberal, while others exaggerate inordinately the moral significance of the fact. Use of the condition as a cover for other impulses was noted some years back, for instance, with the application of the term "totalitarian liberal"; and contrariwise, there is always a contingent that achieves its liberalism only as a by-product in the course of attacking what it started out thinking was "*the* liberal." The very word is an embarrassing historical misnomer in the post-Wilson period. But the more precisely absurd the word becomes, the tighter it sticks—also, one is tempted to say, the looser the connection it presumes to identify, the tighter it sticks. Our liberalism is a great and glorious bag of mixed tricks.

Retreating to a symbolic and somewhat ambiguous definition (for the moment), I will say that the American liberal is someone who participates in the American feast but who then devotes his surplus to an enlarging and reordering of the banquet table rather than to a spirited defense of the caterers. *He is an American with a limited personal perspective in the transcendent matter of general and complete money-making.* (This is the ground on which the patrician *rentier* and the New Class meet, and find each other "strange, but interesting.") Americans can converge on this perspective from opposite directions: from downside there are those who do not have enough and are willing to inhibit somebody else's infinite perspective in order to gain a little more for themselves, while from topside come an increasing number of people in the affluent conclave who find themselves in a state of shock from their discovery of what it means to win out (reasonably) under a system that seems to be devoted exclusively (and unreasonably) to winning out. The first is materially motivated, while the second has more of a cultural problem.* Roughly speaking, the confused roots of these conflicting groups are Populism and Progressivism—which, again roughly speaking, came together with mixed love and lust (and a touch of loathing) in the New Deal, and spawned our postwar society. Special progeny that we are, we do nevertheless have a firm basis in the history of these United States: *to wit,* that a major new society was organized around money-making and almost nothing else, and that this was probably inevitable and has certainly proven to be unbearable, the latter increasingly more than the former as time marches on.

Now on this left/right matter we may note that there can be great daring in looking backward, and rich nostalgia leading one by the nose into a thoroughly misconceived future. This explains why the liberals are at last beginning to lose some of the intellectuals not members of the clergy or the academy; on the other side, it also helps explain some of the upper-level successes of the Communists here and elsewhere. The reason one must look forward anyway is that the

---

* Lipset says "it has been discovered that people poorly informed on public issues are more likely to be both *more liberal* on economic issues and *less liberal* on noneconomic ones." The New Coalition, though necessary, is not necessarily easy to bring about.

past is *too* real and the future is not real *enough*—which should be sufficient reason for real folks, intellectual or otherwise.

The liberal is not an outsider any longer, although he still presumes—sometimes with a heavy hand—to represent all the real outsiders. Since the New Deal was halted and the counterattack began, the liberals have "settled." They have settled for symbolic power and for jobs—electing liberal presidents and participating in their administrations, for instance. By and large, the liberal in America has achieved too much in terms of status and the wide acceptance of his rhetoric, too little by way of durable reform (or, the same thing, New Class advance of a structural kind). It is greatly significant that the right-wingers speak of "the liberal establishment," and even honor its members by substituting their imagined view of liberal workings for the entire course of history itself since the Great Depression. But they should not be permitted to fool the rest of us while they fool themselves: we dare not share their absurd impulse to simplify the world beyond recognition. This is where the liberal himself, in canonizing New Deal happenstance, has participated in the post-Depression trauma of American Individualism (and has helped cause the heated right-wing emanations therefrom).*

The true liberal, I suggest, is not an ideologue at all. Nor is he properly to be understood as a pale radical—although many liberals like to see themselves as "careful" ones. He is not an all-outer: he mostly plays along. He is not all-out about money-making, which gives him his opportunity to be liberal; and he is not all-out about his liberalism, once he indulges that first opportunity. He is simply a fellow with a "surplus" and a generous impulse in disposing of it: basically, he is just a nice American with an education. *Poor people and uneducated people are not "liberals"; they are the natural allies of the liberals.* And since poor people are a minority nowadays, they need the liberals in a new and urgent fashion. The liberals of course need them to become a majority, and as natural objects of their generosity. To such effect, the liberal in this new and truly post-New Deal period must pursue the currently occurring alteration in the

---

* In one sense, the right wing is thoroughly phony and may even prove therefore to be ephemeral: the rightists are mere carbon-opposites of the liberals, and this may well be *because* both are members of the New Class and the right-wingers are mostly objecting to liberal style and rhetoric for the fact that it dominates them as New Class members, whereas they would prefer another style more suitable to their sources and their allies. Clearly, they are not as serious politically (non-style) as the liberals.

real meaning of his role—from the Depression-bred "liberal" who infringes propriety in favor of economic advance, to the postwar "liberal" who deploys his surplus generously.

Poor people are becoming superfluous in the United States—they will soon be unnecessary even for the purpose of exploitation. The issue will one day become that of including them in or institutionalizing them out, the difference being one of price and conscience. (Watch this concept of superfluous people, this black mushroom, grow: first you pay the price of extra guards, then you cut overhead by, let us say, encouraging early death.)

The liberal is a person within the trained and affluent section of society who can, and is still willing to, look outside of it. Also, he has a broader conception of the inside area itself, and of ways and means of improving it, than does the rigid and ungenerous right-winger. He is our best hope for a reasonably innovative politics.

In the past, radicals could dream of awakening the sleeping masses, the silent giants of history. Today, in this country and in countries like it, the majority is well-off: so the radicals can only be goads and gadflies to the lazy or myopic generosity of Insiders.

The greatest dream of all was that of a Prometheus transfixed by the vision of the earth's dispossessed seizing the power of their own destiny by means of the primitive self-consciousness of their overwhelming numbers, similarly situated. But the amoeba that was Marx's proletariat has divided into the Under Class, the Unionized Worker, and the New Class. Those fragments can now be recruited politically for limited purposes, if at all, and then only through a new consciousness sophisticated enough to create an effective existential coalition.

The Working Class is dead. Long live the memory of the Working Class!

The thing I like about American liberals is that they favor positive "programs" of one kind or another.

8 The liberal—the generous man who is willing to suffer the shedding of Scarcity—is apt to be as horrified as the right-winger by the image of rationally organized abundance. But he doesn't panic; he doesn't fall over backward into

the eighteenth century; and best of all, wallowing in his golden con-fusion, he keeps pushing his "programs." And when he dreams, naïf that he is, he thinks beyond 1984 to 1994.

Like most Good Americans, the liberal has not lost the baby of self-interest while throwing out some of the traditional eighteenth cen-tury bath water. Most people most of the time will pursue this "self-interest" of theirs and, having satisfied it perforce, will then proceed to surround the achievement with as much protective cotton batting as may be possible. But some people, certainly, would like to ex-change their surplus for fancier goods than cotton batting. This pin-points both the problem and the opportunity.

A radical, moralistic, either/or approach will not work—not any longer, not in America, not really. That requires well-drawn class lines as well as an overwhelming majority outside the favored circle of participation. Thankfully, both of these factors are lacking here. But this means that we have a new and unique political problem, namely, how to get the best out of a system that works too well at much less than its best level; and which, moreover, is far superior at its actual level to any other—at least until one gets to the purely cultural problems: that is, with all this wealth of ours, we really ought to be much friendlier—and certainly happier. If technological disemployment progresses as some have predicted, and we remain inactive in the face of the event, then—somewhere between ten and fifteen million unemployed—we will have arrived at a major radical crisis. But such inactivity would seem almost inconceivable. Mean-while, the more serious but less dramatic political problems of the human adjustment to affluence remain.

The point is to realize the potential effectiveness of the existing "liberal" consensus, for the limited purpose of ushering ourselves into the new world before the rightists (or some other hysterics) drag us back to theirs. This requires an organization of the surplus rather than an attack on the web of conclave-relations which sus-tains it. The latter would be a direct assault on the conditions of existence of most of the individuals we want and may reasonably expect to have with us; it would be both ultra-moralistic and ineffec-tive; we should not make it a question of quitting the jobs and un-dertaking hair-shirt hardships. That might confirm the worst danger in our situation, namely, the devotion of all surplus to the defense of the conclave-web. Guilt is a bad route to anything: today we all set-tle, who can, and all feel guilty about it—which is a waste of psychic time and effort. *Guilt is the quicksand of the web.* Short of a break-down crisis—that is, urgent demands from outside the system which the system cannot or will not satisfy—our purpose must be to organize the surplus for greater effectiveness, and to manage this without a direct attack on the web and without overexploiting the indigenous guilt of affluence. *If* we want to build the best majoritarian coalition, which is the only democratic thing to do.

Which raises an important question: What is there that we can finally say that might make a difference in the emerging relations between the administrators and the inevitable objects of administration—the unemployed, children, poor people, Negroes, addicts, alcoholics, criminals, the mentally ill, etc.? As for what we used to call "justice" among socially competent men—that has always been a matter of *self*-administration, the muscle for the achievement of which can only be adequately toned by straining to raise the farthest fallen of our brothers.

THIRTEEN

The
New
Coalition

1 The big contradiction in American life concerns money. Money is an institution intended to express the full range of motive, and many of us still think it does. But now we have a New Class that has been freed from the old conception of American money—the infinite perspective of unending accumulation, completely encompassing all motive. As to money, they have settled for a mere standard of living: they say—To hell with the principal, we'll take the interest. This is a spiritual revolution. It is one of the first really specific efforts to enter the new world of technological abundance.

I do not mean to suggest that they know what they are doing, but only that great numbers of them have already done it. In 1965, they maneuvered within a free range, say, of $15,000 to $45,000, with age, aptitude, and accompanying factors the major determinants within this range. Which may strike many readers as quite presumptuous; and the absence of "infinite perspective" will, consequently, go unnoticed. Forty-five thousand a year, indeed! For a four-person family, that would require a national income of over two trillion dollars. A likely prospect! *But fifty million $15,000-a-year incomes is about three years of normal growth of our GNP beyond where we* *were in mid-1965—if our GNP were divided equally.** Even with these rough figures it can be noticed how very close we are to achieving the basic financial side of the minimal reality of the New Class.

Our future is not apt to work out quite so neatly. And it won't work out at all unless the New Class achieves sufficient control of the federal government to ensure at least the 5 per cent rate of growth we have had since 1961; an after-surfeit limitation of the take of the very wealthy; a somewhat democratic sharing among its own recognizable members; and a non-police, welfare-type pacification of the sizable minority that did not quite come up to snuff according to the New Class terms of membership. But, having identified finally with the state or state-like institutions rather than with accumulated principal, the empowered New Class could easily inaugurate a 10 or 15 per cent rate of growth as well as a more serious effort at reasonable redistribution—and that would solve a great number of special-situation problems.

Making fantasy with figures just a bit longer (in order to pose the issue sharply), let us assume these three things: 1) two million really wealthy individuals disposing of $50,000 of GNP each (which would include a large part of the $88 billion of gross domestic investment in 1964 that is included in the total GNP figure); 2) our fifty million poor commanding an average of $3,000 for a family of four (which would include a minor portion of total government expenditures in 1964 of $176 billion, most of the advantage of which goes elsewhere); and 3) the remaining 148 million people in a population of 200 million benefiting from GNP at the rate of $15,000 for the benchmark family of four. What do these rough fantasy-figures come to? For two million people at the top, $100 billion; for 148 million Real Americans, $555 billion; and for fifty million at the bottom, $35.5 billion—making a grand total of $690.5 billion, which GNP figure, at a 5 per cent rate of growth and *without* full employment or full use of capacity, *was reached and surpassed in the first quarter of 1966.*

Assuming an annual three million growth in population, about $10.4 billion out of a $33 billion increase of GNP—not even 5 per cent of $676 billion, the 1965 amount—would cover the inclusion of these new people according to the foregoing percentage distribution.

---

* It is not; it is also not the same thing as personal income, of course. In 1965, personal consumption expenditures were a bit less than two-thirds of the total GNP.

Another $22.6 billion could raise the poverty-family income from $3,000 to $5,000 in one year, or it could be used (figuratively) to purchase a $600 color television set for thirty-seven million $15,000-a-year families.

If you are interested in morality, and are willing to consider it in conjunction with Money, then there you have the moral issue of our day stated rather starkly.

2 Even if you are not over-whelmingly involved in this kind of moral perception, you must be concerned—as long as you continue to live in this technological society—in maintaining the present dull 5 per cent rate of increase, or achieving full use and growth, or in the actual fairness of the division of the product, or the quality of it, or the financial and spiritual costs of inclusion or exclusion of the disadvantaged minority existing at the bottom, and so on.

You see, what has happened is that our present technology has overcome our well-remembered scarcity, but we haven't—not for its extensive effects. Meanwhile, a growing group of our citizens has accepted a life-estate* in this technology in lieu of the accumulation of owned capital, which was the former endeavor of spirited individuals. The passive *rentier* owns a great deal of property, but he, too, has not much more than a life-estate in the technological system which is now run by others: whether the family money was honestly made, shrewdly stolen, or just luckily come by, it is no longer a moral certification nor necessarily a dynamic factor of power. The owning group which still has a sensible reason to believe in the sanctity of private possessory property (and all of the historically related prerogatives and prejudices) has been decisively reduced in size and in significance. And the very poor have become a minority of the underlying population. Thus is capitalism in its classic understanding via Malthus-Ricardo-and-Marx replaced by an organized technological order which creates two kinds of political imperatives: 1) the maintenance and growth (and dampened destructiveness) of the system itself, according to its own revolutionary terms; and 2) the

* This nice term is taken from the law of trusts, in which it identifies a trust device whereby a donor leaves the income from specified property to Joe Blow while Joe lives; on Joe's death, the principal goes to Sam. Joe Blow has a life-estate in the property.

defense and division of life-estates in the product thereof by the individuals living in it—some of whom are true commanders, others of whom are mere historical survivals, and most of whom are the new elevated proletariat (non-owning workers) who operate the machine; or, finally, the discarded humanity which the machine has rejected, also according to its own revolutionary terms.

The maintenance, etc., of the technological order is not the primary political problem. The main issue is to assert ourselves to keep it from destroying us—first physically, then spiritually Physical destruction can result from nuclear and other advanced methods of warfare, and from the further pollution of the environment; our spiritual destruction, however, is a far-ranging and intractable matter that must be faced unendingly into the future, and without waiting on the development of new techniques of management, or better political managers. It is something we must handle on our own. The root of the problem lies within ourselves. A majority of us must decide to be friends instead of pigs; and this majority must rule.

I do not believe, however, that middle-aged men who have scratched their way up from the bottom are able to instruct their families that, beginning on the first of next month, all concerned shall cease to be pigs. It wouldn't work. The kids, however, are not born technological pigs—greedy animals, yes; unfriendly pigs, no. This is our *entrée* to sanity, if any: let us follow, let us even try a little to lead the kids into an order founded on the choice of technological friendliness. Let us stop grabbing so many trinkets each for himself. In fact, it has not been all that much fun—even in the suburbs and away from the niggers.

Having proceeded beyond the personal accumulation of capital, we must take the next step, a positive one, toward sensible consumption all around.

To pin down the issue: We are engaged in a strategic retreat from profit-making as a total view of life—led by the *rentier*/New Class coalition which is already well beyond it in fact. The devotion to profit-making had two uses, historically: 1) it ensured that not everything produced would be consumed. but that a portion would be devoted to the expansion of our capacity for production; and 2) along with interest and rent—the other names for the income from property as distinct from mere work—profits were the occasion for an unequal distribution of the product that was in fact consumed. Many were paupers, few were kings—which caused considerable bad feeling throughout society, also known as class warfare. On occasion, troops were used. But the first part of the profit-proposition remained active, and so the industrial order was in fact being built while the unpleasant argument between the kings and the paupers continued. All this is called "the primitive accumulation of capital," and thank God we are finished with it. No people have looked very good while accomplishing it—not the English, not we Americans, and certainly not the self-righteous Russians, who denied it was happening while it was happening in the worst way imaginable.

But it is not worth arguing about any more. Even the two million American kings—who cares? Take, as an example, their restaurants and resorts (they had to give up the mansions some time back: the servant problem, y'know); none remain insulated from expense-account invasions, and American labor leaders discuss the current class struggle at the Fontainebleau, just as the Politburo meets at various summer palaces formerly graced by the Czar's presence. The point I am making is that these special accoutrements of the life of the wealthy, as they already exist, must serve the purpose of one elite or another—that is their nature physically. And in America, all expense-account elites are welcomed or tolerated, almost everywhere. And, in short, the masses cannot be served lunch at Voisin, or find surcease from their particular *Weltschmerz* in Palm Beach. The places are too small. At most, I would favor Peasant Weeks at Newport, and bus tours through Grosse Pointe, for purely educational purposes—like seeing the Carlsbad Caverns once.

I urge the reader to forget about the profit problem. It is not the main thing, any longer. The main thing, now, is the non-profit problem. We became so unspeakably accustomed to thinking of all of life in terms of profit that we are now in the position of toddlers learning how to accomplish the humanly obvious—like getting from here to there without making a dollar, transferring objects or sentiments from A to B without commercial reasons, and so on. Our trained inability to entertain non-profit motives and engage in non-profit activities was nearly complete when we arrived at the present technological watershed: we require many baby steps, and much reconception, in order to transcend profit-making as the only good reason to get up in the morning; and thus at last to become somewhat human again. We have to do this: the alternative would be to stay with profit-making—a nasty activity which was always Good only because it was Necessary—merely out of fear and ineptitude.

We are the first Surplus Society. Only idiots would deny the fact by concerted make-belief in Scarcity Retained—or profit-making as established ritual.

3 The first dragon on the road back is Charity. And charity (which, incidentally, stinks) should be seen as the historically previous mode of the administration of surplus. The charitable mode is not only outdated but inherently authoritarian: the administrative energy involved is devoted at least as much to the preservation of the spiritual deprivation of all parties as it is to the amelioration of the material condition of the deprived party by the surplus party. It is an attempt by the well-fed to feed the hungry in a very unfriendly fashion, as if the giver might at any moment change his mind and gobble up the morsel himself. The fact that he could not possibly ingest anything further without great damage to himself is denied to the disadvantage of all concerned.

Charity is the monarchical mode of the distribution of surplus. (The king sits on his throne and says, *You*—you get Shlomo's house. Shlomo, you get the axe.) We need a telescoped Magna Carta/Declaration of Independence, and soon, in order to set up a friendly Republic of Reasonable Welfare.

Emotionally, our problem is that we have not yet established a deep belief in our great good fortune, and so still keep a weather eye out for the next rainy day, which is certain to come (we almost hope). We are still ants instead of grasshoppers. Only we are phony ants, in fact. There is featherbedding in the front office, and planned obsolescence back in the shop; meanwhile, we have our greatest prosperity while using 90 per cent of our capacity and under-employing many of our young men. Ants, indeed! Better a few more half-assed grasshoppers than this current mob of phony ants. (And that is exactly the way more and more of our young people sense the situation.)

The next dragon after charity to be met by the new Saint Georges is a mechanical Oz-character by the name of Efficient Administration. This is the charity-type concoction not of the kings, but of the kings' ministers. It constitutes a very great danger in the emerging social order. Our administrative attitudes and techniques are derived either from the process of production or from the authoritarian whimsy of charity, and neither is an appropriate source for an organized effort at offering non-profit assistance to disadvantaged or damaged human beings. We must feel, instead, that they are entitled to our help, that it is a very meaningful non-profit fulfillment for us to try to help them, and that we want them as soon as possible to help themselves by using "our" money, which in fact is "theirs." Also, since we ourselves are not exactly perfect, the reservoir of uncontaminated human emotion and perception which some of the outsiders may bring inside with them, when they are finally allowed in, may be worth a great deal to us who have been inside too long or too much. Note the simple inter-identity advantage merely of abandoning our nasty projective images: if the Negroes do in fact have a real talent for laziness, maybe they can teach us something about how to take it easy. Certainly they can teach us more—the men have already taught us a great deal—about the fluid movement of the human body even in an urban environment.

But this means that the poor are not to be taken merely as messy objects of administration, to be spiritually deloused, bathed, dressed in clean, second-hand clothing, and fed a balanced plateful of nutrition. They are not merely incompetent or recalcitrant Us-es. We may indeed, even using the best ideas, ruin them by trying to help them. But we must try—and we must use the best ideas. The best idea of all is that they are entitled to this new allocation of resources for their benefit; that their new teachers, doctors, counselors, and so on are working *for* them and not *on* them; that the recipients are subjects and citizens, not objects and supplicants; that they need not be humble; and that the administrators have as much to learn about the new non-profit administration of the losers as the losers themselves do in order to overcome their earlier losses.

But it's a problem all around. The present limited war against poverty is being fought by guerrillas in white collars and white uniforms; and non-profit still implies charity or at least efficiency-in-triplicate. This will finally be altered only by the poor fighting back, under imported leadership: after all, a fair war requires two combatants; otherwise it is a mere massacre.

In presenting the initial anti-poverty program to Congress early in 1964, the President said: "Having the power, we have the duty." That was interesting for openers, but the tone was not quite right— certainly not for the long pull. Having the power that our surplus gives us, we have the opportunity to improve ourselves as stewards of it, by using it in a fresh non-profit manner. ("Duty" is for people who would really rather not; "opportunity," however, is something you had better run and get before somebody else grabs it.) We have a great *opportunity* to use our new non-profit power in a fresh way. And it is an opportunity for *us,* and not alone for the "objects of our generosity."

Meanwhile, Westinghouse has concocted a "computerized class-room" as a profitable battleground for the war against poverty; IT&T, GE, Litton Industries, and Philco are building or running Job Corps camps for the objects called "drop-outs"; and other big corporations are seizing opportunities to join the colors and make a dollar in the new welfare/education industry. Just as well—otherwise they might object to the whole activity. Indeed, the first stage of the war on poverty very likely will consist of pouring billions into balance-sheet joy for industry and, even more important, to be soaked up by old, dry welfare administrations—private agencies and public municipal departments—around the country. They have been so hungry for so long that it would be inhuman to bypass them and simply distribute benefits to the needy directly or through new, small, energetic agen-cies. Besides, the vested drones feel they deserve this "back pay" and they will not allow any new fellows in the neighborhood until they get theirs—any more than the AF of L would have stood by quietly if the original New Deal had bestowed all of the manna on the CIO industrial organizing drives. There are various forms of poverty that must be accounted for in any serious war thereagainst.

4 The educated New Class will, in the coming administrative wars, supply more and more of the officers all around. One way and another, the members of the New Class will each have to make a specific choice: they can join with the Under Class, and humanize themselves as they help to educate, make room for, and otherwise advance the disadvantaged; or they can proceed woodenly to administer everybody and everything. The latter choice would indicate that the Soviets do in fact, unmistakably and unalterably, proffer the image of the future technological world order. Because—be very clear about it—what we do here in the United States in disposing of our surplus will largely determine the patterns to be available elsewhere and later. The Soviets have the

administration before they have the surplus; we, having accumulated our primitive capital under another system and before they did under theirs, have an actual surplus requiring a new administration. We got to *that* moon before they did.

And here we confront the true democratic imperative of a society founded upon organized technology. Democracy means individual participation and choice, and the majority as the legitimate source of power. Viewed historically rather than as an absolute ideal invented by ancient Greeks or eighteenth century Europeans or our own colonial Fathers, it must change in order to survive. The basic direction of change has been and remains obvious enough—toward broadening the scope of participation to include various elements of the propertyless. To date, this has meant organized members of the working class, and members of the New Class whether or not organized (and whether or not identified, usually as leaders, with the traditional proletariat). In the United States, with its massive population of immigrants, the process of inclusion has also had a special ethnic side to it. (And the farmers, of course, fought and died for justice and parity, before they moved to the cities.)

At the same time that this broadening was under way, another major historical movement was occurring—the growth of big organizations within the society but more or less outside of the formal political system. Pessimistically, one may say that what was gained in one direction was then lost in the other. More sanguinely—glancing over our shoulder at what has happened in Russia—we may thank the stars above that the democratic impulse at least had the arena of the formal political system within which to assert itself and to grow. And, in the United States, there has not yet been any final showdown between the two systems of power. (I do not mean to suggest that a one-time, deadly showdown is inevitable; we may very well avoid it altogether.) But one reason this has not occurred (and we should not rely on it much longer) is that the extra-legal power system of big organizations is not recognized for what it is—a primary political area not yet constitutionalized or brought within the ambit of majoritarian, democratic control.

Meanwhile, each system is maturing in its own terms; and the inevitable intertwinings between them are also occurring—indeed, ever more tightly. With reapportionment, the overblown obstructionist power of small-town property-owners is being reduced, thus preparing the stage for the coming drama of engagement between the central cities and the suburbs, and also providing the very welcome prospect of some genuine local government. With the enfranchisement of the Southern Negro, the white South as a monolithic obstructionist bloc is finally being reduced to manageable stature, both in Congress and even more particularly within the Democratic Party. As for the interconnections between the two systems of power, the primary one has been the growing acceptance by the corporate order of the utility of the federal government's fiscal power in underwriting mass consumption, by one means or another. The maturation of the technological order itself is, of course, obvious.

With so much inevitable organization, the eternal problem of the future is clearly the development of a relevant individuality—based on, responsive to, and capable of surviving and growing in the new circumstances. One should persevere to be an individual *within* organizations, and to admit this necessity while confronting it. In our kind of society, one is a lost atom outside of organized life—not a Jeffersonian Individual, nor even a mediocre Cowboy.

But the first next great encounter involving this unending issue will be that of the New Class of organizers and the Under Class of those still-to-be-organized. Many elements of the New Class may complete their lives still primarily concerned with self-discovery in relation to the institutional Over Class, to ethnic background, or to feelings about the Possessory Class or the Patricians. But the cultural stew of the future is in fact being cooked on this other burner: it is there that the new individuality will be determined.

The great experiences of nations, I imagine, are never erased no matter how heroically or ignobly dealt with by succeeding generations. Germany and Nazism; Russia and the epoch of Stalin; the French and their still unresolved bourgeois/rational revolution; England with its magnificent but strange history in which the underlying population was so devastatingly domesticated by each victory—these histories will preoccupy fresh generations far into the future.

And what of the young giant of the West? Our basic problems are still unresolved: the robber barons and their heirs have ruled or threatened to rule for no more than one hundred years. And that time span also measures the period of "Negro freedom." The acknowledged rule of property before the Civil War, including property in persons, did not involve the deeply corrosive aspects of the post-

Civil War rule of the plutocrats and the corporations, nor the social devastation of chained freedom following the Emancipation Proclamation. These issues are, today, not yet resolved. But they will be soon, in the qualities-of-life which emerge from the administration of the Under Class by the New Class, especially when the latter has assumed its dominant place in American society.

Since the event has not yet taken place, a moral statement may be excusable. Please excuse the following one of mine.

5 *We should begin at the bottom.* To give an actual and not merely an ideal meaning to the term "American Citizen"—which, once given, would surely be heard around the world more clearly even than the shot fired at Concord—is our great national opportunity. This is the initial indicated use of our surplus. We cannot help being wealthier than everyone else in the world, and this is not an immediately exportable entity; but we can use our wealth with more humane democratic intention than any other society ever thought of doing. This, once accomplished in our own backyard, would do more than anything conceivable to defeat Communism—and much other evil besides. We have the first, best opportunity; no one else does. And it may be a decisive one, since the future of the planet is now being determined in these days of the earliest maturation of technology.

What God-in-His-Heaven has meant to most of humanity is that Somebody with the power to do so actually did care about *your* fate. If this feeling were ever non-fraudulently secularized, mankind would have traveled through a great spiritual desert into a dramatic mode of terrestrial life in which the opportunity to take a reasonable personal responsibility for the fact of one's own death would be a live option even for those of us who are less than heroes. The consequential effect of this new form of living-and-dying would be very much like being born again: we could even enjoy, so to speak, the survival of our children.

Everyone—no matter what anybody thinks is wrong with him—would have a right, and would be included-in. Certainly a very expensive, time-consuming, and infinitely annoying form of citizenship. Ah, but the spiritual advantage—even unto the kings of the earth! (All of whom will die; any one of whom may be lowered before death.)

So, how does one go about this experiment of beginning at the bottom? There must be income-plus-opportunity, and an absence of established disadvantage, for everyone born within the geographical confines of the American jurisdiction. *Henceforth, speak law to no born loser:* to him, if he happens, special concern is due—as if the fault were ours as well as his. Thus we undertake with our wealth to re-do reality from birth; the capacity, whatever it may be, is committed. (Necessarily, births must be limited, since the designated capacity to re-do them is.)

The relation between income and jobs began to separate long before we imagined the possibility of this great decision about the meaning of American Citizenship. Morally, the bigger issue is between income and real work, which has never been measured and probably is not measurable. So we will skip it altogether. The concept to be ingested now is that there is no longer any good reason from anybody's point of view to deny a minimally adequate income to anyone. Stated with warm assertion, *everybody should eat, nobody should beg for what-with*, and it should become our greatest social triumph to upgrade this minimal income as and when we are able—and we certainly are right now. Those who can work, should—preferably at something worth doing, without humiliation, not to aggrandize a superior, etc. However we manage with these close questions, there must in the first instance be a federal obligation to provide a job at a living wage for anyone who wants one. Thus, as we proceed toward non-profit notions of work or occupation or even effort, this will be accomplished without straining the credulity of those least able to bear the strain. The Job is a metaphysical concept which should not be transgressed against the will of the individual suffering from it.

Next, we may observe that "poverty" is a lousy word for describing our interest in this large human process of creating substantial American Citizenship. For example, old people—our parents—who have worked as much as they could, as much as our society demanded or allowed, should not be required to continue the charade unto but a single day this side of the grave, or to suffer for their inability to do so. The cost of providing for the elderly poor has been estimated to be not much more than $7 billion annually. *Enough:*

they participated in building the world for their children and grand-children—for us—so this is a good place to begin practicing realistic decency. Next-to-death is the true bottom, so let us begin there.

That is both easy and cheap: the next move is more complicated. Welfare for the aged hardly needs to be administered at all, it is so obvious. But we should not even begin the serious administration of other problem-populations until we have shaken out the employa-bles, the merely job-deprived. Here the simple answer is to surpass the aggregate-demand approach and just create jobs. At the same time, we are then and thereby compelled to confront the necessity of upgrading the working poor, which involves serious minimum wages, the concerted effort to create non-profit jobs, and finally a fed-eral yardstick minimum-wage job: e.g., everybody can become a federal trash collector and highway beautifier or one-year student of Anything at two dollars an hour instead of a rural slave or an urban laundry worker or other exploited servant—and, yes, we will have more expensive fruits and vegetables and clean clothes. And a cleaner America, in more ways than one.

It would be utterly vicious to administer simple unemployment as a social disease. Narcotic addiction, yes; mere unemployment, no. The lack of a job must never be associated again with anyone's moral condition: that was the "disease of the Depression," a moral equivalent of the bubonic plague, and as a self-constituted social health officer I will not allow the first beginning of a second tolera-tion of that particular piece of nonsense. At the bottom, the people who want jobs have no responsibility whatsoever for the existence of the jobs they want, period: enter a new epoch.

If only that kind of vicious morality would disappear once and for all, the New World would not only be a better world, once arrived; it might also arrive more readily.

6 In that whole large area of human relation and need—must it be called "welfare"?—stretching from basic education through medical care and diet and housing all the way to the treatment of incorrigible criminals, *administration and politics begin to merge.* And the underlying issue then emerges as being an elitist or participatory mode. Where the alteration of human beings for their benefit is the purpose of the activity rather

than merely the dollar profit to the supplier, the ideology of the market with its image of economic man is replaced by the moral culture of the administrator with his particular image of a perfected man. The possibilities here are nearly endless—from *categorical* administration (Eichmann carrying out the Final Solution of the Jewish problem), to *sacrificial* administration (Saint Francis embracing the leper). Freedom, participation, politics—these require constant consultation with the Jew and the leper, even though each is what he is (or perhaps exactly because of the condition and the resulting "expertise" of the inhabitant).

Eichmann was very efficient; but Saint Francis didn't have the whisper of a hope of curing leprosy that way. Divided by efficiency, they are joined by something else: each was "ingesting" an object, rather than assisting another subject. I am a Jew, so it will impress no one that I prefer the approach of Saint Francis. Still, I find it dangerous—on principle. Anyway, things are different in this country. Imagine an American leper dying in a charity ward: he would prefer a carton of cigarettes or his own TV set to a human embrace. Is that so terrible? On the other hand, I suppose that once you create untouchables, nothing can quite do the job of a sincere touch.

But why create them in the first place? Only to avoid the curse of equality. It is interesting, thinking about this, to ask: What is the most equal thing about human beings, the first and foremost common denominator? A heart, a liver, arms and legs? No. The man sitting next to you on the subway has a heart with an unknown defect: he will be dead tomorrow. Yours, however, will last another twenty years: the hearts were not equal. There is only one equality, and that unfortunately is subject both to the unknown and to manipulation: all men have had a day of life, and all men will one day die. All inequalities are treasured because of the who, how, while, when, and where of this final event.

So primary equality is the treasuring of any life, as long as may be.

But only generously, not sacrificially. Generously according to your means. (Sacrifice is for helpless lovers and other fools.) So what is realistic generosity? Now there, granted our undeniable means, is the nub of the issue. I suggest the following principle for determining it: If I have a hundred loaves and eat a loaf a year, I still will not give a crumb to a beggar if I expect to live another hundred years—*but never to gain another loaf.*

Now, I ask you, is that an *American* story?

There is an infinite perspective with regard to consumption, just as there was with capital accumulation. Let us skip the Split-Level Barbecue and move on directly to the Christmas Thing ($27 billion in 1964). I confess that it terrifies me. The mania to purchase at the end of the year—without reason, against all self-interest, in violation of every year-long principle of prudence—is like nothing so much as the last few weeks of a speculative investment boom, where the infinite perspective becomes immediate and therefore insane. If this savage impulse is not domesticated—or at least diverted in an organized way to serve the purposes, say, of the war against poverty—I breathe rapidly for the future of my native land. (There's an idea—how about anti-poverty bonds for Christmas, like during that other war?)

But really, how long can this go on? Pigs, every one of us. And isn't it, underneath, mostly an example of confused peasants acting toward consumption (in mistaken imitation) the way the lords of the manor behaved toward capital? How much can *one* person eat—of anything? Two per cent of GNP—not even one-third of the annual increase—would give every family at least $3,000 a year. That's with no strain at all, accomplished with the "sacrifice" of one-third of what we don't even have yet.

No strain except the psychological one of tolerating primary equality. The suggested federal guaranty—a merely minimal redistribution of our immense and growing product—would help alleviate the administrative problems of both Eichmann and Saint Francis. Constructing an income-floor under everyone, there would be no absolute outcasts; devoting some ameliorative rather than punitive resource to the specific problems of the ruined remnant, there need be no categorical solutions to insanity, criminality, self-destructive addiction, age, miscellaneous disease and handicap, pacifism, laziness, atrocious manners, rigid ideology, other uneducability, satyriasis, excessive saving of old newspapers or coins, absenteeism, hi-jinx, pimples, obesity, balding, flat-chestedness, spitting in public, pasty skin color with a greenish tinge, black skin color, colorless skin color, self-righteousness, frigidity, impotence, humorlessness, facial twitches, boring conversation, and general unfriendliness. All these basic problems of the human condition can, instead, be researched and administered with patient, sympathetic coaxing of the participating subjects and with a view to the long pull.

Once again: Why does the prospect of putting a Social Floor under all of life terrify us so much? To the factors of primary-equality revulsion and the inhibition of the infinite perspective, let us now add the consideration that every bum would be included-in. If *you* are not saved unless all are saved, and so we set up a system wherein all are saved, anybody could be a bum and still be saved. Each man would then be tested for the genuineness of his desire not to be one. Horrors. Who could bear such a realistic and honest system of morality? How can we ever manage without the hypocrisy of Being Better by virtue of pushing others down rather than pulling ourselves up? (As for the general opportunity to go to pot comfortably, without daring too much, the wealthy few have been living with it for some time, making out *comme çi, comme ça;* but it was their unshared opportunity, so not comparable to our future problem.)

On the positive side, the Social Floor would have the sanguine effect of forestalling the worst of the anxieties and protective impulses of guild-type or exclusionary groups, and other similarly vested interests, e.g., mediocre teachers, master plumbers and carpenters, bureaucratically established time-servers, members in good standing of the military-industrial complex, and maybe even the dead horse printer and the featherbird pilot, etc. Of course this problem is broader and even more serious, since it involves the hidden bum in everyone. To do away with useless "work" and improve the quality of the remainder involves the reeducation of an entire society. Still, anything that helps to establish confidence in non-scarcity —or provides defense against the scarcity-type fear of death-and-destruction by the slightest change—is helpful.

7 If our wealth is not used to firm up and then to raise the Social Floor, we may discover it being applied to the construction of hidden trapdoors in what seemed to be a solid Second Floor of affluence.

It will cost a great deal, both in material and spiritual resource, to keep selected patches of humanity on the outside looking in at all the nice people living so well inside. Already the central city ghettos require many more police (and, incidentally, genuinely require much better police) to maintain the suburban policy of containment. It might even be cheaper to assist them in becoming like us (*ugh!*). The way the situation is going, and is apt to continue to go, police barriers are not necessarily cheaper than welfare barriers—dollar-wise, as they say in some bureaus.

But much more important, lifewise, is that the New Class members need the Under Class as an ally to protect them from their own generals: if they take them as objects to be restrained, they hand themselves over to their own worst enemies—the institutional elites of the Over Class. Technology creates organization as well as all this wealth of ours: organization is power—but not necessarily for the individual member. If he wants power, especially something like personal power in relation to the organization under which he is involved, he needs to organize against the organization. That means allies. He needs to belong to a coalition that threatens to control the organizational elites.

The subject of a possible New Class/Under Class coalition entices me back, again, to money.

Having brought us this far, Money—the bloody beating heart of the American experience—is now about to carry us into the promised land. But, in doing so, it will transcend itself. Money can become human, even friendly, or it can ruin us once and for all; that will depend on the character of our political effort. Since the matter concerns organization/power (the sometime-subject of this book), we may interrupt ourselves and look it over for a few pages before proceeding to our final thunder with respect to the New Coalition. As follows:

We have operated not with an appropriately industrial but with a loudly inadequate sense of money. In a productive technological society, money should be nothing but a paper technique—a dependent matter of primary political choices and of secondary bookkeeping. Notice the contrast with the past: In an agrarian order, money represents a shadowy relation to distant, ominous powers, including God, the railroad companies, and Wall Street. There is never enough of it, you had better be extremely careful with it, and if it is incoming it had better be in gold—and, as a matter of simple prudence, it ought not to be outgoing at all. Finally, all money is capital or principal, properly conceived, and therefore should not be spent on living but only to produce more money by being let out at interest or invested at a profit.

That is scarcity-money, unfortunately appropriate to a period covering the primitive accumulation of capital, where everything is being sacrificed to the growth of trade and industry. The welfare of farmers and workers, even the spiritual welfare of the accumulating capitalist himself, is greedily sacrificed to this Mammon of Tomorrow. (A few bums invade principal and live it up inordinately; very big winners imitate the dignified gluttonies of the previous aristocrats; there are generalized drop-outs; all these are exceptions.)

But when the trade and industry have in fact grown? And when their continued growth—without question the first charge levied against production—is the most firmly built-in feature of the system? What then? Why, *then*, the system and the people in it must change —or make believe that what has happened has not really happened. That's where we are now, struggling with the intractable issue of belief in our great good fortune.

Scientific abundance, properly administered, would create a new kind of money, and a new personal psychology and public politics supporting it and expressing it—in fact, *constituting* it. Money *is* a form of psychology and politics; it is certainly not a thing in itself. What kind of money we are to have under technological abundance will be determined by us—by our psychology and our politics. And the main issue here, as noted, is whether we are to perpetuate reservations of scarcity, or spread the blessings.

The disjunction between the money-making and money-spending periods of American history, which we are now experiencing, could not be more severe: it is—we all know of examples—disruptively sharp in the single careers of many American individuals.

If we accept the idea that no one is to be left out altogether, thereby deciding against genocide and all the various social techniques of inducing early death, we have—almost by inadvertence— chosen as well the brotherhood of man, amen. (But, naturally, with a certain amount of sibling rivalry retained.) The alternative to this choice will be horrible: great power greatly misused. The power at the heights of the institutional apexes will be enormous; and what will our powerful leaders have experienced in clawing their way to the top? That is the key: We must train them on the way up.

We are moving toward a Bookkeeping Order of society, one way or another. The computer will do our dear or dirty work for us. Our productive technology leads compellingly beyond old-fashioned money to computerized bookkeeping—of "abundant entries," so to speak. No longer merely a further watering down of Private Property and Individualism, not just a spot of welfarism here and there, but the clear redirection and final unleashing of technology and its administration for the minimal life-use and benefit of everyone, and a national accounting mechanism appropriate thereto.

But this will also mean an acceptance of the society of organization, and its appropriate mode of thought: power.

Computerized bookkeeping would (or could) go beyond money, as we have known it, most decisively in this: life-values would no longer be expressed in simple quantitative relations—"better" people, more dollars; "not-so-good" people, fewer dollars. Money always expressed non-dollar values in that certain personal qualities were correlated more highly with money-making activities—and others had a negative correlation. But once we have decided to value life-itself beyond money-itself, and we make this decision at a time and in a society where we really do have the resource and capacity to act on it, old-fashioned scarcity-money is finished. The social books must be kept on a greater variety of human values than under the old system—for example, economists are already talking of capitalizing education—whether or not the effort is made to express this expanded range of values in terms of dollars. Eventually the computer may demand its own new unit of value, beyond dollars *and* birth certificates, diplomas and other certifications: a fungible unit of value (and dis-value) beyond gross status or mere economics.

It would seem inescapable that we must retain a system of sanctions and incentives embedded in the primary bookkeeping—but in line with our Shall-Live decision, these would not be heavy-handed and could not touch the basic right and means of life. A. A. Berle reminds us: "Classical economics included an assumption that every man will be as lazy as he dares be." The Bookkeeping Order will be uninterested in this daring, to a point, just as the money system was uninterested in the laziness of propertied persons (or left the problem to unenforced morality). Besides, it isn't so daring to be lazy if nobody cares—after a while, this may even take all the fun out of it. But the human race has worked hard enough to be entitled to a generation or two of laziness, if that's what it wants.

More interesting than the boring prospect of extended sloth will be the transmutation of justice in the Bookkeeping Order. What will happen to the idea of justice when the deep sting of injustice is removed? More specifically, with life assured, what's to get sore about? Berle gives us a clue in the course of his own ruminations about advances in bookkeeping:

Some day we shall have true "social cost accounting," which will show not merely what it cost a producer to produce . . . but also what it cost society to produce. . . . All we can say, now, is that the value of the aggregated things and organizations, in motion and in use, depends in part, perhaps in very large part, on their strategic position in a highly organized society.

This suggests that when injustice no longer strikes at the root of life, the suffering or the combating of it may well become an exclusive entertainment of ambitious seekers after strategic position. Thus, it may even be assimilated to pique.*

8 Money is what holds a modern community together (or vice versa). Money, of course, is an act of faith: it *assumes* community, being a bargain among three parties— the buyer, the seller, and an unknown future seller—in which life-values are exchanged, including things. By definition, the connections represented by money create or maintain, by themselves, no more than a commercial community. But for many people in our society, this is the only important public community they ever experience (either making the money or spending it). From barter to gold to negotiable paper to central banking to governmental fiscal policy and on into the Bookkeeping Order of society all involves a continuing extension of the interconnectedness, the faith, that makes and maintains community. Meanwhile, money is clearly not a thing in itself but merely attempts to represent the technological and other —remaining—social order. (Unless it becomes a fetish, in which case a doctor should be called.)

So we are now entering a stage in history wherein money can more and more be used consciously, rationally, even shrewdly, and certainly with increasing effect, to create the quality of community we think we lack. From now on, what money means depends on what we do with it, as never before, because now we genuinely do have an augmented range of choice. As the military men say, we are in a position to search out targets of opportunity.

* In discussing bookkeeping, which is even today zooming beyond traditional money, Berle is very suggestive. The first principle in thinking about these matters could be his statement: "Audit, to be real, becomes matter of philosophy."

In its root-meaning, the word "profit" refers to the value or advantage or other good that may accrue from an act—as in the Biblical, "For what shall it profit a man," etc. It is, if you will excuse an old-fashioned expression, a bourgeois distortion that has limited the word to mean a money-return on the expenditure of money or effort. Since there is more and more money, spending or otherwise getting rid of it consumes more and more of our time—and also determines the quality and character of our living. *Consumption is a non-profit activity*—the major American form of what the right-wingers, if they bothered with relevant consistency, ought to call galloping socialism.

So, the primary non-profit issue being how we shall profit ourselves by spending or otherwise getting rid of our money, I have a suggestion: the liberals should open a bank.

Non-profit "banks" to finance various non-profit activities other than consumption already exist, both government agencies and private foundations. And there are also political "funds" (if not banks) of various kinds, although these are often enough not to be thought of as non-profit in intent. But it is the liberals—the forward-looking intellectual types—who need particularly to move forward in an intellectually financial way, thus becoming serious about non-profit activity that is not merely educational or governmental, but distinctly and exactly political on their own. Activity that will represent a serious material cost to them, a decided-upon piece of "consumption," a specific use of their surplus, a personal payment applied to the social design they dream about. They must learn to vote as well with their dollars; indeed, to put their money where their mouths are.

Ah, but the evil heritage that prescribes two separate orders of existence to money and to ideas! Well, that is just the point. If the New Class liberal—our new bearer of culture as well as the beneficiary of our current affluence—cannot be made to see the evil of the heritage, or just does not desire to overcome it after he comprehends it, then we will indeed end up with an overorganized world with most of the human and individual assertion against it consisting of conversation. It is clear today, as it was abundantly apparent throughout the bourgeois epoch, that one's surplus can be devoted to self-righteousness as well as to material overconsumption. Moral capital, too, can be accumulated with an infinite perspective.

The American liberal tradition, we have noted many times, was always burdened with moralism. And what the liberals have always needed was to accept organization in order to fight organization, instead of merely opposing it on moral grounds while irresponsibly acquiescing in its material benefits. And since organization is power, this attitude has defined as well their attitude toward that: somebody else should dirty their hands with it, while they are simply— most characteristically—"against" it.

Let's state the matter as a cold proposition:

Organization is power: what the liberals need is more power: the one resource constituting power that they most lack is money: therefore, the liberals should devote their greatest effort to perfecting the organization of their collection and disbursement of money.

When it comes to money rather than people, I am a pure Leninist— favoring the highest order of the most up-to-date democratic centralism.

The liberals, however, even abhor patronage—but only if a dollar changes hands. The Democratic Reformers—in California, for example—are very lustful with respect to the psychic satisfaction of "honorific patronage." As reported by Professor James Q. Wilson, Governor Brown in 1959 "made at least 346 discretionary appointments to persons in Los Angeles County alone, the majority of which carried no salary. . . ." Summing up the difference between the new Reformer and the old machine politico, Professor Wilson says of the former:

He seeks to mobilize intellectual, not material, discontent; to obtain recognition for the cosmopolitan middle-class, not for the disadvantaged lower class; and to press for the rationalization of the social order on the basis of general principles rather than for the distribution of tangible benefits on the basis of personal mediation.

But the liberal must not think that "politics" consists only of taking care of himself—*morally.* One's allies must also be taken care of, and some of these are interested in material benefits—as the liberal himself would be, if he didn't already have his.

Perhaps the greatest loss to American politics, over the long decades, has been the repugnance of too many of the "better elements" to engage in the grubby game at all. This is no longer a respectable position, and respectable people must now recognize the fact. Especially since, with the growth of educated affluence among the New

Class, the better elements are no longer limited to the old families. Along with the more needful elements, they can comprise our best majority; and they belong together, under any realistic conception of social decency.

The American reformer can look back over the course of his contribution to our history with some pride in effect achieved as well as a good deal of embarrassment for the naïve moralism of many of his predecessors and contemporaries. Politics is most decidedly a power game, and only by squeamishly avoiding it altogether can one fail to understand this most obvious of the facts about it. But that does not mean that only power-driven and money-hungry people belong in it. These types will, certainly, find their way into political activity, as the bee unto the honey; but that needn't require the more culturally ambitious people to retire inevitably to nicer surroundings. Quite the contrary. They are very much needed for balance, to keep the fast boys and other single-minded types from running away with the game, table and all. And it should not embarrass us to stand up and assert that politics is *also* a deeply spiritual enterprise. In democratic political activity, we participate in building the world that our children will inhabit—when we are no longer here to insulate them from the world that "the others" would provide for them.

So the liberals should open a bank of their own.*

9

The liberal bank, most hopefully, would later become an institution with something of the neutral integrity of the American Civil Liberties Union—but, also hopefully, with a lot more money and a much greater range. It could not expect to begin in business with quite that quantum of dignity, however. And—if you like precedents—neither did the National City or the Chase Manhattan (or the ACLU, for that matter). But note that all of the traditional morality of the liberals could be well applied to ensure the fairness and the honesty of *their* bank; and in that way, which has always been the banker's way, they could achieve for once an equal measure of piety and effectiveness, banks being special temples in which the golden idols are worshiped by being melted down into coin of the realm.

* Incidentally, they have already begun: the civil rights and Viet Nam fund-raising has been rather impressive.

As higher forms of effective organization—therefore, power—banks rank with the Greek phalanx, the Roman legion, the castle keep, the Tweed and Leninist and then Maoist party, and even approach the effectiveness, say, of an early General Motors. But the basic form must undergo some serious adaptation to serve our present American purposes.

To begin with, deposits and investments both are contributions, this being a non-profit bank. Secondly, control over the management of the bank—the election and recall of directors, for example—resides in the depositors, not in the stockholders: there are none of the latter, the bank being a membership organization of depositors. Next, with the usual bank or fund the bigger depositors have inordinate influence with the managers as to investments, while the mass of small depositors are lucky to be given greasy commercial smiles, one to a customer, as they stand in line at the teller's window to make their small deposits. With the stockholder and depositor status merged, and the merged-one interested neither in dividends nor in interest but only and very actively (dollarwise and otherwise) in the management decisions as to non-profit political investments, we proceed substantially in the direction of adapting the big depositor to the new order of business. But, hopefully, without losing him altogether. The more small deposits and depositors there are, even with their votes controlling the management and its investment decisions, the less the big liberal depositor can afford to pass up the opportunity to join his giveaway-money with theirs. True, he previously had the field to himself and, indeed, it was nearly left to his whimsical discretion, as in the charitable game. He is long overdue for an organizational lesson, similar to the one Mark Hanna impressed upon the big business winners nearly three-quarters of a century ago: buy whimsically, buy retail; buy shrewd and organized, and we can get it for you wholesale.

The subject under discussion will be recognized, by the cognoscenti, as that of "fund-raising." You bet your life. Only money will get us out of the ridiculous mess that money got us into. Not money alone, of course: I am talking about money on the left—money on the right and at the center needs no advice from me, certainly none that will be listened to politely. You say there isn't any on the "left"? The hell you say, as follows:

The left in this country, if it is Leninist or Maoist or even traditionally Marxist, is insane. Again, in even more traditional terms, it would be guilty and convicted of "left-wing infantilism" if it had risen, which it hasn't, to a level deserving of that particular revolutionary insult. I say it hasn't. I say it is guilty, when guilty, of nothing more egregious (or impressive) than regular hysterical American moralism. It is only the *chutzpah** of the well-fed fantasist that leads so many noble white warriors to imagine recent Negro activism as a high road to revolutionary purity. Fellows, I tell you in loud, firm tones: you misread Marx if you read him as a moral loudmouth. He was not one of those; he was very serious, and thoughtful. He did not make up the world in his head: he had a theory of revolution derived from and continuously referred back to historical circumstance and other occurrence which had nothing to do with what went on, in pure mental freedom, in his head. He thought that the factory worker everywhere and always was inevitably and exceptionally revolutionary. He had very good reasons for thinking so at the time; but he was wrong. He would be the first to acknowledge this obvious fact today.

As for Lenin, he had an organizational idea (and capacity) also very good for his time and place. That is what we need—what anyone with a revolutionary or even a seriously innovative impulse needs—but for *his* own particular time and *his* own particular place. That is always in order, it is part of the game; and in business, certainly, all of the players understand the need for good organizational ideas.

From the 1830's to the 1930's, from Jackson to Roosevelt, the popular forces in America moved from an ultimately unsuccessful attack against the other side's bank to the finally successful establishment of their own bank. Now, if as a liberal you are still content to rely on this *governmental* bank of ours, then you will be content to ignore the imperative of a higher form of organization which implies the establishment of a *non-governmental* but still very political liberal bank: a tight little private bank to fight for control of the loosely held state bank. And ignoring this imperative will be the end of the liberal tradition in America, to the extent that it might remain non-governmental—except, of course, for loud moral noise.

The deposits will come from the liberal patricians who give now; from the fresh New Class intellectuals who have not yet learned to purchase politics along with their Roualt prints and finely engi-

* Greek translation: *hubris*.

neered kitchens, but soon will; and the deposits will come in kind—
time and effort of all kinds, especially from the young who have no
money, and then from the frustrated, the ungrown, and the otherwise disappointed, for whom our present money buys not enough or
the wrong things.

The investments are more of a problem. Here we get back to the
ugly question of patronage, that is, the support of our friends and
allies for the purpose of carrying on our political activity for us. I
hardly know how to sympathize sufficiently with the revolted reader
for imposing this necessity. On the other hand, what exactly did you
think politics consisted of if it did not include paying the rent, etc.,
for those people who devote themselves full-time to doing our work
for us?

The investments are also troublesome in that decisions concerning them will certainly involve competitive interests. (Liberals are
so noisy.) Shall we collect a few dozen yards of signatures to secure
the admission of mainland China to the UN? Or open a storefront
aiding-and-organizing center in Harlem, Newark, or Cleveland, with
hired hands? These conflicts, which will most often concern which
pronouncement-to-the-wind or actual organizing work shall be accomplished to satisfy which particular group, must be resolved by compromise. Compromise is the wry acceptance of the other fellow's inadequacy—his lack of education, or of rich human feeling, or any
other disability which keeps him from understanding how right you
are in the first place.

The making of these compromises and trade-off adjustments will
be the work of the board of directors of the bank. Elected by the
contributing membership, they will represent the constituent elements of the New Coalition—the New Class liberals, enlightened
patricians, Negro activists, some pieces of organized labor, and elements of the to-be-organized Under Class. They don't have to like or
admire each other; some may even be expected to lack mutual respect. They only need to recognize and remember the substantial
imperatives of organizational power that brought them together in
the first place. Coalition, the native road to effectiveness, is the necessitous community; it does not begin as an ideal one; and some
Moseses will (thankfully?) expire in the desert. None of us are good
enough, still we have to live together—that is *why* we must engage
in politics, which in America can only be coalitional.

And the kind of politics that assumes the conclusion in the beginning is not politics at all: it is mere moral assertiveness, a mode of spiritual overconsumption that comes to little more (if you are not in fact an Isaiah) than an indulgent waste of one's American surplus.

10 Couldn't happen, could it?

The "liberals" and their natural and necessary allies, making up the 51 per cent most-desirable majority of Americans, could never achieve such a high level of effective organization, could they?

Why not? Only because they do not recognize the need, are not accustomed to thinking in relevant power terms, are still satisfied enough with moral postures and other Correct Positions. But the merely moral answer is very boring over the long run; they are learning about the terms of power simply by living in this organized society; and when someone like Goldwater runs for the Presidency, they recognize the need readily enough. The fear of one clear enemy creates a great deal of cohesion: the Jews became such superlative fund-raisers and contributors only after Hitler, and especially after the Crystal Night in 1938. Having learned the lesson, however, they have stayed with it. (And there is a lesson in *that*, too.)

Besides, the liberals *are* very busy; they *do* raise a lot of money. And the moral positions are also functional, at least in serving as a primitive or initial means of identifying like-minded persons to each other. The mass excitement of the anti-war moralism connected with Viet Nam, we noted, has had the important virtue of enheartening the participants with an awareness of their numbers and their fervor. This in itself is a significant power factor, although as a proposition directed not toward creating community among themselves but actually affecting the character of American military policy or the course of events in Southeast Asia . . . well, they never really had a chance. (And perhaps just as well, since they never really had an alternative policy, either.)

But with this costly "sense of themselves" once achieved, they might learn to take on smaller dragons, at least to begin with. The principle of power requires: 1) self-awareness sufficient to distinguish between one's desires and moral beliefs as against the more intractable elements of circumstance; and 2) the creative shrewdness to apply one's limited leverage with the greatest effect. Without achieving 1), the participant hardly arrives at the opportunities of 2), but only wanders farther into the eternal no man's land of *The Problem:* the conflict between an assessment of what exists and is possible, and the freer exercise of creative imagination. There is no virtue in despising the first part; indeed, doing so often enough leads to merely mediocre imagination.

But the fear and the shame of beholding the world, *with you in it,* in power terms! Why? Because you then perceive your own weakness, and consequently the depth of your involvement with others. The weak need community—they find their strength in numbers. When they overassert moral principle in meeting this need, it is done as a piece of unmitigated magic designed to forestall betrayal. But it can't and it doesn't: it only forestalls, at best and for a while, one's own *fear* of betrayal.

Unilateral morality that is not magic is for powerful people; and with whomsoever, it always functions in a close relation with power. If a rule of behavior is shared, based either on tradition or on contract (a deal), the situation is clear and raises no problems—until the contract is broken or the tradition decays. Morality as a unilateral "instead of" view of circumstance, when undertaken with serious awareness, also obviously has a close relation to power in that it is then a generous offering which only a person with the capacity can afford. When genuinely put forth in this way, it is like love— *Here,* I offer you something better than either of us now has. Why is there any difference, then, between love and power? The answer is simple, if painful: Either there is not enough love in the world, or the love that is here is not powerful enough to overcome its enemies just by being itself. (Yes, even Real Love has enemies.)

The difference between love and power—once we uncover it—will turn out to be as grand an issue as the older one between means and ends. Now, we can only say that love involves power-*for* more than power-*over*. But the last issue will be power-over-power, while it still remains power. Indeed, what would "power" be if we did in fact have power over it? *I think it would be very much like shrewdly effective love.*

11 Liberal power in America is irrelevant to the conduct of American foreign and military affairs. In power terms, the liberals are not adequate to any such engagement. But, as we know, that does not inhibit them. Indeed, the fact hardly seems to concern them. That is because right is right, and the government is all wrong in its militaristic foreign policy.

This is a long subject, much too lengthy to come to at the conclusion of this essay. But I want to explain myself—why I have discussed politics only from a domestic viewpoint—and also I am sadly aware that once again the liberals are mobilizing for war and anti-war, and I must join up or find me a new ivory tower.

As for belief, I presumed to be a revolutionary socialist when I was young. It was a Position. Not being strong enough, I never revolutioned anyone. But in the course of fooling around with Positions, I contracted a severe and consistent hatred for the Stalinist betrayal of the Russian Revolution and the resulting totalitarian terror in the name of socialism. That was the emotional and intellectual experience of a very worthwhile element of my generation, and I do not apologize for it—either to those of *my* generation, or of the *new* generation, who did not have the experience.

Anyway, after World War II, I felt that whatever finally happened to the various revolutions in the world it would be an important advantage if the peoples of the planet were given time and other opportunity in which to choose against Communism. So, suffering no delusion that "my" views were being followed by any United States government, I favored the military containment policy. It would buy time. That was twenty years ago. The time bought was well used in Europe, but not impressively so anywhere else. Meanwhile, the problems around the world have become considerably more complicated, while American policy has taken on an increasingly simple-minded military aspect—while at the same time losing much of the European endorsement it inherited after the War. These developments have not made Communism more acceptable in my view (nor has polycentrism enticed me into forgetting the totalitarian nature of Communist society); they have, however, given me a severe pause as to the virtue and even the significance of buying more time—at the new prices. Twenty years have passed.

America has nothing whatsoever to offer the world, at the present time, to fill the void it creates by containing Communism by military means. We support military dictatorships which are, from the most rigidly realistic viewpoint, mere stopgaps; and we have no social policy to be utilized thereafter. This country is revolutionary only in its devotion to technological competence; it is barely adequate in using this competence either fully or sensibly, even here at home. If we could export technological competence neatly wrapped in a cellophane package, well and good. We don't, and I doubt the feasibility of any such thing. The social adaptation to a mature technology is proving almost too much for us. What then have we to offer—and to aroused primitives—for the solution of the much more abrasive problems of the social adaptation to nascent technology? Only a negative view: Don't do it the Communist way—and here's a gun and a tank and a bomb to help you solve your problems.

Notice how much the Soviet-American standoff in nuclear power has in common with the crisis of trench warfare in World War I. In each case, a new point in the development of technology was realized in terms of war and, because war is so difficult to be reasonable about, neither side was able to extricate itself from a suicidal position. It is altogether an awe-inspiring conjunction of history that has placed the fate of the planet in the keeping of two such opposite and similar super-powers as Russia and the United States. The similarities are technological, geographic, and obvious. The opposition is mostly thought to be ideological, between capitalism and Communism; but I would suggest that it is more profound, being the contradiction between an ancient tradition of central authority in Russia, and our amazing absence thereof. If they backed down and we climbed up a bit in this matter of central power, we would be so similar that a disarmament alliance (enforced by a planetary condominium) could be said to be indicated by the course of our history as well as by the requirements of our future. (If we climbed up unilaterally, our social technology would be so commandingly superior that they would have to back down to meet the challenge of our competence.)

If there were no nuclear technology, we could fight the Communists and win. We are that much farther advanced. But there is such technology, and war is no longer a sane man's alternative. Still, there is something like a "war" and, still, we are more advanced technologically. So, theoretically, we could fulfill our anti-Communism by fighting a war for the undetermined areas of the world by the same kind of strenuous deployment of our industrial capacity that bested Hitler. That is our proven power, unequaled by any other nation. If our thinking had proceeded to this point, we would know exactly what to do with the void created by military containment—we would translate our superior industrial capacity into a World War II-type victory-without-guns. But this answer is equally obvious and "impossible." We have not yet accomplished that here in the United States; so we are not yet ready for export.

Any future offering from America must result from domestic changes occurring within America. We need not an Army, not a Peace Corps, but a *Free Force*—enlisted, trained, disposed like an army, but useful instead of destructive to the recipients. And as our Army was created in building America, so will our Free Force be. By helping other Americans, our very next-door neighbors, we will learn how to help the rest of the people on this planet—just as we learned to kill effectively by annihilating the Indians (and each other). Meanwhile, a new world initiative to fill the void created by our military containment must come from some other quarter. I always looked for something from a social-democratic Britain; but Americans of all kinds have looked despairingly for all manner of manna from Mother England. Whether an initiative in fact comes—from somewhere, anywhere—is an infinitely more significant issue than whether we stay in or get out of Viet Nam or even more generally limit our military containment policy, if such were in fact a live option. (And if it were a polite police action in Viet Nam instead of a dirty little war, you would favor staying there? And please note that the wrong face slapped is, in our circumstance, a potential act of escalation.)

A Lodge goes to Viet Nam and a Lowell refuses to go to the White House that sent him there. So much for educated class rule in America. But, for the rest of us, our dream was not merely national—it was as international as our sources. How could we have forgotten that America represents the world by other, better means than its ICBM's?

Well, we are still not Russia, and maybe we will never be. Maybe military containment takes thirty not twenty years before it becomes a virulent infection. And in the meantime, there must have been this place here and that place there where, because of it, the young men did not sing the song of the Russian labor camps, where twenty million died in twenty years:

They finished me, bastards, they finished me,
They destroyed my youth;
My golden hair has turned white,
And I am on the brink of ruin.

12 Finally a word to the young men—a Letter to the Next Generation.

There are two great treasures in life: youth itself, the very animal irreplaceable thing, and the ruminations of older men and dead men about that. Here, I am an utter nationalist. The most beautiful thing about this country of mine is its abject devotion to the simple fact of youth. In this, it is almost Polynesian. But not quite. Because there is an unresolved issue as to whether this unique national feeling amounts to true adoration—something as profoundly institutional as the opposite ancestor worship in some other societies—or is, underneath, a desperate metaphysical envy: warm, intimate hatred.

If there is anything worth talking about in America after the subject of money has been exhausted, then surely it is this father/son thing. For the mothers and the daughters, the worship of youth can only create natural enemies (recognizing some of the other, lesser elements of our culture). But the fathers and the sons: that is different. It is more serious; and, in the American matriarchy, the need is greater. Men know and share the anguish of life in ways that, like their success, are only reflected on their women. The females, with a close, unspoken, biological sense of the generations, experience the piercing awareness only through childlessness—one of the more profound experiences of modern educated women. For the men, the generational yearning is there like a fox at the breast from the beginning, and without end: all that ever happens is that the roles are one day reversed.

The great sacrilege of homosexuality is that the physical act willfully reduces this superior metaphysical issue to a minor matter of nervous manipulation. What a foolish way to become oneself! But if one presumes physically to engage the issue of identity with a woman, this particular pursuit of the impossible is creative, even when disastrous. How else can you discover your own limitations? In homosexuality, your greatest achievement will be an elevated confusion of yours with his—both limitations and achievements.

So, first of all, I hope and I urge that the next generation of serious young men not settle for anything so mean. Homosexuality is a personal disaster far beyond a bad marriage. With the latter, one may perhaps grow; with the former, one can only become an accomplished whore to oneself.

Next, avoid a rigid acceptance of your own superiority: that can only lead to authoritarianism. Superiority is a fact that can never be substantiated intellectually—no one is ever superior enough, considering the tasks at hand—and therefore no final Ritual Fact should be pursued. Within this perspective of limitation, the problem is not to prove it but to give it an arbitrary acceptance-as-proven. In a word: don't measure it; use it.

Third, your most creative posture will be to assume no deep distinction between intellectual endeavor and practical action. Inform the one with the other; always and everywhere remember the opposite. Each proceeds best under this direction. You will discover only one major difficulty in following this rather obvious prescription—the priestly inheritance governing the administration of culture. The defensive lack of interest in intellectuality among men who have nothing but their practicality to recommend themselves will not bother you over a long period. The infinitude of practicality is a ridiculous concept; the notion that you can read everything before speaking or acting has, however, a once-honorable tradition behind it. Therefore, contest it more ruthlessly.

Now, fourth, the day after I die, your excessive idealism will no longer worry me. It is your world—live in it as you please. Until then, I act out my old man's role. Why can't you be smart as well as enthusiastic? And who gave you this big embossed license to be exactly as primitive as your audience? The moral posture, no matter how sincerely taken, is a low mode of behavior. Primitivism, of any kind and in any place and for whatever reason, is a rhetoric that is acceptable only if shrewdly decided upon. Otherwise, it is what it is—mere primitivism.

Fifth and finally, I wish you well. Only you can create a new world. And only you will have to live in it. But remember *les vieux*. You think each one of us was a madman interested in money only? We wanted everything you want; having less, we perhaps wanted more.

Understand one thing clearly: Now that we are dead, we accept our helpless superiority, such as it was: and it is now at last merged in our unending love for the Next Generation. *Et vous, aussi, mon cher*, all in good time.

Author's Acknowledgments

This book was made inevitable by the grant of a two-year visiting fellowship at the newly formed Institute for Policy Studies in Washington, D.C. I went to Washington in September 1963 with little written, and returned to New York in February 1966 with most of the manuscript.

There, I learned even more than I was able to incorporate into these pages. For all that was given to me in Washington (including the unincorporated remainder), my outstanding debt runs to many persons, only a handful of whom may here and now be mentioned adequately: first, to my dear friend, Dr. Leslie H. Farber, surely the most courageous, enlightened listener a hard-pressed writer might imagine; to Oscar Gass, whose astute intellect and emotional oppositeness were so comprehending as often to be exquisitely apposite; to my wife, Mary, who undertook the burden of so much of my research on the subject of traditional American power; to Marcus G. Raskin and Richard J. Barnet, friendly entrepreneurs of the mind from a strange, new generation; to my uncle, Chief Judge David L. Bazelon of the federal appellate court in the District, who was so helpful in his characteristic way; and to Jackie Lushin, Pat Gaddy, and Janet Kotler, typists and manuscript-tenders beyond compare.

Some ideas and even paragraphs contained herein were first enthusiastically inflicted upon several hundred acquaintances of Arthur I. Waskow, Stanley H. Newman, and myself. This exceptional feat was accomplished (with the assistance of Mrs. Carolyn Nichols) by a mail-order enterprise known as the National Coalition for a New Congress, Inc. It was an early political Happening.

Who knows what I took (or failed to get) from my other colleagues at the Institute: Paul Goodman, the inventor of political plastic; Christopher Jencks, a displaced realist on the staff; Donald N. Michael, our leased-out scientist; and Milton Kotler, my cherished metaphysician of survival. To all of them, for both statement and gesture-innuendo, my aware gratitude.

The following are due for recognition with respect to previously published material, portions of which have been included in this book:

1. *Commentary*—for "Non-Rule in America" (December 1963); a review of *Congress: The Sapless Branch*, by Joseph S. Clark, and *The Senate Establishment*, by Joseph S. Clark and Other Senators (December 1964); *Big Business & the Democrats* (May 1965); a review of *House Out of Order*, by Richard Bolling (December 1965); and "The New Class" (August 1966).

2. *Book Week*—for a review of *The Economists of the New Frontier: An Anthology*, edited by B. H. Wilkins and C. B. Friday (January 26, 1964).

3. The American Institute of Planners—for a panel talk on "Advancing Technology and Its Implications for Urban Life," published in the *Proceedings of the 1963 Annual Conference*.

4. Point Films, Inc., W. W. Norton and Company, Inc., and Columbia Records—for material relating to the documentary film, *Point of Order!*

5. *Dissent*—for "Mr. Clapp's Wonderful Book" (Autumn 1964); and "The Kids and the Cockers" (Autumn 1965).

And I wish to thank the city of Washington itself. The osmosis was nearly overwhelming. After one has tried to live there, what the professionals call Basic Research seems like nit-picking. I didn't pick many, but I did live there. And before I left, I had agreed with myself on the essence: *elevated sameness*. Of income, of education, of style, of hope, and even of despair. Washington is the one and true tour of duty, even the home or the asylum, of the New Class. Beginners properly come there to learn: learners cannot live there long enough. In that ultimate setting, many propositions in this book might be nicely referenced-out. There, it is not the institutions of power, but the emotions of the people in and under them, that will tell the longer story—the one I have tried here only to begin to tell.

In the cold, editorial light of the morning, a writer sees ghostly sentences along with the others in the copy on his desk before him. Not everything gets said. What I most deeply intended here was to convey the emotional insides of the growth-points of power to the liberal, or at least the more generous-minded, members of the New

Class. In making this effort at uninvited mutual self-consciousness, either I discovered that to convey was to act, and that this could only consist of tearing down every last brick of the mental walls that still separate the issues of morality and the issues of power; or, I simply failed. I may never know which; but surely some readers will. In any event, I first set out briefly to elaborate Chapters Fifteen and Sixteen (the last two save one) of my earlier book, *The Paper Economy;* then passed through a period of being transfixed by the House of Representatives, and attendant details; and ended up convinced of (and surprised by) the importance of the New Class phenomenon in the United States and the *Götterdammerung*-character of the coming engagements 1) between the New Class and established business interests, as for power prismed through style, and 2) with the new Under Class of the central-city ghettos, as for pelf refracted by a pointedly modern image of the human connection. Thus a new organized America now emerges and, I would hope, with the useful imprint of prior self-consciousness, known as serious intention, rather than the later kind, known as regret.

Before we came to numbered pages, this book was dedicated to my son; here, at the last numbered page—and for a final acknowledgment—I want to reaffirm that dedication: this book was written for a son, the only truly modern American Muse for writers of my kind.

Index

Abolitionists, 35, 274
Absentee Ownership and Business Enter-prise in Recent Times (Veblen), 140
Abundance, *see* Affluence
Academicism, 196–98
Administration, merging of politics with, 372–73
See also Organization
Affluence
in Bookkeeping Order of society, 377–379
increased possibility of, 360–62
potential for increased, 374
poverty and, *see* Poverty
right to, 371
Affluent Society, The (Galbraith), 206
Afterlife and religion, 172
Age of Reform, The (Hofstadter), 138–39
Aiken, Henry David, 145
Alabama Christian Movement for Human Rights, The, 272
Albert, Carl, 82
Altgeld, John P., 46
Amateur Democrat, The (Wilson), 336, 342
American Capitalism (Galbraith), 12n, 16, 192
American Medical Association (AMA), 122, 176, 198, 330
Americans for Democratic Action (ADA), 138, 156, 160, 316
Anarchism
community and, 137
native, 138, 161, 329
Spanish, 137
Ancient Law (Maine), 214–15
Anderson, Jack, 124
Animality of man, 201–2
lying and, 216
Antipoverty program, 366
business community and, 115
See also Poverty
Apathy, political, 126
Apportionment, *see* Reapportionment
Apportionment and Representative Government (de Grazia), 259, 262–63

Baker, Russell, 286
Baker v. Carr, 237, 241, 243–46, 248, 252–53, 259
Baldwin, James, 272–74, 280–81, 287

Banks and bankers, 334
declining role of, 37–38
government role in, 14
Hoover and, 37
liberals and, 380, 382–83
national role of, 38–39
non-profit, 380–83
Barkley, Alben, 69
Bell, Daniel, 145–46
Bennett, Hugh Hammond, 318
Berle, A. A., 18, 313, 379n
on fragmentation of property, 18
on New Deal, 41
on "social cost accounting," 378–79
Berlin crisis, 106
Bevel, James, 282–83
Bickel, Alexander M., 252–53, 258–59
Biddle, Nicholas, 39, 316
Binkley, Wilfred E., 73–74, 126
Black, Hugo, 245
Black Belt, 294
economy of, 300
importance of, 304–5
Black Muslims, *see* Muslims
Black Power slogan, 288
Blaine, James G., 135
Body-mind dualism, 203, 206
Bolling, Richard, 88, 120n
Bookkeeping, social, 377–79
Bourgeoisie, *see* Capitalism
Bovay, Alvan E., 93
Branton, Wiley A., 299
Brokerage politics, *see* Gang-type politics
Brown, Edmund P., 381
Brown v. Board of Education, 238, 244
Bryan, William Jennings, 8–9, 13, 94
Buckley, Charles, 85
Burns, James MacGregor, 62, 75, 94, 111, 122, 123, 321
Business community
divisions in, 113–18
Goldwater and, 98, 101–2
inflation and, 104–5
Johnson and, 97–101, 107–8, 113, 116–117
Kennedy opposed by, 98–99, 103–4, 107
NRA and, 40, 108–9, 114n
needs of, 115–16
New Deal opposed by, 92
NEP and, 105–8

science and, 183
shift toward Democrats, 97–101, 107–
108, 113, 115–18
South and, 115
tariffs and, 39
Business Council, 100
Byrd, Harry F., 87

California Democratic Council (CDC),
336–40, 381
Campaign contributions, 123–25
by liberals, 381–83
Campbell, Phillip, 71
Cannon, Clarence, 84
Cannon, Joseph, 71, 88
Capital paper inflation, 104
Capitalism
classical, 362
corporate revolution and, 17–19, 309–
310, 362–64
New Class and, 308
strategic retreat from, 363–64
Carpetbaggers, 293
Carter, Barbara, 289, 300, 302
Cash, W. J., 135, 280, 301
Cater, Douglass, 83, 120
Catholics, 149, 336, 347
Caucusing, Democratic Party, 119–25
Centrist coalition
Democratic Party and, 95–118
Johnson's role in, 22
New Class and, 344–45
NEP as, 107
See also Liberals; New Coalition
Charity, 365
Chesterton, G. K., 164
Christianity and rationality, 183
Churchill, Winston, 342n
Cities, 6
culture and, 144–45
devaluation of ballot in, 264
Individualism in, 140
metropolitan, 320n
myths in, 140, 143
Nazis and, 142
Negroes in, 272, 284–88, 322
New Coalition in, 269
as organizations, 140
poor in, 288
reapportionment and, 62, 239, 264
rural influence in, 141
suburbs and, 239–40
unsolved problems of, 268
upstate conflict with, 265
"Civil Rights and Legal Wrongs" (Virginia Commission on Constitutional
Government), 290, 296
Civil Rights Act of 1964, 92
Civil Rights Commission, 302
Civil rights movement
emergence of, 243
in North, 284–89
in South, 286–306
See also Negroes
Civil War, 33, 38, 46, 158
failure of, 34
impact of, 32, 153
Clapp, Charles L., 81, 119, 122

Clark, Joseph S., 86, 89
Class conflict
antagonisms engendered by, 363
Marx's theory of, 20, 190
New Class and, 20–21
proletariat and, 357
See also New Class
Class in Suburbia (Dobriner), 148, 319
Cleveland, Grover, 46n, 94
Coalitions
between generations, 231–33
building of, 6–7
business in, 115–18
centrist, see Centrist coalition
conservative, 64–66
current reshaping of, 92
Democratic Party's, 95–96
Democratic-Republican, 113
majority-rule and, 251
New, see New Coalition
New Class, 344–45
NEP as, 107
power through, 268
problem of, 267
reapportionment and, 243
Cold War, 106
foreign policy and, 388–90
government-by-crisis and, 127
need for, 38
Colegrove v. Green, 245
Communism
foreign policy and, 24, 388–89
in 1930's, 154
religion and, 169–72, 182–83
See also Cold War; Marx, Karl; Mc-
Carthy, Joseph
"Community"
anarchism and, 137
bases of, 229–33
lack of, 148
in Mead's philosophy, 205
religion and, 165, 178–84
suburbs and, 239–40
Traditional, 256
weak and, 387
Compromise, defined, 385
Conformism, 151–52
Congress
created by South, 89
Democratic Party and, 49, 119–21
important role of, 56–57
See also House of Representatives;
Senate
Congress of Racial Equality (CORE),
282
Congressional districts, 62–63, 122–23
Congressional Government (Wilson), 72
Congressman: His Work as He Sees It,
The (Clapp), 81
Conservative coalition, 64–66
See also Right wing
Constitution
amending of, 240
early purpose of, 32–34
limitations of, 32–34, 36
private national governments and, 41
Consumption
mania for, 374

as modern social focus, 192
See also Affluence
Coolidge, Calvin, 5, 31, 77
Copeland, Lammot du Pont, 98
Corporate order
   capitalism compared with, 309–10
   growth-to-dominance of, 307–9
   lying in, 216
   See also Business community; New
     Class; New Coalition
Corporate revolution
   capitalism and, 17–19, 309–10, 362–64
   property and, 17–19
Corporations
   military and, 6n
   property and, 19
   technologists and, 317–18
   See also Business community *and*
     corporation names
Cost accounting, social, 377–79
Coudert, Frederick R., 36
Cox, W. Harold, 300
Crisis of the Old Order, The (Schlesinger),
   314
Crossman, Richard, 327–28
Cuban missile crisis and *détente*, 92, 106
Culture, 315
   cities and, 145
   defined, 1–2
   importance of, 128
   as law of generational succession, 231–
     232
   myths in, 181
   problem of changing, 298–99
   religion and, 178–84
   ruling class and, 47

Dale, Edwin L., Jr., 106
Daniels, Jonathan, 287
Darwinism, 166
David, Paul T., 264
Davis, Sammy, Jr., 282
De Grazia, Alfred, 253, 259–60, 262–64
De Sapio, Carmine, 4, 343–44
Deadlock of Democracy, The (Burns), 74
Death
   power and, 174–75
   religion and, 172–78
Democracy, 250–51, 254, 368
Democratic Party
   business support for, 97–101, 107–8,
     113, 115–18
   caucusing in, 119–25
   centrist coalition in, 95–118
   Congress and, 49, 119–21
   economic innovations of, 106–9
   as Establishment party, 49, 112, 116–17,
     119
   gerrymandering by, 258
   growth of, 94–95
   liberals in, 116, 118
   reapportionment and, 242
   reformers in, *see* Reform Democrats
   in South, 301
   suburban vote and, 265, 322
   See also New Deal; *and names of*
     Democratic presidents

Devaluation of the Urban and Suburban
   Vote (David and Eisenberg), 264
Dewey, John, 203
Dewey, Thomas E., 46n, 111, 113
Dillon, Douglas, 102, 105
Djilas, Milovan, 51
Dobriner, William M., 148, 319, 320n
Dos Passos, John, 315
Dostoievski, Feodor, 218, 329, 351
Douglas, Harlan, 319
Douglas, Lewis, 14, 101, 314
Douglas, Paul, 87
Dual government
   gang structure and, 42–47
   nature of, 38–41
   political parties and, 45, 49
   power and, 41
   reformers and, 46–47
Duty, Johnson on, 366

Eastland, James O., 64, 289, 300
Economic theory, classical, 191–92
Economy
   capacities of, 365
   growth of, 360–62
   Southern, 292–93, 300
   workability of, 358
   See also Affluence; Business commu-
     nity; Poverty; Unemployment
Education
   community and, 231
   lying and, 218–19
   New Class and, 195, 197–99, 310–11,
     331
Eichmann, Adolf, 373, 374
Eisenberg, Ralph, 264
Eisenhower, Dwight D., 103, 108, 350
   campaign against Stevenson, 22
   center and, 96
   inadequacy of, 23, 49, 77, 83n
   McCarthy and, 159, 160
   on racism, 305
   suburbs and, 265, 321
Elijah Muhammad, 281–82
Eliot, T. S., 128, 152, 182
Elitism, de Grazia's, 262
England
   New Class in, 327–28
   parliamentary government in, 72
Evans, Rowland, 344
Executive, *see* Presidency

Farmers, 37
   cities influenced by, 141
   demands of, 48
   Individualism of, 140–41
   land-buying by, 140
   Populism and, 48
   rural socialism of, 140
Fascism
   cities and, 142
   defined, 109n
   myths deployed by, 142
   New, *see* New Fascism; Right wing
Faulkner, William, 287
Federal Bureau of Investigation, 299–300
Federal debt, 15
Federal government

dual government and, *see* Dual government
early restrictions of, 32–34
growing role of, 16, 55
See also Congress; Constitution; Presidency
Federal Reserve System, 19
See also Banks and bankers
Federalist/Republican conflict, 34
Filene, Edward A., 15
Ford, Henry, II, 100
Ford Motor Corporation, 114
Foreign policy, 388–91
  Cold War and, 388–90
  Communism and, 24, 388–89
  Free Force and, 390
  liberal power and, 388
  limited goals of, 24–25, 389
  national power and, 29, 55–56
  nuclear technology and, 389–90
Forge of Democracy (MacNeil), 58, 122
Founding Fathers, 7
  negative approach of, 33–34
  rationalism of, 32
Fourteenth Amendment, 246, 248
Fowler, Henry H., 100–1
Franchise
  Congressional districts and, 62–63
  gerrymandering and, 60
  House of Representatives and, 60–63
  Negroes and, 24, 295–96, 301–3
  reapportionment and, *see* Reapportionment
  restriction of, 240–41
Frankfurter, Felix, 245, 248, 259
Free competition, 16, 136–38
Free Enterprisers: Kennedy, Johnson and the Business Establishment, The (Rowen), 107
Free Force policy, 390
Freud, Sigmund, 179–80

Galbraith, J. K., 206
  on economic theology, 192
  on free competition, 16
  on liberal approach to private economic power, 41
  on Mellon, 36
  on property in boom periods, 135
  on role of power, 12n
  on women, 222–23
Gang-type politics
  defined, 43
  family and, 42–43
  of political parties, 45
  of reformers, 46–47
  sources of, 44–45
Garner, John Nance, 78
Gass, Oscar, 249
General Electric, 114
General Motors Corporation, 11, 105
General Theory, The (Keynes), 315
Gerrymandering
  franchise and, 60
  "natural," 284
  principles of, 258
  Supreme Court's jurisdiction over, 257
  See also Franchise; Reapportionment

God, 173
  See also Religion
Goebbels, Joseph, 217
Goldwater, Barry, 7, 22, 96, 135, 301n, 321
  apparent sincerity of, 220
  business community and, 98, 101–2
  electoral strategy of, 90
  ethnic background and views of, 347n
  issues created by, 6, 152
  New Class and, 324
  racist support for, 92
  significance of, 267, 341
  suburbs and, 321, 322
Goldwater movement
  electoral outcome of, 93
  moralism of, 353–54
  New Fascism of, 117
  political context of, 334
  prudent anarchy of, 161
  Republican Party and, 109–10
Goodman, Paul, 138
Grant administration, 44n, 45
Grazia, Alfred de, 253, 259–60, 262–64
Great Crash, The (Galbraith), 135
Grenier, John, 110, 344
Griswold, Erwin, 291
Gross National Product (GNP), 360–62

Habits, nature of, 11
Hacker, Andrew, 265
Halleck, Charles A., 121, 321, 322n
Hamilton, Alexander, 48, 73, 238
Hanna, Mark, 39, 45, 50–51, 94, 383
Harlan, John Marshall, 245–48
Harriman, William Averell, 347
Havemeyer, Henry, 40
Hawes, Gene R., 310
Hayes-Tilden election, 34, 94, 293
Himmler, Heinrich, 217
Hiss, Alger, 157–58
History and religion, 178–84
Hitler, Adolf, 202, 216, 347n
Hofstadter, Richard, 35, 47
  on agriculture in America, 140
  on American moral problem, 8
  on Bank of the United States, 38
  on Grover Cleveland, 46n
  on Hoover, 139
  on intent of Constitutionalists, 33–34
  on Jefferson, 289
  on Lincoln, 75–76
  on NRA, 114n
  on pre-New Deal reformers, 48, 137–138, 155, 274, 314
  on tariffs, 40
Holmes, Oliver Wendell, 226
Homosexuality, 391–92
Hoover, Herbert, 37, 94–95, 137, 139, 318n
Hopkins, Harry, 151
House of Representatives, 21, 58–90
  committee-rule in, 64–66, 71, 79–82
  Democratic Party in, 119–21
  democratic role of, 7, 118
  early positive role of, 70
  Executive and, 73–79

franchise and, 60–63
lack of Democratic caucusing in, 119–
    121
obstructive role of, 64–65
reforming of, 86–90
structure of, 68–70, 127
Wilcox plan for, 69
House Out of Order (Bolling), 88
Hudson Institute, 202
Humphrey, George, 102
Humphrey, Hubert H., 100, 113
Huxley, Thomas, 166

Ideals and New Class, 21–22
    See also Moralism
Income
    jobs and, 371
    social floor for, 374–75
Individualism, 6, 8, 42, 344
    anti-majoritarian bias of, 161
    community and, 148
    farmers, 140
    myth of, 133–62, 248, 344
    need to abandon, 267
    New Fascism and, 138, 162
    urban, 140
Inflation, postwar, 104
Integration, Supreme Court decisions on,
    238, 244
    See also Civil rights movement; Ne-
        groes
Intellectuals
    body-shame of, 185–86
    fellow-traveling, 155
    moralism of, 47
    negative power and, 11
    New Class and, 196, 307, 314
    political realism and, 1
    right wing, 150
    technician-participants and, 196
    technology and, 2
    working, 307, 314
    See also New Class
International Business Machines Corp.
    (IBM), 114

Jackson, Andrew, 48, 94, 384
    King Caucus dethroned by, 70
    spoils system created by, 45
Jackson administration, 14, 38, 48
James, William, 213–14
Javits, Jacob, 110
Jazz, 272–74
Jefferson, Thomas, 94, 161
    compromised by racial issue, 34
    Congressional committee-system and,
        73–74
    farmers and, 48
    fee-simple empire projected by, 140
    personal dependence on slaves, 5, 289
    system of Presidency, 73, 276, 336
Jews, 149, 267
    Nazi persecution of, 373, 386
    Negroes and, 282
JFK: The Man and the Myth (Lasky),
    225–26
Jobs and income, 271
    See also Affluence; Unemployment

Johnson, Andrew, 70
Johnson, Hugh, 40
Johnson, Lyndon B., 106
    achievement of, 56
    business community and, 97–101, 107–
        108, 113, 116–17
    centrist coalition of, 22
    coalition developed by, 96
    Me-tooism of, 108
    New Deal and, 7
    on power and duty, 366
    role of, 24
    suburban support for, 321
    use of power, 77*n*
Jones, Jesse, 14
Josephson, Matthew, 13, 35, 39, 45, 70–71

Kahn, Herman, 185, 202
Kelley, "Pig Iron," 80
Kempton, Murray, 80, 164
Kennedy, John F., 100, 283, 300
    assassination of, 21, 244
    business opposition to, 98–99, 103–4,
        107
    centrist program of, 102
    New Economic Policy of, 105–8
    New Frontier and, 268
    sense of departure conveyed by, 49
    style of, 22, 316
    suburbs and, 321
    use of power by, 78
Kennedy, Robert F., 107
Kennedy administration, 65, 96, 124,
    225, 268, 300
    New Deal compared with, 56
Kennedy government-in-exile, 107
Key, V. O., 264
Keynes, John Maynard, 315
Khrushchev, Nikita, 106
King, Martin Luther, 272
Knowledge, action as, 206
Ku Klux Klan, 299

La Follette, Robert, 46
La Follette, Susan, 138*n*
Land and farmers, 140
Lasky, Victor, 225–26
Law
    immoral, 274
    language of, 248
    power and, 297–300
    rationality and, 203
Lawrence, D. H., 180
Lease, Mary Ellen, 48
Lefkowitz, Louis J., 60
Left wing, insanity of, 383–84
Legal fictions, 214–15, 220
Lehman, Herbert, 337, 347–48
Lenin, Vladimir Ilyich, 384
Lewis, Anthony, 303
Liberals, 23, 333–59
    California Democratic Council (CDC),
        336–40, 381
    in Democratic Party, 116, 118
    foreign policy and, 388
    McCarthy and, 157–62
    moralism of, 352–57
    need for ideology, 154

in New Class, 2, 336–38, 347–48
New Deal and, 116, 355
in 1930's, 154, 156
organization and, 381
political use of funds, 380–83
psychic needs of, 381
reform movements of, *see* Reform
    Democrats
South and, 287
split among, 156
Lincoln, Abraham, 137
coalition behind, 93
originality of, 79
on unconstitutional measures, 74
use of power, 75–76
Lindsay, John, 110–11, 111n, 322
Lippmann, Walter, 95, 315
Lipset, Seymour Martin, 95, 123n, 142,
    146, 190
Literacy tests, 63
Liuzzo case, 300n
Lodge, Henry Cabot, 390
Long, Huey, 301
Love and power, 387
Lowell, Robert, 390
Lubell, Samuel, 94
Lying, 207–25
animality and, 216
by corporate order, 216
education and, 218–19
force and, 217
by Goldwater supporters, 90
importance of, 207–12
patterns of, 218
as personal power, 220–21
physical strain in, 222–23
politics and, 207
pragmatism and, 213–14
rhetoric and, 224–25
Southern, 289
truth and, 211
Lynching in South, 135

McCarthy, Joseph, 341, 347, 350–51
effect of, 159–62
Eisenhower and, 160
influence of, 150
liberals and, 157–62
momentum of, 159
Populism and, 138n
power of, 157
public hysteria and, 352
significance of, 267
McCarthyism, 22
nature of, 149
soil of, 158
McGill, Ralph, 296
McKinley, William, 79
McNamara, Robert, 100n
MacNeil, Neil, 58, 65–66, 69, 80, 122
Madisonian system of Presidency, 75
Maine, Sir Henry, 214
Majority rule
coalitions and, 251
critiques of, 259–64
nature of, 248–55
Supreme Court decisions on, 243–48,
    255–59

Malcolm X, 272
Mansfield, Mike, 87
Marcantonio, Vito, 351
Marshall, John, 73, 238, 244
Marshall, Thurgood, 300
Martin, Joseph, 82, 121, 344
Marx, Karl, 190
concept of freedom, 148
contribution of, 20
rationality of, 179
seriousness of, 384
Marxism
Bell and, 145
inapplicability of, 383–84
Mead, George Herbert, 203, 213n
concept of meaning, 204
concept of truth, 205–6
unity of action and language, 206
will and, 214
Meaning, Mead's concept of, 204
Medicine, 122, 176, 198
Mellon, Andrew, 36
Merton, Robert K., 337
Military and corporations, 6n
Miller, Clem, 79
Mills, C. Wright, 103, 126, 345
Mills, Wilbur, 84, 85, 122
Mind of the South, The (Cash), 135, 301
Mission for My Country (Mohammad
    Reza Shah, Shah of Iran), 218
Mississippi Advisory Committee, 296, 302
Moley, Raymond, 313, 315
Money, 12
farmers' demands for, 48
humanizing, 376–79
Party organization and, 123–25, 381–83
shift from, 192
social role of, 379
values beyond, 15
Moos, Malcolm, 110–11
Moralism, 7–8
anti-war, 386
as failed initiative, 229
of Goldwater movement, 353–54
intellectuals and, 47
of liberals, 352–57
New Class and, 21
power and, 227
of Reform Democrats, 341
of right wing, 341, 353–54
social complexity and, 52–53
unilateral, 387
Morality
American attitude toward, 5
for its own sake, 10
Morgan, J. P., 14, 31–32, 38–39, 46
Moscow Trials, 218, 224
Mugwumps, 35, 343
Muhammad Speaks (Muslim newspaper),
    281
Murray-Wagner-Dingell bill, 78
Muslims
achievement of, 274, 278, 281–82
beliefs of, 165, 281–83
negative religiosity of, 272
Myrdal, Gunnar, 44
Myths, 215
in cities, 140, 143

cultural critic and, 168–69
culture and, 181
current vitality of, 162
defined, 133
differences in, 168
falsehoods in, 215–16
Fascism and, 142
of Free Enterprise, 136–38
of God, *see* Religion
historical bases of, 184
of Individualism, *see* Individualism
politics and, 182
power versus, 147
rationality and, 147–48
right wing, 151

National Association of Manufacturers
    (NAM), 114, 115
National government, *see* Federal gov-
    ernment
National Independent Committee for
    President Johnson and Senator
    Humphrey, 100–1, 113
National Recovery Act (NRA)
    business attitudes toward, 40, 114*n*
    failure of, 40
    purpose of, 91
Nationalism, inverted, 148
Nazis
    cities and, 142
    Jews persecuted by, 373, 386
    19th century sources of, 180
Nazi-Soviet Pact, 156
Negative power, 266
    Congress and, 57
    Constitution and, 32–34
    dual government and, 38–41, 49
    early problem of, 29–31
    gang politics and, 42–47
    intellectuals and, 11
    party structure and, 50–53
    reformers and, 48–49
Negro government-in-exile, 287–88
Negroes
    catalytic role of, 274, 349–50
    civil rights movement of, 243, 270,
        284–306
    cultural contributions of, 279
    family life of, 287
    government-in-exile, 287–88
    Hayes-Tilden election and, 34–35
    Jews and, 282
    jobs and, 283–84
    male rage among, 271
    migrations to North, 273–74
    New Deal and, 276
    in Northern ghettos, 273–74, 284–89,
        322
    planter control of, 294–95
    poor whites and, 128
    racial strains among, 271
    racism and, *see* Racism
    Reconstruction and, 35
    religion and, 165, 272
    Republican Party and, 95
    right to over-representation, 250
    Second Reconstruction and, 24, 275,
        300*n*

sexual humiliation of, 271–73
skin color valued by, 278
in South, 270–73, 286–306
suffrage restrictions of, 24, 295–96,
    301–3
urban role of, 285
New Class, 25, 307–32
    adjustments of, 326–29
    alliances of, 344–45
    basic features of, 195, 308, 335, 336
    class conflict and, 20–21
    class consciousness of, 349
    as cream of proletariat, 20
    defined, 308
    education and, 195, 197–99, 310–11,
        323–24, 331
    frustrations of, 324–26
    growing power of, 37
    ideals and, 21–22
    identity, 349
    intellectuals in, 196, 307, 314
    liberalism and, 2, 336–38, 347–48
    moralism and, 21
    New Deal and, 313–16
    as non-owning, 317–18
    occupational pattern of, 327, 331
    organizational basis of, 195
    power of, 21
    property and, 195
    right wing in, 344–47
    scientism and, 199
    size of, 312
    society staffed by, 367–69
    suburbs and, 319–23
    technology and, 317–18
    tension in, 341
    Under Class coalition, 376
    workers and, 368
New Coalition, 21
    allies in, 269
    Bookkeeping Order of society and,
        378–79
    charity and, 365
    in cities, 269
    democracy and, 368
    economy and, 360–62
    foreign policy and, 388–90
    left and, 383–84
    money and, 360–62, 376–79
    non-profit banks and, 380–85
    poor and, 366, 370–72
    "Social Floor" and, 374–75
    technological order and, 362–64
    youth and, 391–93
New Deal, 36, 41
    blocking of, 92
    business and, 40, 108–9, 114*n*
    canonized by ADA, 156
    completion of, 91–93
    importance of, 91
    innovative role of, 23
    Johnson administration and, 7, 56
    Kennedy administration and, 56
    liberals and, 116, 355
    NRA period, *see* National Recovery
        Act
    Negroes and, 276
    New Class and, 313–16

non-revolutionary nature of, 41
  roots of, 48–49
  sources of, 48
  Truman administration and, 107
  See also Roosevelt, Franklin D.
New Economic Policy (NEP)
  business and, 105–8
  Johnson and, 106
  as new political coalition, 107
  technological unemployment and, 115
New Fascism, 118, 162
  of Goldwater movement, 117
  Individualism and, 138, 162
  myths deployed by, 142
  See also Goldwater, Barry; Right wing
New Left, 116n
New York City, Reform Democrats in, 89n, 243, 336–38, 340
New York State, legislative malapportionment in, 260
Nixon, Richard, 97, 102, 321
Non-rule, *see* Negative power
Nonviolence, 288
Norris, George W., 88
North, 32
  in Federalist/Republican conflict, 34
  gerrymandering in, 258
  migration of Negroes to, 273–74
  racial ghettos in, 273–74, 284–89, 322
  reapportionment in, 242
Novak, Robert, 344
Nuclear technology and foreign policy, 389–90
Nuclear warriors, rationality of, 202
  See also Cold War

Organ transplants, 177
Organization
  archaic forms of, 365–66
  negative attitude toward, 149
  power as, 381
  See also Corporate order; Corporate revolution
Origins of the New South, The (Woodward), 31–32, 292–95

Pacifism, 227
Paper Economy, 18, 330
Paperwork, scale of, 312
Parity, 48, 140
Parliamentary government
  Constitutionalists and, 72–3
  division of powers and, 73–76
  English, 72
Party organization
  campaign contributions and, 51, 123–25, 380–83
  creative role of, 50–52
  ganglike structure of, 45
  gerrymandering and, 258
  Leninist-type, 51
  nature of, 50–52
  Reform Democrats and, 342
  See also Democratic Party; Republican Party
Patronage
  "honorific," 381
  Reform Democrats and, 89n, 340

Peace Corps, 351
Pepper, Claude, 226
Phillips, Wendell, 274
Pirandello, Luigi, 225
Planning, New Class, 331
  See also New Economic Policy
Plessy v. Ferguson, 35, 238, 244
Political apathy, 126
Political Man (Lipset), 146, 190
Political realism and intellectuals, 1
Political style, *see* Style
Politicos, The (Josephson), 35, 45
Politics
  defined, 11, 334–35
  emotionality of, 203
  free competition and, 16
  gang-type, 42–47
  God mythology and, 182
  importance of, 3
  lying and, 207
  merging of administration with, 372
  popular attitudes toward, 4–5
  power and, 11
  rationality and, 194
  See also Coalitions; Democratic Party; Party organization; Power; Republican Party
Popular Front, 154
Population movements
  franchise and, 264
  of Negroes, 273–74
Populists, 8
  conservative ideology and, 138
  farmers and, 48
  moralism of, 47
  political demands of, 48
  racism and, 67n
  relevance of, 158
  in South, 294–95, 304
Poverty, 15, 288, 357, 366–67
  Negroes and, 128, 284
  New Coalition and, 366, 370–72
  See also Affluence; Unemployment
Power
  acts of delegation and, 3–4
  coalition and, 268–69
  competitive economic model and, 16
  defined, 9
  dual government and, 41
  facets of, 53–55
  fear of death and, 174–75
  for its own sake, 10
  Galbraith on, 12n
  gang structure and, 44
  Johnson on, 366
  law and, 297–300
  logic of, 17
  love and, 387
  as modern social focus, 192
  moralism and, 227
  myth versus, 147
  national, need for, 55–56
  as organization, 381
  politics and, 11
  Presidential uses of, 74–79
  private constituencies and, 194n
  private property and, 17–19
  psychological roots of, 11

social and individual compared, 10
  See also Coalitions; Democratic Party;
    Party organization; Politics; Repub-
    lican Party
Power in Washington (Cater), 120
Power Elite, The (Mills), 345
Pragmatism, 20, 203
  concept of meaning, 204
  concept of truth, 205–6
  lying and, 213–14
  unity of action and language, 206
  will and, 214
Presidency, 57, 58
  growth of, 78
  House of Representatives and, 73–79
  uses of power, 75–79
  See also names of Presidents
President and Congress (Binkley), 73,
  126
Presidential Commission on Registration
  and Voting Participation, 63
Price inflation, 104
Priestly class, 197
Private property
  early rule of, 369–70
  fragmentation of, 18–19
  New Class and, 195
  planning and, 331
  power and, 17–19
  shift from, 192
Profit-making
  non-profit issue and, 380
  strategic retreat from, 363–64
Profumo scandal, 328*n*
Progressives, 8
  conservative ideology and, 35
  development of, 155
  individualism of, 138
  social criticism of, 35–36, 155
Property, *see* Private property
Protestants, 149, 272, 285, 325
Proudhon, Pierre Joseph, 19
Puritanism, 8, 52

Racism
  business community and, 115
  effects of, 34, 277–80
  Goldwater and, 92
  impact on democratic elements, 34
  institutionalization of, 276
  local interests and, 275
  Populists and, 67*n*
  and Redeemers, 293
  sex and, 271–72, 279, 281
  See also Negroes
Radical Republicans
  failure of, 35, 293
  Hayes-Tilden election and, 293
  positive Congressional leadership and,
    70
Radical right wingers, *see* Right wing
Railroads and Reconstruction, 32
RAND Corporation, 199, 331, 348
Rationality, 201, 252
  Christianity and, 183
  Founders and, 32
  of law, 203
  limits of, 193–94

Marx's, 179
  myth and, 147–48
  of nuclear warriors, 202
  politics and, 194
  primary thought and, 193
  supra-historical, 253
Rayburn, Sam, 49, 82, 120*n*, 121, **344**
Rayburn-Martin Rule, 82, 121
Reapportionment
  coalitions and, 243
  de Grazia's critique of, 259–64
  Democratic Party and, 242
  legal aspects of, 244–49
  as nationwide problem, 62
  Republican Party and, 242
  South and, 242
  suburbs and, 239
Reconstruction Finance Corp., **14**
Reconstruction Period
  end of, 34–35
  failure of, 293
  railroads and, 32
  Second, 24, 275, 300*n*
Redistricting suits, 242
  See also Reapportionment
Reed, Thomas B., 70–71
Reform Democrats
  in California, 336–40, 381
  "honorific patronage" and, **381**
  moralism of, 341
  in New York City, 89*n*, 243, 336–38,
    340
  patronage and, 89*n*, 340
  political organization by, 342
Reformers, *see* Liberals; Populists; Pro-
    gressives; Reform Democrats
Regionalism, 44
  See also North; South
Reid, John Edward, 222–23
Religion
  Communism and, 169–72, 182–83
  community and, 165, 178–84
  conflicts stemming from, 276
  culture and, 178–84
  death and, 172–78
  decline of, 162–84
  defined, 166
  God and, 173
  history and, 178–84
  intentions of, 231
  Negroes and, 165, 272
  science and, 166–68
  virtue of, 164
Republican Party, 50
  divisions in, 109–12
  dual government and, 39
  failure of, 94–97
  founders of, 93–94
  gerrymandering by, 258
  Goldwater supporters and, *see* Gold-
    water, Barry; Goldwater movement
  Me-tooism of, 111–13
  Negroes and, 95
  post-Civil War, 39–40
  reapportionment and, 242
  Reconstruction Radicals in, 35, 70, 293
  right wing in, *see* Goldwater, Barry;
    Goldwater movement

South and, 34–35, 70, 293, 305
suburban vote and, 265, 322
tariff and, 39
See also Right wing; *and names of Republican Presidents*
Reynolds v. Sims, 247, 248, 256
Rhetoric and lying, 224–25
Richberg, Donald, 315–16
Rickover, Hyman G., 318
Right wing, 53
as carbon-opposites of liberals, 356n
danger of, 341
growing unity of, 340
Individualism of, 151
intellectuals in, 150
money of, 340
moralism of, 341
in New Class, 344–47
paranoia of, 53
prospects of, 341
radicalism of, 152
See also Goldwater movement; McCarthyism; New Fascism
Rockefeller, Nelson A., 60, 110–11
Rogers, Will, 119
Roosevelt, Eleanor, 337
Roosevelt, Franklin D., 72, 78, 232, 347, 384
ad hoc progress of, 151, 160
coalition developed by, 95, 154
Morgan interests and, 13
originality of, 79, 139
personality of, 212
on rescuing business, 14
style of, 316
use of power, 76–78
on Wilson administration, 313
See also New Deal
Roosevelt, Theodore, 35, 39, 77–78, 93–95, 124
Rosenman, Samuel, 313
Rovere, Richard, 153, 160n
Rowen, Hobart, 107
Russell, Richard B., 87, 89
Russia, *see* Soviet Union

Saunders, Stuart T., 100
Scammon, Richard M., 62
Scarcity, 228–29
as useful idea, 228
See also Affluence; Economy; Poverty; Unemployment
Schattschneider, E. E., 264
Schlesinger, Arthur M., Jr., 232, 318
on antecedents of NRA, 40
on brain trust, 313–14
club-like view of history, 316
on conflicts in New Deal, 14
as historian of New Class, 316
on Hoover, 36–37
on Progressive movement, 35–36
on Republican obstructionism, 68n
on Roosevelt's mail, 77
on Roosevelt's simplicity, 212
Science
achievement of, 186
beauty of, 189
business and, 183

origins of, 187
religion and, 166–68
spiritual exaggeration of, *see* Scientism
technology and, 187–88
triumph of, 188
Scientific method
defined, 189
elements of, 167
focus of, 190
Scientism, 185–206
defined, 185
rhetorical method of, 190
Scientists and Engineers for Johnson and Humphrey, 99
Scopes Trial, 48
Scotto, Anthony M., 311
Scranton, William W., 110–11
Second Reconstruction, 24, 275, 300n
Senate, 58, 87, 250
committee assignments in, 87
liberalism of, 66
Senate Establishment, The (Clark), 87
Senator Joe McCarthy (Rovere), 160n
Sex and racism, 271–72, 279, 281
Seymour, Horatio, 46
Shanahan, Eileen, 99, 101–2
Sit-ins, 243
Sitton, Claude, 283, 300
Smathers, George, 225
Smith, Alfred E., 94, 139, 318n
Smith, Bessie, 272–73
Smith, Howard W., 63–64, 83
Snow, C. P., 196
Social classes
conflict between, *see* Class conflict
Marx's theories of, 20, 190
parties and, 50–51
See also Capitalism; New Class; Workers
Social Floor, need for, 374–75
Socialism, 20
rural, 140–41
weakness in America, 20
See also Marx, Karl
Sociology, 191
South, 32
Black Belt in, 294, 300, 304–5
business community and, 115
Congress created by, 89
Democratic Party and, 301
economic exploitation of, 292–93
in Federalist/Republican conflict, 34
hypocrisy of, 67, 289–91
lawlessness in, 135, 290n, 291
liberals and, 287
lynching in, 135
Negroes in, 270–73, 286–306
New Deal opposed by, 92
non-racial conflict in, 293–95
obstructionist role of, 34, 67, 92
Populists in, 294–95, 304
problem of, 67
reapportionment and, 242
Reconstruction in, *see* Reconstruction Period
Republican Party and, 34–35, 70, 293, 305–6
tariff and, 40

unfair advantage of, 61
white supremacy movement in, 295
See also Negroes; Racism
Southern Christian Leadership Conference (SCLC), 282–83
Soviet Union
bureaucratic development of, 51
Cold War and, 388–90
lying in, 216
medicine in, 176
Nazi pact with, 156
Spanish anarchists, 137
Spoilsmen, 39, 343
Stalin, Joseph, 176, 216
bureaucracy consolidated by, 51, 198
fear of death, 176
Stalinism, 154
Stern, Phillip M., 124
Stevenson, Adlai, 22, 96, 347
Student movements, 349–52
Student Nonviolent Coordinating Committee (SNCC), 282
Style
as issue in suburbs, 321
Kennedy's, 22, 77*n*
of New Class, 335–36
public yearning for, 77*n*
Roosevelt's, 316
Truman's, 23, 48
Suburbs, 148
cities and, 239–40
community and, 239–40
increasing power of, 265–66
New Class in, 319–23
party vote in, 265, 321–22
reapportionment in, 239
Supreme Court
courage of, 244–45, 249
gerrymandering and, 257
integration decisions of, 238, 244
reapportionment decisions of, 62, 237, 243–48, 255–59
role of, 238–40
Surplus persons, 268
Sylvester, Arthur, 217

Taft, Robert A., 159
Talleyrand, 53
Tariff
business community and, 39
South and, 40
Taxation, Filene on, 15
Technology
democracy and, 368
intellectuals and, 2
New Class and, 317–18
science and, 187–88
See also Corporate order; Corporate revolution
Theory of Business Enterprise, The (Veblen), 217
Tilden, Samuel, 46
Tilden-Hayes election, 34, 94, 293
Tocqueville, Alexis de, 58, 136
Transplants, organ, 177
Trevor-Roper, H., 261
Trotsky, Leon, 198, 321

Truman, Harry S.
New Deal and, 49, 107
political style of, 23, 48
use of power, 76
Trumbull, Robert, 310
Truth
compulsive telling of, 210–12
dangers in, 211
public lie and, 212
role of, 225–28
as social convention, 206
uninhibited pursuit of, 210
Tugwell, Rexford, 212, 313–14
Turner, Nat, 281
Tweed, "Boss," 45, 46

Unemployment
dealing with, 372
potential impact of, 358
technological disemployment, 358
See also Jobs and income; Poverty
United States Steel Corp., 103
Universities, 196–98, 328
See also Education; Student movements

Veblen, Thorstein, 104, 140
on lying, 217
Vice Presidency, unimportance of, 78
Viet Nam War, 53, 93, 116*n*, 349, 390
Violence in South, 290*n*, 291
Viorst, Milton, 112
Virginia Commission on Constitutional Government, 290, 296
VISTA, 351
Voting rights, *see* Franchise; Reapportionment

Wagner Act, 146
Wallace, George, 298
Wallace, Henry A., 156
War Against the States, *see* Civil War
Watson, James E., 68*n*
Weltner, Charles Longstreet, 306
Wesberry v. Sanders, 62, 245, 255, 306
What Is Property? (Proudhon), 19
Whiskey Ring, 44*n*
White, William Allen, 79
White Collar, The (Mills), 126
White supremacy movement, emergence of, 295
See also Negroes; Racism; South
Wholeness, dream of, 146
Wilkins, Roy, 296
Willcox, Walter, F., 69
Wilson, Harold, 327
Wilson, James Q., 336–37, 342–43, 381
Wilson administration, 313
Wilson, Woodrow, 14, 72, 78, 137–38, 232
on Congress, 88
use of power, 76–77
Woodward, C. Vann, 31, 290*n*, 292–96
Workers, 146, 330, 357
new, 363
New Class and, 357, 368

Yagoda, Henry, 218
Youth, message to, 391–93

ABOUT THE AUTHOR

David T. Bazelon has been publishing in the intellectual magazines since 1943, when he was twenty years old. He was associated with Dwight Macdonald's famous journal, *Politics,* in the mid-forties, and has been a frequent contributor to such magazines as *Commentary, Dissent, The New Republic,* and *The New York Review of Books.* (He was recently identified—and some of the ideas in this book referred to—in the Sunday *New York Times Magazine* article describing the New York Intellectual Establishment.) A lawyer by training— he practiced at one time with Adlai Stevenson's law firm—he is currently a Visiting Professor at Rutgers University Law School. He was recently a fellow at the Institute for Policy Studies in Washington, D. C., and of course is the author of the widely acclaimed essay of social criticism *The Paper Economy.* Mr. Bazelon ranks among the most original and provocative social critics of the day who are continuing the tradition initiated by Thorstein Veblen, and pursued by Adolf Berle, Gardiner Means, Thurman Arnold, and others. He lives in New York City; his son, Cole—to whom this book is dedicated—is nearly three years old.